POWER AND PRINCIPLE

POWER and PRINCIPLE

Armed Intervention in Wilsonian Foreign Policy

FREDERICK S. CALHOUN

The force of America is the force of moral principle.
Woodrow Wilson
June 5, 1914

THE KENT STATE UNIVERSITY PRESS

Copyright © 1986 by The Kent State University Press
All rights reserved
Library of Congress Catalog Card Number 85-24086
ISBN 0-87338-327-3
Manufactured in the United States of America

The paper in this book meets the guidelines for permanence and durability of the Committee on Production Guidelines for Book Longevity of the Council on Library Resources.

Library of Congress Cataloging-in-Publication Data

Calhoun, Frederick S.
  Power and principle.

  Bibliography: p.
  Includes index.
  1. United States—Foreign relations—1913–1921:
  2. World War, 1914–1918—Diplomatic history.
  3. Wilson, Woodrow, 1856–1924. 4. United States—
  Military policy. 5. Intervention (International law)
  I. Calhoun, Frederick S.   Wilsonian way of war.
  II. Title.
  E768.C35   1986   327.73   85-24086
  ISBN 0-87338-327-3

To Austin James and Eleanor M. Calhoun
And to Leslie B. Calhoun

CONTENTS

Preface and Acknowledgments ... ix

INTRODUCTION   Force as Power: The Wilsonian Example ... 1

1. The Power of Ideals: The Wilsonian Framework ... 8
   The Wilsonian Leader
   The Wilsonian President
   The Wilsonian Administrator
   The Wilsonian Diplomat
   The Wilsonian Warrior
   The Wilsonian Advisers

2. The Power of Civilian Control: Mexico ... 34
   The Occupation of Veracruz, 1914
   The Punitive Expedition, 1916
   Civilian Supremacy and the Interventions in Haiti, Santo Domingo, World War I, and Russia

3. The Power of Ideology: Santo Domingo and Haiti ... 69
   American Democratic Ideology and the Mexican Interventions
   Defining Policy: The Dominican Republic, 1913–1915
   The Occupation of Haiti, 1915
   The Occupation of the Dominican Republic, 1916
   American Democratic Ideology During World War I and the Russian Interventions

4. The Power of the Law: The Period of Neutrality ... 114
   International Law During the Interventions in Mexico, Haiti, and Santo Domingo
   Defining American Neutrality
   Promoting Mediation
   Defending Neutrality

5. The Power of Cooperation: World War I ... 155
   Cooperation During the Interventions in Mexico, Haiti, and Santo Domingo
   Establishing Cooperation at Home
   Establishing Cooperation Abroad

6. The Power of Collective Security: Russia ... 185
   Collective Action Before World War I
   Collective Security and the Interventions in Russia
   Collective Pressures for Intervention

7. The Limits of Force: Russia, Bolshevism, and the Paris Peace
    Conference   219
        The Limits of Force in Mexico, Haiti, Santo Domingo, and World
          War I
        Collective Failure in Russia
        Reaching the Limits of Force

EPILOGUE   The Wilsonian Way of War: Veracruz to Vladivostok   250

Notes   268

Bibliography   303

Index   323

PREFACE and ACKNOWLEDGMENTS

The uses of force characterize twentieth-century American foreign policy. Other centuries saw other wars, but none as frequently or on as grand a scale as those witnessed by this century. For the past seventy-odd years, hardly a decade has escaped without some form of armed intervention or full-scale war. William Howard Taft began the trend with an intervention in Nicaragua in 1911 and the majority of his successors have also found ways or occasions to use force. Yet, more than any other president, Woodrow Wilson defined the various ways armed interventions could support foreign policy. During his two terms as president, Wilson embarked on seven interventions, a record as yet unsurpassed by his successors.

The forceful precedents Wilson established served as models for later generations of Americans confronting such problems as international aggression or revolution. The justifications he used in defending force, such as preserving order, promoting democracy, upholding international law, or thwarting aggression, were reiterated by those who came after him and who also saw a need for an armed intervention. Wilson's responses to the revolution in Mexico, the turmoil in Haiti and Santo Domingo, the problems of World War I, and the birth of Russian communism set a pattern for later presidents who faced similar crises in World War II, Korea, Vietnam, the Dominican Republic, and Grenada. Force has become an important tactic in American foreign policy in large part because Wilson showed how convenient an alternative it was.

Thus, studying the role of force in Wilsonian foreign policy offers an introduction to twentieth-century American foreign relations. To a remarkable extent, Wilson identified the goals, established the methods, and defined the terms of U.S. foreign policy in this century. Although his individual style of manifest idealism fell into disfavor, his influence on American policy remains strong, primarily because he embraced traditional values and mores. Similarly, the methods Wilson used to achieve those goals, including the uses of force, underwent little change in the years since he left office.

Wilsonian foreign policy can be broadly defined as the search for principled applications of power in the relations between nations. During each of his interventions, Wilson pursued such traditional American policies as support for democracy, respect for international law, and the protection of freedom of trade, freedom of the seas, and self-determination. He invested the full range of American power to achieve these policies. Toward the end of his administration, he called on all other nations to use their collective power to support them. Wilson's success in achieving these goals through force is measured in the following study.

But the measurement is more than a simple evaluation of Wilson's performance as commander-in-chief or military strategist. It is also an assessment of the various ways, appropriate and inappropriate, that force can support national policy and can be used in conjunction with other forms of power. Further, this study emphasizes several ways Wilson found to limit force to particular, well-defined objectives. Thus, the study goes beyond Woodrow Wilson and the circumstances existing during 1914–19 by putting the uses of force in the context of twentieth-century American policy.

The ideas, conclusions, interpretations, and errors in this study are purely my own and do not represent the views of the many friends and advisers who helped me with it. Nor are they the views or interpretations of any of my employers, past or present.

Nevertheless, I am deeply grateful for the assistance I received from a variety of sources. The staffs of the University of Chicago libraries, the National Archives, the Library of Congress, the Marine Corps Historical Center, the Navy Operations Center, the Kansas State Historical Society, and the University of Missouri Library patiently and professionally responded to my incessant requests for books and records.

Steven Wheatley and Jack Michael, two of my fellow students at the University of Chicago, witnessed the launching of this study. Their enthusiasm for the work and their willingness to debate my ideas set me in the right direction. Michael Doyle and Scott Jones introduced me to professional research and gave me models to follow in my career as a researcher.

Dr. Glen Robinson, President of the Educational Research Service, loaned me office equipment, including a word processor, to make the writing of this book considerably easier. I am grateful for his encouragement.

Deborah Gough and Nancy Protheroe, two of my friends at the Educational Research Service, volunteered to read the manuscript, and each spared me from a number of clumsy errors. Deborah, who edited all my publications, proved time and again that she has the gift of the truly great editor. She forced me to say what I meant, not what she thought I should say.

David Trask of the Center for Military History read each of the many drafts of this book and offered numerous suggestions to improve it. It would not be published now but for his help. Yet, for all that he did to improve it and help get it into print, I am most indebted to him for encouraging me to continue working on it, despite setbacks and disappointments. He continually bolstered my faith in the work, and for that I will always be grateful.

Friedrich Katz and Barry Karl served on my dissertation committee and provided invaluable advice and assistance in improving the manuscript. In particular, Mr. Katz shared with me his understanding of Wilson's Mexican policy and Mr. Karl made many suggestions on Wilson's theories and style of administration.

I have been privileged to study under two great teachers. Jonathan Utley of the University of Tennessee-Knoxville first introduced me to American diplomatic history many years ago. His enthusiasm for the subject was infectious and has remained with me for over a decade. Akira Iriye, under whom I studied at the University of Chicago, demanded the best from me and accepted no excuses. Those familiar with his work will recognize his influence on this book by its title, which reflects the profound influence he has exerted on my views of Wilsonian foreign policy and international relations.

Ken and Holly Hargreaves share my commitment to research. Their eagerness to discuss my work and criticize my ideas helped give shape and form to the study. As a fellow researcher, Ken taught me that the approaches of the scientist and those of the historian are the same. We each ask questions, letting the answers serve as the basis for more questions.

My parents, Austin James and Eleanor M. Calhoun, and my wife Leslie, supported me, financially and emotionally, through school and beyond, yet asked nothing in return. Dedicating this book to them is small recompense for all that they have done for me. With that dedication goes my love.

As the author of this book, I hope that my children Austin and Emily will one day read it. As their father, I hope that the subject of war and armed intervention will be so foreign to their world that they will read it without comprehension. But as a realist, I am saddened by the thought that they will know all too well what I am talking about. To them and their cohorts, I can only say that the first step toward change is understanding. I have tried to take that step.

Introduction
FORCE as POWER:
The Wilsonian Example

International power assumes many forms. These guises include diplomatic, economic, moral, military (the threat of force), and armed power. Among them, armed power is the most brutal expression of a nation's ability to influence events. Force compels through violence the imposition of one nation's will upon another. Other forms of international power can be subtle and insidious, but force never is. Its uses are blatant and readily apparent, for they result in bloodshed, death, and destruction.

As the most obvious manifestation of a nation's strength, armed power is the easiest to study. Nations resort to it for many reasons—to defend their honor, territory, or people, for instance, or to steal another country's land or wealth. But always, it is a product of policy, no matter how rational or how absurd, controlled by the purposes and motives of national leaders. Precisely because policy directs armed power, force can be understood by examining the motives of the leaders who employ it. In the following study, power is the subject, force the example, and policy the theme. The presidency of Woodrow Wilson provides the setting.

More precisely, this study is an analysis of why force was used and how the uses of it changed the course of events. Force is defined as the employment of a nation's military to impose the national will through military combat. Excluded from the definition are the uses of threats or warnings, for the focus is on actual combat. By examining this particular form of power, some of the reasons nations turn to force can be identified and some measure taken of how successful force can be in achieving a country's goals.

The reliance on a nation's military requires that leaders give orders through a chain of command. These orders, implicitly or explicitly, reveal the motives and purposes underlying the decisions to go to war.

Even the most powerful dictator must offer some explanation to his subjects to justify the sacrifices he is calling upon them to make. This is more apparent in a democracy because the power of a leader is limited to his ability to enlist a majority of his people to his cause.

The presidency of Woodrow Wilson offers the best case study for analyzing the employment of armed power in international affairs. No other American president before or since used force more often than he. Within four years, from April 1914 to July 1918, Wilson resorted to force twice in Mexico, in Haiti, in the Dominican Republic, in World War I, in northern Russia, and in Siberia. Thus, his presidency provides a wide range of examples of the uses of force. Wilson's eloquence in explaining each intervention also ensures a ready access to evidence of his motives and policies.

By building on the precedents set by Theodore Roosevelt and William Howard Taft, Wilson introduced the United States to international politics. Both Roosevelt and Taft took an active interest in the international scene, but their activities never reached the same scale as Wilson's. He surpassed his predecessors because he was willing to commit the nation's entire resources, including the military, to an issue, and because world events offered him more opportunities to do so. In Wilson's hands, the ingredients of American power became tools with which to construct a better world.

In many ways, Wilson symbolized the uncertainty and discomfort that pervaded the country during the Progressive Era. The Progressive movement, which began in the closing decade of the nineteenth century and lasted until America's entry into World War I, responded to the Industrial Revolution in the United States. No clear or coherently formulated philosophy underlay the movement, nor was it restricted to any party or faction. Such disparate leaders as Theodore Roosevelt and Woodrow Wilson considered themselves Progressives and each offered his own vision of reform. Thus, generalizations about the period are difficult to formulate. However, conceived in broad terms, the Progressive movement reacted to the shift in the domestic power balance from rural areas to the cities, from the farmer and small shopkeeper to wealthy industrialists, and from an idealized democracy to corrupt city bosses. The growth of professions and bureaucracies also influenced the course of the movement, since these, too, meant that power was taken away from the individual and invested in the group.

Throughout his several careers as college professor, president of Princeton, governor of New Jersey, and president of the United States, Wilson struggled to recapture the lost influence of the individual on America's destiny. His policies attempted to regulate and control the changes brought about by industrialization. He attacked, with both his rhetoric and his reforms, the control of the privileged few over the many. In its stead, Wilson proposed a new cooperation based on democratic principles that would allow common citizens a united voice in the running of their own affairs. When he became president of the country, he moved to put this vision into effect. At the same time, world events enabled him to translate his domestic ideas into the language of foreign policy.

The coincidence of Wilson's own predilection to assume world leadership with the opportunity to do so allowed him to step beyond the limited activities of his predecessors to become the premier figure of his generation. His diplomacy reflected a larger vision. "We have preferred to be provincial," he admonished his contemporaries in January 1916. "We have preferred to stand behind protecting devices. And now, whether we will or no, we are thrust out to do on a scale never dreamed of by recent generations in America the business of the world. We can not any longer be a provincial nation."[1] Central to his policies was the recognition that the United States was tied irrevocably with events beyond its borders. By business, Wilson meant more than commercial or economic entanglements, but political and moral ones as well. On this assumption, he constructed a comprehensive framework that not only recognized the interests of America in global events, but which also assigned it an important voice in determining their course. Wilson did more than accept the responsibilities of his nation toward the rest of the world; he tried to ensure that he and his successors would have an essential role in the conduct of international relations.

As he rushed headlong into world politics, Wilson grabbed for every advantage. Force, he soon learned, offered many benefits, not least of which was its ability to create new opportunities for charting a course through the swirling confusion of world events. During the course of each intervention, Wilson found that the deployment of American troops created situations that he could exploit with new policies and other types of power, such as diplomatic or economic. If, in the end, his policies did not always achieve his central goals, this failure should not be interpreted to mean that force did not assist him. However clumsy and high-handed, Wilson's efforts to assist the downtrodden achieve democracy were helped by the interventions. Force opened new doors for diplomatic, moral, and economic powers to enter. This flexibility in responding to the situations created by the uses of force was a central feature of the Wilsonian way of war.

The seven interventions undertaken by Wilson were limited to the objectives he defined in response to certain crises. Since each is examined in detail later, it is sufficient to observe here that, in general, Wilson's greatest abilities as commander-in-chief were his recognition of the limits of force and his talent of keeping it closely tied to his political goals. On each occasion, he clearly defined his purposes and the results he sought. In doing so, Wilson maintained an exceedingly tight control over the military, rejecting any attempt to broaden the role that he assigned it. Force created new opportunities for him that he exploited, not with armed power, but with other, less violent, tactics. As soon as the troops accomplished the missions he gave them, Wilson turned to different forms of power, most often diplomatic, but sometimes economic and moral, to take advantage of the new situations. Even with the First World War, which was an unlimited commitment of the nation's strength and resources, Wilson restrained the military's participation to victory against Germany and its allies. Immediately after their defeat, he began relying exclusively on diplomatic, economic, and moral power to gain the kind of peace he envisioned. American servicemen were sent home as quickly as possible.

Wilson's ability to limit force, even as he increased its uses, offers a reasonable alternative to mass destruction. The development of the atomic bomb changed the stakes of total war, not the nature of limited war. During each of his seven interventions, Wilson prohibited force from getting out of control, using it, instead, in conjunction with diplomatic, economic, moral, and military power in such ways that each complemented the others in the pursuit of national objectives. Force was but one weapon in the large arsenal of American international power, and Wilson treated it as such.

Wilsonian diplomacy exerted a profound impact on the conduct of American foreign policy in the twentieth century. The principles he enunciated, the methods he adopted, and the goals he sought became the standards for his successors, not because he was so good or so successful, but because he was so American. His influence extended even to the uses of armed power. Force, as power, changed little after the Wilson period. Weapons became more sophisticated and powerful, but using them followed fairly traditional methods. Although the development of atomic bombs threatened to change the nature of war, their major impact was the imposition of stricter limits on the uses of force. Nations were unwilling to use nuclear weapons, particularly after the achievement of nuclear parity between the United States and the Soviet Union. No leader was willing to accept the complete destruction of his own country as the price for the annihilation of the enemy. The evenly weighted balance of terror between the U.S. and the U.S.S.R. produced the ironic result that nuclear arms fell into disuse as a weapon of war, even as their political utility in the foreign policies of each nation assumed a controlling influence.

In effect, the atomic bomb became a weapon of military and diplomatic power, not armed power. On only two occasions were nuclear devices used in war. After the bombings of Hiroshima and Nagasaki in August 1945, no nation dared resort to them again in armed conflict. Instead, nations continued to rely on conventional arms and traditional methods of using force. The obsolescence of nuclear weapons as instruments of war breathed new life into the role of limited military interventions. For this reason, the Wilsonian example of limited interventions is remarkably pertinent to today's world, despite the passage of over seventy years since his first election.

Elected to the presidency on a platform of domestic reforms, Wilson took office expecting to devote his energies to national issues, not international problems. Yet, if he lacked a detailed program for the conduct of foreign policy prior to his inauguration, little time passed before he filled the void. The methods and policies he adopted were controversial among his contemporaries. Historians have echoed those debates. Such scholars as George Kennan and Robert Osgood have pointed to Wilson's idealism as the major factor in his diplomacy. They have ignored the essentially realistic tactics Wilson developed by emphasizing the idealistic goals he pursued. Unfairly, and inaccurately, these students have criticized Wilson for sacrificing the national interest by chasing impossible, albeit greater, dreams. Arthur Link has met these critics on their own ground by describing Wilson's "higher realism." His argument centers not on the daily conduct of Wilsonian foreign policy, but on the president's perceptive realization that the future boded ill for mankind unless world leaders created a better international system.[2]

But the debate misses the point. Wilson was a self-proclaimed idealist who understood, as well as any man can, the international problems and dangers of his time. He spoke openly of his ideals because he believed in them and because he expected his listeners to approve his plans. Yet, he dealt with the world as it was by trying to make it what he wanted it to be. Wilson used his idealism realistically to attack the problems confronting him.

Other analysts have offered different interpretations of the period. Arno Mayer and N. Gordon Levin have developed the best definition of Wilsonian diplomacy for the years 1917–19. According to them, Wilson attempted to employ America's "liberal-capitalist internationalism" as a method for a reformed system of international relations that took a middle stance between the "atavistic imperialism" of the Right and the "revolutionary socialism" of the Left. This program recognized the national interest, but merged it with a liberal ideology to such an extent that Wilson "could act simultaneously as the champion of American nationalism and as the spokesman for internationalism and anti-imperialism."[3] These interpretations enlighten our understanding of the war years, but they shed little light on the evolution of Wilsonian diplomacy in reaching that point. Nor do they consider to any great extent a major part of Wilson's diplomacy—his varied and multiple uses of force.

Each of the seven interventions undertaken by Wilson have been examined in detail by historians. Arthur Link's multivolume biography of Wilson provides a solid foundation for all but the two Russian interventions. Robert Quirk and Jack Sweetman have done the best work on the occupation of Veracruz. The combined memoir and history of the punitive expedition by Major Frank Tompkins and the biography of John J. Pershing by Donald Smythe are the best references for that intervention. David Healy and Hans Schmidt have written the best histories of the occupation of Haiti. The occupation of Santo Domingo still needs equal attention, but the old study by Sumner Welles and a new one by Bruce Calder adequately cover it. World War I has been extensively addressed by historians. George Kennan's study remains the best source for both Russian interventions and Betty Miller Unterberger's work is excellent for the Siberian expedition. The northern intervention awaits similar treatment.[4]

The following study builds on this rich historiography but goes beyond the individual studies of each intervention to offer fresh interpretations based on an analysis of all the interventions. It addresses the function of armed power in the conduct of Wilsonian foreign policy. Because it looks at each intervention as part of the entire picture of Wilson's reliance on force, original sources have been relied on more than secondary works. No extensive effort has been made to paraphrase, challenge, or praise previous works. Instead, the focus is steadily on the role of armed power in the promotion of Wilsonian foreign policy.

The Wilsonian framework of foreign policy and the role that armed power played in Wilson's conception of the international system is discussed first. This establishes a working definition of Wilson's strategy toward the role of force in international relations. Then, because the American military assumed such an integral place in Wilson's reliance on force, civil-military relations are examined, with concentration on Wilson's tight control over the armed services during the interventions. Mexico provides the setting for this analysis because Mexican policy became the issue over which the relationship between Wilson and his men of force was originally established. Mexico also offers the clearest example of Wilson's ability to bend the army and navy, and through them, his employment of force, to his will. The take-over of Haiti in 1915 and Santo Domingo in 1916 exemplify the American democratic ideology motivating Wilson's foreign policies. The events leading up to the declaration of war against Germany in 1917 witness the importance of international law for Wilson. How he conducted America's part in the war and its participation in the interventions in Russia in 1918 reveal the importance of international cooperation to his foreign policies. Finally, the resolution of World War I and the two Russian interventions, as well as the formulation of the League of Nations, indicate how well Wilson understood the limits of force.

By concentrating on the presidency of Woodrow Wilson, the study offers an introduction to twentieth-century American foreign policy and a framework for analyzing it. It is a tragic commentary that such an introduction should be about war and military interventions.

1.
THE POWER
of IDEALS:

The Wilsonian Framework

The Progressive Era saw a rebirth in the powers of the presidency. Between Abraham Lincoln and Grover Cleveland, these powers were largely dormant, causing many observers, including Woodrow Wilson, to conclude that the real power in America lay elsewhere. But Cleveland began a new trend of action in the presidency and Theodore Roosevelt capitalized on it. Roosevelt proved that the president could get things done, that he could lead the reform movement and effect substantial changes in American legislation and life. Wilson went yet a step further when he internationalized the Progressive movement by incorporating his version of the movement's principles into his foreign policy, including his uses of force.

Ironically, Wilson did not bother to formulate a clear or well-defined foreign policy until after he became president and international events compelled his attention. He shaped his response out of his experiences as scholar, university administrator, and governor. Consequently, Wilson's conception of the role of armed power in the conduct of international affairs cannot be separated from his views on leadership, the presidency, and American ideals. It must also take into account the advice he received from the limited number of advisers to whom he turned.

Wilson's training as a lawyer, historian, and political scientist provided a solid grounding in the history and traditions of the United States and led him to develop a distinctive conception of the proper character of leadership. It also allowed him to investigate the office of the chief executive as a neutral observer, before he had the opportunity to experience it firsthand. Indeed, Wilson jokingly complained that his life as scholar imposed additional burdens on his life as president. He worked harder than previous occupants of the White House because, he explained, it was the penalty for holding a definite view of the duties and obligations of the office: "One ought not to write books until he knows whether he will be called on to do what they say ought to be done. I am now paying the price of having told other people what they ought to do when I never had the slightest idea that I would be thrust into their place." Precisely because Wilson, as Link has noted, was fully prepared by education and training for the development and conduct of foreign policy, his earlier views on leadership and the powers of the presidency need to be discussed.[1]

THE WILSONIAN LEADER

A leader's power, in Wilson's view, consisted of "one's capacity to link his will with the purposes of others, to lead by reason and a gift of cooperation." A leader of men interpreted the hopes and aspirations of his followers by translating them into action. "Men are not led by being told what they don't know," Wilson maintained. "Persuasion is a force, but not information; and persuasion is accomplished by creeping into the confidence of those you would lead." The leader relied on his followers' community of interests; he spoke to them about ideas and issues they could understand. In a word, he sympathized with those whom he desired to lead. "It is not a sympathy that serves," Wilson explained, "but is a sympathy whose power is to command, to command by knowing its instrument." The leader employed this mutual understanding to bend the masses to his will. He cared "little for the internal niceties of other people's characters," but, instead, manipulated their behavior to fulfill his ambitions. Although the leader's object was to enhance the life of the individual, his sympathy lay not with the individual, but with men in groups. In effect, the leader depended on the psychology of the crowd, on the ability of individuals to lose themselves among their fellows by merging their personalities into the larger personality of the mass. He recognized the difference between a single man and men come together, united by shared interests and concerns. The lone man's power meant little—the power of the masses everything. For the leader, the "whole question with him is a question as to the application of force. There are men to be moved; how shall he move them? He supplies the power: others supply only the materials upon which that power operates." Men were like clay to be shaped by the hands of the consummate leader. According to Wilson, the leader was limited to the common understanding or purpose. He could not create opinion, only identify and guide it.[2]

Wilson's understanding of leadership reflected on his personality as much as on his intellect. He often felt more uncomfortable in the presence of individuals than he did before groups. In December 1884, for example, he described to his fiancée, Ellen Axson, his efforts to rename and reorganize the literary society at The Johns Hopkins University, where he was a doctoral candidate. He had drawn up a new constitution for the society and "even wrote a set of by-laws." The members accepted these changes with little dispute during a meeting over which Wilson presided. "I have a sense of power in dealing with men collectively which I do not feel always in dealing with them singly," Wilson explained to Axson. "In the former case the pride of reserve does not stand so much in my way as it does in the latter. One feels no sacrifice of pride necessary in courting the favour of an assembly of men such as he would have to make in seeking to please one man."[3] Throughout his career, Wilson seemed always to prefer the lonely companionship of the crowd over relationships with individuals.

The view of leadership Wilson developed was a peculiar one, not so much undemocratic as oddly democratic. The supposition that a leader could not go beyond the common understanding with his constituents witnessed Wilson's faith in the power of self-government. However, the image he created of the people amounted to the democracy of the mob. The distinction between men en masse and individuals, in which the former were substantially and intellectually different from the latter, was hardly new, but the insistence that the leader depended on the emotional instability of the crowd paid scant attention to personal and minority rights. Wilson, perhaps, counted on the leader's sense of morality for protection, but he never clearly specified this. Indeed, during his administration, minority groups, blacks in particular, fared poorly. Yet, the most disturbing aspect of Wilson's definition concerned the portrayal of the group. He described men bound together as though they were sheep to be cajoled by the leader for their own good. If the common consensus fenced the leader in, he could, nevertheless, create a new community of interests by persuading his followers of the correctness of his position. In a real and distressing sense, Wilson balanced the leader along the thin edge separating democracy from tyranny. Only the leader's sense of morality and propriety protected him from a fall into demagoguery.

Wilson's view of leadership explained the relationship between leaders and followers, independent of any political or governmental office held by the leaders. As president, Wilson held true to his theory.

"Democracy," he said in September 1915, "is the most difficult form of government, because it is the form under which you have to persuade the largest number of persons to do anything in particular."[4] Throughout his administration, he repeatedly showed the strength of his conception of leadership. He took an unprecedented role in congressional leadership by formulating his own distinctive legislative program and pushing it through Congress. On many occasions, he appealed directly to the American people to compel their representatives to vote his program. In 1919 Wilson resorted to the same tactics on an international scale by speaking directly to the peoples of the world to pressure their leaders to accept his peace proposals. He failed on at least one notable occasion when, with his plan for the League of Nations, he stepped beyond the boundaries of the mutual sympathy by trying to lead the American people where they would not go. His own theory of leadership should have alerted him to the mistake of demanding action from his followers before they were prepared to move. Had he worked the ground more thoroughly by leading public discussions over a longer period of time than he actually did, American participation in the league would have had a better chance.

For Wilson's uses of force, his concept of leadership proved decisive. Toward two interventions, Mexico and World War I, Wilson convinced himself that his constituents opposed military involvement. Therefore, he avoided armed conflict as long as he could, turning to the army and navy only when he felt he had no choice or when he perceived that the people approved. He intervened in Mexico on two occasions, both of which resulted from events outside his control. The occupation of Veracruz in 1914 came about because of an insult to the American flag. In ordering the navy to take the port, Wilson felt confident that his constituents expected him to uphold American honor. Two years later, the punitive expedition invaded Mexico in pursuit of an insurgent group that had attacked Columbus, New Mexico. Once again, Wilson perceived that the American people expected him to defend U.S. territory. He finally determined on war with Germany only after deciding that the people supported such a step and that relations with Germany could be conducted on no other level. This is not to say that he did not take advantage of the opportunities created by force; he would have been foolish not to do so. Nonetheless, he did not seek military intervention in Mexico or against Germany until the last moment and as a last resort.

The interventions in Haiti, Santo Domingo, and Russia also showed Wilson's hesitation to turn to force until he felt confident the American people would accept such a step. Judged by press reports and editorials, the American people sympathized with intervention in Haiti and Santo Domingo as a means of assisting an inferior people to achieve true self-government, but events in the two countries were not burning issues in the United States.[5] The lack of widespread public interest in the two countries left Wilson a relatively free hand in the formulation of policy. Although not immune to the bias of seeing the Haitians and Dominicans as inferior, Wilson chose to restrict his interference in the internal affairs of the two nations to diplomatic and economic measures until events offered what he considered a perfect excuse for military action. Riots and anarchy in Haiti excused that intervention, while the request of the Dominican president for assistance justified the take-over of the Dominican Republic. Wilson defended the interventions in Russia as war measures and as an attempt to rescue a group of Czechoslovakian soldiers making their way home through revolution and civil war. In each instance, Wilson felt sure that his constituents concurred in his decision to send in the troops because he was pursuing policies that he had promoted before and that the American people had approved previously.

In Wilson's mind, the powers of a leader were distinct from the powers of the president. The great American leaders of his youth were not presidents, but senators and congressmen. His ideals of leadership were based on the British experience with prime ministers. Not until the presidencies of Grover Cleveland and Theodore Roosevelt did Wilson begin to understand the great potential for power that the office of president held. During his terms of office, then, Wilson transformed the presidency to apply his theory of leadership.

THE WILSONIAN PRESIDENT

The presidents of Wilson's youth were weak leaders who bowed before strong Congresses. Wilson took note of this phenomenon, and it profoundly influenced his early opinions toward the office of the chief executive. His infatuation with the British parliamentary system, which he never entirely outgrew, contributed to his early conclusion that the real power of the country lay in the legislature. His first book, *Congressional Government,* argued that the president, in his role as executive officer, was the "servant of Congress." The only substantial power lay in the veto, which made the president, in effect, "a third branch of the legislature." Wilson went so far as to say that "the President is no greater than his prerogative of veto makes him." Even as an executive, he was limited to the weakest of his cabinet members in controlling the federal government since authority was exercised through them. Although Wilson criticized several aspects of the legislature, particularly the committee system, he clearly believed that power and control rested on the Hill rather than in the White House.[6] Yet as the American presidency moved into the twentieth century, Wilson glimpsed the growing powers of the office, which led him to discard his earlier views of the presidency as weak and subordinate to Congress.

The appearance of such strong leaders as Cleveland and Roosevelt convinced him that the chief executive could perform a larger role than he had previously believed. The expansion of the United States into foreign affairs, particularly with the accession of Cuba and the Philippines, compelled Wilson to reevaluate his earlier opinions. "We have come to full maturity with this new century of our national existence and to full self-consciousness as a nation," he said in 1902; "And the day of our isolation is past." The federal government, too, had changed. Wilson identified the cause of the transformation as the domination of foreign affairs in domestic politics—everyone's attention seemed riveted to it. It reminded him of the first quarter century of U.S. history when concern over the attitude of other governments and questions of diplomacy and war exercised a major influence over the life of the young republic. Stronger executive power resulted from this situation: "Once more it is our place among the nations that we think of; once more our Presidents are our leaders." He no longer described the presidency in terms of the veto alone. In his last book on American politics before embarking on his own political career, Wilson wrote of a more powerful executive, one whose control over the foreign policy of the nation was "very absolute." He still considered the veto an important aspect of presidential power, but added that there was more. "He has become the leader of his party and the guide of the nation in political purpose, and therefore in legal action," he observed in *Constitutional Government in the United States*. Wilson added that "we have grown more and more inclined from generation to generation to look to the President as the unifying force in our complex system, the leader both of his party and of the nation." He finally understood the potential power of the office.[7]

On the eve of his inauguration, Wilson reiterated his mature conclusions toward the office he was soon to enter. This view combined his concept of leadership with his increased understanding of the powers of the president. The office now entailed a double function, he noted in 1911, for presidents "must undertake the business of agitation—that is to say the business of forming and leading opinion, and it will not be very effectual or serviceable for them to do that unless they take the next step and make bold to formulate the measures by which opinion is to be put into effect." Two years later he listed the duties that the people expected their principal representative to perform. They demanded that the president "be the leader of his party as well as the Chief Executive Officer of the Government." In addition, they wanted him to be "prime minister, as much concerned with the guidance of legislation as with the just and orderly execution of law," as well as "the spokesman of the Nation in everything, even in the most momentous and most delicate dealings of the Government with foreign nations." Thus, Wilson realized that the proper platform from which to launch his ideal form of leadership was the presidency, not the Congress. As a leader, he moved to consolidate on all fronts the strengths of the executive and to bring to fruition the programs and changes he believed the American people wanted. He continued the radical transformation of the office begun by his immediate predecessors by his uses of the powers of the presidency.[8]

THE WILSONIAN ADMINISTRATOR

Wilson brought to the presidency not only a clear conception of leadership, but also a precisely formulated theory of administration. The science of administration attracted him early in his scholarly career, and he was one of the American pioneers in this new field of inquiry. By late 1885, he was committing his ideas to paper. Throughout the remainder of that decade and the next, Wilson grappled with the study of administration in a peculiarly Wilsonian manner; that is, he tried to reconcile the requirements of efficient administration with the demands of democratic government. As his subject, he chose the imposition of the principles of self-government on the methods of administration; as his approach, he used a comparative analysis, both historical and contemporary, between various European states and the distinctive American form of self-government.

"Neither the practice nor the theory of administration has ever been reduced to a science either in this country or in England," Wilson observed in November 1885. He determined early that "we must have a new machine of government—a machine which may have *thought* for one of its motive powers, by having officers through whose interest in the public thought, and capacity for catching it, is to be controlled." Administration was the art of governing, the practical application of constitutional theory and design.[9] "Public administration is detailed and systematic execution of public law," Wilson wrote in 1886. "Every particular application of general law is an act of administration." In America, administrative methods were controlled by, and gave expression to, public opinion. But this system was encumbered by two difficulties. First, public opinion was too inchoate and multifarious for the civil servant to understand, much less obey. Second, the professional civil service, through its tenure and anonymity, was in constant danger of becoming unresponsive to a public ignorant of its activities.

The purpose of the science of administration was to "seek to straighten the paths of government, to make its business less unbusinesslike, to strengthen and purify its organization, and to crown its duties with dutifulness." Its guiding principle was that

> administration in the United States must be at all points sensitive to public opinion. A body of thoroughly trained officials serving during good behavior we must have in any case; that is a plain business necessity. But the apprehension that such a body will be anything un-American clears away the moment it is asked, What is to constitute good behavior? For that question obviously carries its own answer on its face. Steady, hearty allegiance to the policy of the government they serve will constitute good behavior. That *policy* will have no taint of officialism about it. It will not be the creation of permanent officials, but of statesmen whose responsibility to public opinion will be direct and inevitable. Bureaucracy can exist only where the whole service of the state is removed from the common political life of the people, its chiefs as well as its rank and file. Its motives, its objects, its policy, its standards, must be bureaucratic. It would be difficult to point out any examples of impudent exclusiveness and arbitrariness on the part of officials doing service under a chief of department who really served the people, as all our chiefs of departments must be made to do.

For Wilson, the ideal administration in America was "a civil service cultured and self-sufficient enough to act with sense and vigor, and yet so intimately connected with the popular thought, by means of elections and constant public counsel, as to find arbitrariness of class spirit quite out of the question."[10] In this way, the public will would find both expression and protection in the leaders chosen by the people.

Wilson's early studies on the science of administration, particularly the publication in 1887 of his essay "The Study of Administration," earned him two three-year appointments as visiting lecturer on administration at The Johns Hopkins University. During the six years he offered his courses, Wilson further refined and delineated his thought on administration. He came to see the subject as a branch of public law, equal in importance to the two other components, international and state law. "Administration cannot be divorced from its intimate connexions with the other branches of Public Law without being distorted and robbed of its true significance. Its foundations are those deep and permanent principles of Politics which have been quarried from history and built into constitutions; and it may by no means properly be considered apart from constitutions," he explained. Administration differed from international and state law insofar as it represented the operation of governments, the day to day implementation of the commands of the sovereign. In the United States, for example, the legislature, whether local, state, or national, expressed the will of the government through laws. The administration of those laws was the performance of the deed. Thus, administration encompassed the entire operation of governments, its purview extended from the legal to the practical.[11]

These many years of study allowed Wilson to develop his own philosophy of administration which he, without hesitation, put into practice as soon as the opportunity presented itself. He envisioned a vital, thriving service to the public, strictly controlled by elected or appointed leaders at the top who were accountable to the people, but run and operated by a professional cadre of civil servants chosen on the basis of ability and competence. In this way, constituents received the most efficient service without the danger of being overrun and ruled over by a professional class accountable to no one and driven by its own will.

The presidency of Princeton, which Wilson achieved in 1902, offered him his first opportunity to show himself as an administrator. He began immediately to implement a series of educational and administrative reforms that strengthened the powers of the president and redefined the concept of liberal education. In June 1903 Princeton's trustees authorized him to reorganize the faculty. Wilson created eleven departments, the chairmen of which reported annually to the president. At Wilson's instigation, the curriculum was also revised. Elective courses were severely restricted and replaced by required courses covering the spectrum of studies at the university.[12]

In 1910 Wilson brought his administrative and political reforms to the capital of New Jersey. As governor, he attacked the machine politics that had helped elect him, thereby bringing New Jersey into the forefront of progressive reform. His objective, as it would be during his presidency, was to bring the people more control over their own destinies through their power over elected leaders. Wilson's study of administration and of the American presidency provided him the framework for the construction of ideas in practical terms. As president, Wilson relied on the professional cadre of civil servants for the daily operation of the federal government, but he tended to impose his own ideas and policies through his appointees and special representatives. He allowed his support of the professional civil service to be weakened early in his term of office by the appointment of "deserving

Democrats" as a way to offset the well-entrenched Republican appointees. Yet, his use of patronage followed fairly traditional patterns. In his view, the most important aspect of administration was the control exercised from the top. He knew best the public will and desire because he was their elected leader.

The combination of Wilson's views on leadership, the presidency, and administration made him a powerful president. Perhaps no other American president has so well understood the theory of power; few have exercised it so precisely and coherently. The reforms of his presidency testified to the strength of his determination to lead and to bring back to the people the chance to control their own future. But, it was in the realm of foreign policy that Wilson discovered his greatest opportunities and his ultimate tragedy as a leader.

THE WILSONIAN DIPLOMAT

A particular set of ideals and a distinctive method of operation characterized Wilsonian foreign policy. The former were typically American, but Wilson developed the latter. He jealously guarded his authority over the international relations of the United States, for he took quite seriously his previous injunction that the president's control in this area was very absolute. According to Link, Wilson made all major policy decisions himself, although he did take counsel from a limited group of advisers. His diplomacy was truly his own creation, especially when it concerned matters that he judged extremely important.[13]

Wilson envisioned a major reorientation in the foreign policy of the United States. He wanted to broaden the scope of its activities from the regionalism of the Monroe Doctrine to a globalism encompassing the entire world as its area of influence. This ambition developed over a long period of time, beginning during the years when he was little more than an observer of the political scene and continuing through both terms of his administration. In part, the course of events allowed him to fulfill this dream, but the drive existed before the opportunity. In other words, the void created by World War I offered him the chance to take a commanding position in world affairs, but the desire to step forth was present before August 1914.

Religion acted as the foremost influence on Wilson's life and activities. Samuel Wells has argued correctly that Wilson cannot be understood without first coming to terms with his Presbyterian ethics. Born into a minister's family, Wilson grew up in an atmosphere of unquestioning obedience to the will of God. He never endured the crisis of conscience that, in modern parlance, is known as being "reborn." For Wilson, there was no need to reenter the breech, for he never doubted the truth of his father's God. As it related to daily life, his religion taught him the necessity of service and convinced him of the preordained sanctity of his life and ambition. It also supplied him with a moral vision that he relied on in his foreign policies. He was, in Wells's terms, a "secular evangelist" in proclaiming a better way of life for other nations through the pursuit of American ideals and in his unceasing attempts to proselytize the countries of the Old World to accept the ideals of the New.[14]

As fervently as Wilson embraced the love of God, so, too, did he believe that the United States, its people, constitution, and system of government came closer than any other nation to the life of Christian brotherhood and love. The nation distinguished itself by adopting a code of honor and a set of ideals that transcended the petty squabbles of most political entities to reach ever higher for ultimate redemption. "Democracy is not so much a form of government as a set of principles," he wrote in March 1901. These guiding rules provided the substance of American life and were the touchstones of its actions. "Do not think, therefore, gentlemen, that the questions of the day are mere questions of policy and diplomacy," he asserted a dozen years later. "They are shot through with the principles of life. We dare not turn from the principle that morality and not expediency is the thing that must guide us."[15] Proud of his nation's heritage and philosophy, secure in his own heavenly future, and convinced of the truth and validity of his ideals, Wilson entered the office of president without fixed ideas or programs for foreign policy. He developed his distinctive foreign policy in response to world events, for originally domestic affairs and reforms captured his imagination and interests.

The world, however, gave him no peace. Questions of diplomacy and international relations impinged on the domestic concerns of the Wilson administration from its earliest moments. Caught without a clear international policy, Wilson turned to the ideals and religion that had guided his life to formulate his foreign policy. Thus, even as he protected American interests, his diplomacy spoke to a larger ambition. He infused his foreign policy with the lessons of his youth, that God's way was the only way and that America was distinguished from other nations by its principles. He embarked upon a crusade to bring to the world a new international system based on a peculiar fraternalism that recognized competition, but disallowed bitter rivalry and aggression. In this milieu, force became a method of compelling brotherly love, not dominating other peoples.

THE WILSONIAN WARRIOR

Force attracted Wilson as a method of exerting power only when he determined that the motives directing it were proper and unselfish. Wars of aggression or injustice received his severe condemnation; those of liberation or service won his praise. He looked not to the individual acts of courage and sacrifice that composed organized combat, but to the issues over which people fought. "There is nothing noble or admirable in war itself," he once said. "But there is something very noble and admirable occasionally in the causes for which war is undertaken."[16] By judging the objectives behind the employment of force, Wilson implicitly recognized that purpose controlled the uses of force in international affairs. Although he never clearly enunciated this, his method of analyzing armed power as a scholar, and his application of it as president, revealed his keen understanding of its utility. In Wilsonian diplomacy, force was a means to implement policy.

As a youth growing up in the South during Reconstruction, Wilson experienced firsthand the destruction wreaked by the Civil War. The memories of his boyhood influenced the vision of his manhood and complemented, if not actually founded, his abiding commitment to peace. Wilson, who neither entered the military nor ever faced hostile fire, spent the majority of his life behind the protective walls of various universities. William Allen White, an early biographer, claimed that Wilson during his entire life never had even a fist fight. Blazing guns and drawn sabers did not stir the romantic hero in him to the same extent that they did in many of his contemporaries, such as his rival, Theodore Roosevelt. While the latter emphasized the cleansing properties of war on societies and its quality of uniting a populace against a common foe, Wilson rarely alluded to these aspects of it. On the few occasions when he did, he attributed these qualities to wars of service and principle, which he distinguished from those of jealous purpose and "ugly ambition."[17] A stranger to the dangerous life of the soldier, Wilson was a peaceful man by inclination, training, and belief. Ironically, this man of peace found in force a capable vehicle for carrying out his policies. Despite the lack of a well-formulated understanding of the uses of armed power, Wilson learned quickly to incorporate it effectively and efficiently with his diplomacy. If he spoke of these uses idealistically, his words should not disguise his ability to employ force courageously, intelligently, and innovatively.

Prior to becoming president, Wilson seldom thought about the role of the military in foreign relations. He showed no aversion to fighting if the end justified the means, an assessment he reached by stringently comparing the objectives with the results and costs. He consistently applied this qualification to each of his interventions as president and, as a student of American history, Wilson applied it to the many wars of the United States. His descriptions of these wars dwelt mainly with the causes of the conflicts and only briefly and superficially with the strategies and tactics involved. This method underlined the importance of policy and cause as the tests for evaluating the uses of force. The habits of the scholar remained with the president. Thus, the Revolutionary War, "fought for the plain right of self-government," fell unquestionably into an acceptable category of legitimate war. The War of 1812, however, was more ambiguous. England's policies of impressment of U.S. sailors and interference with trade "cut America to the quick and had become intolerable." Nevertheless, "it was a tragical but natural accident that the war should be against England, not France," since Great Britain instituted these measures to thwart Napoleon's unprincipled ambitions. Wilson condemned the "ruthless aggression" of the United States during the Mexican War. "We were disposed to snatch everything, concede nothing," he admitted. Although both sides of the Civil War aroused his sympathy, the Union's aims seemed to him more acceptable. The North attempted to infuse the country's unity with power and substance, while the South fought "for a belated principle of government, an outgrown economy, an impossible purpose" that it could not escape. Wilson concluded that "it required the terrible exercise of prolonged war to impart to the national idea diffused vitality and authentic power." Thus an unavoidable clash resulted in a strengthened country.[18]

After some hesitation, Wilson spoke out in favor of the Spanish-American War and the consequent occupation of the Philippines. For a year after the Treaty of Paris ended hostilities, he remained silent before openly endorsing the view that the United States fought to free Cuba. Finally, Wilson decided that it was not a war of conquest, but one to "give Cuba self-government." A "moral obligation" compelled America to fulfill the original task, while a "point of conscience" required its application to the Philippines as well. "It was my personal wish at the time that we should not take the Philippines," Wilson explained in 1899, but he later reconsidered his position. He realized that American possession of the islands offered the opportunity to help the Filipinos, for

Americans would have to train them for the responsibilities of freedom and democracy. The islanders "can have liberty no cheaper than we got it," he argued; "they must first take the discipline of law, must first love order and instinctively yield to it. . . . We are old in this learning and must be their tutors." He added that "if we are indeed bent upon service and not mastery, we shall give them more" than law and self-rule. The United States would give the Filipinos respect, independence, and a model to emulate.[19] Thus, Wilson believed that wars of liberation and service fully excused the costs they imposed on a nation. The yearnings of a people for political and individual liberty could find fulfillment, if necessary, through force. It seemed to him time for the United States to accept the duty of coming to the aid of those less fortunate in their struggle to be free.

Undoubtedly, such practical considerations as trade and economic expansion also encouraged Wilson to support involvement in Cuba and the Philippines. He referred, for instance, to the need for a "free outlet to the markets of the world" and the Philippines appeared to offer one, particularly because of its proximity to China. These considerations, though, remained secondary to the lofty ideals of service and humanitarian aid. Wilson foresaw better opportunities than mere economic advantages for the country. As he wrote at the end of 1901:

> It is by the widening vision that nations, as men, grow and are made great. We need not fear the expanding scene. It was plain destiny that we should come to this, and if we have kept our ideals clear, unmarred, commanding through the great century and the moving scenes that made us a nation, we may keep them also through the century that shall see us a great power in the world. Let us put our leading characters at the front; let us pray that vision may come with power; let us ponder our duties like men of conscience and temper our ambitions like men who seek to serve, not to subdue the world; let us lift our thoughts to the level of the great tasks that await us, and bring a great age in with the coming of our day of strength.[20]

A dozen years before he swore the presidential oath, Wilson here outlined several of the themes that would run through the two terms of his administration. As a result of the uses of force employed during the Spanish-American War, the United States could assume its rightful place of leadership among the nations of the world. Wilson predicted that a new era would be inaugurated that would take its motivation from the highest of ideals and would gain its dignity in the uses of power for the good of all. Armed strength, when applied with proper purposes and softened ambitions, would play a large role in the "expanding scene" of American power.

Early in his career as a scholar, Wilson realized that force had limitations that made it unsuitable for all but a few select purposes. He approvingly quoted Edmund Burke, one of his political heroes, who spoke out against England's attempt to suppress the American Revolution with violence. Burke objected on the grounds that such an expedient would be temporary, uncertain, and destructive. "It may subdue for a moment," he warned Parliament, "but it does not remove the necessity of subduing again; and a nation is not governed which is perpetually to be conquered." Burke advised that force be reserved until no other options were left, for if it failed, no recourse remained. If conciliation proved unsuccessful, arms could still be employed. Finally, Burke pointed out that force destroyed that which it tried to save. "The thing you fought for is not the thing you recover," he argued, "but depreciated, sunk, wasted, and consumed in the contest." Wilson presented these observations as evidence of Burke's "eminently practical system of thought." The future president took most of the warnings to heart. He went beyond the master, however, by recognizing that conditions sometimes necessitated turning to armed power despite its terrible price. For example, Wilson endorsed Burke's view of the French Revolution as "vicious" and "radically evil and corrupting," but added that the Revolution obtained "the way of a free life and a reformed . . . government for the French."[21] As president, Wilson's own uses of force reflected his belief that the yearning for freedom justified the resort to arms. In practice, he accepted only part of Burke's advice, that force could not conquer; he ignored the second half, that it could only destroy.

Wilson echoed Burke's admonitions during his presidency. "Force will not accomplish anything that is permanent," he told the Press Club in New York on June 30, 1916. "Force can sometimes hold things steady until opinion has time to form, but no force that was ever exerted, except in response to that opinion, was ever a conquering and predominant force."[22] Significantly, he made this statement after the navy had taken over Haiti and had landed in Santo Domingo. On these two occasions, when Wilson did overcome entire nations by arms, he employed the military only for the establishment of order and American supervision in areas where disorder and apparent anarchy prevailed. For the remaining time of the occupations, the marines served as policemen, overseeing native constabularies that maintained the peace and enforced their government's authority. Naval forces subdued Haiti in order to create an indigenous government which, though a prisoner to the will of the United States, nonetheless cleansed Wilson of the stain of building an American empire. The reliance on Haitian leaders fell into line with Wilson's speech to the Press Club.

Santo Domingo differed from its neighbor because its leadership refused to bow before U.S. power. An American military government, staffed by navy and marine officers, administered the country, not in the name of the United States, but for the benefit of the people of the Dominican Republic. On that side of the island, Wilson came closest to his definition of conquering, but he excused his actions by maintaining that he worked for the salvation of the Dominicans and not for America's self-interests. Wilson did not perceive the occupation as an attempt to subjugate the populace of Santo Domingo to the permanent and complete control of the United States. In effect, he employed American armed power in both Haiti and the Dominican Republic in order to give himself time to make the publics of both countries responsive to his tutelage.

Over two years after the speech to the Press Club, when Wilson announced the armistice with Germany ending World War I, he expressed once again his belief in the limits of force. "To conquer with arms is to make only a temporary conquest," he advised Congress; "to conquer the world by earning its esteem is to make a permanent conquest." Later, he explained the "colossal blunder" Germany made when it decided to go to war. If it had but waited another generation it would have accomplished all that it wanted through trade and commercial expansion. Instead, Germany's ambitions demanded that it take a short cut to world power and domination. As Wilson explained, "She must needs attempt to conquer by arms, and the world will always acclaim the fact that it is impossible to conquer it by arms, that the only thing that conquers it is the sort of service which can be rendered in trade, in intercourse, in friendship, and that there is no conquering power which can suppress the freedom of the human spirit."[23] Wilson obeyed this general rule with his own uses of force, for he turned to them always as a last resort and only to achieve specific goals. He designed his employment of armed power to fit the problems that confronted him and the policies that he pursued.

Wilson's greatest mistake and the underlying tragedy of all his interventions was to ignore the last of Edmund Burke's warnings, that force destroyed that which it was designed to preserve. Wilson's inability to heed this advice resulted from the American democratic ideology that he embraced so fervently and self-righteously. Wilson wanted to encourage people to obtain more democratic ways of life. He continually took notice of those areas of the world racked by turmoil and revolution by moving to direct that unrest toward his vision of the proper solution. His desire to help marked him as humanitarian, but his definition of the solution branded him as ethnocentric. In his efforts to gain people their liberty, he denied them the right to choose their own destiny.

As president, Wilson assumed the moral obligation to come to the support of democratic revolutions in other nations. He took this stand even in the face of resistance from those whom he wished to save because he did not doubt the righteousness of his cause. "If I cannot retain my moral influence over a man except by occasionally knocking him down, if that is the only basis upon which he will respect me, then for the sake of his soul I have got occasionally to knock him down," he told the National Press Club in May 1916. "If a man will not listen to you quietly in a seat, sit on his neck and make him listen."[24] This statement summarized the approach that Wilson took to help others. He intervened twice in Mexico to assist the Mexicans to achieve the political and social goals that he outlined for them. Similarly, he sent troops into Haiti and Santo Domingo when the peoples of those two nations ignored his efforts to show them the proper forms of political freedom and democracy. The attempts to help these three countries were carried out in a presumptuous fashion that ignored their own national pride and ambitions by demanding of each that they become American in their governments and their ideals. During each of these interventions, Wilson strove to restore order and political stability over the chaos of revolution. If he could accomplish that goal, he hoped next to erect democratic governments, which he saw as the only way to ensure long-term stability. In his ethnocentric, albeit humanitarian, efforts to tutor Mexico, Haiti, and Santo Domingo, Wilson did not spare the rod.

In effect, Wilson was simply too American to understand the absurdity of his position. His ideology blinded him to the fact that this help was unwanted. The Christian in him cried out for a crusade; the American in him defined its nature; and the world offered him opportunities in abundance to embark on reforming expeditions. He refused to renounce armed power as a weapon because he believed it necessary in the battle against oppression. As he forcefully declared in 1911, "there are times in the history of nations when they must take up the crude instruments of bloodshed in order to vindicate spiritual conceptions. For liberty is a spiritual conception, and when men take up arms to set other men free, there is something sacred and holy in the warfare. I will not cry 'peace' so long as there is sin and wrong in the world." He admitted that force was a "clumsy and brutal method" of achieving justice, but he could not recommend its abolition until "just" wars became obsolete.[25]

Wilson expected other nations to realize that his country would resort to arms for no selfish purpose. Other governments might plot ways of extending their domination over other peoples, but the United

States maintained its military establishment only for its self-defense or to serve others. "The idea of America is to serve humanity," Wilson advised the graduates of the naval academy in June 1914; "you are on an errand which other navies have sometimes forgotten; not an errand of conquest, but an errand of service." America nurtured no selfish or aggressive ambitions; it would never again take territory away from a weaker state. This intention, Wilson avowed, resulted from the principles of the country. "The force of America," he said, "is the force of moral principle." America's ideals, its self-defense, and its opposition to aggression were the only things for which the United States would fight.[26]

The vision of America in the service of the world was a favorite theme of Wilson's in his public discussions of force. It grew out of his Presbyterian training and reflected the profound influence that religion exerted on his life. As a leader, it also indicated the kind of selfless idealism that Wilson expected his constituents to understand. "Whether by one process or another," he asserted in January 1916, "we have made ourselves in some sort the champions of free government and national sovereignty in both continents of this hemisphere." At the time, he had occupied Veracruz and Haiti and, within a few months, would send the punitive expedition deep into Mexico and would order the navy to take over Santo Domingo. A year later, the declaration of war against Germany extended this ideal of service to global proportions. The process of becoming champion involved a heavy dose of armed power. Wilson explained these actions as though they inhered in the national character: "America was born into the world to do mankind service, and no man is a true American in whom the desire to do mankind service does not take precedence over the desire to serve himself. If I believed that the might of America was a threat to any free man in the world, I would wish America to be weak, but I believe the might of America is the might of righteous purpose and of a sincere love for the freedom of mankind."[27] The origins and purposes of the United States distinguished it from any other nation in the world. Because it stood alone as representative of a greater truth, Wilson accepted the obligation of promoting the principles it held sacred. For this purpose, he never hesitated to use the entire power and resources of the country, including its armed power.

In addition to emphasizing service, Wilson recognized two other legitimate motives for using force. First, he never questioned the right of self-defense and the protection of American rights under international law and its national interests as an international entity. Second, he became convinced, through his observation of the events surrounding World War I, of the duty to resist aggression, whether or not it threatened the physical well-being of the United States. "We regard war merely as a means of asserting the rights of a people against aggression," Wilson noted in 1915. From that date on, he preached in increasingly stronger language the theme that the United States would stand up against aggression and unprincipled ambitions, that America "would lend her moral influence not only, but her physical force, if other nations will join her, to see to it that no nation and no group of nations tries to take advantage of another nation or group of nations, and that the only thing ever fought for is the common rights of humanity."[28] Both the premise of self-defense and that of resistance to aggression received active support in April 1917 when Wilson decided on war against Germany in order to defend the security of the U.S. by thwarting the former's war aims. Each premise was to find legal substance in the Covenant of the League of Nations.

Wilson's willingness to employ force outside the Western Hemisphere went hand in hand with his growing awareness of the interdependence of the world. This insight played a major role in the development of Wilsonian diplomacy. "The time for provincial thinkers has gone by," he argued in July 1916. "We must play a great part in the world whether we choose it or not." In support of this recognition and as a means of underwriting it, Wilson announced his willingness to "lend the full force of this nation, moral and physical, to a league of nations which shall see to it that nobody disturbs the peace of the world without submitting his case first to the opinion of mankind."[29] The fruition of this commitment came with the decision not only to advocate, but also to design such a league for the future protection of mankind from the evils of the previous international system.

During the first half of 1919, the victorious nations associated in opposition against Germany gathered in Paris to settle the world's affairs. Out of this assembly came the League of Nations, the heart of Wilson's program and ambitions for the United States. The covenant of the league detailed major changes in all areas of international relations. Although essentially designed for peaceful pursuits and to offer peaceful means of resolving disputes, it allowed for the uses of force as well. As Wilson explained, "Armed force is in the background in this program, but it *is* in the background, and if the moral force of the world will not suffice, the physical force of the world shall. But that is the last resort, because this is intended as a constitution of peace, not as a league of war." Implicit in the design was the assumption that wars of the future would resemble those of the past—that is, they would result from the attempts of stronger states to take advantage of weaker ones.

Wilson helped create the league to combat such efforts. Collective security offered "the united protection of the world" against any aggression, with the hope that the mere existence of the combination would be enough to discourage any pretentious ambitions to steal forcibly from the weak.[30] The League of Nations represented, not a break for Wilson with his past, but the product of a slow evolution in his thought that began with the recognition that motive and objective controlled the uses of force, and that ended with his decision to take steps to control the scope of those purposes and the extent of the goals.

THE WILSONIAN ADVISERS

Only a handful of assistants played substantial parts in shaping Wilson's ideas on force and in advising him on the uses of armed power. The civilian advisers occupied precarious positions because they served at the whim and will of the president, subordinating their own independent views to his decisions. Of this select group, two, Secretary of State William Jennings Bryan and Secretary of War Lindley Garrison, eventually resigned in protest over some aspect of Wilson's policies. Two more, Colonel Edward M. House, who held no official position until the Paris Peace Conference, and Secretary of State Robert Lansing, Bryan's successor, fell from grace as a result of their disagreements with the president. In the end, only two, Secretary of the Navy Josephus Daniels and Secretary of War Newton Baker, survived to the last as full members of Wilson's trusted coterie. The separate and individual influences of each of these men on the development and implementation of Wilson's policies is detailed in later chapters, but it is appropriate here to discuss in general terms their respective views on the role of force in international affairs.

William Jennings Bryan proclaimed his pacifism early in his life and wore it on his sleeve ever after. As secretary of state from March 1913 to May 1915, Bryan spent most of his time negotiating "cooling off" treaties with a score and a half of other nations. These treaties were designed to promote peace by imposing arbitration and a compulsory period of waiting before war could be declared. Bryan hoped that this year-long interim would dissipate passions to allow a more rational settlement to develop. He refused to accept war as an alternative and, in 1915, fearing that Wilson's policies toward the sinking of the *Lusitania* would lead to war with Germany, he resigned his office in protest, hoping that this act would compel Wilson to accept more peaceful tactics.

Yet, Bryan's pacifism extended only to the developed or civilized nations of his time and did not apply to the underdeveloped or backward ones. Not only did he support the occupation of Veracruz in 1914, but he also advised Wilson to take that action, despite the explicit warning that it might lead to war. Similarly, he helped define policies toward Haiti and Santo Domingo that not only contemplated the uses of force during his tenure, but that led to the take-over of those two nations after his resignation. He objected, not to force per se, but to that well-defined type of force known as war, when civilized nations consciously and purposefully declare according to legal formats and by legal procedures that they are at war with another country. Interventions in weaker or more primitive countries appeared to Bryan as substantially different and, therefore, more acceptable. The apparent contradictions of his beliefs, which were in tune with many of his contemporaries, make Bryan appear the buffoon, but his confusion and inconstancy did not detract from his important role as Wilson's first secretary of state.

The first secretary of war, Lindley Garrison, shared none of Bryan's concerns about pacifism. Although hardly a warmonger, Garrison saw force as a ready and convenient substitute for more peaceful methods. He played only a small role in the course of Wilsonian interventionism, for his advice on force was limited to the occupation of Veracruz. The army took no part in the Haitian affair, and Garrison resigned prior to the other interventions. Despite this lack of opportunity, Garrison's views were important, for he tended to balance the pacifist sympathies prevalent in the cabinet. He became an early and earnest advocate of armed involvement in Mexico and helped to define the uses of force during the occupation of Veracruz. In effect, Garrison agreed with the president's ultimate aim of bringing democracy to Mexico, but he soon fell out of sympathy with Wilson's tactics.

Wilson turned to a pacifist to take over the War Department in 1916. Ironically, Newton Baker was sworn in on the same day that the decision was made to launch the punitive expedition, an omen that boded ill for the survival of his pacifism. Yet Baker's proclaimed pacifism did allow for exceptions. "I believe in peace and in the proper enforcement of the laws of peace—by force if necessary," he declared on March 10, 1916, the day he became secretary. Questions of war and peace seemed less important to him than the greater issues of liberty and democracy. World War I represented a good example of Baker's ability to convince himself of the necessity of armed power to achieve the better goals. He favored peace "at almost any price" in the summer of 1916, but refused to define the "almost." Later, he determined its meaning by drawing the line short of freedom and democracy. "Each day," he said on November 28, 1917, "is demonstrating more and more that the only thing left worth fighting for is to free the world from the menace of having constantly either to fight or prepare for fighting and, of course, that is the democratic gain." As with Wilson, Baker looked to the motives and goals of armed power before deciding its morality and efficacy. Their pacifism meant only that they judged force harshly by allowing only the highest of ideals and the greatest of principles to motivate them.[31]

Two historians have written that Josephus Daniels, as secretary of the navy, "was an able man in the wrong position."[32] To some extent, the description is an accurate one, for Daniels's pacifism, his liberalism, and his desire to democratize the navy put him at direct odds with his uniformed subordinates. But, in spite of the complaints of navy leaders, Daniels made great strides toward improving the strength and capabilities of the service, as well as the common lot of the individual seaman. Nor did his pacifism interfere with his ability to carry out Wilson's policies loyally and capably. Wilson ordered the occupations of Veracruz, Haiti, and the Dominican Republic through his secretary of the navy. If Daniels felt qualms about these instances of force, he swallowed his objections in subservience to his president.

Early in his tenure, Daniels noted in his diary that "the Administration is sincerely desirous of promoting the peace of the world and to that end they are prepared to lead or inaugurate movements that will result in hastening the day when war shall be ended." No one could know, least of all the secretary of the navy, that these movements would include armed power. Daniels clung to this promise of peace throughout the remainder of his career, explaining, for example, his support of America's entrance into World War I by justifying it as a means toward peace. As he wrote Ray S. Baker in 1933:

> I lived one hundred years in those months and did everything I could, consistent with loyalty to the "Old Man," to keep America out of the war, until the Kaiser laid off the lines of the sea and told us where we could go and where we could not go. That seemed to me to bring the issue clear-cut whether German imperialism should dominate the world or should be checked in its mad career. After living in Gethsemane, I came to the conclusion that we ought to go into the war and was largely influenced to that conviction by the sincere belief that our entrance into the war would end imperialism and would bring about permanent and world peace. I feel quite sure that neither Wilson nor I would ever have voted to go into the war if we could have foreseen the tragedy that resulted from the failure to follow Wilson's lead.[33]

Daniels's pacifism was sincere and heartfelt, but it did not outweigh his desire for final peace and his faith in Wilson. He merely went a step farther than Bryan in confronting, and thereby exacerbating, the contradictions and inconsistencies inherent in the simple act of living in a complex world.

Among Wilson's advisers, Colonel Edward M. House exercised the greatest influence. This honorary colonel held no official position until late in the administration, preferring, instead, to adopt a stance of selfless confidant and friend to the president. He rarely voiced any objections to Wilson's decisions, but influenced his policies by finessing and manipulating Wilson through a combination of "yes man" and schemer. Wilson trusted him implicitly, for, more than any other man, House shared with Wilson a close kinship of ideals and objectives. The president described the colonel as his alter ego. He allowed him a greater degree of independence and self-direction than he did his other advisers. House used that trust, which resembled a blind faith, to advantage, increasing his power steadily by the information and advice he offered Wilson. He carried out independent and private negotiations through a complex network of contacts in furtherance of their common goals. House may have danced to Wilson's music, but he at least chose his own steps.

Like all of Wilson's confidants, and like Wilson himself, House believed in peace and dreamed of a better day when international rivalries would not find resolution in violence. However, he was not uncomfortable with the uses of force during those occasions when armed power appeared as the best method of achieving peace. For example, he concluded long before Wilson did that the United States should enter the war against Germany. Most of his efforts following the sinking of the *Lusitania* were directed at aligning Wilson behind the Entente powers. House accepted force as a means to an end, without, as Wilson did, worrying about the price of the goal. This attitude helped him overcome any moral or principled objections to its uses. He encouraged Wilson to turn to it, and praised him for doing so, when its employment seemed proper and inevitable. For House, as eventually for Wilson, war became the purchase price of peace.

Of all Wilson's advisers, Robert Lansing had the most influence on the uses of force and developed the clearest exposition of their role in foreign policy. An international lawyer of some renown before becoming Wilson's counsellor for the State Department and then the secretary, Lansing relied heavily on the law for his interpretations of armed power. Wilson turned to him for legal justifications of all the interventions and Lansing's advice helped determine the course of each instance of force.

Lansing, for example, defined the occupation of Veracruz as a reprisal, an excuse that allowed Wilson to intervene in the Mexican Revolution without the risk of being branded an aggressor. Lansing held true to Wilsonian ideals, but he approached their realization with a cold logic that supported the emotional faith of the president. As early as July 11, 1915, for instance, he concluded that the United States would have to combat German ambitions to protect the democratic countries from imperial domination. Consequently, from July 1915 to April 1917, he worked steadily toward leading the United States into the war, despite Wilson's doubts and hesitation. The secretary affected Wilson's policies both by his recommendations and by the justifications he supplied. House was the closest adviser Wilson had on questions of overall policy and on detailed negotiations and strategy, but no other confidant played a more vital nor interesting role when it came to the uses of force than Lansing.

Ironically, Wilson fired Lansing in 1920 for trying to usurp presidential power through urging an intervention in Mexico. Two years later, Lansing set down on paper his philosophy on force. "It is a fact, which cannot be successfully denied," he began, "that physical force is the only effective instrumentality for accomplishment in the sphere of international relations as it is within an organized state. Force has built empires, and force has destroyed empires. From the very beginning of political organization force has been a protection and a peril to the independence of communities and to national existence." He identified armed power as the "greatest underlying actuality in all history," which became effective and increasingly potent as civilizations organized themselves into distinct political groupings. As part of this evolution into the modern nation-state, two motivations or drives appeared. Originally, "material impulses" motivated men and nations, and these impulses gained dominance over behavior in primitive societies where man was controlled by animal instincts and unrestrained appetites. The second group of impulses, which Lansing called "moral," grew out of the development of culture and higher thought. Every society traveled through a stage of material desires and only slowly and haltingly acquired moral ones. The process caused conflict both within the society itself and between nations.

In domestic affairs, Lansing believed that moral influences controlled almost every major nation, but that influence did not spill over into the realm of international relations. Here material impulses guided the behavior of states. Nations remained "in a state of barbarism responding to material impulses and exercising force in their intercourse as these impulses dictated." In other words, "a nation deals with its people in a civilized way and with other nations in a savage way." He argued that "force is still dominant in human affairs." It would remain so until the power of moral impulses replaced material ones. Embittered by his last dispute with Wilson, Lansing concluded with a rejection of the ideals that Wilson attempted to infuse into his diplomacy: "To assume that the foreign policy of a nation is based on unselfish purpose or is directed by a sense of moral obligation is to assume a fallacy, and to predicate one's own foreign policy on such an assumption is to commit a gross error."[34] Although he reached this conclusion after leaving office under difficult circumstances, elements of it appeared throughout his policies.

In a sense, Lansing resembled the pessimist in search of hope, while Wilson appeared as the optimist in flight from despair. Social Darwinism obviously influenced the secretary's thinking, for he accepted the slow processes of evolution as the only way to achieve his ideals. Yet, these opinions were less important for our purposes than the fact that he recognized force as a way of life in the international community. As such, it worked along certain regulated lines defined by international law. The law showed him that force fell into different categories, that reprisal, for instance, differed substantially from war because it was meant to be used in a certain fashion in response to certain conditions. This simple realization had a profound impact on the uses of force in Wilsonian diplomacy, for it assumed certain limitations on different types of armed power. These limitations were defined by policy.

Wilson's advisers, then, shared a general agreement that policy and purpose directed the uses of arms, although for policymakers this hardly represented a unique understanding. Some of Wilson's advisers, like Bryan, rejected any employment of force against civilized nations, while others, like Lansing, accepted armed power as a fact of international life. Still others, such as Baker or Daniels, opposed force in general, but found themselves approving it for specific cases. This resulted in a range of views presented to Wilson, which gave him some opportunity to examine alternatives both to force itself and to uses of force. His demand for loyalty and approval from his subordinates tended to limit discussion once a decision was made, but he accepted advice and suggestions before settling on a particular policy. Most of the men he chose to help him held only general and poorly formed views on the role of force; consequently, they were never particularly consistent in their suggestions. But, they all held in common a basic understanding that armed power, under certain circumstances, could play a vital and important part in the promotion and enactment of policy. If they reached no real consensus about the circumstances to which it applied, they at least understood that force was a political creature.

Wilson himself agreed with this understanding. His public discussions of force contained several themes that reflected his uses of it. First, he looked to the motives and objectives behind the resort to arms in judging its morality and efficacy. This tendency underscored his emphasis on the employment of the military as an extension of policy, a characteristic of all his interventions. Wilson never forgot who was in charge. He consistently controlled the armed services to fit his goals and purposes. This aspect was central to the uses of force and will appear throughout this study. Secondly, as a leader, Wilson presented to his constituents three basic justifications for war that he believed acceptable and that he expected his followers to accept. These rationales, the promotion of ideals and principles through service to others, self-defense, and resistance to aggression, each found expression in his resorts to arms and became the strategic bedrock of his policies. Finally, Wilson's unquestioning faith in American ideals distorted his vision of what other peoples desired. If he was humanitarian in his hopes and plans for the less fortunate, he was nevertheless ethnocentric in his efforts to assist them.

2.
THE POWER of CIVILIAN CONTROL:
Mexico

Woodrow Wilson came to power during the formative years of the age of experts. The Progressive movement in the United States, in which he took a leading part, encompassed a variety of reforms that reflected the increasing industrialization and specialization of American life. A vast expansion of information and detail inhered in the transformation from a rural to an industrial society, which resulted in a troubled unrest. The changes, in effect, opened the door to an infinite unknown. No longer could a single man study exhaustively many unrelated fields as Thomas Jefferson had done a century earlier, for knowledge had exceeded the limits of the individually knowable. This excess drove the Renaissance Man into extinction by compelling people to take satisfaction in the mastery of one subject. Men carved out niches for themselves, relying on experts in other areas to supply them with the information necessary to offset their unbalanced learning. To deal with the problems confronting them, these cohorts in ignorance turned to specialists from every field for solutions.

Wilson, for example, specialized in American history and government, but he relied on such men as Louis D. Brandeis, William G. McAdoo, Albert S. Burleson, and David F. Houston for advice and direction in those areas beyond his ken. If no experts were readily available, he enlisted aid from people willing to develop a specialty. Thus, Wilson sent William Bayard Hale and John Lind to investigate the Mexican Revolution; he dispatched John F. Fort and Charles C. Smith to Santo Domingo and Haiti to solve the problems racking those two countries; he assigned Colonel House and Robert Lansing to different aspects of World War I; and he employed William R. Bullitt and Roland Morris to study the Bolshevik Revolution and the Allied intervention in Siberia. These men supplied the expertise that enabled Wilson to grapple with the confusion and turmoil reverberating from the collapse of the world of his youth.

Unfortunately, Wilson's judgment in selecting diplomatic agents was, for the most part, notoriously poor. His method of choosing any individual who expressed a willingness to develop an expertise in a particular area accounted for most of this failure. Lind, for example, knew little of Mexico before embarking on his mission in the summer of 1913. He was of Swedish background, a former governor of Minnesota, and, most importantly in terms of his selection for the mission, he was an old friend and early supporter of William Jennings Bryan, who nominated him to Wilson. These credentials hardly qualified him for the Mexican mission. Wilson's other choices for foreign missions, with a few exceptions, were generally of the same caliber—intelligent, well-meaning men who wanted to help. In selecting these individuals, Wilson looked more at their progressive and humanitarian impulses rather than at their experience. He assumed that they would develop an expertise, so he looked first to be sure that their hearts were in the right place.

The leaders of the American military served as Wilson's body of experts on the application of force by recommending the precise methods for employing arms that adequately met Wilson's policy directives. Wilson established overall policy and guiding principles of action, but he turned to the ranking officers of the armed services for the details of implementation. When individual officers of the armed forces overstepped the artificial and rather arbitrary bounds that Wilson erected to govern their behavior, they paid for their indiscretion by receiving a swift rebuke from the president. He allowed the military little freedom of action, for he expected it to fight only when he ordered it, only for the reasons he felt worthy of battle, and only until he decided to quit. Wilson demanded much from the services, but most of all he claimed their complete subservience to his will.

The two interventions in Mexico, the occupation of Veracruz in 1914 and the punitive expedition in 1916, illustrate the degree of control that Wilson exerted over the armed forces. Both instances of force are useful case studies for understanding the strained relationship between the military and its commander-in-chief. Mexican policy served as the battleground on which the president upheld his leadership in determining America's response to the Mexican Revolution. Yet, even though Wilson successfully subdued the army and navy to his purposes, the leading officers of both services remained inconsolable. They begrudgingly gave him control over their actions, but not their thoughts and not their private views. Consequently, Wilson used the interventions to fit his general framework of foreign policy, but in accomplishing that difficult goal, he lost the sympathy of the military men who served him. In the end, however, the military suffered the greater loss, for their failure to understand the president's policies meant that they could not comfortably fulfill the duties he assigned them. Wilson's policies represented the future of force; their objections echoed the call of a distant era that was silenced by the violence of the twentieth century.

For each of the interventions undertaken during the Wilson years, Wilson relied on his own judgment in determining when and how far to go. The ranking officers in Washington and on the scene were allowed to advise only on how to carry out the intervention, not on when or where to intervene. Nor did Wilson listen to their opinions of what the repercussions would be. The only exception to this general rule was the occupation of Haiti, which was initiated by the ranking naval officer on the scene in response to a bloody riot in Port-au-Prince. Even in this instance, the intervention was clearly in line with the admiral's previous orders, it was subsequently approved, and the Wilson administration escalated the original landing in the capital to the take-over of the whole country. The president drew a strict line between policy issues and military tactics. Few of his uniformed subordinates were allowed to cross it. His civilian advisers–cabinet members and the appointed experts—made recommendations on policy issues. Wilson's military advisers were generally restricted to addressing the tactics necessary for each intervention.

Wilson did not distrust the armed forces when they stayed within the specialty that he recognized them to have. The president realized his own limitations in the area of tactics and fighting and allowed his experts on force to determine the best way to occupy Veracruz, to take over Santo Domingo, or to carry out any of the other tasks he ordered. Civil-military relations deteriorated when Wilson believed certain members of the armed services tried to develop or influence policy, to act in a capacity beyond their expertise; he reacted quickly and severely. Only when understood in this sense can Wilson's administration be recognized as, to borrow Richard Challener's phrase, the "climax of civil supremacy."[1]

In general, the president took little interest in the affairs of the military. He usually approved promotions based on the recommendations of his secretaries of war and of the navy with little question. The selection of the chief of staff, for example, reflected the army's general promotion pattern based on length and quality of service. Wilson showed no particular desire to make personal choices. He did cause an uproar in the navy when he approved Daniels's choice for chief of naval operations. The selection of Captain William S. Benson, who was at the time the commander of the Philadelphia Navy Yard, offended higher ranking officers because of Benson's lack of experience and relatively low rank. Indeed, Daniels selected him in large part because he had not yet been molded by the navy. But this was more Daniels's choice than Wilson's. The president cared only that his military advisers stayed within the roles he assigned them; he did not search the ranks for individuals sympathetic to his policies.

Wilson accepted as a constitutional truth the premise that "the armed forces of the country must be the instruments of authority by which policy was determined." This belief went hand in hand with his assumption that the uses of force reflected basic policies and purposes. Similarly, he assigned to the military the task of carrying forth the ideals of the United States as reflected in the intentions of its leaders. As he said at the Biltmore Hotel in New York City on May 17, 1915:

> The mission of America is the only thing that a sailor or a soldier should think about. He has nothing to do with the formulation of her policy. He is to support her policy whatever it is; but he is to support her policy in the spirit of herself; and the strength of our policy is that we who for the time being administer the affairs of this Nation do not originate her spirit. We attempt to embody it; we attempt to realize it in action; we are dominated by it, we do not dictate it.[2]

So long as the armed forces accepted this duty and acted to further Wilson's policies, he brooked no quarrel with them.

Characterized by pettiness and mutual misunderstandings, Wilson's control over the armed services seemed destined for trouble. The stories of his difficulties with the military are legion and but a few examples will suffice to show their tenor. In the spring of 1913 during a crisis with Japan, the Joint Army and Navy Board offered unsolicited advice on the placement of various warships in preparation for hostilities. Wilson, Bryan, and Daniels demanded the dissolution of the board and punishment of its members. Only after the military retreated by apologizing did Wilson relent, but even then the effectiveness of the Joint Board was destroyed. At the end of 1913, Wilson ordered the secretaries of the army and navy to reprimand the members of the Military Order of the Caraboa, a society of veterans of the Philippine campaigns, because those officers had sung songs and ditties that mocked past and present Philippine policies. The president also resigned his honorary membership in that club only a few weeks after accepting it. Two years later, in the autumn of 1915, Wilson "turned white with passion" after reading in the newspaper that the general staff of the army was preparing war plans against Germany. Thereafter, the War College took pains to hide its efforts from the president, which hampered its work.[3] Other incidents abound. The point is clear enough—Wilson went to great lengths to ensure that his men of force remained within their expertise.

Nevertheless, Wilson relied heavily on those officers who gained his respect. General Hugh L. Scott, for instance, established himself as the expert on Pancho Villa. Wilson entrusted him with delicate negotiations for the protection of the Mexican-American border in the winter of 1915 and over the withdrawal of the punitive expedition in April and May 1916.[4] Scott's influence on American policies toward Mexico far exceeded his military specialty. During the occupation of Veracruz, Admiral Frank F. Fletcher earned the president's admiration and commendation. Before the seizure of the port, Wilson mistrusted Fletcher, for he suspected him of being out of sympathy with the government's intentions. The admiral assured his superiors that the suspicions were groundless.[5] Fletcher redeemed himself during the fight for Veracruz, which he commanded in its early stages. Wilson found much to esteem in the way Fletcher handled this very difficult assignment. The president recognized in these and other members of the armed services qualities that he regarded highly and, in a sense, he forgave them their military background. Unfortunately, the American military had more difficulty forgiving Wilson his background.

Raised to maturity in their careers under Republican tutelage, the military leaders who strove to implement Wilson's uses of force were unfamiliar, at best, with Democratic presidents. "It is rather tragic," General Leonard Wood, the chief of staff, observed in February 1913, "when you think of 16 years of accomplishment and the changes which have taken place in our country and policies, to realize that the party which has had more or less steady control is going out." Most officers found it difficult to adjust to Wilson's style of leadership. They never seemed content with the role that he allotted them. The president, however, insisted on holding the reins of power tightly. After four years of such treatment, General John J. Pershing could not contain his anger. Shortly before Wilson's reelection in 1916, Pershing expressed his frustration and his hope. "The political situation is seething now at home, and the election will probably be over before this note reaches you," he wrote Frederick Palmer. "So I am going to predict Republican success—the red-blooded American is still in the large majority."[6] Constantly suspicious of each other, Wilson and his uniformed subordinates shared a mutual antagonism that prohibited a close kinship between them. Their lack of understanding became increasingly evident during the course of the two Mexican interventions.

Force defined the issues between them, for if nothing else, the American military held dear its title as expert on employing arms. During the years prior to Wilson, the leading officers of the period gained valuable experience in fighting, most of it in underdeveloped countries. The Spanish-American War and the consequent Philippine insurrection gave such officers as Generals Wood, Scott, Pershing, Frederick Funston, and Tasker Bliss invaluable lessons. The navy, too, added to its expertise, not only through fighting, but also intellectually. The writings of Captain Alfred Thayer Mahan, particularly his major work, *The Influence of Sea Power Upon History,* introduced a global view to naval officers and set them to thinking in larger terms. Wilson, however, frustrated these designs by refusing the military a substantial say in the course of American foreign policy. Since much of his early diplomacy dealt with underdeveloped countries, the military felt particularly disgruntled. Had it not blazed the trail in the relations between the United States and such backward states as Cuba and the Philippines?

Simply stated, Wilson believed the answer to that question was irrelevant.

THE OCCUPATION OF VERACRUZ, 1914

Prior to Wilson's inauguration, revolution had swept across Mexico with increasing fury. In November 1910 Francisco Madero launched an insurgent movement against the government of Porfiro Díaz. Madero proved a successful, if clumsy, revolutionary by overthrowing Díaz. Unfortunately, he never solidified his support, particularly with the Mexican military. In February 1912, less than a month before Wilson took office, Madero was overthrown, assassinated, and replaced by General Victoriano Huerta. Opposition within Mexico to the usurper sprang up almost immediately. Venustiano Carranza and Pancho Villa allied together under the Constitutionalist banner to begin a war against the new dictator. The events surrounding Huerta's coup, known as the "Tragic Ten Days," appalled Wilson. He determined to rid Mexico of Huerta by helping to install a liberal, democratic government based on the model of the United States. He would teach Mexicans the proper methods of self-government.

American policy toward the Mexican Revolution during the Wilson period encompassed four major goals. First and foremost, Wilson intended to democratize Mexico by reshaping it in the image of the United States. Second, he determined to keep foreign influences, particularly British during the early years and German after America's entry into World War I, to a minimum. Third, Wilson hoped to keep the revolution from becoming too radicalized by directing it along democratic paths. Finally, after the passage of the new Mexican constitution in 1917, Wilson tried to forestall any attempts at the expropriation of American-owned properties or mineral rights as called for in the constitution. Force, he found, served him best in trying to achieve the first policy of democratizing the Mexican people. It offered few benefits in fulfilling the other aspects of these policies.[7]

Armed power did not become an issue during the spring and summer of 1913. "Intervention must be avoided until a time comes when it is inevitable, which God forbid!" Wilson exclaimed to his wife in August 1913. Secretaries Bryan and Daniels agreed. Bryan believed that intervention meant elevating "property rights ahead of human rights—to put the dollar above the man." Such a base motive seemed comparable to extending the nation's territory by conquest.[8] The Wilson administration intended to rely on other means.

Instead of initiating armed intervention, Wilson refused to recognize the Huerta regime. He embarked on a series of diplomatic maneuvers to oust the dictator. Within a week after becoming president, for example, Wilson released a statement concerning the administration's attitude toward revolutions in the Western Hemisphere. It spoke ominously, if not directly, to Mexico. "We can have no sympathy with those who seek to seize the power of government to advance their own personal interests or ambition," proclaimed the March 12 announcement. Wilson added his pledge of the "genuine disinterested friendship" of the United States in aiding any country to establish a constitutional government. The opposition to revolution and dictatorship enunciated in the press release became the theme of Wilson's policies toward revolutions in the Western Hemisphere, but he applied it first to Mexico.[9]

Before Wilson could do anything about the problem of Mexico, he needed to know what was going on across the border. With this in mind, he dispatched William Bayard Hale, a friend and early supporter, to Mexico on a fact-finding mission in late May 1913. Hale's reports presented a gloomy picture of conditions south of the border, which prompted Wilson to take a more active stand in the course of the revolution. Early in August, Wilson sent John Lind, a former governor of Minnesota and a political colleague of Bryan's, across the border to gain by negotiation the retirement of Huerta, an immediate armistice, and the implementation of free elections. Lind's letter of instructions revealed the attitude of the Wilson administration toward the war-torn country. Wilson described the United States as "Mexico's nearest friend," he disclaimed any selfish motives, and he promised to "act in the interests of Mexico alone." Lind was also to seek assurances that Huerta would not be a candidate for the presidency, that all parties would bind themselves to abide by the results of the vote, and that they would support the new president. It was an ambitious plan. Wilson concluded the instructions by protesting that the United States sought "to counsel Mexico for her own good."[10]

Yet, by the end of the month, Wilson realized that Huerta would not accept the good offices of the United States in solving the problems of the revolution. On August 27 the president announced to the Congress his policy of "watchful waiting," by which he meant that his administration would allow the revolution to take its course without overt interference from the north. The Lind mission gave the promise of success in the fall of 1913 when Huerta promised to hold elections, from which he excused himself as a candidate, but he went back on his word shortly before the scheduled October elections. He compounded the crime of becoming a candidate by arresting a large number of delegates to the Mexican congress. These actions made it clear that Lind's errand of service had failed.

Wilson, frustrated and angered by Huerta's double cross, thought of using force for the first time. He drafted a joint resolution and a speech to accompany it for presentation to Congress. The resolution declared that Huerta should resign, that the Mexican legislature should be reopened, and that constitutional government should be restored. It empowered Wilson "to use the entire land and naval forces of the United States and to call into active service of the United States the militia of the several states to such extent as he may deem necessary to carry these resolutions into effect." The draft disclaimed any intention of seizing Mexican territory or of impeding its sovereignty. The declared purpose was the reinstatement of democratic government. In his proposed speech, Wilson claimed that Americans were "bound by every obligation of honour and by the compulsion of sacred interests which go to the very foundation of constitutional government and of the integrity and independence of free states throughout America, North and South." Wilson never delivered the resolution or the speech, for the United States suffered no injury from Huerta's actions and the obligations of honor and service hardly warranted such drastic measures. In addition, certain powerful congressmen disapproved of the proposal. Huerta's enemies, the Constitutionalists, upon whom Wilson depended for support, also opposed any suggestion of such help from the United States.[11]

This brief aberration from the policy of watchful waiting showed that Wilson's patience with Mexico was wearing thin, but it had not yet reached the breaking point. The temptation to use force in the fall of 1913 was born of frustration at Huerta's seeming treachery, which Wilson took as a personal insult. Having believed that his policies had succeeded when Huerta promised elections, Wilson became all the more infuriated when the Mexican president went back on his word. The episode left Wilson bitter, but even in his irritation he finally realized that Huerta had given him no real grounds for intervention.

Wilson temporarily foreswore armed power and returned to diplomatic power. Throughout November 1913 he worked to isolate Huerta from any European, particularly British, assistance. In February 1914 Wilson introduced commercial power by lifting the arms embargo first imposed by William Howard Taft in 1912. This action allowed the Constitutionalists to purchase weapons and ammunition from the U.S. It represented an active measure in support of their cause.[12] Here the situation stood when, on April 9, 1914, Mexican soldiers arrested a handful of American sailors, taking two from a whaleboat flying flags fore and aft, at a dock in Tampico. This incident initiated a chain of events that led to the occupation of Veracruz, Wilson's first limited intervention.

Limited intervention had no place in the American military's views of the proper solution to the Mexican problem. The Army War College Division, which carried most of the responsibility for formulating the war plans for Mexico for both branches of the service, had no design for a limited invasion of Mexico.[13] Since the War College devoted much time and effort to analyzing the best way to deal with the revolution, its plans can be accepted as the most studious attitude of either the army or the navy. Not everyone agreed with the particular tactics endorsed by the War College, but few soldiers or sailors challenged the most basic assumption—that any intervention meant the complete take-over of Mexico.

The War College developed scores of plans and strategic studies during the Wilson period for dealing with the Mexican Revolution. At first, the division hesitated to incorporate the effects of the revolution into its various war plans and, until June 1913, the plans postulated that an invasion of Mexico would prompt the warring factions to unite in combat against the foreign foe. They contemplated a "war with the Republic of Mexico, whose people are assumed to be in revolt now, but certain to be united against an invader." Most of these earlier studies argued that the conquest of the Central Plateau and Mexico City would result in complete victory for the invaders. The division realized that these plans were not entirely applicable to the revolutionary situation, but, fearing to project otherwise, it hoped that the plans were flexible enough to meet any unforeseen circumstances.[14]

The division's views slowly changed when the revolution, instead of ending quickly, reached such a large magnitude of violence that it consumed the entire country. General William Crozier, chief of the division in June 1913, felt uneasy about the earlier studies. In an attempt to make the war plans more realistic, he introduced the view that Mexico was in chaos and ordered his subordinates to direct their thinking along new lines. His premises recognized that a government controlled Mexico City generally free from opposition, but it did not extend its authority beyond that region. The "long continued state of disorder throughout the country and the exhaustion of the resources of the central government" prohibited the Mexico City administration from marshaling its military power to fight off an invasion. Crozier's arguments, although not fully accepted, initiated a process of revision that brought the Mexican war plans into line with actual conditions across the border.[15]

Crozier alleviated the division's fear of a united Mexico, but he did not completely convince his subordinates. General Hunter H. Liggett, president of the Army War College, submitted a revised plan in July 1913 that showed the influence of Crozier's June memorandum as well as its limitations. The plan contained references to a united Mexico and added a new idea that opposition would come from "such a force as 15,000,000 people could put into the field." This number included Mexican regular troops and irregulars. Liggett's mention of the latter implied that an invasion of Mexico would quickly pass from the traditional style of warfare into a guerrilla war. Obviously influenced by Crozier's ideas, Liggett proposed a novel area of interest for the war planners. He postulated that the unorganized resistance would "always be so great and troublesome that no plan should contemplate for the occupation of Mexico less than the total force provided in the basic plan." He estimated that the invading army should be approximately 246,000 men along the invasion routes, with another 18,000 men in reserve. The key to his arguments lay in the assertion that such a force was needed *"if the territory is to be completely occupied by our troops, and a stable government established."* This plan, built on Crozier's specifications, influenced subsequent studies. Crozier had introduced the idea that Mexico presented a problem not of a healthy nation, but of one trapped in its own disorder. Liggett concluded from that premise that the object of intervention centered on the period after Mexico's army had been defeated.[16] The alternative of a limited intervention to achieve clearly defined political goals seemed to occur to no one except Woodrow Wilson.

The idea that fighting could be contained either geographically or politically was foreign to the education and experience of the military. Despite the precedents of intervention in China in 1900 and Nicaragua in 1911, these men equated war with bloodshed. They assumed that the former, of necessity and by definition, had to be pursued to its final conclusion of victory or defeat. Yet, the precedents themselves were not so clear. The intervention in Nicaragua led to de facto American control over the government, which meant that it was not very limited. The Boxer Rebellion was seen as a rescue operation—what later would be called a police action—and did not seem appropriate for comparison with Mexico, particularly since China was far away and Mexico was a neighbor. The War College assumed that the purpose of intervention in Mexico was the restoration of constitutional government; this objective, in its view, required the defeat of regular and irregular forces and the occupation of the country. Anything less was seen as a waste of men and resources. The military learned little from earlier limited interventions partly because these examples seemed inappropriate to a nation of the size and former strength of Mexico and partly because limited interventions, by definition, restricted the influence, and therefore the power, of the military. The members of the War College, and with them other soldiers and sailors, wanted to believe that any intervention in Mexico would lead to war because it was during war that the military gained its highest prestige and its greatest responsibilities.

Thus, military officers scoffed at any suggestion of limited intervention. When John Lind, for example, outlined a plan for the seizure of the customshouse at Veracruz in the fall of 1913, Admiral Fletcher "called Governor Lind's attention to the fact that such a procedure would be an act of war, possibly attended with serious consequences." General Tasker Bliss, the commander of the southern department during the occupation of Veracruz, summed up the military's views. At the time of the seizure, Bliss objected strenuously to orders limiting his troops to a defensive posture even in the event of a Mexican attack. He explained, with reference to his subordinates, that "their own Government has taught them at expensive military schools and by other forms of expensive military training, ever since their entry into the service, that war is a question of fact; that although it may not have been declared by one side, it may have been declared by the other side; that, whether it be declared by either or both sides or not, the actual status may be created by war like acts."[17] Events, however, proved the military wrong in its assumption that fighting meant war. The seizure of the customshouse and the entire city of Veracruz in April 1914 did not, as Fletcher had predicted, cause a war between the United States and Mexico. Bliss, too, was wrong in believing that war was a question of fact created by warlike acts. Instead, as Wilson intuited, it was a question of policy and intention. Nations could commit warlike acts, such as the occupation of another country's city, without the consequence of war if both sides showed that they had no intention of going to war and if they moved quickly to contain the intervention. Wilson introduced a daring complexity into the military's straightforward formula for war and peace. He showed that battles could be fought outside of a condition of war and that the process of carrying the latter to its ultimate end no longer obtained as a matter of course.

"This is a hell of a war," a marine sentry told Jack London while both served in Veracruz, the one as a fighter, the other as a reporter.[18] The observation aptly summarized the military's attitude toward Wilson's first intervention. Amateurs to the methods of limited interventions, the soldiers and sailors who strove to carry out the president's policies found no benchmarks to guide them as they fought for control of a city but were prohibited from pursuing the battle to what they assumed was its logical conclusion. The issue was further compounded because the war plans designated Veracruz as the landing point for the invasion force—the temptation to put the plans into effect was painful to resist. Although the commanding officers who bore the burdens of responsibility for implementing Wilson's policies successfully carried out their orders, they did so in a fog of confusion and with resentment toward their civilian commander-in-chief. The occupation exacerbated the existing strains in the relationship. Veracruz offered the military the chance to learn new methods for the integration of combat into policy; its unwillingness to learn seriously hampered its education.

Ironically, a military initiative inaugurated the immediate crisis. Admiral Henry T. Mayo, the senior officer present at Tampico, demanded a twenty-one gun salute as an apology for the arrest of his men by Mexican soldiers on April 9, 1914. He did so on his own authority. Mayo interpreted the arrest as a national insult, a view that both Wilson and his civilian and military advisers endorsed. Two other incidents compounded the crime. On April 11 a Mexican censor delayed the transmission of a telegram from the State Department to Chargé d'Affaires Nelson O'Shaughnessy. On the same day, Mexican soldiers at Veracruz arrested an orderly from the USS *Minnesota* as he attempted to pick up mail at the post office. Admiral Fletcher recognized the trivial nature of the latter incident, adding in his report that "the attitude of the Mexican authorities was correct, there is no cause for complaint against them." But Wilson, who despised Huerta for stubbornly refusing American help and who was angered by the Tampico arrest, saw in the detention of the orderly and in the delay of the telegram additional evidence of the Huerta faction's animosity toward the United States. As Secretary of the Navy Daniels later pointed out, the "atmosphere of studied insult by Huerta" was the major grievance that caused the occupation of Veracruz.[19]

The eleven days between April 9 and April 21, when the port was seized, witnessed a flurried exchange of notes between Washington and Mexico City as the Wilson administration tried to compel Huerta by diplomatic power to perform the twenty-one gun salute. The Mexican leader refused to comply, even in the face of Wilson's use of military power through the dispatch of the Atlantic Fleet to Mexican waters. Not even the president's threatened use of armed power could persuade Huerta to give in to the American demands. The situation was further complicated when Wilson learned of the possible arrival at Veracruz of the German-owned SS *Ypiranga* and its cargo of arms and ammunition purchased earlier by the Huerta government. On the night of April 20 Wilson summoned his secretaries of state, war, and navy, his highest military advisers, and John Lind to the White House. They conferred for several hours before deciding to take the city of Veracruz.

Early the next morning, Daniels and Bryan informed the president of the imminent arrival of the *Ypiranga,* and Wilson ordered the navy to seize the Veracruz customshouse. When Daniels transmitted this command to Fletcher, he added that the admiral could expand his operations by occupying the entire city only in the event of Mexican resistance or in case the Mexican authorities fled the city leaving no one in control. Fletcher encountered unorganized fighting shortly after landing his troops, and determined that both conditions obtained. Consequently, by April 23, the United States controlled the entire city.

The seizure of Veracruz revitalized Wilson's moribund diplomatic efforts to help Mexico achieve democracy and stability. The president grasped quickly the opportunities opened for him by the landing of American forces at the port. He transformed the occupation into an attempt to use force to implement a novel diplomatic initiative. The landing of the marines and bluejackets on Mexican soil permitted Wilson to claim a new reason for taking an interest in the solution of Mexico's difficulties. He had to protect his men and the disturbances of the revolution threatened them. Once the troops landed at Veracruz, Wilson used their presence as evidence of his right to settle the problems in Mexico. The presence of American sailors and soldiers gave Wilson, or so he claimed, standing to negotiate. In effect, he changed the type of power from diplomatic—which had failed throughout 1913—to armed. Wilson did not give up on diplomacy, he simply used force to open additional channels through which his diplomacy might then find success.

Wilson quickly maneuvered to bring about discussions in order to exploit his recently established position. Sometime between April 23 and 24, Bryan intimated to the French ambassador the "desirability of mediation by the ABC [Argentina, Brazil, and Chile] people." The ambassador contacted the Argentine minister, Romulo S. Naón. Naón, who had the "greatest love" for Bryan, suggested mediation to his government, which approved and invited Brazil and Chile to join. They extended their offer of a conference on April 25.[20] In effect, Wilson created his own opportunity to capitalize on the power that the presence of American forces on Mexican soil gave him.

On April 30 General Frederick Funston and the Fifth Brigade, as called for in the War College Division's war plans, arrived in Veracruz. Instead of marching toward Mexico City as the plans specified, however, they merely relieved Admiral Fletcher's forces of command of the port. The ABC negotiations began in May at Niagara Falls, but the mediators would not allow the Constitutionalists to participate until they agreed to an armistice. Carranza refused, which meant that one of the strongest powers was not represented at the conference. Despite intense pressures from the Wilson administration, the mediators would not change their conditions. Consequently, Wilson and his representatives were able to achieve very little in reforming Mexico and creating democratic government. In July, Huerta resigned and fled the country. Funston and his men remained in Veracruz until the end of November 1914. The war that was not a war enshrouded them throughout the entire occupation.

"There has been no declaration of war," Daniels cabled Fletcher early in the evening of April 21, but he offered no precise definition of the occupation. The ambiguous situation left the navy confused and uncomfortable; its discomfiture allowed Wilson to control its actions more closely. Fletcher and his subordinates lacked a clear understanding of their presence and responsibilities in Mexico because Wilson chose not to explain his policies to them and because they had no precedent to guide them. Wilson stepped into this melee and, with a sure hand and a strong vision, manipulated his men of force and played them to his purposes. He felt no obligation to defend his policies to his military subordinates. Instead, he expected them to follow orders with unquestioning obedience. Wilson supervised all orders and statements of policy communicated between Washington and the forces in Veracruz. Later, he took steps to guard against a repetition of Admiral Mayo's initiative in demanding the salute without Washington's approval.[21]

The navy received only vague explanations of Wilson's policies. On the eve of Admiral Charles Badger's departure for Mexico with the Atlantic Fleet on April 15, for instance, Daniels's aide for operations, Admiral Bradley Fiske, discussed Wilson's purposes with him. Fiske informed Badger that the salute to the flag would be insisted upon even to the point of using force, but "the Administration earnestly desired to avoid war with Mexico." This nebulous injunction made little sense to someone who assumed, as both Badger and Fiske did, that force meant war.[22] Although Wilson consulted with his military chiefs immediately before his decision to take the port, he brought them into the discussion very late and limited their advice to technical questions of tactics. The General Board of the Navy also answered questions posed to it by the civilian administrators, but the queries were generally confined to issues of international law and decorum regarding the salute. Wilson did not turn to the military for advice on war or peace, nor on the question of how much force to use.

Little changed once the navy landed. "The entire situation is serious," Badger reported on April 23 from Veracruz. "We have seized Vera Cruz but have no belligerent rights other than those we ourselves assume and which may cause international complications." Badger felt "uncertain of his powers in the circumstances," for he was "exercising and must exercise powers which can, with strict legality, only be employed in time of war—for war at this place actually exists." Shortly after Badger arrived, Fletcher met with him to discuss the occupation. Fletcher "impressed upon him the seriousness of the situation," adding that "it is urgently necessary for us to determine how long the Navy is expected to hold Vera Cruz." Fletcher pointed out that the condition of affairs was anomalous because "we have no right to control the movements of soldiers as no organized troops of Mexico have fired upon us or offered any resistance." Admiral Mayo, stationed at Tampico, vented his frustration and confusion in a report to Badger: "The situation seems to be decidedly strange, and the Mexican side regards war as existing. So far as I am able to learn or infer, the Government of the United States does not yet consider that a state of war exists and therefore that no war measures can be taken by any naval commander. It is not believed that such a state of affairs can continue indefinitely . . . it was fully believed by all concerned that war had begun."[23]

Wilson did little to relieve the confusion before the army took over from the navy at the end of April.

Secretary of War Lindley Garrison, after consulting with Wilson, wrote Funston's orders on April 26. The orders were submitted for the president's review before they were sent to Funston when he took command of the port. Wilson made no corrections, except to add a paragraph commending Fletcher's handling of the occupation and urging Funston to establish an "intimate harmony" with the admiral, who would remain in the waters of the port. The remainder of the instructions set out in harsh terms the limits of Funston's duties. The administration strictly limited the occupation to Veracruz and prohibited the army from extending it beyond the areas taken by Fletcher's command. In addition, Garrison told Funston not to initiate "any activities or bring about of [his] own initiative any situation which might tend to increase the tension of the situation" or embarrass the United States.[24] These orders reflected the administration's insistence on civilian control and its distrust of the military.

Garrison waited until May 14 before he defined the occupation by identifying its legal basis for Funston. The secretary defended it as an act of reprisal performed, though he readily admitted that "the circumstances attending our occupation of Vera Cruz are peculiar."[25] Both sets of instructions, those of April 26 and those of May 14, gave General Funston a much clearer idea of his powers than any orders sent Fletcher. They offered no relief, however, for the military's anxiety over fighting battles independent of a state of war.

Confusion over the meaning of limited intervention also reached the Mexican-American border, where General Bliss commanded the Southern Department. Bliss interpreted the landing of the marines and bluejackets at Veracruz to mean the initiation of general hostilities with Mexico. On the assumption that war had begun, or was about to begin, he embargoed on his own authority the exportation of arms and munitions into Mexico. The danger of the embargo was the chance that the Mexicans would interpret it as another sign of hostility or as a sign of an escalation of the intervention. Garrison, although personally "delighted" by the action, pointed out at the insistence of the State Department that no presidential proclamation had been promulgated; the Bliss embargo had no legal foundation.

Consequently, Bliss revoked his earlier orders, but, in the meantime, the War Department took up the issue with the president. By this time, Wilson had learned of Carranza's heated opposition to the occupation of Veracruz. The embargo appealed to him as a way to punish the first chief as well as to protect the United States from the wrath of the

Constitutionalists. Garrison, therefore, in a reversal of his earlier orders, instructed Bliss to maintain the embargo. The sealing of the border never had the support of a proclamation by Wilson, which would have imbued it with legal authority and sanctions. As Bliss admitted, "we have no law to back us up." The lack of legal power caused the army no end of trouble enforcing the embargo and, eventually, the judge advocate general determined that the army's actions were illegal and exposed individual officers to lawsuits. The War Department urged Wilson to lift the embargo, which he finally did on September 8, 1914.[26]

The situation along the border underlined the difficulty the military experienced in trying to understand Wilson's decision to halt the advance of American forces at the Veracruz city limits. "You must admit," Bliss wrote to General W. W. Wotherspoon, who replaced Wood as chief of staff in April, "that to anyone so far away as here from the seat of government, it looked as though the first step of intervention, if not of war, had been taken."[27] Bliss initiated the embargo in order to minimize the danger to the frontier from the outbreak of hostilities. His initiative showed the strength of the military's conviction that fighting meant war and that war had but one end.

Wilson understood the situation differently. In his view, fighting did not necessarily mean war. Interventions could be limited both geographically and politically. They could also be used to introduce or rejuvenate other forms of power. Wilson's initiative in arranging for the ABC conference clearly indicated a shift away from further reliance on armed power and a turn toward diplomatic power. By using the occupation of Veracruz to reopen negotiations with all of the major Mexican factions, Wilson invested armed power with a new purpose. The limited intervention at Veracruz succeeded in gaining the limited goal of giving Wilson new opportunities to exert diplomatic power.

Wilson avoided further hostilities with Mexico by adroit diplomatic maneuvers, but he also lessened the chances of continued fighting by exercising complete control over his military subordinates. Neither General Wotherspoon nor Admiral Fiske reconciled themselves to the restrictive policies of the administration. In large part, this was due to Wilson's decision to keep them ignorant of his policies. Wotherspoon complained frequently of the tight supervision placed over the activities of the army by the president and the State Department. "I suppose it never will be possible by any means, even if we could get a prolonged interview, to give you an idea of how we are cribbed and confined up here by the attitude of our superiors and an associated Department," he wrote his friend Bliss in June. "Even the most reasonable requests in matters presented in the strongest possible light as necessary are refused. We can get no ammunition to our men [in Veracruz], we can get no recruits to our men, and we can get no transportation to our men."[28] Bliss could only sympathize, for he, too, could not understand.

Admiral Fiske raised similar objections. In the fall of 1914 he recommended that the navy be withdrawn from Veracruz and the army reinforced, but Wilson and Daniels refused. Fiske confided to his diary:

> I tried to show the reasonableness of this plan, from all points of view, European and Mexican, military, national, and international. From each standpoint, the wisdom of what the Army and Navy have all the time advised becomes apparent. All of this Mexican tragedy would have been avoided if the recommendations of the Army and Navy had been followed in this Mexican matter. . . . There seems to be almost a determination to deny the fact that the military ingredient exists in our national and international life.[29]

Both Fiske and Wotherspoon failed to understand that the Wilson administration intended not to deny the importance of the "military ingredient," but to keep its importance so limited that it did not overshadow other, equally significant, ingredients of American power.

Veracruz offered the armed forces a lesson in limited intervention. It presented them with a case of a battle contained both politically and geographically, but none of Wilson's uniformed subordinates recognized the subtleties of the operation. The constraints on the occupation so took these men by surprise that they made little attempt to understand Wilson's motives. Instead, they expended a great deal of time and effort bemoaning the president's stubborn resistance to what seemed to them an obvious consequence of the fight for the port. When events did not follow the predicted course, the leading officers of the armed forces refused to analyze their error, preferring, instead, to complain about Wilson's excessive authority over them. Two years later, the punitive expedition offered the army a chance to apply the lessons of Veracruz to another limited intervention, but its actions then revealed that it had learned very little from the occupation of the port.

THE PUNITIVE EXPEDITION, 1916

Mexico did not settle down as Wilson had hoped after the resignation of Huerta in July and the withdrawal of the American forces from Veracruz the following November. The former event left Carranza and Villa the two strongest leaders south of the border. Previously united against Huerta, they separated that summer. By the fall of 1914 their bitter antagonism had become public. The Wilson administration gave limited support to Villa because he seemed most amenable to American influence. Based on this hope, Wilson reverted again to watchful waiting. He decided to wait out the fight, praying that the United States could avoid further active involvement. Meanwhile, Villa's political and military fortunes declined slowly. He met defeat on the field of battle at Puebla in February 1915 and, a few months later, at Celaya. These failures convinced Wilson to act once again to resolve the revolution.

Wilson understood from Celaya that he supported the wrong man, but Carranza held no appeal to the president. The so-called first chief consistently turned down all proffered American aid and, to compound the offense, he openly opposed the occupation of Veracruz. Wilson disliked Carranza's obstinate nationalism. On June 2, 1915, the president sent letters to the leaders of the various Mexican factions demanding that they come together under threat of U.S. intervention, but little came of this initiative. At the end of the month, Wilson promised Carranza recognition if the first chief would convene a peace conference between the warring factions. Robert Lansing, Bryan's successor at the State Department, proposed that the United States withdraw support from the opposing groups in order to establish a new government composed of new individuals. The idea tempted Wilson.

The president convened a Pan-American meeting to establish a common approach to Mexico as a means of inaugurating Lansing's scheme. But Carranza proved too strong, and his strength weakened Wilson's infatuation with the plan. By August, when the Pan-American conference met, Wilson realized that no matter how repulsive, Carranza represented the strongest political organization south of the border and the only individual capable of uniting the country. On September 13 the administration decided to recognize the first chief's government. A month later, it extended de facto recognition.[30]

The recognition of Carranza incensed Villa, who refused to admit defeat. He directed his wrath at the United States, showing the depths of his hatred in a series of murders of individual Americans in Mexico. The vendetta culminated in the surprise attack on Columbus, New Mexico, during the early morning hours of March 9, 1916. Although Villa's intentions have been debated ever since, he probably wanted to bring on a war between his country and the United States that would unite the Mexican people under his banner. The Columbus raid, then, was a desperate act of a desperate man. Villa almost succeeded in starting a war; he came nowhere near as close in aligning his fellow citizens behind his leadership.[31]

The day after the raid, General Funston, by this time the commander of the Southern Department, recommended that his forces be sent in pursuit of the Columbus attackers. "Unless Villa is relentlessly pursued and his forces scattered he will continue raids," he argued. "If we fritter away the whole command guarding towns, ranches and railroads it will accomplish nothing if he can find safe refuge across the line after every raid." Funston buttressed his argument by pointing to the failure of Carranza's troops both to protect their side of the line and to chase Villa. They were, in fact, "accomplishing nothing."[32] Funston's plea found a receptive audience in Washington. In three separate telegrams on March 10, the Wilson administration defined its decision to launch a punitive expedition.

Wilson turned to the War College Division for help in drawing up plans for the chase. Its members, however, were not only unprepared for such a request, but also unwilling to respond to it. During the two years between the occupation of Veracruz and the attack on Columbus, the War College continued to formulate plans for war against Mexico. The experience of 1914 showed little positive influence on these preparations. The plans did not include the possibility of another limited incursion into Mexico. Indeed, the members of the college argued just the opposite, that putting restrictions on an invasion would be self-defeating. Five days before Villa's raid, the War College presented its case against limited interventions. In detailing the forces necessary for war with Mexico, the staff of the division wrote:

> In armed intervention it is axiomatic that an overwhelming force used in vigorous field operations without costly pauses and directed straight and continuously at the organized field forces and centers of resources will most effectively and economically overcome organized resistance and make possible a more orderly and more economical period of pacification. . . . Our war plans accept this axiom. . . . To reject these plans, to use only a part of the plans, or to curtail the forces outlined in the plans, can but invite local disasters and delays lengthening the period of military operations, and make more costly in lives and treasure both this period and the period of pacification.

Veracruz served as a negative precedent of what not to do, rather than as an example of what could be done. "At any rate," the War College memo concluded, "it is neither sound nor logical to attempt a partial occupation of Mexico without being prepared to look squarely in the face of the problem and to carry forward the vigorous operations of our war plans without vacillation or confusion of council."[33] The division stood firmly behind its plans.

In effect, the War College Division revolted against the suggestion of sending an expedition after Villa with strict limits placed on its mission and refused to offer any constructive advice on the tactics to follow. Villa's attack meant war and the United States should respond accordingly. At 2:00 P.M. on March 10, the chief of the division, General M. M. Macomb, and his aides received word that General Scott, the chief of staff, wanted to discuss the proposed mission with them. Before the meeting, Macomb drew up a memorandum in which he announced the division's abdication of the role of adviser on the expedition. Macomb suggested that Funston formulate the plans, proceeding "according to his best judgement in the matter." The War Department should help only by filling Funston's requests for men and materials. "The plans on file in the War College Division refer to larger problems, such as intervention in Mexico or some state thereof," the chief of the division asserted. Neither he nor his assistants wanted any part of the pursuit of Villa.[34]

At the meeting, Scott read the memorandum without comment. Bliss, the assistant chief of staff, endorsed it. Scott ordered him, in consultation with the War College, to prepare another memorandum for the approval of the new secretary of war and for the information of the president. In this second memo, Bliss and Macomb adopted a superior's tone, like a teacher instructing a particularly obdurate pupil. Once again, the division refused to offer any advice on the composition of the expedition or on the strategy and tactics it should adopt. Bliss and Macomb insisted that "existing War College plans for war or intervention in Mexico cover larger problems, but in any case a war plan does not cover the movements of tactical units. The commander on the ground draws up his plans based on his knowledge of the terrain and means of supply. In this case, the Commanding General, Southern Department, should be instructed as to what the Administration desires." However sound the military doctrine behind this argument—and it was axiomatic that the commander in the field was best able to judge the movements of tactical units—the tone and presentation adopted by Bliss and Macomb clearly showed their opposition to the whole idea of limited intervention. The memo, for example, examined the problems involved in chasing a band of outlaws through its home territory. It pointed out that the longer the expedition stayed in Mexico, the greater would be the resentment of the Mexican people. Villa could not be captured quickly; thus, as tensions built, trouble along the border would occur and "eventually lead to war." Bliss and Macomb urged that Funston be reinforced along the frontier and that these troops be prepared for an immediate move into Mexico when the inevitable rupture took place. "In conclusion, it is evident that before attempting this expedition, the probable necessity of intervention should be fully appreciated," they wrote, "for intervention, the War College plan will apply." General Scott endorsed the memorandum over to the new secretary of war, Newton D. Baker, who also signed his approval.[35]

Consequently, Wilson and the War Department drew up the orders to Funston without the constructive advice of the War College. The warnings that the punitive expedition would lead to war were ignored. The first telegram wired to Funston on March 10 instructed him to send an armed force into Mexico "with the sole object of capturing Villa and preventing any further raids by his bands, and with scrupulous regard to the sovereignty of Mexico." Scott pointed out the difficulties of this approach. He recommended that it not be a posse after Villa, but a military expedition intent on breaking up the band that raided Columbus and ensuring that it never crossed into American territory again. He advised Baker that Villa could run as far away as Yucatán—could the army pursue him there? Baker answered with a second telegram to Funston that directed him "to locate and disperse or capture" the outlaws that had attacked Columbus. The secretary also authorized similar tactics of defense and pursuit in the event of future raids. The third set of orders sent to Funston identified General John J. Pershing as the commander of the expedition. The orders specified that the troops would be brought out of Mexico as soon as "the de facto Government of Mexico is able to relieve them of this work" or Villa's band had been broken up.[36]

Tasker Bliss remained uneasy with the orders establishing the punitive expedition and limiting its size and objectives. On March 13, he posed two questions to Scott: would the Mexican government and people interpret the expedition as an act of war and, if they did, was the United States militarily prepared to defend its territory against additional raids? Bliss answered the first question affirmatively, the second negatively. Based on these answers, Bliss concluded that "the situation should be handled solely as a military one." The precedent of Veracruz did not apply, since

> Invasion of Mexico for the purpose of breaking up Villa's bands is a very different one from the seizure of Vera Cruz. It was very easy to say to the commander of that expedition, "When you have seized the city, go no further with your troops; do nothing unless the enemy actually attacks you." But when you tell an American general, with 4,000 or 5,000 troops, to go into Mexico and break up certain bands of bandits, you can put no such limitation on his action. They will soon be beyond assured communication with their home government. They

will be in a hostile country surrounded by enemies, and they will do as soldiers under such circumstances must do.

In pursuit of Villa, Pershing and his men would enter Mexican towns and villages; they would be unable to avoid contact with Carranzista soldiers. These encounters would be irritating to the Mexican people and, Bliss assumed, the consequence would most probably be war. Since the United States could ill afford to gamble on Mexico accepting a large force on its land, it was time to prepare for the worst. As a first step, Bliss urged that preparations be made to seize the Mexican towns directly across the border from American towns. Thus, if hostilities broke out, these cities could be occupied and an insulating strip of Mexican territory created that would protect the United States from raids and artillery bombardment. Bliss wanted 150,000 men of the Organized Militia sent to the frontier in order that his plan could be implemented.[37]

This idea did not originate in 1916, for Bliss had advocated it since April 1913 when he commanded the Southern Department. Wilson, however, was unreceptive to it until the raid on Columbus proved the ease with which Mexican bands could invade the United States. Bliss took the opportunity to press hard for his scheme. In a separate memorandum on March 13, he again urged that the United States assume that the Mexicans would interpret the punitive expedition as an act of war and that "we be prepared for every possible military contingency; and that, first of all, we be prepared to take military possession of Mexican territory immediately opposite all American towns as being the only way in which we can guarantee the protection of the latter."[38] Although the Wilson administration did not act immediately on that plan, Bliss's presence in Washington ensured that it would be before the policymakers at all times. The time for its acceptance would soon come.

Members of the War College worried just as much as Bliss about the response of the Mexican government and people to the expedition. Macomb also wrote to Scott on March 13 to review the number of volunteers needed in any fight with Mexico. The plans called for 400,000 men in the event of war, but only 150,000 men "for emergencies less than war." Nonetheless, Macomb pointed out that to "call for less than 400,000 volunteers in the face of the Mexican situation as it stands, is to set aside our experience in the Civil War and in the Philippines as well as the experience of the British in the Boer War." Inadequate planning and a call-up of too few men made all of these wars long and bloody. Macomb insisted that a call for volunteers be made "as soon as it is evident that Mexican troops will resist the progress of the expedition planned by the President in the pursuit of Villa." Scott acted on this advice, which reinforced that received from Bliss, by asking the secretary of war to send a volunteer force of 150,000 men to the border before a disaster occurred that would compel the administration to flood the border with troops. "This force," he said, "will be recognized as being too small to conquer and occupy Mexico and it is therefore only a defensive measure and should have a quieting rather than a provocative effect."[39] Baker rejected this advice. Not until two months later, after the attack on American forces at Parral and the failure of the Scott-Obregón conference, were reinforcements sent south.

Wilson insisted that his orders be followed to the letter, as he had with the forces occupying Veracruz. He understood better than his military advisers how best to conduct limited military operations against Mexico because he knew what his political goals were. The punitive expedition was designed to support those goals. Consequently, the president ignored the army's pessimism, choosing, instead, to gamble that he could contain the intervention and not allow it to escalate into a full-scale war. To ensure against any escalation of the intervention, he tolerated no show of independence from his military subordinates.

On March 16, the day that Pershing crossed the border into Mexico, Baker dispatched a telegram to Funston specifying the limits and responsibilities of the punitive expedition. The secretary emphasized that any Carranzistas encountered were to be treated with courtesy and cooperation. "Upon no account or pretext, and neither by act, word or attitude, of any American commander, shall this expedition become or be given the appearance of being hostile to the integrity or dignity of the Republic of Mexico, by the courtesy of which this expedition is permitted to pursue an aggressor," commanded Baker. Although Pershing could defend his command from attack, he was not to initiate any trouble between the United States and the de facto government. Baker expected Pershing to stay in close contact with Washington, reporting immediately the slightest sign of hostility or misunderstanding on the part of the Mexican forces. Neither the president nor the secretary wanted to chance a war with Mexico.[40]

The army accepted its orders begrudgingly, for most commanders doubted that Pershing could succeed in his mission. Villa was "loose in a big country" and Carranza refused to cooperate in the chase. Pershing described himself in a favorite metaphor as "a man looking for a needle in a hay stack with an armed guard standing over the stack forbidding you to look in the hay." He did not believe that his command could catch the Columbus raiders soon enough to avoid trouble with the Carranzistas. This pessimism permeated the service, for these soldiers firmly believed that an intervention could not be limited. Funston feared that unless Villa could be caught quickly, which he thought very unlikely, the United States was "going to have to fight and fight hard." He pleaded with Washington to prepare for the possibility of war. "We are not going to gain anything by hiding our heads under the bed clothes like children afraid of the dark," he warned.[41] But, in Wilson's mind, this was a political question and, although he willingly listened to his experts on force on military issues, he refused to abdicate his power on questions of policy. The army's warnings were heard, but their advice went unheeded.

The punitive expedition got off to a slow start, but quickly picked up speed. Two forces, an infantry column from Columbus and a cavalry unit from Hachita, crossed the border into Mexico on March 15 and 16, respectively, almost a week after the raid on Columbus. Once launched, however, the cavalry moved fast throughout the state of Chihuahua searching in vain for Villa's trail. Elements of Pershing's command penetrated over four hundred miles into Mexico before the movements of the expedition were halted in late June. Occasionally, isolated bands of Villa's now-dispersed forces were found and brief battles ensued. But the punitive expedition never laid eyes on its prime target. In the meantime, the anger and resentment of the Mexican population and the Carranza government led to increasingly hostile actions.

The army's predictions of trouble proved true on April 13 when a mob of Mexicans, aided by Carranzista soldiers, attacked a troop of Pershing's cavalry under the command of Major Frank Tompkins at Parral. Tompkins fought a running battle as he and his men sought shelter. By the time they reached a protected position, two Americans were dead and several wounded. Tompkins reported to Pershing that he had tried everything to avoid a battle but was eventually compelled to return the fire of the attackers. He blamed the Mexicans for starting the skirmish, implying that they had set him up for an ambush.[42]

The incident at Parral not only proved to the army the accuracy of its foresight, but it also convinced most soldiers that war or complete intervention was at hand. Pershing claimed that his men had given Carranza no provocation. The Mexicans, he swore, planned the attack. Carranza's general attitude had been "one of obstruction" from the start, Pershing argued, insisting that "in order to prosecute our mission with any promise of success it is therefore absolutely necessary for us to assume complete possession for time being of country through which we must operate. . . .Therefore recommend immediate capture by this command of city and State of Chihuahua."[43] Mexico had no strong leaders capable of pacifying the country, Pershing asserted, for only "anarchy exists." American intervention and "at least partial occupation of the country" seemed to him the only proper solution. Funston reacted similarly. Fearing that Parral was but the beginning of further trouble, he begged for reinforcements. Although he understood that this would endanger the diplomatic settlement of the crisis, nevertheless, the general noted that "I must consider [the] military feature of the situation." Funston agreed that Carranza had done little to help in the chase, but he did not recommend invasion or occupation of Mexico. Instead, he advised waiting until the Mexicans engaged in further hostilities so that they would be "indisputably in the wrong." Then, if a fight occurred, there would be "no more hope of localizing the difficulties than of localizing a typhoon."[44] He demanded only that the United States remain blameless.

The Wilson administration, however, denied the request for reinforcements. It paid scant attention to Pershing's suggestion of a partial occupation of Mexican territory. Wilson evinced no desire to use the Parral affair as an excuse to escalate the conflict or to expand the mission of the expedition. When General Scott prepared to leave Washington on an inspection trip along the border, Baker took the opportunity to remind his subordinates of the nature of their assignment and the limits of their task. The secretary encouraged Scott on April 19 to discuss with Funston "the theory of this expedition as being different from either war against or intervention in Mexico." He emphasized that Funston was to ensure an attitude of respect toward Mexican sovereignty, which would give no cause for the Mexicans to complain about the incursion of American forces into their country. The delicacy of the situation, the sensitivities of the Mexican people, and the general suspicion of Latin America required the utmost tact and circumspection in order to forestall pressures on Carranza to embark on a war with the United States. Baker explained that the fundamental purpose of Pershing's presence south of the border was to compel the de facto government to aid in the pursuit of Villa. Friendly cooperation, therefore, was essential.[45]

Shortly after reaching the frontier, Scott joined the chorus of soldiers demanding that some action be taken to relieve the tension. Neither he nor Funston believed that Carranza exercised much control over his troops. They urged that representations be made to the first chief to keep Mexican reinforcements out of the state of Chihuahua. The two generals drew up three options for the future of the punitive expedition. First, Pershing could fight through the Carranzistas until he found Villa's band. This course would require large reinforcements and seizure of the Mexican railroad to supply the men, but, nevertheless, it would not guarantee success since Villa could "go clear to Yucatán." Second, the War Department could order the expedition to pull in its outlying forces and concentrate in the vicinity of Colonia Dublán, where it could be supplied and protected. This alternative would give Carranza an "incentive . . . to kill or capture Villa." Finally, the expedition could be withdrawn altogether. The longer it stayed in Chihuahua, the greater the chance of additional encounters with unfriendly Mexicans. In addition, there was only a "very small chance" of finding Villa since he was hiding amidst a population largely sympathetic to him. Scott and Funston recommended the second course of concentrating the expedition and pressuring the de facto government forces to destroy the Columbus raiders.[46]

The second option also appealed to the Wilson administration, which approved it on April 23. At about this time, Carranza began hinting that he would like his most able lieutenant, General Álvaro Obregón, to meet with Scott and Funston on the border to discuss the withdrawal of the expedition. Wilson eagerly embraced the opportunity to negotiate, and orders went out to Scott to wait for word from Obregón. Although skeptical of Carranza's motive and doubtful of the possibilities of successful negotiations, Scott agreed to meet with Carranza's representative.[47]

Wilson saw in the conference a chance to explain his policies, as well as to allow tempers on both sides to cool. His administration made a real effort to define its purposes to Obregón, but it did not listen to the other side. "The Government of the United States earnestly desires to avoid anything which has the appearance of intervention in the domestic affairs of the Republic of Mexico," the War Department informed Scott in preparation for the talks. "It desires to cooperate with the *de facto* Government of that Republic, and its pursuit of the bandit Villa and his bands is for the sole purpose of removing a menace to the common security and the friendly relations of the two Republics." The administration emphasized that the punitive expedition entered Mexico in response to an attack on American territory and that it would not be withdrawn until Washington was satisfied that such an incursion would not be repeated. "We must safeguard our people," was the constant refrain.[48]

During the conference in Juárez that began on April 29, Obregón never varied from his insistence on the withdrawal of the punitive expedition. Scott proved just as stubborn in his argument that the expedition would not be pulled out until Carranza proved himself able to protect Mexico's side of the border. Two raids on the United States that took place during the Scott-Obregón talks heightened tensions, but did not alter the basic problems. The Glenn Springs and Boquillas raids, which included Carranzista troops among the raiders, merely supplied additional proof of Carranza's impotence. After an all-day session with Obregón on May 2, Scott obtained an agreement that, though "not altogether satisfactory," did contain the de facto government's assurance that it would carry on a "vigorous pursuit" of any raiding parties. In exchange for the "gradual withdrawal" of U.S. forces, Obregón agreed that his side would distribute its army in order to prevent future attacks on American territory. Withdrawal of American troops depended directly on the performance of the Carranzistas.[49]

Wilson approved the agreement quickly, but Carranza took almost a week before deciding to reject the proposition. In the meantime, General Funston grew "sick with apprehension over [the] safety of [the] border." Scott agreed that the anxiety was justified. On May 8, Scott, Funston, and Obregón met again for the latter's announcement that the first chief found the agreement unacceptable because it contained no firm date for the withdrawal of the expedition. The two Americans immediately protested that a firm date could not be set since the withdrawal hinged on the ability of Mexico to protect its side of the border. They could not budge Obregón. "We feel," they complained, "that whole proposition is redolent with bad faith, that Mexicans are convinced that they are not able to carry out agreement even if ratified and they desire to keep United States troops quiet until Mexican troops are in position to drive them out of Mexico by force." Scott and Funston asked for 150,000 additional men along the border because they feared a surprise attack. "We have struggled for a different result with all our intelligence, patience and courtesy," they said, "hoping against hope for a peaceful solution, but are now convinced that such solution can no longer be hoped for." Both men agreed that war was again on the horizon.[50]

Wilson once more counseled patience. Although aware of the "gravity of the situation," he refused to allow his troops to attack first. If Carranza started hostilities, then Funston could immediately occupy Mexican border towns. The Bliss plan thus received its first official sanction. In addition, the president turned to military power again by mobilizing into the federal service the national guards of the border states. Negotiations continued from May 9 until May 11, long enough for the sense of crisis to pass. An agreement remained out of reach, but, as Scott realized, "the conference furnished much beneficial results in relieving a very acute situation and in demonstrating to General Obregón and other Carranza leaders the intentions of our Government."[51] Thus, though ultimately unsuccessful, the talks did defuse a dangerous situation. They bought Wilson enough time for tempers to cool. The punitive expedition remained based near Colonia Dublán, but the easing of tensions partially freed it to again take up the chase.

The expedition served as a constant reminder to Carranza that Villa remained loose in a big country, but the first chief needed no reminder of the freedom of his most dangerous internal enemy. Unlike the United States, however, he separated that issue from the other danger that confronted him, the presence of the punitive expedition on Mexican soil. On May 22 Carranza's representative delivered to the State Department a long, bitterly hostile note. In undiplomatic terms that threatened war, the de facto government demanded the immediate withdrawal of the expedition.[52] Wilson's attention was concentrated on a crisis with Germany over the sinking of the *Sussex,* and he delayed sending a response until his subordinates in the State and War departments could suggest an appropriate reply. The delay, which lasted almost a month, also helped postpone a confrontation between Mexico and the United States.

In the meantime, the army geared itself for war. The War College submitted a plan for an invasion of Mexico that decried limited interventions, including the Bliss plan. "It seems evident that any further movement of our troops into Mexico, even if only to seize border towns, will so intensify the existing hostile feeling of the Mexican people that nothing short of the occupation and pacification of the entire country will be a final, satisfactory termination of the disturbed conditions," argued the college staff. Scott asked the staff to formulate a plan that shifted the objective to the Mexican army, rather than Mexico City, the goal identified in previous plans. "It has the appearance now," Scott awkwardly wrote, "that difficulty with Mexico can not be long delayed." The War College went to work incorporating the new objective into the Mexican studies.[53]

The war pressure increased again on June 16 when General Jacinto B. Treviño, a Carranzista commander, coldly demanded that Pershing's troops move in no direction but north. Pershing politely but firmly refused to obey orders from a foreign government. Although still headquartered in the vicinity of Colonia Dublán, Pershing sent out scouting parties and pursued bandits, when he could find them. His standing orders to his men were to avoid camps and towns occupied by Carranza's men, "but if attacked, [to] inflict as much damage as possible." Treviño's demand worried Scott, who told Wilson to "look for an attack upon Pershing by the national forces of the Mexican government." Scott believed "we are verging rapidly towards war." Mindful of the

Bliss plan, he wanted to seize the border towns and "shove the Mexicans into the desert beyond" if Carranza started trouble.[54]

Bliss, defending his plan from the criticisms of the War College, continued to promote it with the secretary of war. His influence within the War Department grew steadily. For example, Bliss penned the War Department's analysis of the Mexican note of May 22. He argued that Mexico failed in its duty to protect a friendly country from the violence of the Mexican people. Therefore, Carranza lacked legitimate cause to complain about the presence of Pershing's forces on his nation's soil. Large sections of Bliss's evaluation appeared in the American reply to Carranza. Bliss's only concern was protecting the border; he seemed not to realize the political and military nuances of his plan. Because of his increasing importance as an adviser, he had little trouble convincing the Wilson administration to reaffirm its commitment to his scheme of border protection. Because Wilson understood the political aspects of the plan, it offered him a convenient form of limited intervention that preserved the options of either occupying a larger portion of Mexico or taking the entire country. On June 19 Bliss submitted another memorandum to Scott summarizing the Mexican situation and detailing the number of troops needed to meet the crisis. Bliss advised that, should Carranza begin further hostilities, Funston should be ordered to take the Mexican border towns and, if necessary, all of northern Mexico in order to protect American territory. Scott, under orders from the secretary of war, telegraphed Funston that same day instructing him to seize the various towns should the Mexicans initiate "open hostilities."[55] The army was ready for action.

Wilson was not ready. He ordered the remainder of the Organized Militia to the border on June 18, but made no other overt moves. Two days later the United States answered the Mexican note of the month before in harsh language. The message referred to past raids on American territory as the reason for the refusal to withdraw the expedition. Wilson expected Carranza to prove his cooperation by aiding in the chase after Villa's band, but if the de facto government resorted to war, as its note implied, then it would suffer "the gravest consequences." Wilson preferred to cooperate with Carranza to help him rid the nation of its unruly elements, particularly since Mexico's troubles too often spilled over onto American ground. But, regardless of whether the first chief accepted the proffered aid, Wilson intended to protect the United States from bandit raids.[56]

The clash that everyone expected, but few wanted, occurred on June 22 when two troops of the Tenth Cavalry fought with a large number of Carranzistas outside the small, dusty village of Carrizal. The Americans suffered severe losses, including all but one of the officers. Pershing, frustrated by the limitations placed on his command and incensed by the deaths of his men, assumed immediately that the Mexicans had initiated the skirmish. He demanded "execution of plans seizing Mexican Central [Railroad] and Chihuahua." He was convinced that the Mexicans had tricked Captain Charles T. Boyd, the commander of the two troops, and that the Mexican actions were "premeditated and treacherous." Funston, however, kept a cooler perspective. He refused to endorse Pershing's recommendations, saying only that "this is a matter for the War Department to decide." Baker backed Funston, and both requested more information about the fight before taking any offensive steps.[57]

The Wilson administration insisted that only policymakers could decide between peace and war. Baker told Funston that the secretary intended for him to "act promptly" in the event of an emergency, but before taking any violent actions he was to inform the War Department of the situation "so that the questions as to the actual existence of a state of war can be decided here." Pershing's request to take over Chihuahua and the Mexican railroad was explicitly turned down as being impractical and, besides, he was told "no overt act must be committed in absence of specific orders from Washington."[58] Wilson showed no intention of using the fight at Carrizal as an excuse to expand the intervention.

Meanwhile, information began to trickle in that raised serious questions concerning the innocence of Boyd and his men in starting the fight. The one surviving officer, Captain Lewis Morey, reported that Boyd believed that "the Mexicans would run as soon as we fired." Morey's story made Boyd sound impetuous and headstrong. It implied that the dead captain had been spoiling for a fight with the Carranzistas and that the battle could have been avoided if Boyd had not been so hot-tempered.[59] In a symbolic sense, Boyd represented the frustrations of an army kept too tight on the leash, but if he intended to start a war, he died in vain.

Once again, Wilson refused to turn the punitive expedition into a full-scale war with Mexico. Despite the irritations of dealing with Carranza, his uncooperativeness, and his threats, Wilson was determined to use only a minimum of violence. Instead of sending more troops south of the border, Wilson resorted to the same tactics he had pursued two years earlier during the occupation of Veracruz. He arranged for negotiations with the government of Mexico. After a round of notes had been exchanged, and much time consumed, the Joint Mexican-American Commission opened in the late summer of 1916, a direct result of Boyd's suicidal charge against entrenched Carranzistas. Pershing, his movements again frozen, remained in Mexico as a bargaining chip in the negotiations. The joint commission, like the ABC negotiations before it, failed to achieve a satisfactory diplomatic settlement, but it kept both sides talking rather than fighting. Wilson ordered Pershing's command home early in 1917, by which time the difficulties with Mexico had taken a back seat to the troubles with Germany.

The withdrawal of the expedition ended another painful period in the relations between Wilson and the military. The army's assumption that fighting meant war failed, yet again, to meet the tests of Wilson's understanding of limited intervention. Although the president allowed the army more say in the affairs of the expedition than he had during the occupation of Veracruz, he accepted only part of its advice. The president refused, for example, to send the Organized Militia to the frontier when the army urged him to do so. Instead, he waited until he determined the time was right. Although Wilson trusted Scott in the negotiations with Obregón, nonetheless, Scott worked under closely defined instructions that allowed him little discretion. Pershing, too, endured the tight controls established by Wilson. His demands for a more active pursuit of Villa and for revenge against Carranza were often ignored and sometimes explicitly denied. Shortly before he turned his command north toward home, the commander of the punitive expedition cried into his pillow.[60] As a soldier he obeyed orders; as a man, he rebelled against his president's policies. This rebellion of tears signified that the army finally understood what it had not realized about Veracruz: that the army itself was but one of a number of tools used by Wilson in the conduct of foreign relations. For the first time, some members of the military showed a glimmer of understanding that Wilson used force for more than one purpose and in more than one way.

General Pershing never reconciled himself to the tight controls placed upon his command, but he did recognize that he formed only a part of a larger strategy employed by Wilson toward Mexico. "Matters with reference to this Expedition are entirely at a standstill, as the diplomats have it in hand," Pershing wrote on June 15. "We should have caught Villa long ago if it had not been for interference." Following the skirmish at Parral, "the diplomatic end of the government stepped in," effectively ending the pursuit of Villa. Pershing accepted, stoically if not happily, that his command had become a pawn of the politicians in Washington. His advice was not accepted, and his views only rarely sought. As he wrote Frederick Palmer:

> I have been hoping ever since your letter came that I might be able to cable you to come on that we were "going to it." But no such hint has been given to me. After Carrizal was the time, if ever there was a time,

when red-blooded Americans felt that we should go in, but we did not advance. I need not tell you how this command stood in the least, as you could guess what we thought ought to be done, but it was not done. Soldiers are but to obey no matter what they think, but we can't keep from thinking.

Instead of intervention, Wilson chose negotiation. Pershing could see no military reason for the retention of the expedition in Mexico. Its original purpose had changed, he finally understood, and he realized that his command had become "something of a club that the administration can use over the Mexican government."[61] This perceptive insight showed that Pershing had gone beyond his Veracruz predecessors to see that force, for Wilson, was not an end in itself, but sometimes just the beginning of other tactics in the larger strategy of Wilsonian foreign relations.

Other military leaders gained similar insights into Wilson's purposes in keeping the expedition south of the border. General Scott, for example, originally interpreted the mission of Pershing's command as an act of retribution directed against Villa for his raid on Columbus. During the Scott-Obregón conference, however, Scott saw the expedition from a different angle. The punishment of Villa was of less importance at that time than the protection of the American border. This new policy involved two approaches. First, the frontier guard was reinforced and the Bliss plan accepted, and, second, the punitive expedition was used to compel Carranza to protect his side of the line. "Our troops are on Mexican soil," Scott wrote after the conference, "as a guaranty that the border is going to be protected." The troops would ensure that Carranza fulfilled his promise to rid the areas nearest the United States of bandits.[62]

Finally, Scott, like Pershing, evidenced an imperfect understanding of yet another of Wilson's policies that involved the punitive expedition. Wilson used the expedition as a means of introducing himself to Carranza in order to help solve the problems racking Mexico. "The presence of troops in Mexico is the only way in which we can have influence on the actions of the Mexican government," Scott observed on September 5, but he made little effort to pursue that line of thought.[63] Nevertheless, he and Pershing made important breakthroughs in the military's perception of its role in Wilsonian foreign affairs. Although they never approved the part Wilson assigned to them, these two military leaders, and colleagues who agreed with them, at least partially understood their mission. This was all that was required of them, for Wilson understood exactly what he was doing. In the end, that was all that counted.

The relationship between these men of force and Wilson during the Mexican interventions throws light on Wilson's conduct of foreign policy. First, and most obvious, Wilson rarely allowed the military to wander far from the role he assigned it. He took its advice cautiously and only in areas where the armed services possessed a recognized expertise. Otherwise, Wilson simply refused to listen to the grumblings of individual commanders about the risks of limited interventions and the necessities of war. Second, the military failed to understand Wilson's policies at Veracruz, even after Wilson's motives should have been clear to the leading officers. By shutting their eyes to the lessons of limited interventions at the port, the army and navy lost an excellent opportunity to learn about their assigned role in the Wilson administration. Had they tried, many of their problems during the punitive expedition and other interventions would have been avoided. Two years later, however, the army did gain a clearer understanding of Wilson's intentions and purposes. It at least made the most important discovery: that Wilson's uses of force changed as his policies changed and that the original goal of the expedition was dropped in favor of more important objectives.

CIVILIAN SUPREMACY AND THE INTERVENTIONS IN HAITI, SANTO DOMINGO, WORLD WAR I, AND RUSSIA

This same pattern obtained in all of Wilson's interventions, but not to the same degree since the military was not as opposed to Wilson's policies in Haiti, Santo Domingo, World War I, and Russia. Yet, in each of these instances of force, Wilson insisted on a very tight control of the armed services. During the occupation of Haiti, for example, Daniels ordered Admiral William B. Caperton to cease military actions against outlaw forces over Caperton's protests that they had not been subdued. During World War I, Wilson prohibited General Pershing, the commander of the American Expeditionary Forces, and General Bliss, the American representative among the Allied military advisers to the Supreme War Council, from participating in any political discussions. But during that war, Wilson's tight control over the military loosened somewhat, primarily because of the size and scope of the endeavor. For example, he allowed Pershing to fight the war as Pershing thought best, provided he retained independence from the Allies. Since it was a war and not a limited intervention, Wilson's concern for exercising constraint in the use of force was not as strong as it was during the other, limited interventions. Yet, as a general rule, during each instance of force the president held all his military subordinates strictly to their well-defined sphere of expertise.

In doing so, Wilson retained for himself almost complete control over each intervention. He sought advice from the military on military matters, and from his small group of advisers on matters outside of this limited sphere. Nevertheless, Wilson reserved the final decisions to himself. These were often contrary to the recommendations of his advisers, civilian or military. Wilson's control over each intervention permitted him to limit or expand armed power at will and as he thought best. He was then able to incorporate it fully into his foreign policies, without fear that it would get out of hand. Thus, policy was the most important aspect of each intervention. The occasional Admiral Mayo or Captain Boyd could complicate matters by acting independently, but no military officer ever gained enough power or influence over events or policy to change Wilson in his course.

3.
THE POWER of IDEOLOGY:
Santo Domingo and Haiti

The Progressive movement exalted the rights of the common man. Domestic reforms of the period shared the general goal of freeing various segments of American society from the oppressive power of the privileged few who, by wit and wile, controlled the nation's business, industrial, and political sectors for their own selfish purposes. Progressives sought to allow the small businessman to compete equally without fear of giant trusts and monopolies. They also wanted to return to the people their right to govern themselves without interference from political machines, bosses, or corrupt politicians. Each of the reforms of the era expressed to some degree a common desire to reinvest democratic ideals of equal opportunity and fairness into the newly industrialized society.

Progressives enlisted eagerly in the cause of democratic service. They envisioned themselves as selfless individuals united in battle against a selfish minority of the powerful. Abjuring personal ambition or gain, the Progressives wanted only to help all people share in the benefits accruing from industrialization. The battle was joined against those who, with their enormous wealth and consequent power, represented the antithesis of democracy. The weapons consisted of publicity and the strength of the government. Through newspapers, magazines, and books, the Progressives exposed the abuses committed by the privileged. This exposure galvanized the people to seek justice through legislation and governmental changes. An enlightened populace demanded recovery of its lost influence and power. Thus, the Progressives responded to the changes incurred in industrialization by emphasizing democracy. They wanted each voice to equal every other, and every man to enjoy the same opportunities and the same benefits as his cohorts.

Wilson's campaign platform, the New Freedom, for example, promised to restore economic freedom to small businessmen by using the powers of the federal government to regulate competition and abolish unfair trade practices. In promoting this program, Wilson assumed the role of democratic leader, speaking both to and for the people. He worked closely with senators and congressmen who enlisted in his cause. In addition, he publicized his legislative proposals in public addresses and by taking them directly and in person to both houses of Congress. Using these progressive tactics, he succeeded in obtaining many of the Progressives' goals.

With the Underwood Tariff, Wilson attacked the special protections extended to manufacturers. The Clayton Anti-Trust Act regulated trade and commerce. Similarly, the Federal Reserve System harnessed the power of banks for the good of all, while the Federal Trade Commission refereed the activities of businesses. Eventually, Wilson moved tentatively and slowly into the realm of social reform. The Child Labor Act of 1916 protected the youth of the country from ruthless employers. Woman suffrage offered half the population of the United States the sweet fruit of the franchise, and Prohibition liberated everyone from the tyranny of alcohol. Although not always successful, and certainly by no means complete, Wilson's reforms attempted to extend to all, without favor, the service of the government in the promotion of democratic equality and ideals.

So, too, did Wilson approach foreign affairs. Elected on the basis of the New Freedom's domestic platform, Wilson also turned his reforming zeal to international affairs. The motive was essentially humanitarian. Although he occasionally confused America's self-interest with the best interests of the nations he wanted to help, he never consciously encouraged economic or commercial advantages for the United States in those areas of the world that he saw as truly in need of America's political and moral assistance. Wilson failed to understand that symbiotic relationships rarely survived the harsh climate of the international environment. Blinded by the conviction that what was best for the United States was of equal or greater benefit for the countries that received its aid, Wilson perceived himself not merely as a crusader for justice, but as a Christian savior intent on providing a better life to the struggling masses of the misguided foreign states. These peoples, he reasoned, had for too long been denied the advantages that America had to offer them. In the end, the destruction caused by World War I convinced him that the entire world needed his singular ministrations.

Wilson proffered a peculiar humanitarianism. Stained as it was by the ethnocentrism of his government, the help given other peoples did not distinguish between their needs and those that the American historical experience indicated were requisites for political and moral progress. Wilson and his subordinates made little attempt to identify the uniqueness of other countries; few of them, least of all the president, understood that other states could instill a xenophobic nationalism in their citizenry. These officials, convinced of the purity of their motives, assumed that nations racked by turmoil would accept American aid willingly and without hesitation. Who else could bring such selfless devotion to the cause of progress but the American people? As Arthur Link has pointed out, Wilson believed that the U.S. had been born "that men might be free."[1] America strode nearest the peak of civilization; other states inched upward from various distances along the precipitous climb. The duty of all right-thinking Americans was to help the less fortunate at home and abroad reach the summit.

Wilson embraced the Christian duty of helping others achieve a better life. His speeches and private correspondence were replete with references to the twin ideals of service and duty. "The world sneered when we set out on the liberation of Cuba, but the world sneers no longer," he said in January 1916. "The world now knows, what it was then loath to believe, that a nation can sacrifice its own interests and its own blood for the sake of liberty and happiness of another people." The United States symbolized the perfect life, and Wilson presented it as a tutor to the downtrodden and a model for the more developed states. As he explained on July 4, 1914:

> My dream is that as the years go on and the world knows more and more of America, it will also drink at these fountains of youth and renewal; and it also will turn to America for those moral inspirations which lie at the basis of all freedom; that the world will never fear America unless it feels that it is engaged in some enterprise which is inconsistent with the rights of humanity; and that America will come into the full light of the day when all shall know that she puts human rights above all other rights and that her flag is the flag not only of America but of humanity. What other great people has devoted itself to this exalted ideal?

This conception of the United States as unique imposed upon it a special mission, a duty to be "custodians of the spirit of righteousness, of the spirit of equal-handed justice, of the spirit of hope which believes in the perfectibility of the law with the perfectibility of human life itself."[2] While other nations pursued their selfish interests, the United States approached the world selflessly.

Despite Wilson's claim to America's uniqueness, other nations also saw in imperialism an opportunity to uplift the backward peoples of the world. Each brought to their respective colonies their own culture, their own version of the perfect world. What Rudyard Kipling called the "white man's burden" excused the imperial expansion of the major European powers into Africa, Asia, India, and other less developed areas of the world. The crimes committed in its name were legion; the victims were as often exploited as helped.

Wilson differed from other national leaders and from his American predecessors in the intensity with which he accepted the mission of helping other peoples and the lengths to which he went. Others talked of duty; Wilson acted dutifully. Indeed, his major policy toward such nations as Mexico, Haiti, and Santo Domingo was to help the poor and the powerless gain some level of democracy and freedom. Although Wilson invested his Latin American policies with such traditional concerns as the Monroe Doctrine and the protection of the Panama Canal, he added an insatiable desire to Americanize the backward states. He envisioned the United States as the "standard bearer for all those who love liberty and justice and righteousness in political action."[3] Wilson did not develop this approach entirely independent of precedent—the 1901 Platt Amendment ensuring American control over Cuba, and the 1911 intervention in Nicaragua evidenced earlier attempts to rehabilitate different countries in the image of the United States. Wilson intensified this effort to the point that American democratic ideology, although present in the foreign policies of earlier presidents and (in other forms) of other nations, became the central motive running through much of his diplomacy. It had no less of an influence on his employment of armed power.

AMERICAN DEMOCRATIC IDEOLOGY AND THE MEXICAN INTERVENTIONS

During both Mexican interventions, for instance, Wilson tried to encourage the adoption of liberal and constitutional reforms to free Mexico from the control of wealthy land barons, despots, and military dictators. Immediately after the navy took Veracruz on April 21, 1914, as we have seen, Wilson arranged for Argentina, Brazil, and Chile (the ABC powers) to offer their good offices to mediate the dispute between the United States and Mexico. They extended their invitation to a conference on April 25, four days after the landing of American forces. In effect, Wilson created his own opportunity to capitalize on the power which the presence of American forces on Mexican soil gave him. His next difficulty was to control the topics of the conference.

Wilson found the scope of the ABC invitation too limited. The mediators intended to cover only "the conflict between the United States and Mexico," by which they meant the controversies leading directly to the occupation. Wilson set out to increase the topics under discussion to permit him to address the causes and cure of the Mexican Revolution. In accepting the offer of mediation, Secretary of State Bryan expressed the hope that "the several elements of the Mexican people," and not just the Huerta faction, would be willing to "discuss terms of satisfactory and, therefore, permanent settlement." The United States defined "permanent settlement" quite liberally. Wilson explained his policy to the ABC powers as the "elimination" of Huerta and the establishment of a provisional government pledged to the creation of a permanent one. As Robert Lansing, at that time the counsellor of the State Department, argued, the United States viewed the mediation as "an attempt to restore peace between Mexican factions and to obtain guarantees from them which will insure the reestablishment of constitutional government in Mexico." The "real quarrel of the United States" was not with the individual factions in Mexico, but with the "intolerable conditions" which caused the fighting between these groups. In this sense, the mediation was actually between the various groups of the Mexican people and not between the United States and any single political element. Lansing perceived the role of America to be that of interested and friendly witness.[4]

"Our object," Wilson proclaimed during the conference, "is the pacification of Mexico by reforms and changes instituted by her own leaders and accepted by her own people." Unfortunately, Carranza refused to participate because the ABC powers insisted that an armistice be effected first. Furthermore, the first chief would not consider anything other than the controversies that led directly to the occupation as fitting topics. Wilson, in pressing the mediators to relax their demands for an armistice, shrugged off Carranza's objections to the expanded scope of the discussions. Carranza, he insisted, must be admitted, "for if he participates he will be under the stronger compulsion before all the world to accept the results." Wilson threatened that, if the Constitutionalists were not allowed at the table, the United States would appoint itself as their representative, "to constitute ourselves judges of what would be just to them and reasonable to expect them to accept." But the mediators remained unswayed by Wilson's arguments and threats. They would not relent on their demand for a cease-fire in Mexico. Carranza proved equally adamant.[5]

Without Carranza's cooperation, however, Wilson could do little to help Mexico. The first chief had no intention of allowing anyone but his party to decide the outcome of the revolution. In mid-June, he sent representatives close enough to the scene of the deliberations at Niagara Falls for the American commissioners, Joseph Lamar and Frederick Lehman, to meet with them. Carranza's agents objected strongly to everything the commissioners thought they had done for the Constitutionalists. "They say that Mexican conditions raise no international questions and that they are entitled to fight out their own fight in their own way," Lamar and Lehman reported to the president. The Constitutionalists wanted "no outside interference." The Americans returned to the conference disillusioned and chastened for their ethnocentric efforts to help the Mexicans.[6]

By this time, the Constitutionalists represented the strongest power south of the border. Diplomacy alone could not defeat their intensely nationalistic intention to rule, and Wilson never contemplated the further employment of armed power to force them to accept his aid. Eventually, Carranza was invited to negotiate privately with Huerta's representatives. "We have done what they wanted," Bryan confessed. Carranza, under the excuse that he had to consult his subordinates and daily growing stronger, delayed sending any representatives to the conference. Finally, he refused altogether to participate in negotiations with anyone. His generals, he said, disapproved of the idea.[7] The issue was resolved in July when Huerta resigned and fled the country. The episode exemplified both Wilson's profound desire to promote democracy and liberty in other countries and the clumsiness of his methods.

During the punitive expedition two years later, Wilson pursued a similar course. Following the battle between American cavalrymen and Carranzistas at Carrizal on June 21, 1916, the United States proposed directly to Carranza, who was then the head of the government in Mexico, the establishment of a Joint Mexican-American Commission to discuss the problems plaguing the two countries. Once again, the president insisted that the subject of the discussions go beyond the particulars leading up to the intervention. Instead, as Acting Secretary of State Frank Polk explained, the United States wanted the commission "to consider such other pending questions the settlement of which would tend to improve the relations of the two countries."[8] After considerable negotiations with Carranza over the scope of the negotiations, the matter was left unsettled until the commission could meet to work out an agenda.

The Americans clearly believed that they would have an opportunity to discuss all aspects of Mexico's troubles. Wilson urged Dr. John R.

Mott to serve on the commission because he needed men "who wish to serve the real interests of their fellow men whether those fellow men happen to be their fellow citizens or not. We want a settlement that will help the Mexicans." As Secretary of State Lansing told one of Wilson's first choices for the commission, Richard Olney (who declined to serve for personal reasons): "The scope of the work of the Commission has been left more or less indefinite in order that there may be a very free and informal discussion of the various questions which have arisen between the two countries in addition to the troubles along the border." According to Lansing, Mexico's financial problems, which he believed were at the root of its other troubles, were at the top of the list of topics to be discussed after the delegates worked out a solution to the border problems.[9] With these grand purposes in mind, the American commissioners, Franklin K. Lane, George Gray, and Mott, met their Mexican counterparts at the beginning of September 1916.

For more than three months, the Joint Mexican-American Commission deliberated on the problems between the two countries. Early on in the proceedings, the Mexican commissioners made it plain that Carranza expected them to reach an agreement on the withdrawal of American troops from Mexico before they could even discuss other issues. The Americans tried to make withdrawal conditional on a promise from Carranza to allow discussions of the larger issues, but the first chief would have none of it. The conference adjourned without settlement because Carranza refused to allow the United States to step in with its own solutions to Mexico's troubles. Although Wilson failed in his attempt to use the occupation of Veracruz and the punitive expedition as entrees to propose American solutions to the Mexican Revolution, the efforts underscored the ethnocentric humanitarianism motivating his Mexican policies.[10]

DEFINING POLICY: THE DOMINICAN REPUBLIC, 1913–1915

Revolution and turmoil in the Dominican Republic attracted Wilson's attention soon after he entered office. The lack of stability convinced him of the necessity of teaching the Dominicans not only to live in peace with each other, but also to follow legal and constitutional procedures in governing themselves. The Wilson administration expressed no other interest in the affairs of the country than the desire to help the people grow out of their political immaturity. Because Wilson's earliest policies toward Santo Domingo were important in determining his later intervention, and because he followed a similar course toward Haiti, the events from 1913 until 1915 are reviewed here in some detail.

Prior to the Wilson administration, Santo Domingo enjoyed a brief period of relative peace. In 1905 Teddy Roosevelt, aware that the failure of the Dominicans to pay their debts encouraged European military foreclosure, established a customs receivership with Santo Domingo. The arrangement was formalized by a convention in 1907. Under the customs receivership, the Bureau of Insular Affairs (BIA) of the War Department administered Dominican customs. Representatives of the BIA in Santo Domingo were civilians appointed by the president. They reported to General Frank McIntyre, the chief of the bureau in Washington. The general receiver lived in Santo Domingo City, and his assistants resided in most of the remaining Dominican ports. The receivership's control over the customs revenues gave it substantial power, but it rarely exercised its influence without the express consent of the State Department.

The assassination of the Dominican president, General Ramón Cáceres, on November 19, 1911, shattered the frail peace of the country. His successor faced escalating opposition until, a year later, William Howard Taft compelled the Dominicans to accept a nonpartisan leader, the archbishop, Monsignor Adolpho A. Nouell. The new president managed to maintain the semblance of order for a few months, but poor health forced his resignation in March 1913. A month later, José Bordas Valdés was elected to a year's term as provisional president.

The election of Bordas inaugurated another period of instability in the Dominican Republic. Bordas turned his back on the Horacistas, the political faction led by General Horacio Vásquez that helped elect him, by giving some of the choicest political appointments to the faction headed by General Desiderio Arias. The Horacistas were particularly incensed over the leasing of the national railroad to the Arias group. To show their anger, they revolted against Bordas. This revolt confronted the newly installed Wilson administration with its first Dominican crisis. Its response set the pattern for Wilson's policies leading up to the occupations of Santo Domingo and of Haiti.

Wilson and his advisers decided to help Santo Domingo escape the destitution caused by the violence of its own people. They used the Convention of 1907 as their legal excuse for interfering, but pled neighborliness as their moral justification. As the method for solving Dominican problems, the administration insisted on the form, if not always the substance, of constitutional procedure. Responding quickly to the insurrection against Bordas, for example, Bryan announced "the profound displeasure that is felt by this Government at this pernicious revolutionary activity, the responsibility for which this Government will not fail to fix." He and Wilson decided early in September to support

Bordas as proof of their commitment to legitimate government.[11] This commitment led the United States deeper into Dominican troubles.

"The President directs me to say for your instruction that the influence of this Government will be exerted for the support of lawful authorities in Santo Domingo and for the discouragement of any and all insurrectionary methods," Bryan informed James M. Sullivan, Wilson's choice for ambassador to Santo Domingo, on September 9, shortly before the latter arrived at his new post. The secretary of state pointed to Wilson's March 1913 press release, originally directed at Mexico, as the definitive statement of the government's policy of not countenancing further revolutions in Latin America. Yet, having taken such a harsh stance toward the revolutionaries, Bryan added some friendly advice. Men in power, he wrote, could not be expected to rule without making mistakes, "but mistakes should be corrected by constitutional means." Similarly, reforms could not be effected as quickly as one would like, "but the remedy for this is agitation, not insurrection." The United States stood ready to offer its good offices for the establishment of justice and the promotion of the welfare of the Dominican people. However, the Dominicans themselves would have to take the first step of joining together to secure justice through lawful methods, such as free and fair elections. Thus, although the American government would "employ every legitimate means to assist in the restoration of order and in the prevention of further insurrections," it would not be deaf to those who felt they had a real grievance against the present government. Bryan believed that "when the disinterestedness of our Government is fully understood, its friendship will be appreciated and its advice sought."[12] In effect, the secretary insisted that Santo Domingo adopt, with the Wilson administration's assistance, American methods for solving Dominican problems.

The United States threw its full support behind the Bordas administration, including the powers it derived from the customs receivership. Boaz Long, Bryan's hand-picked chief of the Division of Latin American Affairs, suggested that the receivership exert its influence over Dominican finances. Wilson approved, so Bryan cabled the legation in Santo Domingo its instructions on September 11. He explained that the United States, "firm in its determination to cooperate with legally constituted government to the end that revolutionary movements may cease," disapproved of any increase in the Dominican debt for the purpose of settling the financial claims of the revolutionists, a traditional practice in Santo Domingo. In addition, the Wilson administration viewed with disfavor any intention to increase internal taxes for the same object. Finally, Bryan warned that in the event the revolution succeeded, the United States would withhold its diplomatic recognition from the new regime. This meant that the Dominicans would not receive their percentage of the customs revenues. The secretary referred to the Convention of 1907, which allowed the United States control over the size of the public debt, as the authority for the new policy.[13]

The new American minister, immediately after his arrival in Santo Domingo in mid-September, entered into negotiations with the government and its opponents. The talks lasted over a month before Sullivan wrestled an agreement out of the two factions. The minister held to the insistence on support for the legal government, but exceeded his instructions when he promised that American observers would be sent for the December elections to choose delegates to a constitutional convention. It was one thing to insist on American-style voting, but quite another to ensure that it took place.[14]

The promise caught Washington officials by surprise. Sullivan assured them that sending observers would help establish a stable government in Santo Domingo. Besides, he had already committed both the president and the secretary in writing. "There can be no evasion of our responsibility in the premises," he proclaimed at one point. A fair election made the "salvation of Dominican government possible."[15] The Wilson administration hesitated because the action lacked precedents. In addition, no one wanted to take the responsibility for rectifying improper conduct.

Bryan, for example, recommended that the Dominicans follow standard American practice to ensure the fairness of the vote. He suggested appointing enough judges from the individual political parties so that at least two from each would be present at the various polling and counting places. The secretary did allow that it might be necessary for Sullivan to tour a few of the polling sites in order to show the commitment of the United States. "This Government is, of course, indifferent as to which party succeeds," the secretary avowed. "It merely desires the maintenance of constitutional government, and there, as here, constitutional government means that the people shall rule and have what they want in the way of offices and policies." But this advice was as far as Bryan would go in promoting Dominican democracy; he withheld approval for sending observers.[16]

For American representatives in the country, supervision symbolized Wilson's commitment to the future of Santo Domingo. Charles B. Curtis, Sullivan's assistant, believed that observation would be the "entering wedge for the probably seriously contested Presidential election to follow." Sullivan warned that "the danger lies in the people turning liberty into license and Government taking advantage of same." The delicate state of Dominican politics required American observers to prevent this from occurring. Walter Vick, Wilson's appointee as general receiver, during a visit to Washington in November, met personally with Bryan to urge that supervisors be sent "for the strengthening of the Latin-American policy of the administration." He feared that Bordas might confuse support for constitutional government as support for his regime. Consequently, Vick told Bryan, "certain sinister politicians" were trying to control the upcoming elections. If they won, they would control the reforms of the Dominican constitution. If the United States did not send observers, Vick believed, another revolution would occur. Since the revolutionists depended on American assurances, a failure to carry out the agreement would convince them that the Wilson administration cared little for "a real fulfillment of its free and fair election promises." Wilson, Vick maintained, had no choice.[17]

The arguments of Vick and others in Santo Domingo finally convinced Bryan. He wrote Wilson on December 1 to suggest that they send observers. The observers would not, he assured the president, "act as election officials but could be known as inspectors, sent from the United States to use their moral influence to secure a fair election." On the following day, the secretary informed the American legation of his decision to send three agents from the State Department and thirty from Puerto Rico. He appointed Sullivan in charge of the task force.[18]

Bordas suddenly became uncooperative. When he learned of Bryan's decision, he protested, thereby breaking the settlement reached with the Horacistas. However, his opposition confirmed Bryan in the new course. To soothe the Dominican president's pride, though, Bryan emphasized that the United States intended to send inspectors in order to lend America's "moral support." Wilson endorsed this arrangement—the idea of moral assistance appealed to him. After further negotiations between Sullivan and Bordas, this description became the basis for an agreement.[19] During the three days of the elections, thirty-three observers, stationed at various polling places across the country, watched as the Dominican people cast their votes.

Although Bordas arrested six opposition leaders on the second day of the elections, Sullivan claimed that the voting went very smoothly. He attributed this success to the calming presence of the Americans. Wilson and Bryan interpreted the successful elections as a vindication of their policies. The support of Bordas illustrated their commitment to constitutional government, while supervision showed their faith in the efficacy of democracy. Few officials took much notice of the incarceration of the opposition speakers and leaders. Even fewer paid attention to the final tally, despite the fact that it boded ill for Wilson's policies. The Bordas party suffered an overwhelming defeat.[20]

This episode, although it did not lead directly to Wilson's later employment of armed power, set the pattern of his policies which eventually culminated in the occupation. By establishing early in his administration a commitment to constitutional government in the Dominican Republic, Wilson inadvertently lost any flexibility in responding to future events in the country. The slow degeneration of stability in the country drew the United States further into the morass of Dominican political upheavals. Soon after the elections, the Wilson administration began pressuring the Bordas regime to adopt constitutional and financial reforms, including the appointment of an American comptroller to oversee government expenditures. "We have Constitutional Government and Constitutional reforms jacked up here and resting upon props," Sullivan advised. "It seems to me we should build our foundation at once under this institution because we will never have a better opportunity to do the work." Thus, the Wilson administration increased its efforts to remake the Dominican Republic in the image of the United States.[21]

Unfortunately for American policy, the Wilson administration relied on the Bordas regime as its vehicle for the introduction of democratic methods. Bordas, it soon became clear, was interested only in maintaining his own power. He played along with the United States to retain its support, hoping all the while that it would protect him in office past the expiration of his presidential term on April 14. Walter Vick suspected Bordas's ambitions. "The Government now in power is very naturally playing for an extension of its term by some means or other," he warned General McIntyre. "It does not seem probable that they would be successful in any general election properly conducted." Vick feared that, should Bordas succeed in his plans, "the insistent dissatisfaction is apt to culminate in serious disturbances at any time."[22] Both the general receiver's fears and his predictions were realized soon afterward.

Bordas, convinced that he could engineer his own reelection, announced in February that he intended to run in the April elections. The announcement triggered the basic distrust of the other political factions, primarily because previous presidents found little difficulty in arranging for a convenient electoral count. These groups had not let Bordas's arrests of the opposition in December pass unnoticed. The president's former ally, Desiderio Arias, launched his own revolt. Sullivan advised the State Department to aid Bordas. The president, he said, was "most friendly to our Government," as well as "the best possible agency for implanting American ideas for good Government in this country." Besides, he added, "to remain passive seems to me to be almost shirking our responsibility." However, unknown to Washington officials, Sullivan had personal reasons for praising Bordas's friendship. He was financially involved in various unscrupulous business deals with the Dominican regime. Throughout the spring and summer of 1914, Sullivan continued to urge assistance for Bordas, but it is not clear how much his pocketbook influenced his advice.[23]

Officials in the department agreed to the necessity of supporting Bordas. Since the Bordas government symbolized constitutional authority, Bryan ignored the extent of the dissatisfaction with Bordas throughout the Dominican Republic. Opposition to Bordas equalled opposition to democracy, and Bryan refused to admit the possibility of failure for his earlier policies. The secretary insisted that the United States stood behind the constitutional government, "which all leaders a few months ago claimed to desire." Since the U.S. had no sympathy for any faction that opposed reform of the constitution, Bryan expected all parties to come together, assist in the convention's rewriting of the nation's charter, and then participate honorably in the April elections.[24]

By confusing support for Bordas with support for Dominican democracy, the Wilson administration succeeded only in becoming further enmeshed in the political turmoil of the country without seeing or understanding the larger implications of its policies. Bordas offended the other factions in Santo Domingo because they understood his ambitions, which jeopardized their own. "Rumors of trouble are rife and the entire situation is illustrative of the fact that government in Santo Domingo is either 'Anarchy or Tyranny,'" Vick advised McIntyre on March 24. The machinations of Bordas convinced him that the president intended to continue his reign by any means possible, which meant that "all pretensions of reforms, free and fair elections, are but sham and subterfuge." The general receiver expected violent outbreaks in opposition to the government soon after April 14. "The outlook for the next few months gives cause for nothing but pessimism," he warned McIntyre.[25]

Bryan continued to espouse his faith in Dominican democracy despite the crumbling situation. On March 19 Bordas promised elections on April 1 and 2, which gave his opponents precious little time to campaign against him. In the end, it did not matter. The president cancelled the elections ten days later. Bryan tried a two-pronged approach to solve the problems. On the one hand, he put his faith in elections, avowing that "the United States has no interest except to aid in directing through the medium of free and fair means of the candidate desired by the voters." On the other hand, Bryan finally came to the conclusion that Arias was "an outlaw and enemy in insurrection against the constituted government, to which this Government is lending its moral support." When Bordas decided to take to the field with one thousand troops to suppress the revolt, the United States encouraged him by financing the expedition through a loan and an increase in the percentage of customs revenues. "A crisis has arisen in Santo Domingo which seems to require immediate action," Bryan, in a memo written by Long, told Wilson. "Our pacific measures have not resulted as successfully as I had hoped." He urged financial support for Bordas, declaring that "if there must be violence before peace the more quickly and decisively the government acts the better." After Bryan worked out the details with the Dominican government, the flow of money increased into the coffers of the Bordas regime.[26]

Bordas's attempts to maintain himself in power angered the major factions in the country's politics, as predicted by Vick. The Horacistas, Jiménistas, and Velásquistas allied themselves with Arias against the so-called constitutional government. Bordas continued in office past the expiration of his term, which the parties aligned against him interpreted as a disavowal of the agreement made the previous fall. On April 21 the important province of Puerto Plata and several other provinces became strongholds of the rebels. Acting Secretary of State Lansing asked Daniels to order navy representatives to negotiate an end to the fighting at that port. If negotiations failed, Lansing advised, the United States "will be forced to take such measures as are necessary to protect the assistants of the General Receiver of Customs in the performance of their duties." The negotiations conducted by Captain E. W. Eberle of the USS *Wheeling* failed to effect a truce, even though Eberle continued trying well into August. State Department representatives promised the support of the American navy if Bordas declared a blockade of Puerto Plata.[27] Once again, the United States based its interference on the rights and responsibilities it derived from the Convention of 1907. The convention became the legal shroud covering the corpse of Wilson's first policies toward revolt and turmoil in the Dominican Republic.

The infectious spread of rebellion compelled the Wilson administration to reconsider its support of Bordas, but no ready alternatives to its policies seemed available. Wilson himself addressed his attention to the problem. "What a perplexing question of duty Santo Domingo offers," Wilson exclaimed to Bryan on May 13. Throughout the next week and a half, he contemplated the situation and the method for dealing with it. "I am ashamed of myself that I have not been able to think out a satisfactory solution," Wilson wrote his secretary of state on May 24.

"My thought is a great deal upon the subject."[28] So was everyone else's. During the late spring and into the summer of 1914, the Wilson administration considered a variety of options for solving the problem. These ran the gamut from continued support of Bordas to armed intervention, but none appealed to Wilson.

Bordas eventually destroyed himself. He scheduled elections for June 7 and 8 and then, over the objections of Bryan, held them in selected provinces. The results gave him a landslide victory for the presidency, but a severe loss, in Bryan's view, for democracy. The secretary suggested postponement of the elections until a compromise provisional president could be installed. Sullivan, showing the strength of his financial ties to Bordas, argued that no such man could be found; Bordas was still the only hope for democracy in Santo Domingo. The minister's arguments, however, failed to persuade Bryan, who began insisting on the settlement of the revolution by the selection of a neutral Dominican to serve as a caretaker president.[29]

Other American officials offered their solutions. Lansing strongly urged that the United States determine its policy and follow it relentlessly. He pointed out that the Dominican people distrusted Sullivan's motives, which harmed his usefulness in promoting American policy. "It appears to me that the present conditions are becoming intolerable, and that this Government may be compelled to take drastic measures to establish a stable government in order that the provisions of the Convention of 1907 may be carried out," he asserted. "If something is not done, and done at once, it seems to be certain that the situation will continue to grow worse and worse both politically and economically." Lansing appended to his memo a lengthy review of the situation by Jordan Stabler of the Division of Latin American Affairs. Stabler wanted the commander of the USS *Washington* to notify the conflicting factions that the United States would not allow the revolution to continue. American responsibilities under the Convention of 1907 required forceful action, but Stabler hoped that the threat alone would suffice. The United States could then help the Dominicans to choose a compromise provisional president whose major task would be to supervise, with American assistance, elections for a regular president. Throughout the summer, Stabler continued to press for a stronger stand toward the revolution.[30]

An acceptable solution eluded the Wilson administration until the end of July 1914. Throughout that month, Wilson received advice from his secretary of state and other officials which focused his attention on the chaotic conditions. Early in July, Bryan reiterated his plan of installing a provisional government which would remain in power until "fair elections" could be held. This time, Bryan added the suggestion that the United States take upon itself the task of preventing further insurrections. "Our experience in San Domingo [sic] and Haiti convinces me," the secretary concluded on July 8, "that we can render no more neighborly service than to rid them of constant revolutions which impoverish the country at large and enrich only a few ambitious chieftains."[31] These recommendations encouraged Wilson to develop his own plan.

In a truly amazing feat of energy and concentration, Wilson formulated a proposal toward the end of July for ending revolutions in the Dominican Republic. The summer of 1914 offered the president an agony of personal and international tragedies. As he endured the heat of Washington, Wilson confronted four separate crises. In addition to Santo Domingo, he also set American policy toward the occupation of Veracruz and the continued turmoil in Mexico. World War I began, which shook his faith in the supremacy of Western civilization and compelled him to define American neutrality. Finally, as he dealt with these problems, Wilson sat at the deathbed of his first wife, Ellen Axson Wilson. That he thought of the Dominican Republic at all testified to the depths of his humanitarianism; his solution witnessed the strength of his ethnocentrism.

Wilson informed Bryan on July 23 that he felt "a way is opening up for an adjustment in San Domingo." Four days later, he composed a draft of what later became known as the Wilson Plan. "The Government of the United States desires nothing for itself from the Dominican Republic and no concessions or advantages for its citizens which are not accorded citizens of other countries," it began. Instead, the United States "desires only to prove its sincere and disinterested friendship for the republic and its people and to fulfill its responsibilities as the friend to whom in such crises as the present all the world looks to guide San Domingo out of its difficulties." The draft then outlined three steps to end the rebellion. First, Wilson warned everyone involved to cease hostilities and disband their forces. "This is necessary," he wrote, "and necessary at once." Second, Wilson demanded a "reconstitution of political authority in the republic." He wanted all factions whose leaders had "pretentions to be chosen President" to agree on a "responsible and representative man to act as provisional President." Wilson expected Bordas to surrender his office to this man, who would be recognized by the United States.

If the several factions failed to choose a leader, then the United States would do so. This provisional president would then hold elections which would be supervised by American representatives. If the elections were free and fair, the United States would recognize the winner as the constitutional president. If the elections were not properly conducted, they would be held again. Finally, Wilson insisted that revolutionary movements cease. Further changes in government would be effected by peaceful means. "By no other course can the Government of the United States fulfill its treaty obligations with San Domingo or its tacitly conceded obligations as the nearest friend of San Domingo in her relations with the rest of the world," proclaimed Wilson.[32]

Bryan received the plan enthusiastically, suggesting only that the provisional president take office with the understanding that he could not be a candidate in the elections. The secretary allowed himself to feel "very hopeful about the success of this plan," which, as he wired Sullivan, promised "the restoration of peace and establishment of order in Santo Domingo." Wilson's draft became, without any changes, the final Wilson Plan. To ensure its implementation, Wilson and Bryan appointed a commission headed by John Franklin Fort to go to the Dominican Republic. Charles Cogswell Smith and Minister Sullivan made up the rest of the commission. Wilson and Bryan instructed them to meet with Bordas and the other political leaders, present them the Wilson Plan, and make sure that the Dominicans fulfilled its stipulations. They further explained:

> You will say to the various leaders that the United States will thereafter employ such force as is necessary to maintain constitutional government and put down insurrections. In other words, in the fulfillment of the duties enjoined upon it by its treaty, it will cooperate with the people of Santo Domingo in the maintenance of orderly government. . . . The President feels that the step which he is taking is not only one to which he is compelled by the obligations which the country has assumed, but that this Government will be performing a neighborly act, entirely consistent with the feeling of sincere friendship entertained by the people of the United States for the people of Santo Domingo.[33]

Driven by an humanitarian impulse and the requirements of the Convention of 1907, Wilson determined to end the turmoil in Santo Domingo.

The Fort Commission arrived in the Dominican Republic on August 16. It immediately began a series of meetings with the various leaders to convince them to accept the plan. Although Bordas originally promised his cooperation, he later changed his mind, declaring that he was not only de facto president, but de jure as well. Wilson had had as much as he could take. He instructed the commission to "yield nothing; insist upon full and literal compliance with plan." Bordas needed to realize that "the U.S. means business," Wilson declared. "This government will not brook refusal, change of purpose, or unreasonable delay." The Dominican president, unable to rule without American support, gave up. The commission reported "full acceptance" of the Wilson Plan on August 25. Negotiations continued on the selection of a new provisional president until, finally, Ramón Báez was chosen. He was inaugurated on August 27, and the United States recognized his government the next day.[34]

Báez, with American help, supervised presidential elections on October 25, 26, and 27. Smith reported that the success of the voting "surpasses greatest expectations of Commission and Dominican Government and people." When the votes were finally counted, which took some time because many of the district counts were disputed in the courts, Don Juan Jiménez was declared the new president. He was sworn in on December 5, and the next day, Secretary of the Navy Daniels ordered the commanding officer of the USS *Hancock* to "render President Jiménez such support as may be necessary for proper administration of the government and for maintenance of order." The Wilson Plan worked, Bryan claimed, since the situation has "cleared up and the Government's policy has been vindicated by a fair election and the restoration of peace."[35] The policy of promoting American democratic ideology seemed a successful solution.

During the months immediately following, Jiménez shakily ruled the country. He ended the Arias revolt by appointing its leader secretary of war, an astute political move that co-opted into the government the most explosive element in Dominican politics. The ensuing peace relieved the strain on Wilson and his subordinates. Bryan wasted little time before he began suggesting reforms for the new government to implement. As usual, the secretary blinded himself to the troubled waters beneath the placid surface. Others were more observant, or at least more skeptical. The Fifth Regiment of the Marine Corps, which was assigned aboard the navy's Atlantic Cruiser Squadron, completed its war plans for the occupation of Santo Domingo in December, the same month that Bryan bragged of the presumed victory over Dominican chaos.[36] In the end, the marines proved far more prescient than the secretary of state.

THE OCCUPATION OF HAITI, 1915

The navy, confident of the settled conditions in Santo Domingo, began withdrawing most of the ships stationed there in December 1914. On December 12 Lansing asked Daniels to send one of the warships to

Port-au-Prince, Haiti, to pick up the gold stored in the vaults of the National Bank of Haiti, lest it be repossessed by the native government. Daniels assigned the task to the USS *Machias*. Upon its arrival at the capital, the *Machias* dispatched a detachment of marines to the bank building where they found five hundred thousand dollars worth of gold, which they carried back to the ship. The ship then proceeded to New York to deposit its cargo with the National City Bank, the corporate parent of the Haitian institution.[37] The route of the *Machias* from the Dominican Republic to Haiti symbolized the interrelated character of Wilson's policies toward the two countries; its mission indicated the extent of American involvement in Haiti by the end of 1914.

With the situation in the Dominican Republic temporarily resolved, Wilson and his subordinates decided to settle their difficulties with Haiti, which had been just as troublesome as Santo Domingo. Although Haiti presented Wilson with problems different from those he confronted in Santo Domingo, the president designed his response on the model of his presumed success with the Dominicans. The collapse of this approach led to the American occupation. However, the events culminating in the American intervention can best be understood by examining three interconnected aspects of Haitian-U.S. relations. The first concerned the interest in the Mole St. Nicholas, a natural harbor on the sea lanes to the Panama Canal. The second aspect involved the intention to prohibit foreign powers from gaining predominance in the country. The third, and most important, concerned the desire to establish American control over Haitian finances and politics similar to the influence that the United States enjoyed in the Dominican Republic.

Unlike Wilson's approach to Santo Domingo, his Haitian policies recognized strategic and commercial considerations. Bryan, for example, argued that a white man, rather than a black, should represent the United States in Haiti "in view of the increased importance that Haiti will assume with the opening of the Panama Canal." The interest in the Mole St. Nicholas stemmed from the fear that a foreign power might take possession of it, which would threaten one of the passages to the canal. The Mole seemed to the secretary a convenient coaling station for navy ships. American possession of it would contribute to the security of the canal.[38]

Originally, Bryan urged that the Wilson administration purchase this "very desirable harbor," adding that "I am satisfied that it will be of great value to us and even if it were not valuable to us it is worth while to take it out of the market so that no other nation will attempt to secure a foothold there." Wilson approved the proposal, which prompted Bryan to send one of his assistant secretaries, John E. Osborne, to Haiti to negotiate an agreement for buying the harbor. Haitian law, however, prohibited the sale of land to foreigners. The best Osborne could achieve was a promise from the current president, Michel Oreste, that Haiti would not allow any foreign power to take possession of the Mole. Wilson settled for this, particularly since the navy decided that it did not need an extra coaling station in the Caribbean. Throughout Wilson's dealings with Haiti, the Mole continued to be an issue, but the danger of foreign bases was finally settled when the United States took over the entire country in July 1915.[39]

The second aspect of Wilson's policies, the fear of foreign interference, came to the fore during negotiations for a customs convention with Haiti. In March 1914 both France and Germany requested equal participation. They based their claim on the large investments of their nationals in the country. Neither Bryan nor Wilson looked with favor on this proposal. "It seems to me it would be very unwise to agree to any kind of joint control," Bryan advised. "I quite agree with your judgment that we could not enter into any arrangement in Haiti by which there should be joint control in the customs matter with any foreign nation," Wilson responded. Although the possibility of foreign interference lessened considerably following the outbreak of World War I, the administration's fear never diminished.[40]

Opposition to foreign involvement extended beyond the perceived threat to America's strategic and financial interests in the island. Officials of the Wilson administration perceived themselves as the only ones capable of helping Haiti achieve a higher level of civilization. In their view, foreign meddling would not promote their goal. Boaz Long, in a letter to William Phillips, an aide to Bryan, on May 16, 1914, cogently expressed this aspect of the government's faith in its own American democratic ideology:

> If our Government desires to eliminate the ever present danger of German control, which is today apparently more of a menace because Haiti's tragic political situation affords a favorable opportunity, let us now seize this moment to send a special emissary there to endeavor to bring her to a reasonable basis of financial administration.
>
> The people of Haiti are virtually slaves; their owners a lot of low politicians. The majority of the population desires to be free of the grafting generals and politicians. If we are going to remove the hands of graft from their throats we will have to be very firm, for our opponents are among the most skillful of the world.
>
> As I see it, we have no choice but to sit in this game.[41]

Long's statement indicated the paternalistic attitude that the Wilson administration brought to American policies, whether they concerned the Mole, outside interests, or Haiti's internal affairs.

American democratic ideology also motivated the third aspect of Wilson's policies. The desire to help Haiti with its finances and its politics was neither malicious nor greedy, merely misdirected. Administration officials shared an abysmal ignorance of Haitian history and culture. They found guidance for their policies in racial prejudice (a form of ethnocentrism) and the example of Santo Domingo.[42]

Haitian revolutions typically followed a set pattern. A disgruntled or ambitious leader launched a revolt from the northern hills, where he hired troops from among the *cacos,* various bands of mercenaries and bandits. Rebel forces first took Cape Haitien before proceeding toward Port-au-Prince. Usually, the current president, broke and unable to hire his own *cacos,* fled the country before the rebels reached the capital. The rebel leader then seized Port-au-Prince, arranged for his own election by the national assembly, and disbanded the *cacos,* who returned to the hills to await their next customer. In this way, Haiti had evolved a political system which, though based on violence, was relatively bloodless. The *cacos* were much more interested in spending their pay than in dying for another man's cause.

Haitian President Michel Oreste came to power in May 1913. His tenure ended in early 1914 when he was overthrown by the brothers Oreste and Charles Zamor. At the end of January 1914, American forces, in company with British, French, and German troops, landed in the capital for the protection of foreign interests. They remained until February 9, by which time the Zamors were in power.[43]

"Only one President of Haiti has served out the regular term of office, seven years," Long informed Bryan on January 23. "The political system which obtains throughout the country constitutes a certain form of slavery for the masses," he continued, "and no helping hand has been stretched out to the common people in an effort to improve their condition." Long then briefly reviewed Haitian political history, from which he concluded that the cause of revolutions in the country resulted from the struggle of "professional revolutionists" to take control of the government and its customs revenues. The present situation with the Zamors, Long believed, presented the State Department an opportunity "to take such steps in Haiti as will be likely to produce a great improvement in conditions there, along the lines of our President's policy." Quite simply, Haiti needed money to meet the interest payments on its various loans. Long suggested sending a "competent man" there to negotiate a million-dollar loan under the condition that the Haitian government allow the United States "to assist in inaugurating a more practical system of customs collection and in handling the finances of that country." Such a loan would allow "an opportunity for this Government to assist Haiti."[44] Thus was born the idea of American control of Haitian customs revenues. The key to the idea was the insistence that the Haitians request American help, for until July 1915 the United States shunned imposing its aid on the country.

The abdication of Michel Oreste opened the way for the Wilson administration to gain a foothold in Haiti. "At the present moment it would appear that the United States is in a position to gain that influence which for many years we have desired and needed in the Republic of Haiti," Jordan Stabler advised Bryan on February 3. He argued that the United States should choose a candidate for president, lend him support, and recognize him as president, provided he agreed to several conditions, including customs control. Others picked up on the idea, including Roger L. Farnham, an officer of the National City Bank of New York and its Haitian company, the National Bank of Haiti.[45]

Throughout 1914 Farnham played an important role advising Bryan. The secretary listened to him because he was informed of the conditions in the country and knew its leaders. Also, Farnham wanted what was best for the people, that is, American control of the customs service. Bryan wanted the same. Thus, the two men colluded for the same objective, at least so Bryan thought.

Bryan suggested recognizing the government of Oreste Zamor to Wilson on February 21 because "it would be well for our influence with the new Govt." Two weeks later, Bryan heard rumors, probably from Farnham, that the Zamor government intended to request American aid in the reorganization of its customs service. He instructed the minister to Haiti, Madison Smith, to respond to such an invitation by saying that President Wilson "feels a deep concern in everything that affects the welfare of Haiti." The United States would give serious consideration to the matter. For the minister's own information, Bryan added that "the President is disposed to support the present government against insurrections in so far as it proves itself worthy of confidence by meeting governmental responsibilities," which included, presumably, asking for American help. The new Haitian government, however, though friendly to the idea of customs control, feared that the United States would give it only moral support against further insurrections. Farnham continued to urge U.S. control, arguing that the deplorable conditions in Haiti required it. But the Zamors hesitated to make a formal request and Bryan refused to impose assistance on them.[46]

The situation remained stagnant until the spring, when a new revolution, led by Davilmar Théodore, broke out against the new regime. Bryan reviewed the matter with Wilson toward the end of June, at which time the two men discussed applying a Dominican-type customs receivership to Haiti. The secretary of state forwarded a copy of the convention to Wilson, who read it with Haiti in mind. Wilson concluded that "the general administrative arrangement is no doubt such as we could enter into with Haiti." He asked Bryan to have his assistants draw up a draft convention for the Black Republic.[47]

The decision to apply the Dominican customs convention to Haiti led to the implementation of what department officials variously called "the plan" or the "Farnham plan" after the banker who promoted it with both Bryan and the Zamor brothers. Bryan commissioned the new American minister, Arthur Bailly-Blanchard, to negotiate a request from the Zamor brothers. The department forwarded a proposed treaty to Blanchard in early July. The secretary admitted that it was "fashioned after the Convention with the Dominican Republic, and follows closely its terms and language." The State Department took the opportunity to append an article allowing for the appointment of an American financial adviser which, though absent from the model, resembled the agreement recently reached with the Bordas regime. In addition, the proposed treaty contained an enabling article that made "clear the authority of the United States to aid in the attainment of each and all the objects comprehended within the Convention." Bryan believed that this would assist the Zamors in establishing "the tranquility, security and prosperity of the Republic."[48] However, the continued revolt against the regime threw this objective into doubt.

Intervention seemed a definite possibility. It was not, as Arthur Link has argued, a part of the plan. Bryan asked Daniels on July 10 to send a force of marines sufficient to protect "American interests throughout the island of Haiti" to a point close by in case a landing became necessary. As the secretary explained to Wilson, he made the request because of a "possible disturbance at the capital." A State Department memorandum written some months later explained that the plan involved negotiations between Blanchard and the Zamors—the memo made no mention of a conspiracy for American intervention.[49]

Bryan determined to support Farnham as much as possible. As he told Lemuel W. Livingston, the consul at Cape Haitien, the department "earnestly desires successful carrying out of plan" proposed by Farnham for the "permanent solution of political and financial unrest." In addition, Bryan issued instructions to all consular agents "to cooperate for the advancement of American interests with other Americans now at Cape Haitien," a reference to Farnham, who was in Haiti carrying on discussions with the ruling brothers.[50]

The Haitian government accepted the plan in principle, but its stability was daily being eroded by the spreading revolution. Livingston suggested on July 18 that intervention would "enable Government to save appearances by yielding to superior force and shift responsibility to those who [provoke] landing by taking up arms." Boaz Long approved the idea. The deteriorating situation, including violent outbreaks at Cape Haitien and Port-au-Prince, provided "every excuse for landing a small force to protect foreign property in the capital." Besides, if the opportunity passed and the Zamor government fell, "there would no longer be any prospect of carrying out your plan." Bryan, however, shied away from imposing the plan on Haiti because he wanted the suggestion to come from the Haitians. The secretary considered it "absolutely necessary that the request for the adoption of this plan be given by the Haitian government." If a treaty could be agreed to, then the United States would furnish the necessary assistance "to enforce law and order and insure constitutional government." Bryan pointed to the success the U.S. achieved in Santo Domingo in the fall of 1914 as an example of what could be done for Haiti.[51] But he refused to allow American troops to violate Haitian sovereignty without the express invitation of the native authorities except if force were necessary for the protection of foreign lives and property.

The stalemate continued into the fall of 1914. In October administration officials discussed the possibility of landing marines for the protection of foreigners, but the revolution never got far enough out of hand to require this step. Indeed, the Zamor government fell before action could be taken. The Farnham plan was thrown back to its starting point. Théodore took charge of the affairs of Haiti, leaving the Wilson administration with a new government with which to negotiate. Their success in Santo Domingo encouraged administration officials to apply the Wilson plan to Haiti, but eventually they decided to entice an agreement out of the Théodore regime by withholding diplomatic recognition until Théodore sent three commissioners to the United States empowered to sign a treaty allowing American control over Haiti's finances. Severe domestic opposition, however, compelled Théodore to refuse.[52]

No one wanted yet another revolution, so Bryan backed down. "In expressing a willingness to do in Haiti what we are doing in Santo Domingo," he cabled Blanchard, "this Government was actuated wholly by a disinterested desire to render assistance." The United States would not "press the matter" if the Haitian authorities considered it best not to proceed. Diplomatic recognition would depend on the democratic character of the new regime, as well as its ability to govern. Bryan explained the new approach to Wilson on December 12: "It is intended to present two ideas—first, that we do not insist upon their making an agreement with us against their will; and second, that we must be satisfied of the representative character of the government and of its ability to conduct a government before we recognize them."53 The United States would not force its will on Haiti—only its morals.

The Haitians responded with a counterproject that offered an opportunity for American commercial interests to exploit the country's natural resources. "It is so evidently an attempt to negotiate for concessions that I think it is well for us to let them distinctly understand that this Government is not disposed to make a bargain of that kind," Bryan angrily complained to Wilson about this insulting proposition. The Haitians, he claimed, misunderstood the American position. "While we desire to encourage in every proper way American investments in Haiti," he cabled Blanchard, "we believe that this can be better done by contributing to stability and order than by favoring special concessions to Americans." Investors would flock to Haiti once peace was firmly established. This was the Wilson administration's goal. "If the United States can, as a neighbor and friend, assist the Government and people of Haiti as it has assisted the Government and people of Santo Domingo," Bryan proudly proclaimed, "it will gladly do so provided that assistance is desired." Once again, the Haitians would have to request American help.54

Wilson never extended diplomatic recognition to the Théodore government, which faced its own revolution led by Vilbrun Guillaume Sam shortly after defeating the Zamor brothers. Destitute of funds, and at odds with the national bank over debts and the contractual arrangement between them, the Théodore government seemed desperate enough to take by force the gold stored in the bank vaults. At this point, Lansing asked Daniels to send a ship to pick up the gold in order to keep it out of Théodore's hands. As the *Machias* steamed toward New York with its precious cargo, one phase of Wilson's relations with Haiti ended and another began. Free now of the worrisome Dominican problem, with the situation in Mexico relatively calm and the Veracruz occupation ended, and with World War I yet to infringe seriously on U.S. neutrality, Wilson and Bryan decided to resolve the irritating troubles in Haiti.

In the event that Bryan and Wilson failed again, others readied themselves for the occupation of the country. As it had with Santo Domingo, the Fifth Regiment of the Marine Corps completed in November 1914 its war plans for taking the Black Republic. Based on recent experience, the plans assumed that "the government has been overthrown; all semblance of law and order has ceased; the local authorities admit their inability to protect foreign interests."55 The plan's assumption predicted the situation in July 1915 fairly accurately. The intervening months, however, witnessed the continued but tragically futile efforts of Wilson and his pacifist secretary of state as they struggled to achieve a less drastic solution.

The new year brought the need for a new policy. Throughout the first half of January 1915, Wilson and Bryan grappled with the problem of Haiti. The vice president of the National Bank of Haiti, Henry W. Wakrhave, pleaded with Bryan for armed intervention to forestall loss of life and property of foreigners. Three days later, on January 7, the secretary outlined the situation to Wilson. He stressed the threats to the bank and the continued attempts by the Haitian government to violate its contract with that corporation. "I believe that there will be no peace and progress in Hayti [sic] until we have some such arrangement as we have in Santo Domingo, and, as you remember, we have proposed that to them but have not felt like compelling acceptance of the plan," he wrote. "There is probably sufficient ground for intervention, but I do not like the idea of forcible interference on purely business grounds." Bryan suggested, instead, sending a commission to Haiti similar to the one just returned from Santo Domingo. In addition to arranging for a provisional president and an American supervised election, this Haitian commission would also press for U.S. control over the customs revenues.[56]

Bryan's plan appealed to Wilson. "The more I think about that situation, the more I am convinced that it is our duty to take immediate action there such as we took in San Domingo," he told Bryan on January 13. The president approved sending a commission to insist on a popular election under American supervision. The United States would then uphold the results of the vote, for it "cannot consent to stand by and permit revolutionary conditions constantly to exist there." Within days the two men agreed that Fort and Smith, lately returned from their mission to Santo Domingo, were the best candidates to send. If the new commission could achieve a success equal to its settlement of the Dominican crisis, then "Haiti can be put on the road to prosperity," Bryan believed.[57] Once again, the threads of Wilson's policies stretched across the island from Santo Domingo to Haiti.

The Sam revolt spread successfully across Haiti. Rebel forces captured Cape Haitien in late January before turning toward the capital. The Navy Department ordered the Atlantic Cruiser Squadron under the command of Rear Admiral William B. Caperton, whose flagship was the USS *Washington,* to Haiti. The department assigned Caperton a dual mission: to gather intelligence on the situation and to protect Americans and other foreigners from the violence endemic to the Black

Republic. A paper on the mission of the *Washington,* written aboard the ship, outlined the attitude of the officers toward their tasks:

> The conditions in Haiti are chaotic. The present government is without funds. Some action on our part will be demanded in the immediate future. . . . The ships of the Cruiser Squadron engaged in protecting American interests in the Caribbean and Mexican region do so principally by diplomatic means in conjunction with the diplomatic and consular officers of the United States; by showing force, and upon order of the Government, by seizing and taking control of the customs administration and government finances.

Shortly after arriving in Haitian waters in late January, Caperton received permission to land troops for the protection of the bank's property should the situation require it. Caperton's command formulated plans for such an eventuality, but they were not immediately needed.[58] In the meantime, the Fort Commission prepared to find a solution to the problems.

"This Haitian case, as I understand it," Fort wrote Joe Tumulty, Wilson's private secretary, on February 19, "is squarely under our Monroe Doctrine." With this attitude, he and Smith traveled to Haiti. Bryan prepared for their mission by querying the American minister on conditions in the country and its political system. He learned that Sam had taken office as president in the fashion typical of successful revolutionaries. The new leader awaited the vote of the national assembly to confirm his legal authority. Blanchard also described conditions as desperate—the economy was disrupted by World War I and the government had no money. The minister recommended a delay in the arrival of the Fort Commission, of which he was the third member, until Sam could establish himself as president. Bryan was also informed, much to his chagrin, that Haiti had no popular elections for president. A national assembly, composed of members of the Chamber of Deputies and Senators, selected the president, who was almost always the victor of the most recent revolution.[59]

This meant that the Dominican solution could not be applied in all its particulars to Haiti. As Bryan told Wilson, "we will have to content ourselves with ascertaining whether so far as public opinion can be learned, the man selected by the National Assembly is really the choice of the people." Their ignorance of Haitian politics deterred neither man from advancing with the plan. Bryan did question whether the moment was opportune for establishing American control over the customs, for he preferred to ensure order first. "It is the desire of the President that we shall do in Haiti all that can be done under the circumstances to assist, in a friendly way, the establishment of order and the administration of a government which will safeguard the rights of the people of Haiti as well as protect the rights of foreigners doing business in Haiti," Bryan informed Blanchard on February 27.[60] Consequently, Fort and Smith traveled to Haiti with only vague instructions to guide them.

The secretary's letter of instructions to Fort lacked detail as to how the commission should achieve its goal. "It is the desire of the President to render to Haiti such assistance and disinterested service as are possible under the circumstances," the instructions stated, "but just what the character of that service is to be, or to what extent this Government can be of assistance cannot be determined until the President is fully informed." The commission carried with it copies of the previous instructions for the Santo Domingo mission and a copy of the Wilson Plan, but ignorance of the conditions in Haiti and the attitude of the new government made it impossible for the administration to decide if these approaches were appropriate. Bryan resorted to vague generalities which, though they did not enlighten the commission as to tactics, did reveal the ethnocentric humanitarianism that underlay Wilson's policies. Bryan wrote:

> You will please assure the authorities with whom you have to deal of the genuineness and disinterestedness of this Government's friendship for Haiti. We ask nothing in return but the satisfaction which will come to our people from the knowledge that the assistance rendered has contributed to the peace, progress, and prosperity of a neighboring republic. Our conduct toward other Latin-American countries ought to make the assurance unnecessary, but that there may be no misunderstanding you will, of course, explain to the Haitian authorities that such guarantees as we ask for citizens of this country we also ask for citizens of other countries and that any work entrusted to this Government by Haiti will be performed with entire impartiality toward all foreigners, from whatever nation they may come.[61]

The Wilson administration only wanted to help; the twin calls of Christian duty and service compelled it to action.

The commission arrived in Haiti on March 5, 1915. Daniels assured the presence of ships in Haitian waters to assist Fort and Smith, including a "show of force" if necessary. But the commission remained only a week before it admitted failure and asked to return to the United States. Sam refused to deal with Fort and Smith until Wilson recognized his government. The two commissioners were also discouraged by Blanchard's attitude, which seemed to them suspiciously sympathetic to the Haitian position. Although Wilson expressed surprise at how quickly they gave up, he allowed them to return without delay.[62] Their abrupt departure left Wilson's policies in a shambles and in need of a new approach.

A resort to force tempted Bryan. Disgusted by the attitude of the Haitians and frustrated by the lack of success of his previous policies, Bryan asked Wilson if it were not time to send in troops. "I have been reluctant to favor anything that would require an exercise of force there," he said, "but there are some things that lead me to believe it may be necessary for us to use as much force as may be necessary to compel a supervision [of the customs service] which will be effective." He came to this conclusion on the basis of two perceptions. First, he was convinced that foreign agents were controlling the Haitian government. Second, he was equally sure that the new regime was fostering disorder and revolution in Santo Domingo. Thus, to save Haiti from the influence of selfish interests and to restore stability to the entire island, Bryan contemplated employing America's armed power.[63]

"The time to act is now," Wilson decided, but he remained unsure just what action to take. He suggested making certain demands a condition of recognition, such as U.S. control of the Mole and the appointment of an adviser who would implement the policies of the United States for political and financial stability. Yet, the president was not quite ready to turn to arms to solve the "perplexing" difficulties presented by Haiti. Instead, he determined to exert what Fort called a "firm hand at the helm" of affairs.[64]

Rather than armies, Wilson again sent an emissary. It was, in effect, if not by intent, the last chance for the Haitians to come to terms before the United States settled matters for itself. Wilson, through Bryan, asked Paul Fuller, Jr., to go to the Black Republic as the "Special Representative of the President." His instructions made clear that the administration was fast losing patience with the obstinacy of the Haitians. Bryan directed Fuller to advise Sam that the United States intended to protect Haiti from outside interference and from internal revolution. Wilson took this stand as the friend of the country and as the leading power in the Western Hemisphere. All that he asked in return was the honest and efficient administration of the affairs of the country, which could only be established if the Haitians allowed American representatives to enter into an "intimate and confidential relationship as will enable the American Legation to advise as to such matters as affect the honest and efficient administration of the government." The president of Haiti must promise to follow this advice.[65] At this point, Wilson upped the ante. He and Bryan were no longer willing to settle for customs control alone. They now insisted that the United States should have de facto control over the affairs of the entire country, not just its finances.

The time seemed ripe for such a demand. In May 1915, just as Fuller arrived in Haiti, a new revolution, led by Doctor Rosalvo Bobo, broke out against the Sam regime. Pressed by lack of finances and afraid of the revolutionists, Sam evinced a willingness to talk about American assistance. Fuller, playing on these fears, offered the assistance of U.S. Marines if Sam would agree to establish an intimate relationship between the two nations. The proposed treaty called for American predominance in Haiti, though this would be accomplished not by outright control but through the advice of U.S. representatives. The offer tempted Sam, but the negotiations eventually broke down. Sam insisted on the inclusion of several unacceptable conditions. He also demanded that the United States recognize his government before he signed any agreement. Early in June, Fuller returned to Washington for consultations with Bryan.[66]

In his report on his mission, Fuller described the Sam government as desperate. He felt confident that, as the pressure from the Bobo revolt increased, Sam would become more amenable to American demands. The danger lay in the possibility that Sam might delay too long, gambling that he could defeat Bobo without American help. If he lost his gamble, the United States would also lose yet another opportunity to set Haiti on the proper course toward advancement. Thus, Fuller made a startling recommendation, one which reopened the debate on intervention among members of the Wilson administration. Fuller concluded that

> The paralysis of what may be termed "the governing element," due to the dread of insurrection and revolution, on the low scale of personal revenge, cannot longer endure without danger of a complete disappearance of any semblance of independent nationality, and the time has come when such a convention as that proposed is the only alternative to active intervention in the interests of civilization and humanity. If, unfortunately, even approaching destruction does not soon bring about acquiescence in such treaty, I feel and recommend that the United States should intervene by the landing of its marines and should take necessary steps to establish an honest and efficient administration. When this result has been accomplished, the United States should invite (and would unquestionably obtain) a Treaty along the lines of the Platt Amendment as preliminary to turning over the administration to the Haitians. This beneficent purpose could in my opinion be accomplished without loss of life and without loss of friendship. Only such a thorough reorganization as an American occupation would bring about, will in my opinion ever permanently

change the present conditions which are destructive of freedom, of progress, of peace, and are intolerable to Haitians and foreigners alike.[67]

The administration came back to the Bryan option—intervention for salvation.

The Division of Latin American Affairs endorsed Fuller's recommendations. Wilson, too, was impressed. He asked Lansing, who took over as secretary of state following Bryan's resignation on June 7, to review the report. "It gives me a good deal of concern," Wilson told the new secretary; "Action is evidently necessary and no doubt it would be a mistake to pospone it long." Lansing turned the report over to the Office of the Counsellor, which replied on July 8 with an anonymous analysis. In the opinion of that office, the treaty proposed by Fuller did not go far enough. "It seems to me if we are to guarantee against foreign aggression and internal disorder the Haitian government should be willing to agree to limit its freedom so as to minimize causes for aggression and disorder," argued the reviewer. The author of the memo wanted more than an adviser appointed for Haiti, but someone who could control events on the basis of his own power, not just the willingness of the Haitians to listen.[68]

Sam, instead of running to the United States for help, decided to increase the stakes of his gamble. He broke the rules of Haiti's revolutionary political system. In July he ordered the arrest of 240 political opponents. Secretly, he added instructions to execute these prisoners in the event his government fell before the onslaught of Bobo's forces.

Incensed by the arrest of their friends and colleagues, an insurrectionary mob of Port-au-Prince citizens stormed the presidential palace on July 27. Many members of the mob were supporters of Bobo and other opponents of the Sam government, but the majority were moved to action by the mass arrests of their relatives and friends. This was a break in the pattern of Haitian revolutions; thus, it was met with an unprecedented reaction from the outraged citizens. Sam fled from the mob to the French legation next door. In the jail, the bloody massacre began as Sam had ordered; few of the prisoners survived. The next day another mob, enraged by the deaths of their brethren, attacked the French legation. Some of this group found Sam hiding in a bathroom. They dragged him outside onto the legation grounds, where they chopped his body to bits, throwing the pieces over the wall to their compatriots on the other side. The mob then paraded the remains of Sam through the streets of Port-au-Prince, a last tribute to the independence of Haiti.[69]

Caperton, warned by the American chargé, R. B. Davis, dashed to the capital. He arrived in time to witness the gruesome parade from the bridge of the *Washington*. As soon as the ship moored, the admiral dispatched marines to the city. They landed in the late afternoon. By nightfall, the bloodied mob had exhausted itself. American forces took control of the capital. Lansing, upon learning of the riot, requested Daniels to order a landing, thereby confirming five hours after the fact the course that Caperton decided to take on his own. The twenty-year occupation of Haiti began.[70]

Originally, Caperton intended to protect foreigners from the mob, but the motive was later expanded to encompass protecting the Haitians from themselves. Years afterward, Lansing explained the motives of all the Americans who were involved in the take-over:

> The murders and atrocities perpetrated marked the complete breakdown of Haitian institutions, the culmination of a process of disintegration which had been in progress for a generation or more. It was evident from the state of affairs that there remained no possibility of a civilized government functioning without external assistance. The limit of tolerance for such conditions, which menaced the lives and property of Americans and other foreigners, was finally reached when the French Legation was violated. The restoration of order and government in Haiti was as clearly the duty of the Government of the United States as was the landing of the Marines.[71]

Caperton determined on July 29 that Haiti had no government. Therefore, he decided to consolidate his military control over Port-au-Prince. The landing of the marines compelled the Wilson administration to take further action. With men already ashore, it seemed absurd to withdraw them and let the chaos in Haiti rear up again. Lansing, still unsure about what to do, suggested to Daniels that Caperton remain in possession of Port-au-Prince until the administration could determine its policy. In the meantime, the navy sent reinforcements.[72]

As Caperton moved to ensure his control over the capital, Washington officials discussed their next move. They acted independently, with little or no consultation with other nations in the Pan American Union. Wilson, vacationing on the New Jersey coast with his fiancée, Edith Boling Galt, turned to Daniels and Lansing to handle the problem. "I am sure I can count upon you to maintain peace and order and protect the embassies," he wrote on July 31.[73] Members of the State Department discussed possible alternatives for carrying out this duty during the end of July and the first few days of August.

The discussion showed that most felt only one course was open.

Former Minister Blanchard, who had been withdrawn from Haiti after the Fort mission, recommended that the United States avail "itself of the opportunity to intervene and bring order out of the existing chaos." Boaz Long, after reviewing conditions in the country, concluded that Haiti represented "the failure of an inferior people to maintain the degree of civilization left them by the French, or to develop any capacity of self government entitling them to international respect or confidence." He advised the establishment of a military government to rule for thirty-three years, at the end of which the United States would decide whether to turn over the government to the Haitians or to continue to govern for another thirty-three years. Fuller, conversing with Lansing, reiterated his earlier views that Haiti should be treated similarly to Cuba. Lansing, however, remained undecided. "I have not yet been able to reach a conclusion as to the course this Government should pursue," he wrote Wilson on August 2. "Our naval forces are in control of the city and I believe they should remain there until a definite policy in regard to the Republic can be reached."[74] It was not an easy decision for either man.

The United States lacked legal authority for its actions in Haiti. Although justified in intervening to stop the riot, this justification did not carry over into saving the Haitians from themselves. Wilson hoped that "it will be possible to bring some order out of the chaos," but neither he nor Lansing felt confident of their authority under international law to realize that hope. "The situation in Haiti is distressing and very perplexing," Lansing told Wilson on August 3; "I am not at all sure what we ought to do or what we can legally do." He believed that the only viable solution was to take over the customs, particularly since the country was in desperate straits economically and politically. Port-au-Prince was suffering a severe lack of food, but the United States had no authority to save the situation. "We have no excuse of reprisal as we had at Vera Cruz to take over the city government and administer the offices," Lansing complained. "There would appear to me to be but one reason which could be given for our doing so, and that is the humane duty of furnishing means to relieve the famine situation."[75] But doubts continued to plague him.

Wilson shared his perplexity. "I fear we have not the legal authority to do what we apparently ought to do," he replied the next day. But the United States, whatever the consequences in terms of domestic and international objections, could not ignore its duty. "I suppose there is nothing for it but to take the bull by the horns and restore order," Wilson suggested. He concluded that more troops should be sent to Port-au-Prince "to absolutely control the city." The Haitian congress should be informed that the United States would not accept the election of men in whom it had no faith. Finally, the U.S. should make clear by its actions that it intended to establish constitutional government in Haiti along the model of its own institutions.[76]

Lansing finally realized the absurdity of fretting over legal justifications when Haiti seemed desperately in need of American help. By August 7, he had developed two motives for continuing the intervention. First, "it was in the interest of humanity." Second, if the United States did not take action, some other nation would. Consequently, he agreed that Caperton should be directed to take over the customshouses throughout the small nation. It also appeared to him that, barring some drastic change, "we will be able to arrange matters very much as we please." For the Wilson administration, power became its own authority for action in Haiti, its own justification for occupying the country.[77]

Thus, Caperton took up the task of bringing Haiti under American domination. The admiral dispatched ships to the various ports to take over the customshouses. Marines went into the interior of the country to bring the *cacos* to order. In addition, Caperton, with the able assistance of Captain Edward L. Beach, his executive officer, arranged for the election of the American choice for president, Sudre Dartiguenave, who had given assurances that he would be amenable to the wishes of the United States.

Immediately following Dartiguenave's election on August 12, Caperton, Beach, and American chargé Davis entered into negotiations for a treaty. These resulted in the September 16 signing of a treaty which gave the United States de facto control over all aspects of Haiti's affairs. Although the country retained the fiction of an independent government, it was nothing but an American puppet regime. The treaty gave the United States complete financial control over the country, provided for the disarming of the Haitian army, and allowed the establishment of a native constabulary under officers of the U.S. Marine Corps. Throughout the remainder of the twenty-year occupation, American military officers ruled the country through the Haitian president and legislature.[78] Haiti lost its independence and became, in reality if not in legal terms, a de facto protectorate of the United States.

As Caperton, Beach, and Davis negotiated with the Haitians over the election of a president and the treaty with the United States, naval forces proceeded with the military occupation of the country. They encountered armed opposition from the *cacos,* who were no match for the better-trained and armed marines. Indeed, the marines worked so efficiently that on November 19, Daniels, concerned with the "heavy losses to the Haitians," ordered Caperton to suspend offensive operations in the interior. The admiral, perplexed by the order, protested that the loss of life could not be avoided if the U.S. intended to effect its control over the country. But the Wilson administration wanted to save the Haitians, not kill them. Daniels held firm and the marines turned their attention to the establishment of a gendarmerie to train the populace to maintain order themselves.[79]

The Americans perceived themselves as the saviors of Haiti, not its tyrants. They wanted to civilize the country, not exploit it. A proclamation issued by Caperton for the take-over of Cape Haitien on August 9 revealed the American democratic ideology that motivated these men:

> I am directed by the United States of America Government to assure the Haytian people that the United States of America has no object in view except to insure, establish and help maintain Haytian independence and the establishment of a stable and firm government by the Haytian people.
>
> Every assistance will be given to the Haytian people in their attempt to secure these ends. It is the intention to retain United States of America forces in Hayti only so long as will be necessary for this purpose.

Major General John H. Russell, who became the head of the occupation forces toward the end of the Wilson period, called the take-over of Haiti "one of the outstanding acts of international humanitarianism in world history."[80] Few Americans, military or civilian, disagreed with this view of their actions.

Other examples of this ethnocentric humanitarianism abound. Captain Beach, for instance, wrote that he and Caperton wanted only "to benefit Haiti, to secure good government and prosperity for Haiti." He added that the United States "asked absolutely nothing for herself. Her only gain was the satisfaction of doing a good act for an unfortunate people near her shores." Major Smedley Butler, the ruthless head of the Haitian gendarmerie, declared that his objective was "to make of Haiti a first-class black man's country. . . . What we wanted was clean little towns, with tidy thatch-roofed dwellings." Marines and naval officers, State and Navy Department officials, and Wilson himself saw in the occupation an opportunity to turn Haiti around, to push it into the twentieth century, away from its barbaric past. Russell called it a "laboratory government," but it was much more than that. It was the physical and political manifestation of American democratic ideology, a consequence of the desire to perform good works in a world sorely in need of goodness.[81]

THE OCCUPATION OF THE DOMINICAN REPUBLIC, 1916

Force provided the Wilson administration with a convenient method of imposing its goodwill on Haiti. Meanwhile, the people of Santo Domingo continued to frustrate the administration's peaceful efforts to guide them to modern civilization. The political situation in that country, despite the faith of the administration that it had solved the Dominican problem, passed from unresolved crisis to unresolved crisis. No riots or bloody butcherings offered the United States an opportunity to settle the matter through intervention. Wilson and his advisers struggled to control events through advice and threats; neither approach proved effective. They hesitated to intervene, however, because they lacked sufficient justification to excuse such action. Instead, these officials relied on the Convention of 1907 and interpreted it as allowing them to support the constitutional government they had helped elect in October 1914. In addition, Wilson and the State Department attempted to broaden the terms of the convention by insisting that it gave them the right to interfere in the financial and political affairs of that unhappy country.

Throughout 1915 the Dominicans refused to cooperate in their own salvation. They blocked the unselfish attempts of the Wilson administration to help. Because Wilson's motives were humanitarian, the failure of the Dominican people to follow his advice infuriated American officials. With a bulldog's tenacity, the president and his subordinates grappled with the obstinate nationalism of the Dominicans. The contest of wills centered on two convergent issues. First, Wilson insisted on the prohibition of further revolutions. Second, his administration tried to increase its control over the republic's finances. In neither effort was Wilson able to achieve a satisfactory resolution through peaceful means.

Early in January, a revolt began in Puerto Plata, the hotbed of Dominican chaos, in opposition to President Jiménez's political appointments. Desiderio Arias threatened to resign as secretary of war to protest the increasing American influence. Bryan, after advising Wilson of the situation, recommended that they inform Jiménez that "this Government would furnish whatever force was necessary to help the President maintain order." On January 12, the secretary explained American policy to Sullivan. He wrote the minister that: "You may say to President Jiménez that this Government will support him to the fullest extent in the suppression of any insurrections against his Government. The election having been held and a Government chosen by the people having been established no more revolutions will be permitted. . . . The people of Santo Domingo will be given an opportunity to develop the resources of their country in peace. . . . A naval force will be sent whenever necessary." The Navy Department, at Lansing's request, dispatched the USS *Castine,* under the command of Commander K. M. Bennett, to Puerto Plata.[82]

The resolve to stop further revolutions became the foundation for American policy. Sullivan believed that if the United States allowed the Puerto Plata revolt to continue, "it would encourage the belief that the old revolutionary methods could be again employed with impunity." Bryan expressed his wholehearted agreement. "This Government," he told the minister, "will not permit any interference whatever with the Jiménez Government." Reforms were to be effected by constitutional means only. "This Government will furnish whatever force may be necessary to suppress insurrection and preserve orderly government," Bryan added, and "any attempts there to use force against the Government will be dealt with immediately and firmly." The presence of the *Castine* helped Jiménez put down the Puerto Plata revolt and his victory encouraged the United States in its policy.[83]

Unfortunately, revolutions did not end. Disturbances continued to plague the Jiménez regime, further sapping the strength of an already weak government. The Wilson administration proved unrelenting in its determination to uphold constitutional government. Bryan repeatedly insisted that the United States "meant what it said when it declared that it would tolerate no more insurrections in Santo Domingo and it will furnish whatever force may be necessary to put down insurrections." Lansing, when he assumed the office of secretary of state, did not change the American attitude toward revolutions. As General McIntyre explained to Clarence Baxter, Vick's replacement as general receiver, this policy resulted in a new relationship with the Dominican government. "We are in a position somewhat different from our position in the past; that is, we are going to do more for this government than we have ever promised any Dominican government."[84] The United States was drawn even deeper into the morass of Dominican instability.

At the same time, the Wilson administration insisted on greater control over Dominican finances. Ironically, this demand further weakened Jiménez because it offered his opposition a rallying point around which to gather in revolt. Although the Bordas government had accepted the appointment of an American financial adviser, the agreement was never approved by the Dominican congress. Jiménez was not bound by it. Thus, even as Bryan and his successor promised Jiménez military support, they badgered him to accept the financial adviser. Jiménez, who realized that his people would never accept such an arrangement, stalled throughout the spring and summer of 1915. His attitude incensed the State Department. When a commission of Dominicans went to Washington in March to discuss the issue, Bryan hoped that he could convince its members of "the disinterestedness of our nation and its determination to support the Government and put an end to insurrections." He believed that this compelled the United States to take positive action to improve conditions in the country. A financial adviser was a necessary ingredient in this process. Wilson agreed, but neither he nor the officials in the State Department were able to convince the Dominicans to accept the appointment. The stalemate continued throughout the remainder of Jiménez's tenure.[85]

When Sullivan resigned in disgrace on July 8, it opened the way for redefinition of American policy. The minister quit following an investigation of his conduct by Senator James Phelan, who found him unfit for office because of his financial entanglement in the country. Sullivan's illegal financial ties with the Bordas regime severely damaged Wilson's policy of helping the Dominican Republic achieve stability and democratic government. Appointed as one of Bryan's "deserving democrats" (Bryan first used the phrase in reference to Sullivan), Sullivan sought to promote his own affairs rather than the interests of the Wilson administration. He exemplified one of Wilson's most serious defects as president—appointing incompetents to important diplomatic positions on the basis of their party loyalty. Although Bryan was immediately responsible for most of these choices, Wilson followed the secretary of state's recommendations without reflecting on the potential problems. Thus, he bore ultimate responsibility for the selection of men of Sullivan's caliber.

The appointment of Sullivan's successor led to the development of a tougher approach. Wilson chose William W. Russell, the minister to Santo Domingo during the Taft administration, to take Sullivan's place. As Wilson explained, he wanted the new minister to "exercise a real guiding influence in affairs" commensurate with his policy. The Division of Latin American Affairs urged taking a "strong line" with the Dominicans, so the department began formulating Russell's instructions to reflect this attitude. Lansing, in preparation, asked the Navy Department to station a war vessel, "with a force of marines" aboard, in the vicinity of the Republic. Even the chargé d'affaires, Stewart Johnson, who originally opposed the violation of "the sovereignty of an independent people," came to believe in the efficacy of intervention. According to Johnson, the occupation of Haiti had a most beneficial and sobering effect on the Dominicans. On September 5 he advised that preparations be made for a "comprehensive occupation here at the moment the Department considers that conditions impose upon us the duty to act under our pledge that revolutions must cease."[86] The Wilson administration determined to solve the problem of Dominican recalcitrance.

By September 17 Russell's instructions were ready. Written by Boaz Long, they consisted of a detailed review of events in the country since 1907, with an emphasis on the ever-increasing public debt, which by the fall of 1915 was seven million dollars above the 1907 ceiling. Long summarized the debt issue by writing: "It is, therefore, evident that since 1910 there has been a continuous violation of the provisions of the Convention of 1907," particularly Article III, which specified that Santo Domingo could not increase the size of the debt until it repaid what it owed in 1907. Long, speaking for the State Department, stated that the "wisest course" was to amend the convention to give the United States more influence. He outlined five amendments. The new provisions included the appointment of a financial adviser; the establishment of a native constabulary officered by Americans; an agreement on a protocol for settling financial claims; an arrangement for a survey of the Republic to allow for more efficient tax collection; and a provision to allow the United States "the right to intervene in the Dominican Republic for the maintenance of a Government adequate to protect life, property and individual liberty." If Russell could not persuade the Jiménez administration to accept these amendments, the new minister was ordered to inform the Dominican government:

> that the United States interprets the Convention of 1907 to give it the right—
> A. To compel the observation of Article III of the convention in the appointment of a Financial Adviser.
> B. To provide for the free course of the customs organization, on a much larger scale, of what is now known as the Dominican Customs Guard, or by the creation of a constabulary.

Wilson approved the instructions on September 22.[87] The stage was set for Russell to impose the American will on Santo Domingo, either by agreement or by a broad, albeit unsubstantiated, reinterpretation of the convention.

The administration, however, misjudged the feelings of the Dominican people. A wave of opposition greeted the publication of Russell's instructions. Jiménez refused to accept the five amendments, primarily because his cabinet and his people objected adamantly. Indeed, the widespread opposition to the demands was the last straw for the crumbling Jiménez government.[88]

Once again, diplomatic power failed the Wilson administration. The president and his advisers retreated from their generous interpretation of the convention because of the bitter opposition evidenced in the Republic. Yet, the administration's success in Haiti made its failure in Santo Domingo all the more difficult to swallow. For the first time, the Black Republic became the model for Wilson's Dominican policies. Lansing explained on November 24 that the amendments were absolutely essential for bringing the convention "in line with the treaty with Haiti." That treaty had the effect of establishing a puppet regime controlled by American military forces. The secretary suggested to Wilson that they should wait to see what would happen to the Jiménez government. "If President Jiménez should resign, or a revolution break out for any cause, we should be justified in landing forces to prevent bloodshed and to give the Dominican Congress an opportunity to ratify an amended convention, so it might be presented simultaneously with the Haitian treaty for our Senate's consideration." Although the administration continued to support Jiménez, it waited for the death of order in the Republic. At the appropriate moment, American forces would rush in to save the Dominicans.[89]

They waited longer than anyone expected. Russell predicted trouble on January 19, 1916, but nothing serious developed. J. W. Wright of the Division of Latin American Affairs pointed out to Lansing that "the entire principle that control of the customs in turbulent countries precludes the possibility of revolution is now at stake." Failure in Santo Domingo endangered American relations with all of South America, particularly Haiti. Lansing reaffirmed U.S. support of Jiménez, but he refused to approve any more loans to the beleaguered government.[90]

The door to intervention opened slightly on February 18 when Russell reported that the lower house of the Dominican congress was entertaining a motion to impeach Jiménez for "malfeasance in office." Also on that day, the minister advised the State Department of the outbreak of a revolt led by the "Bandit [Fidel] Ferrer." Lansing, hoping that the time for forceful interference was near, arranged for the *Castine* to go to Santo Domingo City. The "Commanding Officer has received appropriate instructions," he cabled Russell. Yet, Jiménez miraculously settled the Ferrer uprising. Afterwards, he retired to his country estate. When the *Castine* arrived at the capital, Russell informed the department that the political situation was calm.[91]

Arias proved himself the wild card. On April 15 Arias was angered by the arrest of his allies, Mauricio Jimenes, the commandant of the fortress, and Cesário Jimenes, the chief of the national guard. He began a revolt against Jiménez. For the next two weeks, Russell worked to extinguish the new revolution. At the end of the month, Lansing asked Daniels to send more naval reinforcements. The "disturbed conditions" in Santo Domingo and the "intention of this Government to maintain, by all proper means, the constituted authority," he explained, required that the United States furnish "such cooperation as may appear expedient." On April 30 Commander W. S. Crosley of the USS *Prairie* received orders directing him to Santo Domingo. For a moment, it looked as though Russell had arranged a truce, but even he knew it was temporary.[92]

By May 1 Arias controlled the capital. His supporters in the congress continued the impeachment proceedings against Jiménez. Crosley, who arrived on May 2, immediately went into conference with Bennett of the *Castine,* Russell, Jiménez, who had brought a force of loyal Dominican troops to Santo Domingo City, and the Dominican cabinet. The situation convinced Crosley that "it would be necessary to land a force" to protect the American legation, but Russell and the Dominicans objected. Crosley then began negotiations with the Arias faction. It soon became apparent that no settlement could be reached. On May 5, with the advice of the American minister, and after informing Daniels, Crosley landed three hundred marines and bluejackets. They proceeded to the American legation, but made no attempt to take control of the city.[93]

Admiral Caperton, still in Haiti, confided to Admiral William S. Benson, the chief of naval operations, that he felt "very much perturbed and exercised" over Dominican events. At the same time, Benson cabled the admiral suggesting that he contact Crosley about sending additional forces. He granted permission for Caperton to "take whatever action you deem advisable." Caperton interpreted these instructions as permission to proceed to Santo Domingo City. On May 6 he embarked aboard the *Dolphin* (of Veracruz fame). He also instructed the commanders of the *Wyoming* and the *Culgoa* to proceed to the Dominican capital. Each ship carried a full complement of marines.[94]

As Caperton assembled his fleet, Crosley reported that he considered the situation serious. He thought that it might be necessary to bombard Santo Domingo City, but he decided to issue a warning first. During a conference with Russell and Crosley early on May 6, Jiménez asked for assistance in taking the city. "In accordance with the request of the American Minister and President," Crosley radioed Caperton, "will bombard and capture capital." He urged that reinforcements be sent immediately. Russell informed the State Department that Jiménez was out of ammunition "and can not win." The president, he wrote, "has requested us to take the city." Russell, however, had bigger plans. "If we do this," he advised the department, "it should be for ultimate occupation and not for Jiménez." The minister feared that the Dominican congress, which had impeached Jiménez, would claim that he had no authority to arrange for the American landing. Complete occupation of the country would solve the problems in the Republic as well as avoid any legal questions over Jiménez's status.[95]

The United States welcomed Jiménez's request. From the fall of 1915 on, American officials sought a legitimate reason for the take-over of the country. Jiménez, weak and desperate, under pressure from Crosley and Russell, provided the necessary excuse. The way seemed clear for the U.S. to step in to bring order to the Dominicans.

But, in a last minute display of personal courage, Jiménez, troubled by the prospect of spilling the blood of his people, withdrew his request on the afternoon of May 6. The old man, no longer sure of himself, his friends, or his country, then resigned the presidency. This last act of a desperate, demoralized man effectively disrupted the American plans. Caperton cancelled the orders to his makeshift fleet. Crosley held up the bombardment and occupation of the capital. "This is not the end but the beginning of trouble," Russell predicted.[96]

Washington officials took a different view. They decided to ignore Jiménez even as they upheld his presidency. "While naturally desirous that bloodshed be avoided," Lansing, who was aware of Jiménez's resignation, instructed Russell on May 7, "Department believes that manifestly irregular manner of impeachment renders it particularly desirable that President be upheld in every possible and proper means." Admiral Benson ordered Caperton to proceed as planned. His previous instructions to take whatever action seemed necessary remained in effect.[97]

Caperton decided on intervention. He landed troops in Santo Domingo City on May 15. The United States justified the intervention on the grounds that Jiménez requested it. American officials purposefully ignored Jiménez's later change of mind. According to Russell, for example, writing three years later, "a force of Marines, at the request of President Jiménez, had landed on May 15, 1916 to preserve law and order . . . and to protect the lawfully constituted government against the unwarranted and senseless rebellion of General Arias and his political plotters." Caperton considered himself acting in support of constitutional government, despite the fact that Jiménez had resigned.[98]

During the summer of 1916, Caperton extended the occupation across the entire country. He also sought to arrange for the election of a president amenable to American control, but he could find none among the Dominicans. The Dominican congress proceeded to elect its own choice for president. After protracted efforts, the congress settled on Federico Henríquez y Carvajal. The United States disapproved of the choice and Wilson refused to recognize his government. This meant that Henríquez received none of the customs receipts due the Dominicans, which rendered his regime impotent.

It was an awkward situation. Americans ruled by force of arms, without any legal arrangement for their actions. Henríquez ruled in name only, with neither the power nor the finances to make his government any more than a committee of frustrated Dominicans. The situation simply could not continue without some formalization. The United States needed legitimate as well as real authority.[99]

Consequently, in the fall of 1916, Washington officials determined to straighten out the confusion. After a series of conferences between State and Navy Department representatives, they decided to declare martial law in Santo Domingo. Although this would establish an American-run government, it would rule in the name of the Dominican people. It was not seen as a disruption of Dominican sovereignty because the United States made no claim to possessing the country. It merely administered affairs there until such time as the Dominican people could rule themselves.[100]

"It is with the deepest reluctance that I approve and authorize the course here proposed," Wilson wrote Lansing on November 26 when he consented to the establishment of a military government, "but I am convinced that it is the least of the evils in sight in this very perplexing situation." Lansing passed the word to Daniels. "The Department has come to the conclusion that the only possible solution of this serious problem will be the Proclamation of Military Occupation and the establishment of Martial Law in the Republic," he wrote. Two days later, on November 29, 1916, Captain H. S. Knapp issued a proclamation to the Dominican people declaring himself, in the name of the United States, the military governor of the country. He immediately established a government with marines and naval officers in charge of all departments.[101]

The United States based its authority for taking this action on the failure of the Dominican Republic to live up to the terms of the Convention of 1907, particularly Article III. "This Military Occupation is undertaken with no immediate or ulterior object of destroying the sovereignty of the Republic of Santo Domingo," Knapp's proclamation assured the people, "but, on the contrary is designed to give aid to that country in returning to a condition of internal order that will enable it to observe the terms of the Treaty . . . and the obligations resting upon it as one of the family of nations."[102] The Dominicans, dispirited and overpowered by the eighteen hundred marines under Knapp's command, bowed before the power of America's democratic ideology.

Article III of the convention with Santo Domingo provided the pretext for the intervention, giving the cloak of legality to an action largely determined by Wilson's desire to end the political turmoil in the country. Having found Dominican leaders unresponsive and intransigent, it was much simpler to take over the entire country. A period of instruction could then begin during which the United States would teach the Dominicans proper methods of democratic government in the same way as neighboring Haiti was being taught. The country's finances could be put in order, its people could be inculcated to respect the law, and the turmoil that had racked the nation could be brought to an end. Wilson's motives were humanitarian, his methods shrouded in legality, but his aims were ethnocentric. He ignored the Dominican Republic's traditions and historical experiences in his efforts to make it over into a small United States.

AMERICAN DEMOCRATIC IDEOLOGY DURING WORLD WAR I AND THE RUSSIAN INTERVENTIONS

In subsequent interventions, Wilson also tried to export the American form of government. World War I, for example, represented a war to save the world for democracy. By turning the hostilities into a democratic crusade, Wilson underscored the tenacity with which he held to the belief that the United States offered the best form of government for the salvation of the modern world. By defining the war as the ultimate battle between democratic goodness and autocratic evil, Wilson passed over the selfish goals of his allies. The defeat of Germany symbolized the triumph of an enraged democracy.

During the Siberian intervention in 1918–19, Wilson searched again for a democratic Russian to lead his country along the path to salvation. Unfortunately, no candidate appeared on the scene. The United States flirted with the White Army and its leader Admiral Alexander Kolchak, but Wilson was never convinced that Kolchak truly believed in democracy. Consequently, he insisted that the admiral give several promises and assurances, such as land reform and the election of a constituent assembly, even as the White Army was being defeated by the Bolsheviks.

The strength of Wilson's democratic ideology surfaced again at Paris in 1919. In the first place, he convinced himself that the national leaders meeting with him represented the great mass of humanity and not selfish interests. When it became quite apparent that this was not the case, Wilson came to believe that he could speak over the heads of his colleagues to their peoples, whom he never doubted would accept his programs, his ideals, and his humanitarian impulse to help them create a new world order. Finally, the League of Nations codified the ethnocentrism of the United States by requiring that its membership be composed only of democracies. Autocracies such as Germany would not be allowed because, in the forum of international relations, Wilson's new system depended on the freedom and responsiveness of individual citizens.

Thus, Wilson's ethnocentric humanitarianism played an important role in each of his interventions, from the landing of American forces at Veracruz to the dispatch of troops to Siberia. Other concerns, such as the defense of international law, the promotion of international cooperation, and the establishment of collective security, also played important parts.

4.
THE POWER of the LAW:

The Period of Neutrality

Domestic law, in the view of the Progressives, ensured the permanence of civilized institutions. As a step beyond man's primitive state, the law institutionalized God's will. It also offered the Progressives a convenient method for reforming American society without destroying its foundations. The reforms of this period shared the assumption that the excesses of industrialization and the immoral aspects of modernization could be eradicated through governmental power. Wilson, for example, envisioned the law as a system binding men together according to moral precepts. The New Freedom, Wilson's domestic platform, numbered among its major provisions the rationalization of business practices and the establishment of a modern, more equitable currency and banking system. The Clayton Anti-Trust Act, the Federal Reserve Board, and the Federal Trade Commission were the centerpieces of the New Freedom's legislative program. These and other measures underlined the Wilsonian and Progressive faith in the law as the cure for the problems of an advanced society. For almost every abuse the Progressives recognized, they proposed a law as the antidote.

International law, as the Progressives understood it, applied morality to the society of nations. Throughout this period, conferences were held and organizations such as the League to Enforce Peace were formed in order to explore new ways to promote peace. Americans, thrust upon the world stage by the Spanish-American War, began discussing a variety of methods to reform and moralize international relations. Most of these reformers turned to the law as the vehicle for the institutionalization of the changes they advocated. Thus, the growth of American internationalism went hand in hand with a rejuvenated advocacy of international law. Visionaries and pragmatists alike expressed their faith in the importance of morality by urging respect for the law as the best way to guarantee peace among nations.[1]

Wilson shared these beliefs. He taught in classroom lectures at Princeton during the 1890s that international law drew its strength from "a common consciousness and acknowledgement of certain laws of human nature," and that it rested "wholly upon opinion—as morals do." Not "sanction, but opinion, acquiescence, habit" provided it with substance. As Wilson interpreted this system, the law originated as rules for war, with peace its ultimate goal. *"Its* object was to substitute for *barbarity,* humanity," he noted for a lecture in 1892, "to substitute *ordered relationships and recognized obligations* for the license, disorder and invasions of right which provoked war—in short, *to create a moral sense and a community among States."*[2] Thus, international law typified the stability of a civilized community of nations.

This understanding of the law implied cooperation among sovereign states. As Wilson's views matured during his presidency, this belief grew increasingly explicit. Eventually, he saw in cooperation the salvation of the law. In effect, Wilson reversed his earlier views. The law did not guarantee cooperation; rather, cooperation ensured the supremacy of the law. In his vision of a better world, nations worked together to sustain morality. The Covenant of the League of Nations formalized international cooperation by defining a method for nations to work together. The league took its authority from a constitution, but its power derived from the unity of its members. Without the latter, the former went for naught.

This chapter examines Wilson's responses to World War I during the period of American neutrality. The eventual decision to resort to force against Germany resulted from the failure of Wilson's policy to uphold neutral rights and his unsuccessful attempts to mediate an end to the hostilities. During the first year and a half of the war, from August 1914 until the winter of 1916, Wilson demanded not only neutrality from the American people, but complete impartiality in dealing with the belligerents. He purposefully made no attempt to assign responsibility for the war, nor did he allow himself to sympathize with one side over the other. In following this policy, Wilson hoped to keep the United States out of the war at the same time that he made it possible for the United States to participate as a disinterested arbitrator in the eventual peacemaking. Germany's continued violent infringements on American neutral rights, however, made the policy of impartiality impossible to maintain.

Wilson's insistence on neutral rights exemplified the importance of international law, and the several efforts to effect peace witnessed the dawning belief in the importance of international cooperation. From August 1914 to April 1917 international law received the major emphasis in Wilson's foreign policies, with the bid for mediation running a close second. But from April 1917 to the fall of 1919 this framework was reversed. During that period, the dream of international cooperation provided the prime motivation for the Wilson administration; respect for the law was viewed as an important tactic in achieving that goal.

Wilson understood the limitations of international law. He asked no more of it than what it was. As he explained in October 1914:

> We stand now in a peculiar case. Our first thought, I suppose, as lawyers is of international law, of those bonds of right and principle which draw the nations together and hold the community of the world to some standards of action. We know that we see in international law, as it were, the moral processes by which law itself came into existence. I know that as a lawyer I have myself at times felt that there was no real comparison between the law of a nation and the law of nations, because the latter lacked the sanction that gave the former strength and validity. And yet, if you look into the matter more closely, you will find that the two have the same foundations, and that these foundations are more evident and conspicuous in our day than they have ever been before.
>
> The opinion of the world is the mistress of the world; and the processes of international law are the slow processes by which opinion works its will.[3]

Throughout each of the instances of force in which Wilson engaged, he defined his actions according to the precepts of international law. He paid tribute to these "standards of action" because he perceived himself as a moral man and his country as a righteous nation.

INTERNATIONAL LAW DURING THE INTERVENTIONS IN MEXICO, HAITI, AND SANTO DOMINGO

The United States justified the occupation of Veracruz, for example, by calling it a legitimate act of reprisal, a means of "enforcing redress for a specific indignity." The Wilson administration's actions were directed specifically at Huerta and his subordinates for the insults and indignities they perpetrated against the United States. The occupation was not meant as an act of war against the Mexican people. State Department Counsellor Robert Lansing pointed out on April 14, 1914, a week before the landing, that the president was well within his authority in "the enforcing of claims or demands by the display or use of force, or the making of reprisals." Although reprisals had the "characteristics of war in that they are appeals to force rather than to reason," they were "not deemed by Governments to be actual warfare." Lansing offered several examples, including the shelling of Greytown, Nicaragua, in 1853 by the U.S. Navy. Wilson cited the Greytown incident as a precedent in a press conference on April 20, suggesting that the causes of that incident were very similar to the problems he was having with Huerta. On the same day, he took the matter before Congress to discuss using the "armed forces of the United States in such a way and to such an extent as may be necessary to obtain from General Huerta and his adherents the fullest recognition of the rights and dignity of the United States." Although he did not use the word reprisal, it was clearly his term of reference.[4]

Two years later, during the punitive expedition, American officials defended the action on the basis that the expedition constituted a "hot pursuit" of Villa's band of outlaws. General M. M. Macomb explained this legal rationale to the new secretary of war, Newton Baker, by quoting from Francis Wheaton's *A Digest of the International Law of the United States*. According to Wheaton, "when there is no other way of warding off a perilous attack upon a country the sovereignty of such country can intervene by force in the territory from which the attack is threatened to prevent such attack." Wilson maintained from the beginning that the expedition "can and will be done in entirely friendly aid of the constituted authorities in Mexico and with scrupulous respect for the sovereignty of that Republic." Shortly after the Columbus raid, the administration negotiated with the Carranza government for permission to engage in "hot pursuit." Although Carranza claimed that the discussions, which never resulted in a signed agreement, were not retroactive to the Villa attack, State Department officials maintained in good faith that they were.[5] Mexico's failure to protect its side of the border gave the United States the legal right to take action in its own defense.

The occupation of Haiti lacked legal authority, which concerned both Lansing and Wilson. Although the initial landing was justified by the breakdown of civil authority in Port-au-Prince, the take-over of the entire country was a different matter. "We have no excuse of reprisal as we had at Vera Cruz to take over the city government and administer the offices," Lansing complained to the president. Wilson agreed, noting that "I fear we have not the legal authority to do what we apparently ought to do."[6] They eventually decided that the demands of humanity required the continued presence of American forces. They acted, if not legally, at least in a way they considered moral. Ultimately, the treaty with Haiti gave a post facto legitimacy to the occupation by a clause in which the Haitian authorities expressed their consent to the action.

During the occupation of Santo Domingo, Wilson interpreted the Convention of 1907 as giving the United States the right to control Dominican affairs if the Dominicans proved unable to maintain their debt payments. In addition, the request for armed assistance from President Jiménez, although withdrawn the next day, allowed administration officials to claim that they acted at the behest of the constituted government. When Captain Knapp established the U.S. military government in November 1916, he carefully pointed out that he did so, not to the detriment of Dominican national sovereignty, but in order to preserve it until the Dominicans could learn, under American tutelage, to control their own affairs.

Wilson shaped his policies during each of his interventions to fit his understanding of the law. International law neither controlled nor caused these instances of force. Instead, it guided American policies in a moral and righteous manner toward Wilson's objectives. When he lacked legal excuses, as he did in Haiti, he sought some moral rationale to justify his policies to himself and before the world. Wilson's idealism, religious convictions, and the conception of the United States as a force for morality in the world allowed no other course. Wilson simply could not willfully violate the law; to have done so would have been to deny all that he believed. Because he used the law as a standard for judging his own actions and the actions of other nations, the law assumed a central role in the conduct of his diplomacy. This was particularly true during the period of neutrality.

DEFINING AMERICAN NEUTRALITY

"It is plain enough how we were forced into the war," Wilson explained two months after Congress, at his request, declared war on Germany. "The extraordinary insults and aggressions of the Imperial German Government left us no self-respecting choice but to take up arms in defense of our rights as a free people and of our honor as a sovereign government," he continued. "The military masters of Germany denied us the right to be neutral."[7] As the leader of the most powerful neutral nation, Wilson found in the law the rules to govern American policies and the criteria for judging the actions of the belligerents. Violations of these standards by the warring nations represented more than a disregard of the law; they threatened American sovereignty and honor by denying it the rights inherent in its standing as an international entity.

In Wilsonian foreign policy, neutrality meant more than the nonbelligerency of the United States. It became the way to show the world how to live in peace, for the example of the United States would be the example of the just and the good, of a people truly neutral in thought and action. In this way, no belligerent could complain of unfair treatment or favoritism toward its enemies. All would seek the U.S. as an outside, disinterested arbitrator. At the conclusion of hostilities, America, unscathed by the destruction, would be in the best position to help with the reconstruction along lines amenable to a lasting peace. In effect, Wilson conjoined legal neutrality with his efforts to mediate the peace.

This attitude was apparent throughout the period of neutrality. Wilson explained to a gathering of the Associated Press on April 20, 1915, that

> My interest in the neutrality of the United States is not the petty desire to keep out of trouble. To judge by my experience, I have never been able to keep out of trouble. I have never looked for it, but I have always found it. I do not walk around trouble. If any man wants a scrap that is interesting and worthwhile, I am his man. I warn him that he is not going to draw me into the scrap for his advertisement, but if he is looking for trouble that is the trouble of men in general, and I can help a little, why then, I am in for it. But I am interested in neutrality because there is something so much greater to do than fight; there is a distinction waiting for this nation that no nation has ever yet got. That is the distinction of absolute self-control and self-mastery.[8]

This statement caused little controversy in April 1915, but it caused a public outcry when Wilson rephrased the idea less than a month later, following the sinking of the *Lusitania* (which aroused the anger of the country). Yet, the public misunderstood him when he said on May 10, 1915, that "there is such a thing as a man being too proud to fight. There is such a thing as a nation being so right that it does not need to convince others by force that it is right." He meant only that America "must be a special example" because it obeyed the law. Through its actions, the United States would show that "peace is the healing and elevating influence of the world and strife is not." The belligerents would then turn to America for help in effecting a just and lasting peace of hope and reconciliation.[9]

International law offered the way to achieve the goal. The role of the United States was "to preserve the foundations upon which peace can be rebuilt." Wilson insisted on the rights of neutrality because his vision of the future depended on respect for the law. As he proclaimed to the Daughters of the American Revolution in October 1915: "Peace can be rebuilt only upon the ancient and accepted principles of international law, only upon those things which remind nations of their duties to each other, and, deeper than that, of their duties to mankind and to humanity." America, the "great spiritual conception" in the world, stood apart from the struggle and awaited its chance to act as referee. The nation's strength lay in the "moral force of great and triumphant convictions," Wilson argued. This force the world could not long resist.[10]

"The neutrality of the United States has not been a merely formal matter," Wilson explained in January 1916. "It has been a matter of conviction and of the heart." On these convictions lay the basis for peace, for he could find "no other foundations for peace than is laid in justice without aggression."[11] America would fight for only one reason—to defend its self-respect, by which Wilson meant observance by the belligerents of the nation's neutral rights under the law. Otherwise, the warring powers might hesitate to accept the United States as a possible mediator.

"There is no immediate prospect that America's material interests may be seriously affected," Wilson asserted in January 1916, "but there is constant danger, every day of the week, that her spiritual interests may suffer serious affront." America stood ready, when necessary, "to show that the old conceptions of liberty are ready to translate themselves in her hands into conceptions and manifestations of power."[12] The necessity arose in April 1917 when, because of Germany's violations of America's neutral rights, Wilson saw that the road to peace lay through the valley of war. He took that path hesitantly and with regret, but also with the hope that vindication of the law would ensure the peace.

Throughout the period of neutrality, the State Department, particularly Robert Lansing, advised Wilson on the strategy of upholding neutral rights. Colonel House took charge of the second strategy of exploring avenues for mediation. Both reported directly to the president, who carefully directed each policy toward the single objective of peace. This triangular arrangement, with Lansing and House at opposite ends of the base and Wilson at the apex, distinguished the policies in terms of who implemented them, but control of both lay in Wilson's hands.

Both policies went into effect at the beginning of hostilities. On August 4, Wilson appealed to the belligerents to allow him "to act in the interest of European peace." He based this plea on Article III of the

1899 Hague Convention, which called for the settlement of international disputes by third party mediation. "All I wanted to do was to let them know that I was at their service," the president informed House. The administration also moved quickly to define the nation's neutrality. On August 9 Lansing proposed cautioning the American people against public utterances that might "cause hostile feeling by one or more of the belligerents toward the United States and *form* a pretext for involving this Government in the present war." Wilson acted on this advice ten days later by asking the country to remain "impartial in thought as well as in action." Privately, he ordered officers of the military to "refrain from public comment of any kind upon the military or political situation on the other side of the water."[13] This stance would not only help keep the country out of war, it would also prove that the United States could easily adopt the role of objective mediator.

In keeping with this, the Wilson administration accepted the duties and obligations required by the law to preserve its status as a neutral. "Mr. Warren and I agree," James Brown Scott wrote Lansing of their colleague in the Office of the Counsellor, "that international law is part of the law of the United States; that international law imposes duties upon the United States as a neutral which the United States must perform." This approach allowed the administration to exemplify the rule of law and morality. "I do hope by my peace policies to establish such standards in the action of this country that will enable the United States to serve as an unimpeachably just example of the way in which the relations between different countries should be regarded and handled," Wilson declared.[14]

Wilson's original approach to neutrality went well beyond the letter of the law. At Bryan's suggestion, Wilson banned loans to belligerents on the grounds that, as Bryan suggested, "money is the worst of all contrabands because it commands everything else." The ban on loans turned out to be an unneutral act, however, since it worked most harshly against Great Britain, rather than equally against Germany. It also turned out to be unworkable, since the American economy grew increasingly dependent on commerce with the belligerents and the belligerents, particularly Britain and France, grew increasingly short of cash. In the spring of 1915, the House of Morgan requested permission from the State Department to extend a fifty million dollar credit to France. The Wilson administration approved the request, though few bothered to question the difference between banned loans and approved credits.[15]

In November 1914, again at Bryan's instigation, Wilson decided not to sell to the belligerents submarine parts, which could be assembled by the purchaser to make a complete submarine, despite Lansing's opinion that it was within the law. Bryan feared that the American public would not understand the difference between selling a whole submarine and marketing its component parts. Wilson agreed, noting that such a policy was within the "spirit" of the law, even if not actually required.[16]

"We have acted in strict accordance with international law, so far as we know," the president explained to Hugo Munsterberg, a German sympathizer. The rules of war allowed little discretion in determining the American response. "The law standing as it does," Wilson informed one correspondent, "the most I can do is to exercise influence." Although such issues as loans to belligerents and the sale of submarine parts required a political decision from him, in most instances Wilson acted on the supposition that "the precedents of international law are so clear . . . and my lack of power is so evident, that I have felt that I could do nothing else than leave the matter to settle itself."[17] But the president soon discovered that the obligations of neutrality were far more complicated than merely following the rules established by precedent and convention.

Great Britain first ran afoul of the insistence on strict neutrality and respect for neutral rights. The dispute centered on the composition of the contraband list and Britain's establishment of a blockade around German controlled ports. The Wilson administration urged acceptance of the unratified Declaration of London, which offered a fairly liberal categorization of what constituted the list of prohibited items. Foreign Secretary Earl Grey, not surprisingly, wanted to add as many items as possible to the list in order to prevent the German side from receiving American goods. As they had during the Napoleonic Wars a century earlier, the British established Orders in Council and blockades to seal the continent from trade with the United States and other neutrals. The State Department objected strenuously, its complaints spelled out in lengthy legal treatises. "God deliver us or can you from library lawyers," the Anglophilic ambassador to England, Walter Hines Page, cried to House at one point. "They often lose chestnuts while they argue about burns." The British ambassador to the United States, Cecil Spring-Rice, warned Wilson that "the misery caused by the war is not confined only to the belligerents. Neutrals too have their share."[18] But both ambassadors misunderstood Wilson's policy of neutrality.

Wilson insisted on "immediate and vigorous protest" against British violations because neutrality required it. "England should be held to the letter and spirit of the law if we are to maintain our attitude of strict neutrality," House advised the president, who determined to do just that. "I mean that if we are to remain neutral and to afford Europe the legitimate assistance possible in such circumstances," Wilson explained to Page, "the course we have been pursuing is the absolutely necessary course." The United States had no choice but to insist on "the full performance of our utmost duty as the only powerful neutral." This policy would satisfy opinion at home and abroad.[19]

Although the British did not escape the American insistence on respect for neutral rights, Wilson's dealings with Great Britain differed in two significant respects from his problems with Germany. First, British violations did not result in the deaths of Americans, but Germany's actions did, particularly its reliance on the submarine. Disputes with Great Britain could be resolved at war's end because they involved only money and property. "My own idea is that we cannot afford to make merchandise a cause for the use of force," Bryan told Wilson. "If we have any disputes about merchandise which cannot be settled during the war, they can be settled afterwards."[20] Wilson shared this opinion, one of the few issues about which he and his first secretary of state agreed in regard to the war.

"I have been through all the intricacies of our controversy regarding neutrality with the several belligerent powers, and it seems to me that the blockade and the submarine matter stand on different grounds," the president explained in April 1916. Upon accepting the Democratic nomination for reelection the following September, Wilson reflected on his policies toward the warring powers:

> The rights of our own citizens of course became involved; that was inevitable. Where they did, this was our guiding principle: that property rights can be vindicated by claims for damages when the war is over, and no modern nation can decline to arbitrate such claims; but the fundamental rights of humanity can not be. The loss of life is irreparable. Neither can direct violations of a nation's sovereignty await vindication in suits for damages. The nation that violates these essential rights must expect to be checked and called to account by direct challenge and resistance. It at once makes the quarrel in part our own.

German violations were different from British incursions because the Germans attacked the "rights, commerce, and the citizens of the United States." Wilson later claimed that "the list is long and overwhelming. No nation that respected itself or the rights of humanity could have borne those wrongs any longer."[21] Thus, the United States eventually went to war to vindicate its rights as a neutral.

Second, the British played the American game much better than Germany did. They shared a common tradition and sympathy with the

United States, and Grey and his colleagues depended on this to avoid arousing American anger to too high a pitch. The Foreign Office engaged in lengthy debates over the law, which helped tempers to cool. It also made correspondence with Great Britain "less dramatic" than the controversies with the Imperial Government. Disputes with England moved, Wilson wrote, "as slowly as cold molasses, but it would be a mistake to think that we are not exercising as much pressure in the case of our rights in one direction as in the other."[22] As part of their general strategy to court American goodwill, the British were more receptive to considerations of American mediation. Without ever really committing themselves, they encouraged Wilson to believe that, at some indefinite time in the future, he would be allowed to help end the war. This played on the egos of both Wilson and House, but at little cost to the British. It also led American officials to identify with the Entente cause, a perception that the British exploited.

Germany, however, failed miserably to attract the sympathy of the United States. Its reliance on the submarine shocked American sensibilities about humane warfare and symbolized the total disregard for legality and international comity on the part of the Imperial Government. The exposure of an elaborate espionage system and plans for sabotage in the fall of 1915 compounded the outrage. British propaganda effectively portrayed the "Huns" as barbarians, a reputation that Germany was never able to offset adequately. Nor was the Imperial Government as patient when arguing legal technicalities, an attitude revealed at the opening of hostilities when German troops invaded Belgium in flagrant violation of a treaty guaranteeing its neutrality. The claim that the necessities of war excused this and other actions did not wash with the American government and people, who expected every nation to follow the standards that the United States did. Germany's unwillingness to talk peace added further substance to the charges. Thus, the attitude of both sides toward American neutrality played a major role in the decision to form an armed association with the Entente side in April 1917.

Sunken ships littered the route that took the United States and Germany to war. Early in February 1915, the German government announced the establishment of a war zone around the British Isles within which U-boats would attack enemy shipping. The announcement warned the neutral nations of the possible dangers to their ships if they ventured into the proscribed area. This method of warfare immediately put Wilson's neutrality policy at risk because it introduced an element heretofore not covered by the law. Under the rules developed over the centuries, belligerent warships were required to stop and search enemy and neutral merchant ships for contraband and other violations. The warships could condemn the merchant ships either by sinking them or taking them captive, but not before allowing the crew and passengers adequate protection. In this gentleman's method of warfare, surprise attacks were not permitted.

But submarines, because of their small size and vulnerability when surfaced, depended on unannounced attacks. The new German policy provided for the destruction of enemy shipping without warning, a clear departure from international law. Neither Wilson nor Lansing sympathized with the German claim that this weapon required new law. When asked at a press conference about the submarine's challenge to the rules of war, Wilson replied emphatically that the law could not be unilaterally amended. "No nation has the right to change the rules of war," the president said, "I think that it would be more precise to say that the conditions of war have changed radically; the rules of war have not."[23]

The American reply to the German announcement was no less insistent. In a note drafted primarily by Lansing and Wilson, the United States declared that it found the prospect of submarine warfare intolerable. The note warned that Germany would be held to a "strict accountability" for the unlawful destruction of American ships and lives, which implied that, if necessary, the United States would protect its rights upon the high seas. The note did not contemplate what would happen if belligerent ships carrying American passengers were sunk because, at the time, the greater threat seemed directed against the rights of American shipping. Submarines directly challenged Wilson's fundamental policy of following and upholding international law. Over this challenge, the great diplomatic battles of the war were waged. Ultimately, peace itself was the victim.[24]

Trouble began in late March 1915 off the coast of England when, without warning, a German U-boat torpedoed the British steamer *Falaba*. Among the drowned was Leon C. Thrasher, an American whose death raised the issue of the responsibility of the U.S. government to protect its citizens when they traveled on belligerent passenger vessels. At first, Wilson could not decide how firmly to press the issue, for the death of one American hardly warranted even an outside chance of American involvement in the war. Bryan and Lansing immediately raised opposing viewpoints as to the appropriate response. Bryan questioned the right of a citizen to involve his nation in a dispute by risking his life on personal business. "It seems to me that the doctrine of contributory negligence has some bearing on this case," he wrote Wilson on April 2; "that is, the American who takes passage upon a

British vessel knowing that this method of warfare will be employed stands in a different position from that occupied by one who suffers without any fault of his own." Later, the secretary raised the issues of Britain's policies of arming its merchant ships and of flying neutral flags. But his basic objection was Thrasher's own responsibility for being aboard the ship in the first place.[25]

Lansing offered a much harsher view of Germany's responsibility. "If it is decided to denounce the sinking of the FALABA as an act indefensible legally and morally, we will have to say so, and I do not see how we can say it in a pleasant way," he advised Bryan. "We are dealing with a tragedy." The government "must assert our rights, condemn the violation and state the remedy which we expect." As for Bryan's argument that Thrasher contributed to his own death, Lansing felt that taking this position would "amount to an admission of Germany's right to perform lawless acts in that area." In a draft note to the Imperial Government, he wrote that the sinking of the *Falaba* indicated "a wantonness and indifference to the rules of civilized warfare by the German naval officer responsible for the deed, which are without palliation or excuse." The attack was "a flagrant violation of international law and international morality" that required a prompt protest from the United States. The draft note demanded punishment of the German U-boat captain, a disavowal of submarine warfare by the Imperial Government, and reparation for Thrasher's death. If the issue involved only the loss of property, Lansing argued, the administration "might continue to show that patience and forbearance which it has manifested so often during the progress of this deplorable conflict." But the death of an American by "an act of lawlessness and cruelty" required that the Wilson administration not remain silent.[26]

The opposing views of Bryan and Lansing helped clarify the controversy for Wilson. "The Thrasher case is constantly in my mind," he told Bryan on April 6. At one point, Wilson decided to adopt a moral tone in the protest to Germany. He suggested to the secretary of state that they "put the whole note on very high grounds,—not on the loss of this single man's life, but on the interests of mankind which are involved and which Germany has always stood for; on the manifest impropriety of a single nation's essaying to alter the understanding of nations; and as all arising out of her mistake in employing an instrument against her enemy's commerce which it is impossible to employ in accordance with any rules that the world is likely to be willing to accept." Yet, Bryan's continued objections raised doubts in the president's mind. At the end of April, Wilson rejected Bryan's suggestion that the administration use the incident as an excuse for proposing mediation because he feared that such an offer would interfere with the efforts of House, who was then in Europe exploring the attitudes of the belligerents toward the United States as mediator. The president told the secretary, however, that "I am not at all confident that we are on the right track." He hoped that it would not be "necessary to make formal representations in the matter at all."[27] Here the matter stood as events overcame the discussion.

On April 29 a German plane dropped two bombs on the American freighter *Cushing*. Fortunately, no injuries resulted from the attack. Two days later, the German embassy published a warning to the American people in various newspapers across the country advising travelers not to sail into the war zone. Both incidents infuriated Lansing, who considered the attack on the *Cushing* a "more flagrant violation of neutral rights on the high seas" than the Thrasher case, despite the absence of injuries. "German naval policy is one of wanton and indiscriminate destruction of vessels regardless of nationality," he wrote Bryan. As for the German embassy's warning, Lansing considered it a "formal threat" that bypassed proper diplomatic procedures. "Everything seems to point to a determined effort to affront this Government and force it to an open rupture of diplomatic relations," Lansing concluded. Bryan, when he forwarded these comments to the president, suggested bringing the *Cushing* incident to the attention of the German government, but he opposed the idea of protesting the warning.[28]

Before the administration could formulate a response to either event, however, it received word that a German submarine had attacked the American tanker *Gulflight*. Two American sailors drowned as a result of the torpedoing. At a cabinet meeting on May 4, Secretary of War Garrison argued strongly in favor of a harsh protest to the Imperial Government. As trustees of the American people, Garrison said, the administration must defend the national honor, no matter what the risks. "It may be that there is no way to meet a situation like this except by war," Wilson replied. "It is important that we should show how sincere is our belief that there are other ways to settle questions like this." Bryan contributed nothing to the discussion until the end of the meeting, when he approved of Wilson's position.[29]

Thus far, the question of how far to go in defending the rights of the United States as a neutral power remained unanswered. Three days after the cabinet meeting, the issue was put in stark relief. On May 7 a German submarine launched a single torpedo into the bowels of the British passenger liner *Lusitania*. Eleven hundred noncombatants, including 120 Americans, went down with the ship. The resultant controversy compelled the Wilson administration to determine finally its stance toward the use of the submarine against belligerent shipping and the effects on neutral rights. The issue turned on the rules of war, but the eventual decision was made at a high cost. Bryan resigned in protest over the possibility of war and, in making the decision to insist on respect for American neutrality, Wilson sacrificed much of the flexibility in his policies.

Throughout the debate within the administration over the response to the *Lusitania* crisis, Wilson and his advisers turned to the law as their point of reference. They discussed the requirements of visit and search, the difference between unarmed and unresisting ships, and the right of neutral citizens to travel abroad. "These acts on the part of Germany are indefensible violations of the law applicable between the German nation and the United States," Garrison advised the president. House, still in England seeking a way to mediate an end to the war, wrote that "I cannot see any way out unless Germany promises to cease her policy of making war upon non-combatants." Wilson agreed, for he had concluded that the role of the United States as the most powerful neutral required it to defend its rights against both Germany and England, even if the result might be war. "I think we might say to them," Wilson told House in reference to the Germans, "that this Government is not engaged in arranging passenger traffic, but in defining neutral and human rights." He told James W. Gerard, the American ambassador to Germany, to convey to the Imperial Government that the United States intended to "confine itself to the protection of its own clear rights," although it would be willing to help arrange peace discussions between the two sides.[30]

In a series of three notes to the German government, the Wilson administration defined its attitude toward U-boats. Wilson sided with Lansing against the advice of Bryan, and the notes took the high moral tone the president had considered employing in the response to Thrasher's death. The first note, cabled to Gerard on May 13, demanded that the Imperial Government quit its strategy of submarine warfare against "unarmed merchantmen." The objection to the U-boat rested on the rule of visit and search. As Lansing later described this protest, the administration based it on "principles of law and humanity." Neutral citizens were entitled to travel on the high seas aboard merchant vessels of any nationality. International law protected these travelers because it required the belligerents to ensure their safety by placing them on enemy or neutral vessels prior to the destruction of their ship. "To destroy a merchant vessel without safeguarding the lives of the persons on board," Lansing told Bryan, "is inhuman and morally wrong." In the counsellor's view, "the essential issue between the

Governments is one of principle and not of fact." Germany must be held accountable to the law.[31]

Germany argued that British violations of contraband law forced it to attack merchant ships and the vulnerability of the submarine required that the attacks be made without warning. Wilson refused to accept this line of reasoning. He insisted on compliance with the law, for "no matter what England does to Germany or Germany to England our rights are neutral and we cannot abate them in the least. They cannot depend on instances of war which do not . . . recognize international law." Indeed, he believed that "England's violation of neutral rights is different from Germany's violations of the rights of humanity." The two issues were clearly separate, though the United States would defend its rights against both sides.[32]

In the second *Lusitania* note, Wilson appealed to Germany to respect "the rights of humanity, which every Government honors itself in respecting." The third note warned that a continuation of the policy of sinking ships without warning would be regarded by the United States as "deliberately unfriendly."[33] This constituted a refinement of strict accountability by putting the Imperial Government on notice that its diplomatic relations with the United States depended on the proper use of the submarine. Despite the warning, Germany refused to admit liability for the *Lusitania;* negotiations over the settlement of claims continued without resolution.

The secretary of state understood that war might result from the position of the Wilson administration. He raised a number of objections to Wilson's course, but to little avail. Each of the suggestions involved some curtailment of America's neutral rights, but by this time the president was unwilling to sacrifice these rights for the expediency of peace. For example, Bryan urged that passengers be prohibited from ships carrying contraband. Allowing them to travel on these ships seemed like "putting women and children in front of an army," particularly since Bryan believed that "Germany has the right to prevent contraband from going to the Allies." He also pleaded for the United States to proceed slowly in resolving the issue. Strict accountability, he wrote Wilson, meant that they could await the end of the war before resolving the controversy, which would be in line with the "cooling off" treaties that he had negotiated with thirty nations, though Germany was not among the signatories. In addition, the secretary accused the administration of acting in an unneutral way because it protested German actions, but not British violations of the law.

Despite these objections, Wilson could not see Bryan's point of view. In frustration and disappointment, Bryan resigned his commission as secretary of state rather than sign the second *Lusitania* note. To join with Wilson in transmitting that protest would violate, Bryan explained, "what I deem to be an obligation to my country." He preferred to work for peace in the capacity of a private citizen rather than run the risk of war by insisting on respect for neutral rights.[34]

Bryan's opposition merely confused Wilson. "It is the possibility of war from which I shrink," the secretary explained, but this made little sense to the president, who had complained several months earlier to House that "while Mr. Bryan was always using the 'soft' pedal in negotiations with Germany, he had to restrain him when he was dealing with Santo Domingo, Haiti and such small republics."[35] Wilson failed to understand that, when it came to force, Bryan applied a double standard.

The secretary feared war with civilized, which he defined as European, powers, but he considered interventions in less developed lands a duty from which America could not escape. Thus, he participated in the decision to occupy Veracruz because the Mexicans desperately needed American help; force in that case was a sacred obligation, no matter how distasteful. Similarly, his policies toward Haiti and Santo Domingo contemplated a resort to arms because these peoples needed the uplifting presence of U.S. troops. Germany, however, was a developed nation and a full-fledged member of the international community. War with such a power was inconceivable to Bryan and against his pacifist principles because he believed that civilized gentlemen could settle their disputes amicably if given time for reason to prevail over emotions. This philosophy undergirded the cooling off treaties in which he took such pride; for Bryan to admit the necessity or even the potential of war with a developed power would have meant giving up his view of the world. He resigned from Wilson's cabinet, not over the issue of intervention in Mexico, nor even over war with Germany, but over the possibility of hostilities with a developed, civilized power.

Wilson's other advisers reached a different conclusion, for they now saw Germany as the greatest threat to the United States and the American insistence on strict neutrality. "There is no doubt that the position you have taken with both Germany and Great Britain is correct," House wrote the president on May 25, "but I feel that our position with the Allies is somewhat different, for we are bound up more or less on their success, and I do not think we should do anything that can possibly be avoided to alienate the good feeling that they now have for us." Lansing, Bryan's successor, also began to see Germany as a dangerous enemy. "I have come to the conclusion that the German Government is utterly hostile to all nations with democratic institutions because those who compose it see in democracy a menace to absolutism and the defeat of the German ambition for world domination," he wrote on July 11. The new secretary decided that Germany must not be allowed to win the war, even if it meant the participation of the United States on the side of the Entente powers. Lansing used his influence in favor of England and its allies, working just as steadily to ensure that Germany was held to a strict regard for neutral rights.[36]

The submarine continued to plague relations between the United States and Germany. The Imperial Government, anxious to avoid further difficulties, yet unwilling to concede publicly to American demands, secretly issued orders to avoid attacks on neutral shipping and passenger vessels. These instructions represented a victory for the civilians, headed by Chancellor Theobald von Bethmann-Hollweg and Undersecretary of State Arthur Zimmermann, over the military, but their success was sustained only by the weak and easily suaded will of the kaiser. U-boats continued to prey on protected shipping, but no clear-cut violations of the law occurred during the first few months after the *Lusitania* went down.[37]

Then, on August 19, 1915, U-boat 24 mistook the White Star liner *Arabic* for a cargo ship. The torpedo, fired without warning, found its mark, resulting in the deaths of forty-four people, two of whom were American. The sinking shocked Wilson, not only because of the deaths, but also because it flagrantly disregarded the American attitude that he had so meticulously spelled out in the *Lusitania* correspondence. Even before he learned the details of the incident, Wilson steeled himself for a confrontation with Germany. "If American passengers were on board and no opportunity was given for them to escape before the torpedo was fired at the vessel, there would appear to be what we told Germany we should regard as 'a deliberately unfriendly act,' knowing the significance of the words we used," he wrote his fiancée, Edith Boling Galt, on the day of the attack. Wilson could not understand why the Germans refused to heed his warnings. "Certainly the Germans are blood mad," he told her.

This latest sinking struck him as "an act of wanton disregard of international law and of brutal defiance of the opinion and power of the United States." Yet, war must be avoided, he wrote Galt, because "the one thing that is clear or, rather, the two things that are clear are that the people of this country rely upon me to keep them out of war and that the worst thing that could possibly happen *to the world* would be for the United States to be drawn actively into this contest,—to become one of the belligerents and lose all chance of moderating the results of the war by her counsel as an outsider." Wilson contemplated nothing harsher than breaking off relations by sending the German ambassador, Count Johann von Bernstorff, home and recalling Gerard. Should further action prove necessary, Wilson believed the best course lay in calling a conference of all neutral nations to determine a common response "calculated to make neutral rights more secure."[38] Once again, Wilson's twin perceptions of the United States as a neutral and as a potential mediator merged to determine his policies. Force still seemed an unattractive alternative because it would negate the efforts to end the hostilities through American mediation.

Nevertheless, the *Arabic* crisis tested the American resolve to hold Germany and the submarine accountable to international law. None of the president's major advisers thought war the answer, but they unanimously urged a tough response. Lansing wrote the day after the incident that "I proceed on the assumption that we do not want to enter the war, and that the American people do not wish it but are greatly incensed over this last submarine outrage." Yet, the administration "must act," otherwise its *Lusitania* warning would appear as "mere 'bluff,'" which would put the United States "in a humiliating position." Tumulty, upon whom the president relied for advice on public opinion, reported that the people did not want war, nor even such radical action as breaking relations. However, Tumulty sensed "a universal demand for the recall of von Bernstorff and the withdrawal of Gerard." This should be done as quickly, he recommended, as the facts could be established. Diplomatic relations could continue, but at a lower level.[39]

Colonel House privately expressed surprise at Wilson's hesitation. The colonel believed that Wilson should have set his course when he determined the response to the *Lusitania* incident; surely the third note already defined the U.S. attitude toward additional sinkings. But still Wilson appeared to shy from a firm stand. He wrote House on August 21 pleading for advice. The American people "count on me to keep them out of the war," Wilson said, adding that "it would be a calamity to the world at large if we should be drawn actively into the conflict and so deprived of all disinterested influence over the settlement." House noted in his diary that "I am surprised at the attitude he takes. He evidently will go to great lengths to avoid war."[40] In his replies, however, House kept his opinions to himself.

House urged the president to settle this latest incident with Germany before taking up British violations of neutrality. In a second letter, the colonel pointed out the possible repercussions of various actions. "Our people do not want war," he told Wilson, "but even less do they want you to recede from the position you have taken." If Bernstorff were sent home and Gerard recalled, it "would be the first act of war."

Another alternative was to call Congress into emergency session, but this was a "dangerous move" since "there is no telling what Congress would do in the circumstances." Wilson could send Bernstorff back to Germany, bring Gerard back to the U.S., and wait for Germany to commit another offense. He could then call Congress into session, at which time it would probably be more willing to follow his lead. "Unless Germany disavows the act and promises not to repeat it," House observed, "some decisive action on our part is inevitable, otherwise we will have no influence when peace is made or afterwards." Wilson should move carefully, for if his response to the *Arabic* "hurt our pride of nationality," then the president would lose the "commanding position" that he had achieved during the *Lusitania* crisis.[41]

"You see he [House] does not advise, he puts it up to me!" Wilson exclaimed when he forwarded the second letter to Galt, but he should have expected nothing else. The possibility of war quite naturally frightened him, yet he did not want to lose the respect for neutral rights that he had demanded throughout the hostilities. House was right, of course; Wilson risked going to war with Germany on the one hand and losing all hope to influence the peace on the other. In the end, he feared the latter more than the former. On August 22 he explained his decision to Galt:

> The Germans have admitted all along that they had no right to sink any ship carrying our flag without first making themselves responsible for the safety of the lives of those on board. . . . The case we based our protest on was that of the *Lusitania,* chiefly, a British ship, and the case of the *Arabic* is the same in principle and worse in fact. It was your friend W. J. B. [Bryan—the reference to friend is facetious] who took the ground that we must let Americans understand that they took passage on British ships, or any other ships owned by belligerents, at their own risk and peril. Beware of heresies! It may very well be that this Bryan and Albany doctrine is the more reasonable and practical one, my precious Sweetheart, but it is not the doctrine of international law, and we must base our claims of right on the undoubted practice of nations,—for which Germany is showing such crass and brutal contempt. The road is hard to travel, but it is plain before us. She has no right whatever to deal with ships owned by *belligerents* as she has dealt with the *Lusitania* and the *Arabic,* and the *Falaba* before them, and when our own people are on board we must tell her so. It was another *Lusitania* incident we told her we should regard as "deliberately unfriendly."

The *Arabic* incident was "just a clear and simple case of insolently ignoring the protest and the warning of our three notes." Wilson determined to "go forward," perhaps by sending Bernstorff back to Germany and bringing Gerard home. This course might not lead to war, but there was a definite possibility that it would.[42] Nonetheless, Wilson resolved to act purposefully in demanding that Germany respect the legal rights of the United States.

In a series of lengthy meetings between Lansing and Bernstorff, the United States demanded an apology and reparations for the sinking of the *Arabic* and for the loss of American lives, as well as a promise that it would not be repeated. "The disavowal must be very explicit and must involve a virtual promise that these barbarities will stop," Wilson informed Galt. The Germans stalled, their government thrown into a crisis as the kaiser's civilian and military advisers battled for his support. Wilson and Lansing increased the pressure by demanding a response, which helped the civilian side, for no one in Germany yet wanted to risk war with the U.S. Finally, early in September, the kaiser sided with the imperial chancellor, who issued instructions to Bernstorff to tell Lansing that submarine commanders were under orders not to sink ocean liners. Bernstorff exceeded these instructions by delivering a written promise to Lansing that "liners will not be sunk by our submarines without warning and without safety of the lives of noncombatants, provided that the liners do not try to escape or offer resistance." Although the German government privately reprimanded its ambassador, his actions effectively defused the crisis. A month later, Germany apologized for the sinking and offered an indemnity for the loss of American lives.[43]

Bernstorff's *Arabic* pledge and the subsequent apology by the Imperial Government signaled a significant victory for Wilson's insistence on upholding the law. During the *Lusitania* crisis, Wilson defined his stand; with the *Arabic* crisis, he proved that he meant what he said. War's shadow hung constantly over him and the strain was often overpowering, but still he faced the issue squarely, ever mindful that neutrality imposed responsibilities as well as rights. In the months to come, he turned to England to insist that it, too, show more respect for the rights of the United States. The long and complicated story of these negotiations need not detain us, for others have described these diplomatic exchanges and, more importantly, at no time was war a possible consequence. As Lansing pointed out in mid-September 1915, "It seems to me that we must keep clearly in mind the distinction between the case of Germany and the case of Great Britain, in that the latter relates to violations of the rights involving loss of property."[44] The administration made a clear distinction between German infringements of neutral rights, which too often resulted in the death of Americans, and British violations of the law, which injured only property rights. The former required a tougher and, ultimately, a more forceful response from the United States.

For the purposes of this study, the details of England's interference with American trade is of less importance than the fact that Wilson demanded that Great Britain show the same respect for neutral rights that he expected from Germany. In this way, the United States confirmed its position as the leading neutral power. This confirmation encouraged Wilson to believe that some day he would be allowed to step in as mediator. This hope played a substantial role in Wilson's eventual decision to turn to force against Germany.

PROMOTING MEDIATION

Legality defined Wilson's neutrality policy, but ideology determined the character of America's mediation efforts. During the period of neutrality, Wilson and House developed a definite conception of the future international system. International cooperation would guarantee peace because nations would work together according to legal constructs. Even before the outbreak of the war, the president and his adviser began thinking along these lines. House traveled to Europe in the spring of 1914 to meet with British and German leaders in an attempt to bring about a common understanding among the major world powers. As he explained to Wilson on June 26, 1914, "I have suggested that America, England, France, and Germany and the other money lending and developing nations have some sort of tentative understanding among themselves for the purpose of establishing some plan by which investors on the one hand, may be encouraged to lend money at reasonable rates and to develop, upon favorable terms, the waste places of the earth." House, in his usual self-effacing way, flattered Wilson that both men were set on a revolutionary course to reshape world diplomacy. "I have a keen desire for you to become the world figure of your time," the colonel wrote Wilson a month before World War I began. "Never again can the old order of statesmen hold sway, and you are and will continue to be the prophet of a new day."[45] The opening shots of the war, however, dashed all hope that this purpose could be realized soon.

Even as Wilson outlined American neutrality, he adopted a particular role for the United States in regard to the world struggle. The United States, he told a press conference on August 3, 1914, "owes it to mankind to remain in such a condition and in such a state of mind that she can help the rest of the world. I want to have the pride of feeling that America, if nobody else, has her self-possession and stands ready with calmness of thought and steadiness of purpose to help the rest of the world."[46] Throughout the period of neutrality, Wilson held to this understanding of the American part in the struggle. International law guided Wilson's response to events, but the dream of future cooperation between nations increasingly became the central motivation behind his policies.

House took charge of the mediation effort in the fall of 1914. Based in New York, he arranged meetings between himself and Cecil Spring-Rice on the one hand and with Bernstorff on the other. The essential purpose of these conferences was to prove the interest of the United States in resolving the conflict. The discussions remained at a fairly general level, for neither ambassador either was willing or had the authority to enter into detailed negotiations. Both Wilson and House kept their hopes tightly harnessed. "I am looking for the right opportunity to influence, if I may, the course of events toward peace," Wilson explained to Thomas Nelson Page, the American ambassador to Italy.[47] For the moment, it was enough to keep before both sides the idea that America offered the best channel for the arrangement of the eventual peace talks.

In order to confirm as well as strengthen this idea, House returned to Europe in the winter of 1915. The president's instructions expressed succinctly the purpose of the mission. Wilson wrote:

> Please state, therefore, very clearly to all with whom you may confer that we have no thought of suggesting, either now or at another time, the terms and conditions of peace, except as we may possibly be asked to do so as the spokesman of those whose fortunes are involved in the present war. Our single object is to be serviceable, if we may, in bringing about the preliminary willingness to parley which must be the first step towards discussing and determining the conditions of peace. If we can be instrumental in ascertaining for each side in the contest what is the real disposition, the real wish, the real purpose of the other with regard to a settlement, your mission and my whole desire in the matter will have been accomplished.

Wilson intended, through House, to offer the belligerents a "channel of confidential communication" for exchanging views on peace. The United States "sought no advantage for ourselves," but, rather, wished only "to play the part of disinterested friends who have nothing at stake except their interest in the peace of the world."[48] House set sail with good intentions, but limited hopes.

As an effort to establish a conduit for the exchange of views, the second House mission succeeded. The colonel engaged in lengthy, private talks with Grey and other British officials during which they explored a wide range of propositions and conditions for achieving peace, as well as for reconstructing the shattered international system. House also went to Germany for similar discussions with members of the Imperial Government, including the kaiser. In order to gain favor with the British, the colonel offered an understanding sympathy for the cause of democracy and the rights of trade; for the Germans, House emphasized freedom of the seas as an essential condition of peace. The sinking of the *Lusitania,* however, ended any further effectiveness for the second mission, and shortly thereafter House returned to the United States. But from New York, he maintained correspondence with Grey and Zimmermann, as well as with their ambassadors. At least the talk, if not the immediate possibility of peace, was kept alive.[49]

The second mission also helped stimulate the thinking of Wilson and House in regard to plans for the postwar world. Throughout the period of neutrality, both men considered a variety of ideas. Since neither was a particularly original thinker, they borrowed proposals from a wide range of sources. House, for instance, suggested to the belligerents that, when the time came to end the war, two international conferences be held. The first, which would be attended by the belligerents, would settle the issues between them. The second and more important convention would be chaired by Wilson and would include all important nations, belligerent and neutral. This conference would arrange the postwar international system based on a spirit of cooperation and respect for the law. This was the grand dream that evolved in the minds of Wilson and House, but which had roots extending deep into the internationalist community of the United States. Eventually, it came to life in the form of the League of Nations.[50]

Originally, House believed that a spirit of militarism pervaded all of Europe, but his discussions with British leaders convinced him differently. Upon his return to the United States in the summer of 1915, he began promoting a conception of the war that Wilson ultimately adopted with vigor. House now saw the hostilities as a great battle between the forces of democracy arrayed against militarism and autocracy. "The difficulty," he wrote Wilson, "is not with the German Civil Authorities, but with the Military and Naval as represented by the Kaiser, [Admiral] von Tirpitz, and [General] Falkayn." The colonel suspected that the Germans would continue submarine warfare at the insistence of the military because a substantial faction in that branch of the German government saw war with the U.S. as "a good rather than a bad thing for Germany." Indeed, House advised the president on June 16, 1915, that American entry into the fight would not be an altogether tragic event. "The war would be more speedily ended and we would be in a strong position to aid the other great democracies in turning the world into the right paths," he explained. "It is something that we may have to face with fortitude being consoled by the thought that no matter what sacrifices we make, the end will justify them."[51] Wilson did not accept this interpretation immediately, but Germany's continued violations of international law added credence to House's view. It was merely a question of time before Wilson committed himself to fighting a war to save the world for democracy.

For Wilson, democracy extended into all areas of human endeavor. The postwar world, inasmuch as he could influence its character, would be based on liberal humanitarian foundations, a system of free trade, and shared economic interests. Democratic governments would be encouraged in all nations, and capitalist internationalism would characterize the world economic system. The major powers would unite together to assist the weak and the poor. The Open Door policy of the United States would be adopted as a world policy; the seas would be freed for use by all powers. Cooperative competition, regulated by international law and agreement, would replace the previous system of hostile competition. Arms and naval races, such a notable characteristic of the previous generation, would become obsolete, for nations would no longer need to fear other nations—all would be united together for the common good. Outlaw countries would be opposed by the world acting in concert. And, finally, the United States would accept the position of leadership to which it was born.

House's conception of the war as a battle between democracy and militarism came to control Wilson's thinking. The president's acceptance of this view during the fall and winter of 1915–16 privately compromised American neutrality, although publicly the Wilson administration continued to adhere to its original policy. During the third House mission to Europe in the winter of 1915–16, the private constraints on American sympathies became apparent. Wilson explained to House that the United States had "nothing to do with local settlements,—territorial questions, indemnities and the like." But, the president was concerned with "the future peace of the world." To guarantee that peace, he insisted on "(a) military and naval disarmament and (b) a league of nations to secure each nation against aggression and maintain the absolute freedom of the seas." Wilson now wanted mediation talks to begin soon. He instructed House that "if either party to the present war will let us say to the other that they are willing to discuss peace on such terms it will clearly be our duty to use our utmost moral force to oblige the other to parley."[52] In House's conferences with leading members of the British government, he took these instructions well beyond the meaning of strict neutrality, for he informally allied the United States to the British cause.

In talks with the British, House spoke of peace, but he accepted war as an intervening step. He emphasized that American entry into the conflict at the present time would be a mistake, yet he also gave assurances of American belligerency in the event Germany refused to negotiate. The contradiction stemmed from the timing; the United States would not go to war until Germany turned down its offer of mediation, which would be made after the Entente powers signaled their readiness. With this in mind, House signed the House-Grey Memorandum with the British foreign secretary on February 22, 1916. It provided that, upon notice from Great Britain, Wilson would make a formal offer of mediation to both sides. As House told the president, "the Allies will agree to the conference and if Germany does not, I have promised for you that we would throw all our weight in order to bring her to terms." Wilson approved the memorandum after toning down the promise by stating that the United States would "probably" enter the war against Germany in the event it refused to negotiate.[53]

Peace shone on the horizon and the prospect excited Wilson. House, however, continued to counsel the possible necessity of war. "Our becoming a belligerent would not be without its advantages in as much as it would strengthen your position at home and with the Allies," he wrote Wilson on April 3, 1916. "It would eliminate the necessity for calling in the conference any neutral because the only purpose in calling them in was to include ourselves." American belligerency would enhance its role in the peace conference because "we would be the only nation at the conference desiring nothing except the ultimate good of mankind."[54] This objective, House well knew, greatly appealed to the president.

Yet, Wilson accepted the possibility of war only if it represented the last opportunity to achieve a just peace and the complete alteration of the international system. The Wilsonian way of war, if it came to that, would be nothing less than a fight for justice and an end to all wars. By the winter of 1915–16, Wilson had fully, albeit privately, embraced the concept of a League of Nations and an expanded role for the United States in world affairs. Wilsonian internationalism was based on international cooperation and respect for the law, the only goals worthy of the sacrifice of American lives. Wilson intended to fight for nothing less. Still, he clung to the hope that he could shape the peace without the necessity of American intervention because he believed that the United States occupied such a central position in world affairs, even as a nonbelligerent, that when the time came, he could step in to help end the hostilities. The dream of a reformed international system was not motive enough to justify American participation in the war. The realist in him knew that he could not take the country to war for ideals alone; the people would break out of their isolationist shell only after they had been shown the intimate involvement of the nation in world affairs. Only through injury to their interests would the American people be convinced that they could not escape the world's tragedies. Thus, though Wilson would fight for nothing less than the good of mankind, he was unwilling (and, he knew, unable) to make that the *causus belli*.

From August 1914 to the beginning of 1916, Wilson's policies evolved from strict neutrality to a benign sympathy with the Entente cause, from patiently waiting for the belligerents to request his arbitration to an active desire to end the war through mediation or, possibly, through American participation. This evolution mimicked the change in Wilson from slumbering isolationist to awakened internationalist. Like most Americans in August 1914, Wilson confidently expected the expanse of two oceans to protect the United States from the insanity on the other sides of the water. At first, for example, he opposed increasing the size of the military establishment because of the historic American opposition to large armies. As he explained to Congress in December 1914:

> We are at peace with all the world. No one who speaks counsel based on fact or drawn from a just and candid interpretation of realities can say that there is reason to fear that from any quarters our independence or the integrity of our territory is threatened. Dread of the power of any other nation we are incapable of. We are not jealous of rivalry in the fields of commerce or of any other peaceful achievement. We mean to live our own lives as we will; but we mean also to let live. We are, indeed, a true friend to all the nations of the world, because we threaten none, covet the possessions of none, desire the overthrow of none. Our friendship can be accepted and is accepted without reservation because it is offered in a spirit and for a purpose which no one need ever question or suspect. Therein lies our greatness. We are the champions of peace and of concord.

Military preparedness was unnecessary because the United States was always able to defend itself without maintaining a large standing army during times of peace. Wilson saw no need to change that traditional policy because of events far across the seas.[55]

Events during 1915 convinced him otherwise. A growing preparedness movement in the country, spearheaded by such popular figures as Teddy Roosevelt, showed the growing attraction of expanding the military. General Leonard Wood's Plattsburg training camps, where young men volunteered to receive military training, exemplified the willingness of a substantial section of the populace to make the sacrifice of military indoctrination. The crises with Germany witnessed the inability of America to separate itself from war on distant shores; will it or not, the United States was now a part of the world. The possibility that the U.S. might have to join the battle in order to force Germany to the negotiating table also helped convince Wilson that military preparations should begin.

Thus, a year after denying the necessity of preparedness, the president recommended to Congress a plan for increasing the army and navy. He asked the legislature in December 1915 to provide for the addition of forty thousand officers and men to the army rolls, as well as to finance the training of four hundred thousand citizens in the bearing of arms. For the navy, Wilson outlined an ambitious construction program that included building ten battleships, sixteen cruisers, and fifty destroyers. The request soothed the complaints of the preparedness group, but the president carefully pointed out that the use of the expanded army and navy would be confined to the national defense and to peaceful endeavors. "We will not maintain a standing army except for uses which are as necessary in times of peace as in times of war," he promised Congress and, through it, the American people, "and we shall always see to it that our military peace establishment is no larger than is actually needed for the uses of days in which no enemies move against us."[56]

At the same time that he enlisted in the preparedness cause, Wilson continued to shy from military involvement in the war. Although informally tied to the British through the House-Grey Memorandum, Wilson hoped that its conditional promise would not have to be fulfilled. The American people, he believed, expected him to keep them out of war. The growth of the peace movement in the nation confirmed his belief, and even the preparedness advocates argued that military preparations would ensure the peace rather than lead to war. Thus, the president walked a tightwire. Convinced that the majority of the people disapproved of American entry into the war, he nevertheless allowed House to promise that the United States would "probably" go to war with Germany if it refused an offer of mediation. It was an uncomfortable balancing act between neutrality and internationalism, between the fear of involvement in the hostilities and the great desire to help bring them to a close. Wilson, uncertain of his ability to maintain the balance, determined to spend 1916 preparing the American people for war and the belligerents for peace. Perhaps in this way he could end the hostilities before the country was dragged into the conflict.

DEFENDING NEUTRALITY

During the early months of 1916, Wilson made a speaking tour of the midwestern states from Ohio to Kansas. In a series of almost daily speeches, he urged the acceptance of his preparedness program in the heartland of American isolationism. He chided his audiences that they expected him to keep the nation out of war at the same time that they insisted he defend the country's rights and honor. These expectations, Wilson repeatedly said, were contradictory and might well prove irreconcilable. Over and over again, he announced his intention to uphold the nation's honor and rights, even at the cost of war. "You have laid upon me this double obligation: 'We are relying upon you, Mr. President, to keep us out of this war, but we are relying upon you, Mr. President, to keep the honor of the Nation unstained,'" he told listeners in Cleveland, Ohio. "Do you not see that a time may come when it is impossible to do both of these things?" Honor came first. "You may count upon my heart and resolution to keep you out of war, but you must be ready if it is necessary that I should maintain your honor," he said, for "the Nation's honor is dearer than the Nation's comfort and the Nation's peace and the Nation's life itself." For this purpose, for the possibility of war, the United States needed more men under arms and more ships on the seas.[57]

By defending honor and rights, Wilson meant that he intended to protect the United States against any infringement on its neutrality by the belligerent powers. "It may be necessary to use the force of the United States to vindicate the rights of American citizens everywhere to enjoy the protection of international law," he told an audience in Topeka, Kansas, on February 2. Indeed, the warring powers themselves expected America to uphold the law. Honor and rights, then, entailed responsibilities, and from these Wilson would not shrink. "Somebody must keep the great stable foundations of the life of nations untouched and undisturbed," he proclaimed in Chicago. "Look at the task that is assigned to the United States, to assert the principles of law in a world in which the principles of law have broken down—not the technical principles of law, but the essential principles of right dealing and humanity as between nation and nation," he added. "What is America expected to do?" Wilson asked in Des Moines, Iowa. He answered himself: "She is expected to do nothing less than keep the law alive while the rest of the world burns."[58] This task was both the honor and the duty of the United States to perform.

It was the American way, founded in tradition, to uphold honor and self-respect as defined by the law. Neither Wilson nor the nation could escape that past, but surely, Wilson believed, no one really wanted to avoid this duty. They were, after all, Americans, and the president based his policies on the true spirit of the country:

> I know the spirit of America to be this: We respect other nations, and absolutely respect their rights so long as they respect our rights. We do not claim anything for ourselves, which they would not in like circumstances claim for themselves. Every statement of right that we have made is grounded upon the previous utterances of their own public men and their own judges. There is no dispute about the rights of nations under the understandings of international law. America has drawn no fine points. America has raised no novel issue. America has merely asserted the rights of her citizens and her Government upon what is written plain upon all the documents of international intercourse. Therefore America is not selfish in claiming her rights; she is merely standing for the rights of mankind when the life of mankind is being disturbed by an unprecedented war between the greatest nations of the world. Some of these days we shall be able to call the statesmen of the older nations to witness that it was we who kept the quiet flame of international principle burning upon its altars while the winds of passion were sweeping every other altar in the world.[59]

This was true neutrality, and Wilson wanted the American people ready to defend these principles of humanity.

Still, the administration remained uncertain of the country's determination to uphold the nation's honor and rights. Lansing believed that a large segment of the population desperately wanted to stay out of the war, no matter the provocation. "Our people are not aroused to a sufficient pitch of indignation at the barbarism of the Germans," he noted in his diary. "It is hard to comprehend this apparent indifference, but the fact that it exists cannot be doubted." The secretary feared that Congress would not support any "drastic action" against Germany, even if the Imperial Government resumed unrestricted submarine warfare. Yet, for him, the issue was clear: "It is my opinion that the military oligarchy which rules Germany is a bitter enemy to democracy in every form; that, if that oligarchy triumphs over the liberal governments of Great Britain and France, it will then turn upon us as its next obstacle to imperial rule over the world; and that it is safer and surer and wiser for us to be one of many enemies than to be in the future alone against a victorious Germany."[60] The attempted passage of the Gore-McLemore resolutions in February, which prohibited Americans from traveling on armed or contraband-carrying vessels, confirmed the impression that Congress sympathized with the desire to avoid a confrontation with Germany, even if it meant restricting the rights of Americans under internationl law.

Although the resolutions, which challenged both Wilson's leadership and the basic philosophy undergirding his policies, failed to pass, they attracted a substantial number of congressmen. The president dealt with this congressional insurgency firmly, using not only his powers as president, but also his considerable talents as a national leader and spokesman. Wilson spoke out against the resolutions on his midwestern tour and, once back in Washington, he met with leaders of the Senate Committee on Foreign Relations and the House Committee on Foreign Affairs to defend his policies and his leadership in international affairs. In an open letter to Senator William J. Stone, the president left no doubt as to his course. "But in any event our duty is clear," he wrote. "No nation, no group of nations, has the right while war is in progress to alter or disregard the principles which all nations have agreed upon in mitigation of the horrors and sufferings of war; and if the clear rights of American citizens should ever unhappily be abridged or denied by any such action, we should, it seems to me, have in honor no choice as to what our own course should be." Wilson would never consent "to any abridgement of the rights of American citizens in any respect." American honor and its responsibilities to the world as the leading neutral demanded no other attitude.[61] Even though he effectively stifled this attack against his policies, the congressional opposition emphasized what Wilson already knew—a substantial portion of Congress and the American people were determined to avoid war at all costs.

At the end of March 1916 Germany forced the confrontation that both Wilson and Lansing dreaded. Submarines attacked two Dutch vessels, including the passenger liner *Tubantia,* on March 16 and 18. Although the sinkings violated the *Arabic* pledge, the United States lacked standing to complain because neither ship carried Americans. Then, on March 24, U-boat 29 torpedoed without warning the French channel steamer *Sussex,* causing the deaths of almost eighty people and the injury of four Americans. The nation's resolve to stand up for its rights as a neutral was put to the test once again.[62]

Both Lansing and House recommended strong action against the Imperial Government. On March 27 the secretary advised Wilson either to break relations or issue an ultimatum demanding that Germany admit the illegality of its submarine operations. The dignity of the United States required a prompt, firm response. House rushed to Washington from New York to attend his friend. He found Wilson hesitant "to back up his former notes to Germany." House noted in his diary that Wilson "does not seem to realize that one of the main points of criticism against him is that he talks boldly, but acts weakly." Throughout his two-day stay at the White House, the colonel emphasized the necessity of action. On his last day, he told the president that the United States stood to lose all influence with the Entente powers and, therefore, all hope of shaping the peace unless it met Germany's challenge head on. Despite these high stakes, or perhaps because of them, Wilson withheld judgment. He asked House to meet with Bernstorff in order to convey the seriousness of the situation to the German ambassador. The U.S., the colonel was to say, would join the war unless Germany drastically changed its use of the submarine.[63] Yet, it was not clear if this message was intended as threat or bluff.

Wilson seemed in retreat from the stance he assumed during the *Lusitania* and *Arabic* crises. He wrote Lansing on March 30 indicating that the evidence that a U-boat attacked the *Sussex* was weak. In addition, Wilson said that "there are many particulars to be considered about the course we should pursue as well as the principle of it." The next day, the president described his quandary to Thomas Nelson Page, the American ambassador to Italy. "The German submarine policy is making an extremely complicated and difficult situation for us, and sometimes there seems to be little prospect of extricating ourselves from it without serious conflict, but we are still hoping that it will be possible," wrote the worried president.[64] Wilson's recent difficulties with Congress, combined with the desire of the American people to avoid involvement in the war, raised doubts in his mind about his ability to lead the country into a fight with Germany. The hope of mediation, which the House-Grey Memorandum strengthened, also contributed to Wilson's apparent indecision.

Early in April, House proposed sending a cable to Grey asking him to put their agreement into effect. Wilson himself wrote the message in which House suggested that the British foreign secretary act on their plan immediately by consulting with Britain's allies to determine their receptiveness to an American offer of mediation. The cable indicated that Grey should allow Wilson to propose the good offices of the United States. If the Germans refused the invitation, the United States would probably enter the war. But Grey refused, reasoning that the *Sussex* crisis might bring the U.S. into the war without any interference by the Americans with the possible peace settlement at that stage of the hostilities. With nothing to lose, the Entente powers could afford to await the outcome of the controversy. That Wilson sent the message showed his desperation to avoid a possible confrontation with the Imperial Government over the submarine. Yet, he also knew that the law required a protest from him. From this responsibility, no matter how heavy a burden, he could not escape.[65]

In the meantime, Lansing, at the president's request, drafted a note to the German government protesting the attack on the French channel steamer. The wording of Lansing's protest proved too strong for Wilson's taste, so he spent several days toning it down. Lansing, House, and even the second Mrs. Wilson found the president's version too weak. After further conferences and rewritings, the note was finally ready by April 17; the State Department dispatched it to Gerard the next day. In it, the United States demanded that Germany abandon "its present method of submarine warfare against passenger and freight-carrying vessels." The Wilson administration insisted on an "immediate declaration" from the Imperial Government expressing its disavowal of the practice of attack without warning.[66]

Wilson went before Congress on April 19 to explain his policy. International law, he said, justified the protest to Germany. The United States based its original protests against the use of submarines on the time-honored law of nations, which was based "upon manifest and imperative principles of humanity." The president reviewed the actions of the Imperial Government in regard to submarine warfare. "Tragedy has followed tragedy on the seas in such a fashion, with such attendant circumstances, as to make it grossly evident that warfare of such a sort, if warfare it be, can not be carried on without the most palpable violations of the dictates alike of right and of humanity," Wilson asserted. "Whatever the disposition and intention of the Imperial German Government, it has manifestly proved impossible for it to keep such methods of attack upon the commerce of its enemies within the bounds set by either reason or the heart of mankind." Despite German promises to protect unarmed merchant and passenger vessels, the assurances had gone unrealized. Indeed, Wilson said, "the lives of noncombatants, passengers and crew have been sacrificed wholesale, in a manner which the Government of the United States cannot but regard as wanton and without the slightest color of justification." Despite the patience of the American government and people, despite their willingness to accept the promises of the Germans to respect the law of the seas, attacks and sinkings continued. Not only did Germany infringe on the rights of the United States as a neutral, but it also insulted the honor of the country by ignoring its demands.

This review of the Imperial Government's past practices brought Wilson to the latest submarine incident, the attack on the *Sussex*. He spoke harshly of this episode, calling it one of the "most shocking instances of this method of warfare" which clearly showed the inhumanity of relying on U-boats to conduct naval operations against the enemy. For Wilson, the torpedoing of the French channel steamer meant but one thing:

> The facts are susceptible of but one interpretation. The Imperial German Government has been unable to put any limits or restraints upon its warfare against either freight or passenger ships. It has therefore become painfully evident that the position which this Government took at the very outset is inevitable, namely, that the use of submarines for the destruction of an enemy's commerce is of necessity, because of the very character of the vessels employed and the very methods of attack which their employment of course involves, incompatible with the principles of humanity, the long established and incontrovertible rights of neutrals, and the sacred immunities of noncombatants.

Consequently, if the Imperial Government did not "immediately declare and effect an abandonment of its present methods of warfare against passenger and freight carrying vessels," the United States would have no alternative but to sever its diplomatic relations with Germany. The "sacred and indisputable rules of international law" allowed no other course.[67]

In the *Sussex* note and in the speech to Congress, Wilson increased the demands on Germany. The *Arabic* pledge covered only passenger liners, but the United States now insisted that the submarine obey the rules of war in regard to freighters as well. In addition, Wilson threw the decision of continued relations between the two countries, which almost certainly meant the decision between war and peace, to the Imperial Government. By making the demand on Germany to cease its present method of submarine warfare or face a rupture in relations, the president, in an astute diplomatic maneuver, spared himself from responsibility for deciding the issue. He could have broken relations himself, which is what Lansing advised, but given his concern over the pacifist attitude prevalent in the Congress and across the country, Wilson had no assurance how far he could go before losing the nation's support. Thus, he made a demand on Germany which the nation would recognize as reasonable; if the Imperial Government refused to accept the terms, then the United States could react to that refusal. Everything now depended on the decision of the kaiser about whom he would heed among his advisers, the civilians or the military.

The civilians won the kaiser's support by linking Germany's acceptance of international law with the demand of its own that the United

States compel England to obey the law in its blockade of the continent. This represented not only a face-saving solution, but, in the German view, a reasonable one as well. In the reply to the American note, the Imperial Government gave the appropriate assurances that its U-boats would observe the proper rules of the seas, but it added that it expected the United States to require Britain to observe the law. The assurances were made conditional on the expectation. A second note expressed Germany's apology for the *Sussex* incident, offered an indemnity, and stated that the submarine commander had been duly punished.[68]

The German reply was not well received by the Wilson administration. Lansing's first impression of the note was "bad," his second impression was "good," but his third was "unsatisfactory." He wrote Wilson that "the more I study the reply the less I like it. It has all the elements of the 'gold brick' swindle with a decidedly insolent tone."[69] The conditions that Germany outlined in its acceptance of international law put Wilson in an awkward position. To accept the terms would have been embarrassing; to reject them would have meant breaking relations, the consequence of which might well have meant war.

The president, in a diplomatic soft-shoe, neatly sidestepped the problem. The American government refused to recognize that any conditions had been set on Germany's promise. Although the German note could be interpreted in several ways, the American reply read, the United States believed that no conditions had been placed on the pledge. Wilson would accept no interference in America's relations with other countries. Since Germany obviously had no right to interfere, the logic of the reply went, it could not possibly have meant what some might think it said. Thus, Wilson accepted Germany's assurances that the submarine would be bound by the rules of naval warfare, but he made it clear that obedience to the law could not be made dependent on any action that the United States might or might not take in its relations with other nations.[70]

The *Sussex* crisis thus ended ambiguously, with neither side quite sure that its interpretation of the outcome coincided with what the other side believed. Nevertheless, the peaceful termination of the controversy bought Wilson more time. He had avoided war with Germany for yet another indefinite period. Perhaps, he hoped, in that time he could exert his influence to convince the warring powers to allow him to mediate their dispute. At the same time, he continued the efforts to prepare the American people for war.

Throughout the remainder of the year, the president engaged in two important campaigns—the first to bring the belligerents to the peace table and the second to win reelection. At House's suggestion, the president accepted an invitation to speak at the annual meeting of the League to Enforce Peace. He took the opportunity to announce publicly for the first time his endorsement of the proposal to form a concert of nations at war's end. At the same time, he pledged America's willingness to join in such an association, which would ensure the supremacy of the law and morality in international affairs.[71] Thus, in the summer of 1916, Wilson embarked on his efforts to form what would become the League of Nations. This objective became one of the prime motives behind his policies both in peace and in war, for Wilson saw in it the solution to many of his problems. Through international cooperation, the nations of the world could guarantee the freedom of the seas, the right of all nations to a peaceful existence, and respect for the law.

The nebulous resolution of the *Sussex* crisis allowed House to approach Grey at a more propitious time to suggest that the foreign minister implement the terms of their memorandum. But Grey again put him off, claiming that the time was not opportune and that England's allies would be unwilling to have Wilson offer mediation. Once again, Grey suggested that they wait a little longer, perhaps until after the summer military campaigns. Although discouraged by the answer, House and the president continued to discuss when and how to call for a peace conference. House, while conferring periodically with Bernstorff and Spring-Rice, maintained his correspondence with their superiors. This helped pass the time during the summer, but had little practical result. The great move for peace was stalled.[72]

During the election campaign in the fall, Wilson ran on the slogan "He kept us out of war." The past tense of the verb made it a statement of fact, not a promise for the next four years. Nonetheless, Wilson feared that the American people would expect too much from him. During the campaign against Charles Evans Hughes, the Republican nominee, Wilson took advantage of the fear of American participation in the war. Yet he hoped that the people would understand the risky position of the country. The race was hard run and the outcome extremely close, but Wilson won a second term. Throughout the campaign, the central issue remained unanswered: How long could the president maintain the precarious balance between neutrality and the nation's honor? The solution lay, not in depending on Germany to fulfill its promises, for war prohibits firm assurances, but in the ability of America to bring about peace.

Immediately after the election, Wilson renewed his peacemaking efforts. Neither House nor Lansing supported his latest move, so the president developed a plan on his own. He worked steadily on a note to the belligerents, but the task was complicated when Germany issued a statement on December 16 inviting its enemies to the conference table. Although the Entente powers were certain to reject the dubious offer, Wilson did not want his invitation linked to the German one. Yet, he also feared that time was fast escaping. Thus, on December 18 Wilson sent his peace note, which expressly disavowed any connection with the German offer, to the belligerents. The note requested the participants to communicate to the United States their list of war aims. Perhaps in that way, through a comparison of goals and demands, a road to peace could be found.[73]

Wilson's subordinates, however, sabotaged the effort. Ambassador Page made no attempt to hide his disapproval when he delivered the message to the new British administration, headed by David Lloyd George. House sent word through an English acquaintance that the note did not signify any change in American policies toward the Allies, and Lansing publicly denied that it was a peace note at all. Rather, he told representatives of the press on December 21, Wilson sent the message because the United States was teetering on the verge of war. The secretary seemed to imply that before entering the war, the administration wanted to discover which side had the more reasonable demands. The president ordered Lansing to retract the statement, but by then the damage had been done.[74]

Germany replied first. The Imperial Government promised to reveal its war aims at the peace conference among the belligerents, to which, the answer clearly implied, the United States would not be invited. The Allies delayed their response until mid-January 1917, partly because they were waiting for Germany to go first and partly because it took that long to get their answer approved by all the governments. They submitted a list of demands, which was better than Germany's reply, but their war aims required major concessions from the Imperial Government, which encouraged little hope for peace. In the end, it was quite clear that Wilson's fall 1916 peace offensive had failed.[75]

Although the answers disappointed Wilson, he refused to give up. Convinced that each day might bring a new crisis to draw the United States into the hostilities, he searched desperately for a way to ward off the inevitable. The answers to his request for war aims gave him the idea to propose a "peace without victory," which he did in a speech to Congress on January 22, 1917. He also pledged the cooperation of the nation in any fair settlement of the war, which, he hoped, would include some form of a congress of nations. The United States could no longer deny its intimate participation in world affairs and Wilson made it clear that he intended to lead the country in the direction of greater involvement. But it would be on his terms, not on the basis of power politics.[76]

Neither side approved of Wilson's proposal for a peace without victory. The war had lasted too long and the stakes were too high. The German government decided to take a last, desperate gamble. Ambassador Bernstorff informed Lansing on January 31 that, effective the next day, U-boats would resume unrestricted attacks on all neutral and belligerent shipping. The military had finally won the kaiser's support, and even Chancellor Bethmann-Hollweg agreed that now was the time for the final effort to destroy Britain's lifeline to the United States. The Imperial Government gambled that its submarines could win the war before America's entry could be decisive.

For Wilson, the complete renunciation of the promises he had extracted at such a great cost was intolerable. Still, he shied from joining the war. On February 3 he announced the complete severance of diplomatic relations with Germany, adding that "actual overt acts" in violation of the Imperial Government's pledges would compel a harsher response from the United States. The threat, however, had little effect, for Germany had prepared itself for making America an enemy. The longer the delay, the better for it. And Wilson continued to delay, despite the occurrence of several sinkings from torpedoes. At the end of February, he requested authority from Congress to arm U.S. merchantmen, but "a little group of willful men," led by Robert M. LaFollette, successfully filibustered the bill in the Senate. The administration proceeded to arm the ships on its own authority.[77]

Throughout this time, submarines exacted a heavy toll on neutral and belligerent shipping. Among the targets were many American-owned vessels, including the *City of Memphis,* the *Illinois,* the *Vigilancia,* and the *Healdton.* These sinkings confirmed the complete failure of Wilson's policy to uphold the law. The interception of the Zimmermann telegram to Mexico by British naval intelligence revealed Germany's willingness to accept the United States as an active enemy. The telegram outlined the terms of a proposed alliance between the Imperial Government and the Carranza regime whereby, in exchange for a declaration of war by Mexico against the United States, Germany would assist Mexico in regaining the territory it lost in the Mexican War of 1846. The major effect of the proposal was to infuriate Americans; its appeal to Carranza, who had his hands full consolidating his own power, was limited.[78]

These events gave further proof that Germany had decided to give up on any effort to appease the United States. Wilson's policy of neutrality was in a shambles; his insistence on respect for international law and the rights of neutrals no longer carried weight with the Imperial Government. Whatever influence the American government had mustered before in bringing Germany to accept its interpretation of the law grew from Germany's respect for American power and its fear of making the U.S. an enemy. Once the kaiser and his advisers determined that defeat of Britain on the seas was worth the price of active American hostility, the Wilson administration lost all power to hold Germany to respect for the rules of war. The failure of Wilson's peace policies compounded the problem by limiting the alternatives open to him.

Germany's lack of respect for freedom of the seas and the loss of any hope of mediating an end to the war meant that only one avenue remained open. Throughout February and March, members of the Wilson administration discussed the necessity of war. Secretary of War Baker began preparing the army by the purchase of supplies and equipment and by the formulation of war plans. Secretary of the Navy Daniels worked on the navy in the same way and Admiral William Sims was secretly dispatched to Great Britain to open consultations looking toward cooperation with the British navy.[79] Wilson approved of all these measures, even though he continued to postpone the decision to join the war.

Despite the previous resorts to force in Mexico, Haiti, and Santo Domingo, the prospect of war against a developed power was both depressing and frightening. Those interventions, in Wilson's view, had been necessary steps in the process of enlightening backward peoples. This conceptual framework hardly fit a developed power like Germany until Wilson accepted the House and Lansing view that Germany symbolized the power of darkness, the Allies the power of light. The war represented the last, cataclysmic clash between autocracy and democracy, militarism and freedom. The outbreak of the first, democratic revolution in Russia in March added further proof to this interpretation. Wilson asked himself: Could the United States, not only the strongest neutral, but, more importantly, the greatest democracy, remain on the sidelines during so important a struggle?[80]

Throughout March, Wilson secluded himself from public appearances and from most visitors. He had difficulty accepting the failure of his policies, for, as he explained early in April, "I was for a little while unable to believe that such things would in fact be done by any government that had hitherto subscribed to the humane practices of civilized nations." Members of the administration continued to advise American entry into the war. On March 20 the cabinet, in a heartrending scene that left Daniels in tears, unanimously recommended a declaration of war against the Imperial Government. The illegal use of the submarine was the overriding reason the various secretaries gave.[81] The next day, Wilson called for a special joint session of Congress to convene on April 2.

The speech to Congress asking for a declaration of war mirrored the bifurcation of Wilson's policies during the period of neutrality. In the first half of the speech, in which Wilson described the causes of the trouble, he addressed the issue of neutrality and the refusal of the Imperial Government to respect the dictates of international law, particularly Germany's use of submarines. "International law had its origin in the attempt to set up some law which would be respected and observed upon the seas, where no nation had right of dominion and where lay the free highways of the world," the president explained. The slow, painful evolution of this system had been dealt a grievous injury during the present conflict. "This minimum of right the German Government has swept aside under the plea of retaliation and necessity and because it had no weapons which it could use at sea except these which it is impossible to employ as it is employing them without throwing to the winds all scruples of humanity or of respect for the understandings that were supposed to underlie the intercourse of the world," Wilson added. Germany's use of the submarine represented a "warfare against mankind" and a "war against all nations." America had been unable to escape the insult and injury resulting from the illegal methods of submarine warfare.

For this reason, because of the high cost in life and self-respect, the president asked Congress to recognize that Germany's course amounted to war against the United States. He expected Congress to formalize America's status as a belligerent by a declaration of war. "Our object now . . . is to vindicate the principles of peace and justice in the life of the world as against selfish and autocratic power and to set up amongst the really free and self-governed peoples of the world such a concert of purpose and of action as will henceforth insure the observance of these principles," Wilson declared. "Neutrality is no longer feasible or desirable where the peace of the world is involved and the freedom of its peoples." The United States must take its place among the democratic nations in the struggle against autocracy and militarism.[82]

Wilson asked for a declaration of war because of the refusal of the Imperial Government to obey the law. This represented the cause of the war, not its purpose. Once Wilson identified the reason that required American belligerency, he went on to define the objectives for which the United States would fight. As he had during the period of neutrality, the president adopted two policies, the first to enforce respect for international law, the second to ensure the future peace. Germany's use of the submarine compelled the United States to resort to force to defend its international rights, but once he accepted the necessity for this action, Wilson proceeded to define a greater purpose. America would take advantage of the unfortunate situation by bringing to the world a vision of a perfect postwar system. Americans would fight because Germany left them no choice, but they would use the opportunity to make the world safe for democracy. The United States went to war, not against the German people, but against the German government. It fought, not for selfish purposes, but for the greater honor of bringing to the world a just and lasting peace. The death of American neutrality allowed the birth of Wilsonian internationalism.

The separation in Wilson's mind of the cause of the war from its purpose reflected his approach to the hostilities during the period of neutrality. The United States went to war to defend its rights under the law, but it fought for a better world in which the necessity of defending international law would be borne by all nations. "But the right is more precious than peace," Wilson said, "and we shall fight for the things which we have always carried nearest our hearts,—for democracy, for the right of those who submit to authority to have a voice in their own Governments, for the rights and liberties of small nations, for a universal dominion of right by such a concert of free peoples as shall bring peace and safety to all nations and make the world itself at last free."[83] Thus, Wilson married the practical aspects of defending neutral rights with the ideological vision of erecting a better international system.

During the war, international law assumed less importance than it had during the period of neutrality. In its stead, Wilson pushed for the institutionalization of international cooperation. In his vision, cooperation would ensure all other aspects of his program. It would protect international rights and freedom, as well as ensure the supremacy of the law and a lasting peace.

5.
THE POWER of COOPERATION:

World War I

The recognition of the federal government as an agent for reform during the era of the Progressive movement confirmed the results of the Civil War. The powers of the national government were consolidated, giving it precedence over state and local governments. Awakened from its slumber during the Gilded Age, Washington involved itself in all facets of American life. By using federal power to direct commerce, social behavior, and the economy, the Progressives injected Congress and the presidency with a revitalizing strength. Such leaders as Roosevelt and Wilson gave a fresh interpretation to the role of the executive. The impetus behind this governmental revolution grew out of the abiding belief in the power of men united under democratic rule.

The Progressives saw the law as their instrument of change, but the root of their reforms was their compelling faith in the sanctity of democracy. People united by common consent could change the world; democracy was the salvation of modern man. "It is for this that we love democracy," Wilson wrote in 1901, "for its tendency to exalt the purposes of the average man to some high level of endeavor; for its just principle of common consent in matters in which all are concerned; for its ideals of duty and its sense of brotherhood."[1] The Progressive Era represented the triumph of faith in democracy and constitutional government.

Wilson epitomized the resurgent belief in democratic action. Throughout his careers as scholar, public speaker, and politician, he peppered his writings and speeches with loving references to an idealized democracy. During the 1890s, for example, he repeated his favorite address, titled simply "Democracy," more often than any of his other set lectures. It summarized his thinking on the subject, and, more than that, it captured his devotion to democratic government. He spoke here of *modern* democracy

> in which the people who are said to govern are not the people of a commune or a township, but all the people of a great nation, a vast population which never musters into any single assembly, whose members never see each others' faces or hear each others' voices, but live, millions strong, up and down the reaches of continents; building scores of great cities throughout fair provinces that would in other days have been separate kingdoms; following all callings under all climes; and yet not *separate,* but standing fast in a vital union of thought and of institutions, conceiving themselves a corporate whole; acting so, and so accepted by the world. There is no simplicity here! The new democracy is manifold, intense, dramatic, thrilled through and through with a new life, facing a new destiny,—with many questionings, but also with high and confident hope.

The people, Wilson explained, did not actually govern. Rather, they selected a few among them to lead. The power of democracy derived from the people's respect for honesty and openness in the conduct of their affairs. The strength of democratic man lay "in cooperation, in combined and regulated social effort." The power that defined personal rights and liberty was stronger than the individual because it depended on the strength of men united. This power was the salvation of modern man. The individual's greatest obligation was "to preserve and to transmit" the liberty bestowed upon him to his descendents.[2]

A faith in freedom for all humanity and an urge for individual liberty transformed the individual into an American. "America was created to unite mankind by those passions which lift and not by the passions which separate and debase," Wilson told a group of newly naturalized citizens, several thousand strong. This was the cement that held the country together. He added that

> We came to America, either by ourselves or in the persons of our ancestors, to better the ideals of men, to make them see finer things than they had seen before, to get rid of the things that divide and to make sure of the things that unite. It was but an historical accident no doubt that this great country was called the "United States"; yet I am very thankful that it has that word "United" in its title, and the man who seeks to divide man from man, group from group, interest from interest, in this great Union is striking at its very heart.[3]

The unity of the American people depended on shared ideals, not similar personalities, traditions, or backgrounds. In the United States, all were free to follow their own pursuits, to be individuals and adventurers in the common experiment to promote freedom and democracy. The duty of the citizen was to protect liberty, not to enforce conformity.

The responsibilities that inhered in democratic citizenship extended into the realm of foreign affairs. For Wilson, America was more than a city upon a hill serving democracy by example. Instead, it was a living entity, actively involved in the promotion of united self-government. He believed that

> All mankind deem us the representatives of the moderate and sensible discipline which makes free men good citizens, of enlightened systems of law and a temperate justice of the best experience in the reasonable methods and principles of self-government, of public force made consistent with individual liberty; and we shall not realize these ideals at home, if we suffer them to be hopelessly discredited amongst the peoples who have yet to see liberty and the peaceable days of order and comfortable progress. We should lose hope ourselves, did we suffer the world to lose faith in us as the champions of these things.

Americans, Wilson claimed, "have sympathized with freedom everywhere . . . have deemed it niggardly to deny an equal degree of freedom to any race or community that desired it; have pressed handsome principles of equity in international dealings; have rejoiced to believe that our principles might some day make every government a servant, not a master, of its people."[4] Upon assuming the presidency, Wilson consistently showed how truly he believed that it was not enough for Americans to have democracy. He offered it to all the world.

During the First World War, Wilson relied on the ideal of cooperative action in his relations with the Entente powers. He applied his understanding of national unity—people working together as equals for the greater good—to the international sphere. Wilson hoped to transform the reliance on national power into a dependence on the community of nations. Individual countries would no longer be compelled to rely solely on their own strength. Instead, they could find protection in each other. The war offered the president the opportunity to encourage this spirit of cooperation. Coalition warfare would prove how nations could work together against a common enemy. After the war, cooperation would provide a firm foundation upon which to rebuild the international system according to the design of collective security. The previous system, which was based on national jealousy and competition, would be torn asunder.

COOPERATION DURING THE INTERVENTIONS IN MEXICO, HAITI, AND SANTO DOMINGO

The search for cooperation ran through each of Wilson's interventions. It took varied forms in each, depending on the opportunities and circumstances within each nation. In general, Wilson's actions during each intervention followed a similar pattern. He consistently sought some internal political group with which he could work. Once he identified potential allies, he lent them American support in an effort to solidify their power within the country. But, at best, Wilson was clumsy in his method of cooperating. He often tried to force American assistance onto unwilling allies in order to guide them along democratic paths that he blazed. Wilson cared little for the objectives of his selected allies. He demanded only that they adopt American goals. When, as happened in Mexico and Santo Domingo, the internal groups opposed those designs, Wilson was incensed. Nevertheless, whether or not the other side sought to cooperate with Wilson, he always tried to work with them.

In Mexico, for example, Wilson sought a national leader who could rally the Mexican people against the usurper Huerta. He turned first to the Constitutionalist alliance of Carranza and Villa, hoping that both men could overcome their petty ambitions to work together for the greater good of the Mexican people. The occupation of Veracruz in 1914 offered Wilson a chance to negotiate an end to the revolution. The discussions at the ABC conference at Niagara Falls centered on who could lead the country in place of Huerta and what program that leader should adopt. Carranza's stubborn refusal to cooperate with his American saviors effectively destroyed Wilson's chance to establish a national government, but Huerta's resignation in July raised the president's hopes that the Constitutionalists could continue working together. When Villa and Carranza split in the fall of 1914, Wilson began his search anew.

At first, Wilson settled on Villa, but Carranza's growing military power soon proved the error of that choice. In the summer of 1915, Lansing proposed dropping both Villa and Carranza in favor of an as yet unidentified leader who, with American backing, would assume leadership of the revolution-torn country. The idea tempted Wilson, who called together representatives of other Latin American countries to help make the selection in a show of unity. But by this time, Carranza was too firmly in control, his power too deeply rooted throughout Mexico. The United States granted his government de facto recognition in October, not because Wilson approved of the first chief, but because Carranza met the essential test of uniting a substantial number of

Mexicans behind him. Wilson hoped that American recognition would help the first chief further solidify his power.

Villa, though weakened by military defeat and loss of support, retained just enough strength to cause problems. Carranza's inability to deliver a death blow to his adversary was compounded in March 1916 by Villa's attack on Columbus, New Mexico. Once again, Wilson sent American troops into Mexico and then used their presence to propose negotiations. The discussions at the Joint Mexican-American Conference focused on various ways that Carranza could strengthen his leadership by implementing social and political reforms. The first chief, incensed at this blatant interference in his country's affairs, demanded that the punitive expedition be withdrawn. Faced with this hostile opposition, Wilson washed his hands of Mexico, but not before he satisfied himself that Carranza was strong enough to maintain Mexican unity and that Villa no longer posed a serious threat. In January 1917 Wilson withdrew Pershing's forces and turned his attention to the larger problems presented by World War I.

Affairs in Haiti offered more fertile ground for Wilson's efforts to plant the seeds of democratic unity through cooperation with internal political elements. The Haitians were too disorganized, their political system too primitive, to muster effective opposition against outside interference. Indeed, Haiti's method of changing leaders evolved within its national disunity. The *cacos* sold their loyalty to the highest bidder, with no compunction about overthrowing a leader installed by them in a previous rebellion. Wilson's policies, defined by the ethnocentric humanitarianism of his administration, assumed that the Haitians could learn from America the proper methods of self-government. Installing democracy in the small republic depended on fostering a sense of unity among the Haitian people. The breakdown of civil authority in Port-au-Prince in July 1915, combined with the gruesome coup against Guillaume Sam, gave Wilson the chance he sought to turn Haiti around.

Shortly after Admiral Caperton's forces took over the administration of the Haitian capital, Wilson ordered them to effect control over the remainder of the country. The Marine Corps subdued the *cacos* and the Haitians settled into an uneasy obeisance to American military rule. But bringing peace and order to the country was not enough for Wilson. Soon after the naval forces established their authority, he searched for a Haitian leader behind whom the people could unite and who would obey American direction. Caperton found such a man in Sudre Dartiguenave. Immediately following Dartiguenave's election on August 12, the admiral and his aides inaugurated negotiations for a treaty that gave the United States effective control over all aspects of Haiti's affairs. During the remainder of Wilson's administration, President Dartiguenave and his successors ruled a united Haiti because of the support given them by the U.S. Navy and Marine Corps. In addition, the marines trained a Haitian gendarmerie to enforce national unification.

Santo Domingo presented a more difficult problem. Not only were the Dominicans unable to unite among themselves, they also resisted American efforts to bring them under control. At first through diplomatic and economic power, then through intervention, Wilson sought some way to establish a truly national government to rule the Dominican Republic. None of his policies succeeded. Throughout the summer of 1916, with American marines spread across the country, the United States struggled with the Dominicans to make them choose a leader amenable to American direction, yet also able to unite the nation. The refusal of members of the Dominican legislature to cooperate—indeed, their insistence on choosing their own man as the new president—convinced Wilson to impose an American military government on the country. Once again, he hoped to compel political unification by teaching the Dominican people the American form of democracy.

The military government stabilized the country's affairs, but the Dominicans proved poor students. Wilson's instructions about the advantages of unity under democratic government never took hold. Eventually, world problems drew the president's attention away; he left Santo Domingo to its own resources. Although the military government remained in control until the early 1920s, Wilson had little time left to teach the Dominicans properly.

Tragically, both Haiti and Santo Domingo learned from their experiences that a national police force best controlled the people. The American-trained gendarmerie in each country became the instrument of ambitious leaders. Whoever controlled it could impose himself as leader of the country. Although Wilson's efforts to instill democracy failed despite the strength of his ethnocentric humanitarianism, his insistence on national unity succeeded with a bitter vengeance.

ESTABLISHING COOPERATION AT HOME

For Wilson, World War I represented the breakdown of international order. He approached it with the same intention to establish cooperation and stability that appeared in his earlier interventions. The German government, he finally realized, left him no choice but to achieve through force what he failed to accomplish through diplomacy. Throughout the period of neutrality, Wilson searched for some avenue to peace that would uphold the principles of international law and cooperation. On April 2, 1917, a dark day in the president's life, he admitted that the road to peace could be cleared only through force. In asking Congress for a declaration of war, Wilson pointed to the necessity of uniting the American people and the Allied nations in a cooperative effort against Germany. For Wilson, the search for international cooperation defined the war effort.

Winning the war, the president advised Congress, "will involve the utmost practicable cooperation in counsel and action with the governments now at war with Germany," and he added that "it will involve the organization and mobilization of all the material resources of the country." To meet the needs of the army and navy, Wilson urged the legislature to adopt the principle of universal liability for military service. He spoke also of his hope for cooperation among the nations at war's end. In concluding the thirty-six minute address, Wilson reached a stirring eloquence, born of "a distressing and oppressive duty," to preach the necessity of national unity:

> It is a fearful thing to lead this great peaceful people into war, into the most terrible and disastrous of all wars, civilization itself seeming to be in the balance. But the right is more precious than peace, and we shall fight for the things which we have always carried nearest our hearts, for democracy, for the right of those who submit to authority to have a voice in their own governments, for the rights and liberties of small nations, for a universal dominion of right by such a concert of free peoples as shall bring peace and safety to all nations and make the world itself at last free. To such a task we can dedicate our lives and our fortunes, everything that we are and everything that we have, with the pride of those who know that the day has come when America is privileged to spend her blood and her might for the principles that gave her birth and happiness and the peace which she has treasured. God helping her, she can do no other.

American dedication to principle, combined with a spirit of cooperation amongst all peoples and democracies, offered the only hope for the world. "The supreme test of the nation has come," Wilson later proclaimed to the American people. "We must all speak, act, and serve together."[5]

Others in the administration also saw the war as a great challenge to democracy which required a united effort. Sometime in February 1917, Admiral William S. Benson, the chief of naval operations, outlined for Secretary of the Navy Daniels the measures he considered necessary to win the war. "No diplomacy that is unsupported by ability to use force can hope to achieve its ends when these conflict with important interests of other governments," advised the admiral. In short, he said, everything must be subordinated to the war effort. "Diplomacy, statesmanship, commercial and scientific endeavor—all must bring their full energy to support and reinforce the effort of the fighting forces in the manner that the supreme commanders of these forces indicate as most effective," Benson told Daniels.[6] Only by rallying the country behind the military could America defeat Germany.

Colonel House saw Wilson as the spokesman for democracy in "a world at arms, not against the German people, but against Prussian military oligarchy." The kaiser spoke for autocracy, and the war represented a battle for supremacy between those two systems of government. Secretary of War Baker also interpreted the war as a great challenge to democracy requiring the unity of the American people. "But what America is actually fighting for is not England and France," he stated; "we are fighting for what they are fighting, and that is, Liberty." Each day it became clearer to him that the war "bespeaks the unfathomable hostility between divergent philosophies of government; that it portrays the inevitable conflict between irresponsible and immoral government, and responsible and moral government." To meet the challenge, America needed to create a democratic army supported by all the people united in their struggle.[7]

The need for a cooperative effort defined the approach to the war. Daniels had introduced this idea to the navy almost as soon as he took over as secretary in 1913. "I had not long to wait," he later remembered, "before learning that the most serious defect in the Navy was the lack of democracy." By mixing enlisted men and officers, easing the way for enlisted men to move up the ranks, and turning every ship into a school where officers taught their men the rudiments of an education, Daniels fought tradition to establish a democratized navy. "But I had no liking for the chasm that separated the officers from the enlisted men, upon whose united efforts Naval efficiency depends," explained the secretary.[8] The war added further encouragement to his reforms.

The desire for a united effort extended into all areas of society. The War Industries Board, for example, coordinated the production and distribution of war materials. The board depended on "the patriotic cooperation of manufacturers, merchants, and the public." Its success resulted not from statutory authority, but from the "dynamic force from the spirit of cooperation it encouraged." Through a decentralized administration, the board fostered unity at the same time it preserved American individuality. By the simple procedure of establishing priorities for the war effort, the board avoided massive governmental regulations on the wartime distribution of materials. Instead, it encouraged individual producers and distributors to see themselves as part of a larger, more important effort to win the war.[9]

Yet, nothing symbolized the drive toward united cooperation during World War I better than the implementation of selective service. Based on the principle of universal liability for military service, the draft channeled the spirit of American cooperation into the war effort. Through local administration of the selection process, but central control from Washington of the entire system, the draft embodied democracy in action. The Wilson administration promoted it as the American answer to German militarism. "Militarism is a philosophy; it is the designation given to a selfish or ambitious political system which uses arms as a means of accomplishing its objects," Secretary of War Baker explained to the House Committee on Military Affairs. "The mobilization and arming of a democracy in defense of the principles on which it is founded, and in vindication of the common rights of man, is an entirely different thing."[10] Selective service required the citizenry to work or fight, depending on priorities set in Washington. Through its design and administration, the draft became the ultimate Progressive measure, for it marshaled all the American people to accomplish their greatest reform yet—the salvation of the world for democracy.

On February 4, 1917, Wilson visited Baker at the War Department to ask the secretary to formulate a plan for a draft. Baker turned to Judge Advocate General Enoch H. Crowder to carry out the task. Crowder, a wiry little man who had devoted his professional life to the administration of military justice, brought to the assignment a clear conception of the necessity of uniting the people. For him, the war was more than the mere clash of armies and countries; instead, he saw it as a "contest of ideals of government. It had become a struggle of democracy against autocracy; of international honor against international perfidy; of international justice against international tyranny; of altruism against avarice; of civilization against chaos." Working through the night of February 4, Crowder and his assistants drew up a selective service bill. The president submitted it to Congress within days of the declaration of war; it passed, with a few revisions, a month later.[11] During the intervening months, Crowder engineered the administrative machinery necessary for effecting the registration and selection of the citizenry to fight a war.

Ever conscious of the failure of the Civil War draft to overcome the animosity of the American people, who on occasion had erupted in violent protest against it, Crowder sought some method to administer selective service without relying on an obvious resort to the overwhelming power of the federal government. The army had run the draft during the Civil War even at the local level, which Crowder believed was a mistake since it represented blatant interference by the federal government in the private lives of the people. For the current draft, "the strong arm of the military must not be too apparent," wrote one of his assistants. Crowder needed to foster the cooperation of all the people and of local, state, and federal agencies. The nation could not afford internal opposition in its war against Germany. "The ultimate goal of America," he determined, "was to organize not only an army, but a nation for war." The quandary presented to him was to create a national force while avoiding the appearance of the national government and the military overtly disrupting the lives of ordinary citizens.[12]

At first unable to find a satisfactory method to resolve the contradiction, the administration settled on local post offices as registration centers. But a better solution came from an offhand question from a member of Congress. "Why cannot the registration be conducted in the voting-precincts throughout the country?" the congressman asked Crowder. "It was a simple inquiry born of a casual thought," Crowder later remembered, "but the thought was pregnant with the germ of a new idea of government." He soon realized that the administrative organization used for elections suited his purposes perfectly. Local precincts served as registration and selection points and were overseen by county agencies which, in turn, were supervised by state commissions controlled by each governor. The Provost Marshal General's Office in the War Department ran the entire system at the national level, setting quotas and issuing regulations. This scheme, Crowder envisioned,

> would put the administration of the draft into the hands of the friends and neighbors of the men to be affected; it would operate through familiar, well-known instrumentalities; it would be speedy; it would be easily controlled; it would be fair; and it would instantly invite the aid and cooperation of every local community throughout the land. Finally, it was the enunciation of the true democratic doctrine of local self-government, yet withal, a local administration the guiding star of which was a uniform national policy, nationally directed.

He came to call this organizational framework "supervised decentralization." It seemed to embody American ideals by integrating state and federal agencies in the common cause.[13]

By gambling on the spirit of cooperation pervading the country, Crowder avoided lowering the heavy hand of the federal government. "The adoption of the decentralized plan was the result of the conviction, which I think I alone entertained for a time, that it would succeed in a conspicuous way if the country supported the war; that, in common with all other plans, it would fail if the country was not behind the war," he explained later. He eased the burden of the draft by relying on precinct, county, and state organizations familiar to the American people. But the success he achieved as provost marshal general depended on "the coming into being for the first time of a national spirit." The response to selective service, Crowder later wrote, showed an "Americanism without selfishness. It is a pride of country plus a brotherhood of man."[14]

The selective service system "taught practical Democracy practically applied to a human problem." Local boards across the country offered the American people "a great school in Citizenship." In the proclamation promulgated by Wilson setting June 5, 1917, as the first registration day, the president urged the country to unite against Germany. "It is not an army that we must shape and train for war; it is a nation," read the proclamation. "To this end our people must draw close in one compact front against a common foe." Modern warfare went beyond the clash of armies; it now consisted of "entire nations armed." Each man had a part to play, whether on the fields of battle or in the fields for harvest. "All must pursue one purpose," Wilson announced, adding that "the whole nation must be a team in which each man shall play the part for which he is best fitted." Through the various classifications established by Washington, each man was expected either to work or fight, depending on which was more important to America at war.[15] Although women were not registered under selective service, their support of the war was sought and they were expected to show that support by maintaining the home front, helping the men, and other activities.

The appeal to nationalism, defined by Crowder as "Americanism plus brotherhood," helped make the draft more palatable to the people. The method of supervised decentralization was able to "popularize the unpopular" because it emphasized the role of the individual. Crowder encouraged the members of the local boards to become actively involved in the lives of the registrants so that they could ease the burdens imposed on the men. After the war, he explained his views to Miss Miriam Jones, a former member of a local board in New York who was worried that she had abused the franking privilege by writing personal letters to the registrants in her community. Crowder offered her reassurance:

> An important part of the work of the Local Boards was to compose the minds of registrants and their families; to adjust them to an unprecedented situation which the law created for them; to instill into the hearts of the registrants and their relatives an attitude of co-operation with Local Boards and the spirit of sacrifice which the military service entails; and to assist them with friendly counsel and words of advice

and encouragement in getting themselves placed in the military service. . . . Remember, we were keeping the great Human Ledger, and every entry therein was not in dollars and cents but in human beings. The Local Boards in the development of their work became the centres from which radiated the whole life of the war-time community. They became the consolers of the anxious wives and mothers, the preceptors of the doubting and the confessors of the weak in spirit. Their duties embraced the entrainment of quotas, the furnishing of the latest news from the theatre of war and even the arbitration of domestic disputes. They were sought out and solicited to participate in every phase of local life. It was necessary, if they were to be successful, that they win the confidence of the communities they served.[16]

By promoting a sense of community and participation in a great cause, the local boards enhanced the sense of unity among the people. All were expected to carry their share of the load.

The American people responded to the call to arms. On June 5, 1917, 9,586,508 men between the ages of twenty-one and thirty registered with their local boards. During the eighteen months of the war, the selective service system classified 24,234,021 men. Two million men served in France, and at war's end an additional two million were in training camps across the country.[17] This unprecedented accomplishment, achieved through an organization designed during the hectic weeks immediately before and after the declaration of war, sustained Wilson's faith in the unity of the nation. It strengthened his determination to see a similar spirit of cooperation effected on an international scale.

ESTABLISHING COOPERATION ABROAD

The thirty-five months between the declaration of war against Germany and the rejection of the Versailles peace treaty by the Senate witnessed not only Wilson's triumphant progression from national to international leader, but also his greatest defeat as president. He succeeded in uniting the people of the United States and the Allied nations in the prosecution of the war, yet he could not carry this consensus across the threshold of peace. When the Senate defiantly snatched defeat from the jaws of victory in early 1920 by rejecting the peace treaty, it proved the dependence of American foreign policy on the personality and good health of the tired, stricken president, whose natural stubbornness was exacerbated in October 1919 by a stroke. His refusal to compromise with the Senate represented the breakdown of his efforts to encourage cooperation and unity.

Wilson's ideals invigorated the world; his visionary rhetoric stirred the hearts of men everywhere with its promise of a better day. But eloquence alone was not enough to ensure the implementation of his plans after the war. By 1919 it could no longer feed the hungry nationalism at the Paris Peace Conference nor soothe the shy isolationism that resurged in the United States. The epic story of this tragedy, of the prophet scorned in his own land, has been told before. It is sufficient here to sketch the silhouette of the president's policies to show how the theme of international cooperation ran through his climb to the highest peak of power and his final free fall into the depths of rejection.

Both symbolically and practically, Wilson emphasized unity. During the war, sheep grazed on the White House lawn to underline the need for winter woolens. Practically, the sheep were fleeced every year; symbolically, the flock exemplified the need to stick together. When officers of the British and American navies debated how best to combat the submarine, Wilson came down heavily in favor of convoys. The choice was supported practically by the relative ease with which convoys could be protected from prowling German U-boats. Symbolically, the decision stressed the principle that only through international unity could the Allies achieve victory. The flock of sheep and the fleets of ships illustrated the administration's overriding desire to effect the closest cooperation at home and abroad.

Modern methods of warfare exacerbated the unprecedented need for cooperation among nations. This convinced Wilson that previous military tactics and strategies obtained no longer. He called the Great War one for amateurs, by which he meant that the armed forces would have to adapt to international cooperation and to modern weapons. The president continued to rely on his experts on force, but he encouraged them to shed the blinders of the past in order to develop novel approaches for the incorporation of new technologies. As he told the officers of the Atlantic Fleet on August 11, 1917,

> Now, the point that is constantly in my mind, gentlemen, is this: this is an unprecedented war and, therefore, it is a war in one sense for amateurs. Nobody ever before conductd a war like this and, therefore, nobody can pretend to be a professional in a war like this. . . . The experienced soldier—experienced in previous wars—is a back number so far as his experience is concerned; not so far as his intelligence is concerned. His experience does not count, because he never fought a war as this is being fought, and, therefore, he is an amateur along with the rest of us.

Disappointed with the way the professionals had thus far fought the war, Wilson pressed the British and American navies to adopt convoys and to attack the "hornet's nests," the ports used by the U-boats. Consequently, a combined British-American operation was conducted in 1918 to mine the submarine bases. The success of the "Northern Barrage" added further evidence to the importance of Allied unity.[18]

The desperate condition of the Allies in 1917, combined with the American military's lack of preparation for total war, made it easier for Wilson to impose his plan of cooperation on the war effort. Britain and France, teetering on the brink of bankruptcy, their manpower reserves nearly depleted, and their ally Russia racked by domestic strife, sought American help, but on their own terms. Their original plan was to use American men and material to beef up their own fighting forces, feeding U.S. troops piecemeal into their own ranks. But Wilson insisted on cooperation, not the absorption of his soldiers. By keeping his army independent of the Allies, yet working closely with them, the president was able to prove the practical utility of unity among equals.

The American military, lacking set notions of how to conduct the war, was receptive to the creation of intimate ties with the Allies. Indeed, the military seemed blissfully ignorant of the massive effort required for the defeat of Germany. The War College Division, for example, made few plans for fighting Germany and none for fighting a coalition war against Germany until early 1917. This lack of foresight is difficult to understand, except that Wilson opposed any planning for war during the period of neutrality. Military officers seemed to have shared the general belief that the United States could stay out of the war. Consequently, no one advocated planning for it. Many of these officers saw the preparedness movement as far more important, and that took up most of their time and intellectual effort. Yet, even preparedness worked against planning for war. Preparedness advocates argued that making the United States militarily strong would lessen the chance for war, since no nation would dare challenge a fully prepared and militarily strong America.

The plans drawn up in early 1917 bore little relevance to the true situation. They took no account of the necessity to establish an industrial base for the army, nor did they broach the issue of how to organize the whole of American society to fight the war. Crowder, for example, did not develop plans for the draft until Wilson suggested doing so in February 1917. As Grosvenor Clarkson, a member of the War Industries Board, pointed out, the unpreparedness of the military "resulted in the almost incredible circumstance that even six weeks before war was declared the army had not even hypothetical plans for the organization and equipment of a force of any size. Not only that, but it did not even have a formula for undertaking such a task." Clarkson complained that the General Staff "had made no study, and, as a body, had no comprehension, of the fact that in modern war the whole industrial activity of the Nation becomes the commissariat of the army."[19] All of this had to be envisioned and put into effect after the declaration of war.

The plans that the War College drew up indicated the army's reliance on Britain and France to continue carrying the brunt of the fighting until American recruits could be trained adequately. At the same time, the army feared the dispersion of its forces in minor attacks on the flanks of Germany's Imperial Army. Brigadier General J. E. Kuhn, head of the War College Division, reported to the chief of staff, General Hugh Scott, that the division was "unanimously of the opinion that the United States should engage in no operations abroad except in sufficient force to exert an appreciable influence upon the issue of the war." Kuhn estimated that this force "must not be less than 500,000 men," a remarkable underestimation of the situation. As late as 1917, Kuhn identified the most pressing problem confronting the United States as "one of training, equipping, and shipping to Europe as strong a force as is possible with the available shipping." There was time enough later, he added, to formulate a war strategy.[20] The startling feature of this estimate was not the accurate recognition of the need to train and equip an army, but the failure to understand the urgency of the problem and the scope of the effort. Trained in such relatively minor scrapes as the Spanish-American War, the conquest of the Philippines, and, more recently, the interventions in Mexico, Haiti, and Santo Domingo, the American armed forces were unprepared intellectually and by experience for a total, international war.

In order to avoid involvement in flank attacks, the military began giving high estimates of the men needed to fight the war. General Tasker Bliss, the assistant chief of staff, summarized the thinking of the military in late March 1917. Operations in Macedonia would require half a million men and ten months for preparations. An invasion of Holland would require a million men, fourteen months for preparations, and absolute secrecy to ensure a surprise attack. Consequently, Bliss wrote, "the War College Division is of the opinion that there must be no yielding to a popular demand to send small expeditions composed of one or two divisions of our regular army." Bliss and the War College considered that sending one million men to Europe would require training two million men from the beginning, since the American public would never allow the administration to leave "no trained force at home." They estimated that it would take a year to organize, train, and equip a force of this size, after which it would take another fourteen months to transport it to Europe. Thus, the army needed at least two years and two months "before there could be active participation by the United States in war on land." Even a force of five hundred thousand men would take two years from the initiation of training until they actively participated in the war.

The conclusions Bliss and the War College drew from these estimates revealed the military's dependence on international cooperation with the Allies, as well as its naiveté in assuming that Britain and France could continue to carry the burden of the war effort. Bliss outlined four conclusions based on various War College studies:

> 1. As soon as a rupture occurs a basis of cooperation between our Government and those of the Entente nations must be established;
> 2. Our action must be based upon a definite understanding between ourselves and the above powers engaged in seeking a common end;
> 3. In the beginning our cooperation must be solely naval and economic;
> 4. Ultimately it may include joint military operations in some theatre of war to be agreed upon between the United States and the other nations.
>
> A summing up of all . . . studies seems to be that the war must last practically two years longer before we can have other than naval and economic participation.[21]

Although these plans were not unreasonable, they were, as the army soon learned, unrealistic given the debilitated state of England, France, and Russia. Yet, the most important realization evident in these studies was the army's recognition of the necessity of working closely with the Entente powers. This was the Wilsonian way of war aimed at achieving the Wilsonian vision of peace.

American entry into the war corresponded with the accelerating decline in the military fortunes of the Entente powers. France suffered a disastrous setback with the failure of the Neville offensive, which cost 120,000 casualties and resulted in a series of mutinies throughout the army. In early May an Allied mission, headed by Britain's Arthur Balfour and France's Marshal Joffre, arrived in Washington for discussions with Wilson and the War Department. Their review of the desperate situation frightened American officials, but it also convinced them of the need to speed up America's contribution of men and materials. In summing up his meetings with the Allied mission, Bliss told Baker that "as the foreign gentlemen spoke more and more freely it became evident that what they want and need is men, whether trained or not." Although both Wilson and the War Department resisted the suggestion to incorporate American men into British and French units, Wilson did promise to send a small force—about twelve thousand men—immediately in order to stimulate morale on both sides of the ocean.[22]

To command this initial force, Wilson and Baker chose General John J. Pershing, lately returned from Mexico, as head of the American Expeditionary Force. Pershing's orders, written by Bliss for Baker, gave him almost complete control over the tactical operation of America's participation, with the proviso that U.S. forces retain their independence of Britain and France. "In military operations against the Imperial German Government," Baker instructed, "you are directed to cooperate with the forces of the other countries employed against the enemy; but in so doing the underlying idea must be kept in view that the forces of the United States are a separate and distinct component of the combined forces, the identity of which must be preserved."[23] These orders conveyed the central theme of Wilson's policies toward the war. The United States would cooperate with Britain and France as an equal, not as a subordinate.

Unity and cooperation, then, became the method of the American war effort. But the desperate condition of the Allies also convinced American officials that the survival of democracy depended on the United States. Baker, for example, wrote in a magazine article that "I shall not attempt to describe the size of our American duty beyond saying that the human race is a waif left to die unless we, as trustees, accept the task of rescuing it." At the end of May 1917, the secretary advised Wilson to forgo the long period of training for American troops earlier recommended by the General Staff. "I think it essential," he wrote, "to keep the country of the spirit which made it necessary for us to go into this war. That spirit, I think to be a compound of two motives; first, the determination expressed by you to make the world safe for democracy, and second, the desire to bring the war to the earliest possible conclusion." A long period of training exposed the administration to three criticisms. First, "it would be said that our part in the war was too slow." Second, the administration could be accused of taking the chance that France and Russia might collapse, which would increase "the size of our own task later." Finally, "it would be said that the immediate and overwhelming aggregation of forces, including our own, is the way most speedily to terminate the war, and not to feed nations to the German machine in detail." Baker sympathized with this last view, adding that the administration could trust its military officers not to expose inexperienced troops to too much danger until they were ready.[24]

Other members of Wilson's inner circle also saw the war as a united effort in which the United States must play an important role. "This is a combination of the Democracies of the world against feudalism and autocracy," Secretary of the Interior Franklin K. Lane told his brother.[25] Lansing explained the meaning of the war in similar terms:

> The United States has entered the great world war because it could no longer doubt the evil character of the autocratic Government of Germany and its vast ambition for world empire threatened the national safety and peace of this country. It is the final struggle between autocracy and democracy, between tyranny and liberty. There can be but one outcome. Those who rest their cause on right and justice must triumph over those who are seeking by force to impose their will upon the nations. The overthrowing of the malignant forces which menace humanity will bring the dawn of universal peace.[26]

The interpretation of the war as an ideological struggle between democracy and autocracy underlined the view that the United States was not alone in the struggle, indeed, that the struggle itself went beyond national boundaries because it represented a battle of ideas and forms of government. The Allies embodied Democracy in action; the Germans epitomized the evil nature of Militarism and Tyranny. Thus, for the United States at least, the war became a great battle of ideals that united nations of similar faiths.

Not surprisingly, Wilson himself gave the clearest expression to this interpretation of the war. He understood it as more than reprisal against Germany for its unrestricted submarine warfare. It was also more than a reaction against German aggression and territorial aggrandizement. Rather, the war entered a philosophical plane to become a great ideological battle that would determine the future character of the world and its people. "We have at the end of a long and patient experience discovered that the world cannot be rescued from slaughter and destruction by any other process than a major exercise of the great martial force of this Republic," Wilson explained to a gathering of college presidents in early May 1917, "but we ought never to lose sight of the fact that the purpose of this war is not aggression, is not punishment; it is not inspired by resentment nor fed by ambition, but it is loyalty to an ideal, and that ideal is freeing the world from an impossible international philosophy, a philosophy in which, if it should prevail, no freedom is left or is safe."[27] These statements went beyond propaganda, though they served that purpose as well. They went beyond self-delusion and an effort to convince everyone that the war was somehow more noble than suffering in muddy trenches, bloodshed, and death. They showed that the Wilson administration accepted force as *idea*. Victory would prove the worth of a system of government; the defeat of

Germany would illustrate the strength of democracy over autocracy, of liberty over militarism.

Wilson used armed power in World War I to advance a concept of government against its opposite philosophy. He refused to join the alliance of Britain, France, Russia, Italy, and Japan, preferring, instead, to associate American power with the power of other democracies. This stance allowed him to abjure the nationalistic aspirations for territory expressed in the several secret treaties and agreements among the Allies while, at the same time, he embraced the political hope of saving the world for democracy by conquering autocracy. While one may chide Wilson and his advisers for their innocence and naiveté, the fact stands out starkly that they understood the war as force applied for a distinct purpose: to save an ideal and to promote a concept of self-determination known as democracy.

During the war, the Wilson administration purposefully avoided discussions with the Allies concerning postwar territorial arrangements. "I hope you will agree with me that the best policy now is to avoid a discussion of peace settlements," House advised the president in late April 1917, explaining that "if the Allies begin to discuss terms among themselves, they will soon hate one another worse than they do Germany." House believed that "the only thing to be considered at present is how to beat Germany in the quickest way." Wilson agreed completely. "Our people and Congress will not fight for any selfish aim on the part of any belligerent," he told House months later. In the spring of 1917, Wilson learned of the various secret treaties between Britain, France, Italy, and Japan that specified territorial divisions at the successful termination of the war. Italy, for example, was promised Fiume, while Japan for its part in the war was assured the Shantung peninsula and other German possessions in the Pacific. Wilson chose to take no official position on the treaties because he did not want to risk breaking up the coalition during the war by challenging their terms. Instead, he postponed any territorial discussions until war's end, leaving to the peace conference the settlement of boundaries and national claims. During 1917, then, the president confined his statements about the postwar world to his conception of the purpose of the fight, that is, to the philosophical and political, rather than territorial, aspects of the peace. "We are fighting for Freedom," he said in December 1917, "not to obtain it for a favored few or for a group of nations. It must embrace mankind; it is for all."[28]

The Bolshevik Revolution in November 1917 increased the importance of the philosophical and political aspects of the war. Bolshevism competed directly with Wilson's efforts to offer the world a new system of international relations and threatened his liberalism with radicalism. While Wilson promoted the unity of nations derived from a community of interests and common philosophies of government, the Bolsheviks spoke of the unity of the workers based on class, not national interests. With their publication of the secret treaties and agreements between the Allies, they offered evidence of the degenerate nature of the capitalist war.

In response to the Bolshevik criticisms, Wilson spelled out the philosophical, territorial, and political goals of the war in the Fourteen Points speech, which he delivered to Congress on January 8, 1918. The philosophical points covered such issues as open diplomacy, freedom of the seas, freedom of trade, disarmament, and self-determination, which was implicit in his proposed territorial settlements. The territorial points promised hope for colonial peoples to have an equal say in their own affairs; self-determination for all of Russia, including those areas presently occupied by Germany; the restoration of Belgium; the return to France of Alsace-Lorraine and other occupied areas; changes in Italy's borders to reflect more accurately the nationalities of the people; the autonomous development of the people of Austria-Hungary; restoration and independence for Rumania, Serbia, and Montenegro; sovereignty for Turkey; and independence for Poland. The political point proposed an association of nations to protect the peace and the territorial integrity of all nations through international cooperation. These war aims responded to the Bolshevik competition at the same time that they pressured the Allies to liberalize their own goals.[29]

Throughout the remainder of the war, Wilson continued to emphasize its philosophical and political aspects over its territorial disputes. At various times during 1918, Wilson added additional points to the original fourteen. On February 11, in another address to a joint session of Congress, he outlined four principles upon which peace must be negotiated. These specified that the settlement of all issues must be guided by justice; peoples should not be bought or traded to affect any balance of power, an international system now discredited before the world; territorial settlements were to be made solely for the good of the peoples who lived in the areas; and well-defined national aspirations were to be fulfilled if possible.

On July 4 the president added another four points. He called for the destruction of any arbitrary power with the potential for disturbing the peace, a reference to the German military establishment. In addition, territorial and other settlements were to be freely accepted by the peoples most directly affected, and all nations were to agree to abide by principles of honor and law in their international relations. Wilson also called for the creation of a peace organization to assure that "the combined power of free nations will check every invasion of right and serve to make peace and justice . . . secure."

Finally, on September 27, 1918, Wilson added a last five points to his list of twenty-two. These required, first, that the peace be based on equal justice to all peoples. Second, special interests were to be prohibited from overwhelming the common interest. Third, special understandings or agreements were to be barred between members of the League of Nations. Fourth, selfish economic combinations and any type of economic coercion were to be banned within the league, unless in accordance with a league request to prevent aggression. Fifth, all international agreements were to be publicized to the world.[30] These twenty-seven points, though some were redundant, clearly outlined Wilson's ambitious peace program.

At the center of Wilson's plan stood the proposed League of Nations, which would see that all other points would be implemented and protected. Wilson hoped to prepare the American people and the people of other countries to come together in such an organization. "In other words, the United States, as spokesman of the allied world, voices the principle that the Democratic form of government is worth spending the lives of millions of men and billions of treasure to preserve," he said on February 22, 1918. "This is our reason for being today in arms. It has been agreed to by our allies as an all-sufficient reason for them as well." In this battle, America had a special role to play. As Wilson asked one correspondent, "Please tell the people for me that this seems to me to be a war in which the American people are privileged to play a singular and noble part because they have no selfish ends to serve and are fighting for the principles and ideals which have always lain at the very foundation of our own nation's life. We are trying to extend to the world the gift of liberty and conscience and disinterested service of mankind."[31] Through the enunciation of his vision of the postwar world, Wilson tried to lay the groundwork for peace. Democracy and unity were the themes, cooperation was the key. By pointing to a community of interests and ideals, he hoped to persuade the world to follow his lead. Wilson's approach to the conduct of the war also reflected his desire to create a firm foundation upon which to build his cherished league of nations. The establishment of a unified command over the Allied armies and the decision to intervene in Russia clearly showed the strength of Wilson's desire to effect cooperation among the democracies involved in the war.

From the beginning, American participation in the war revolved around the key policy of cooperation with the Allies. Cooperation, however, did not mean blind acceptance of the goals of the Entente powers, which Wilson knew were not in line with his ideas. On September 2, 1917, the president asked House to begin studying "just what the several parties to this war on our side of it will be inclined to insist upon as part of the final peace arrangements." The United States could then determine its own position "whether for or against them and begin to gather the influences we wish to employ—or at least ascertain what influences we can use: in brief, prepare our case with a full knowledge of the position of all the litigants." In response, House began setting up the Inquiry under his brother-in-law Sidney Mezes to prepare for the peace conference.[32] Wilson intended to cooperate with the Allies in the defeat of Germany, but this did not mean that he accepted their political and territorial ambitions. Once Germany was defeated, he fully intended to use his power to negotiate a peace in line with his own vision, not that of the Allies.

Pershing sailed to Europe at the end of May 1917 aboard the British steamship *Baltic*. His original mission was to survey the situation on the western front in order to develop recommendations for American participation. Shortly after setting sail, however, Pershing determined to ask the War Department for an army of one million men. Upon his arrival at Liverpool on Sunday, June 10, he told an assemblage of British and American reporters, "Speaking for myself personally, the officers of my staff, and the members of my command, we are very glad indeed to be the standard bearers of our country in this great war for civilization. . . . We expect in course of time to be playing our part, and we hope it will be a very large part, on the Western Front." Within a month, he cabled the War Department that "plans should contemplate sending over at least 1,000,000 men by next May." Further, he recommended that the department consult with the Allies in order to arrange for the transportation of these troops. Pershing added that his advice should not be construed as the absolute total necessary to win the war. Rather, plans should provide for the doubling in size of this army.[33]

Wilson hardly expected that the commitment to save democracy would require such large numbers of American men. Yet, he accepted Pershing's recommendations with little question, and the War Department geared up to induct new soldiers into the service. At the same time, the administration settled on the strategy of concentrating its effort on the western front, rather than attacking the Germans through Russia or across Turkey. The reasons for this, in retrospect, are obvious. The shorter lines of communication across the Atlantic to France, combined with the desperate condition of the British and

French armies, demanded an American presence there. It was the easiest and shortest route to fight Germany.

At the time, however, various people seriously questioned where best to apply American strength. In response to a letter from Senator George Chamberlain, the chairman of the Committee on Military Affairs, the War College explained its reasons for selecting the western front. "In this war success for us and our Allies depends upon: first, an agreement among all as to what operations shall be conducted, and thorough cooperation among all in carrying out the details of these operations." Sound military doctrine dictated that the United States commit its troops in France. As the War College explained:

> The distance to France being so much less than to Russia, the difficulties of transportation and supply are much more easily overcome. We can strike more quickly and with greater force and security there than in Russia or any other proposed theater. The necessity for men to aid France is much greater, too, than in Russia where there are plenty of men, or on other fronts where the pressure has not been so great as in France. We are carrying out the request of our Allies, particularly England and France, that our military aid on land should go to France. . . . It is vitally essential that we devote all our efforts at this time to putting into France a trained army that will aid her armies in the actual fighting as well as prevent discouragement among her civil population.

Even had they understood the impending breakdown in Russia's fighting ability, it is doubtful that members of the General Staff would have changed their minds about sending American troops to France. Baker endorsed this view to Wilson, who also approved it.[34] Having settled on the overall strategy, the task then became to implement it in the quickest and most efficient manner. In the president's view, this efficiency depended on the utmost cooperation with the Allies. His next step was to ensure a unified effort with Britain and France. Consequently, he moved to establish a united command over all the armies fighting Germany on the western front.

In the fall of 1917, Wilson sent Colonel House and General Bliss to Europe for consultations with the Allies. Shortly after their arrival, they submitted a joint memorandum to the president in which they urged the creation of an Allied council to determine joint military operations. Although both believed that unity of command would be a better solution, they did not think the Allies were quite ready to accept it. Bliss, in particular, worked assiduously toward appointing a single commander-in-chief during his service in Europe, but he felt obliged to move slowly so as not to risk a controversy that might tear the coalition apart. Both he and House clearly hoped that a joint Allied committee would lead to unity of command. Wilson heartily approved the idea. "Please take the position that we not only accede to the plan for a single war council but insist on it," he instructed House. As discussions at Rapallo, Italy, continued, the president grew impatient. In a note to himself, he wrote under the heading "Immediate Business" the message: "To House: Take the whip hand. We not only accede to the plan for a unified conduct of the war but insist upon it. It is not practicable for us to be represented *in the same way* as the other governments on the civil side, but we will be on the military." The last sentence was in keeping with Wilson's consistent efforts to avoid involvement in settling territorial issues during the war, a policy in which House concurred and which he obeyed.[35]

On November 27 the Allies agreed to the establishment of a Supreme War Council, composed of the prime ministers of each nation, except the United States, and military representatives from each country. The council assumed responsibility for setting the general direction of the war effort and for determining the best allocation of resources. Each nation, however, retained independence in deciding how and when it would fight Germany. Although it fell far short of a unified military command, the Supreme War Council was a move in that direction.

Bliss, the American representative on the military committee, continued to urge the creation of a single command to direct the war effort. In mid-December he wrote Wilson that "national jealousies and suspicions and susceptibilities of national temperament must be put aside in favor of this unified control; even going if necessary (as I believe it is) to the limit of unified command." The collapse of Russia, a process which became apparent in late November, allowed Germany to concentrate on the western front. This made a united command all the more imperative.[36]

Instead, the Allied and Associated nations wasted a considerable amount of time and effort arguing about the amalgamation of American soldiers into British and French armies. The Allies wanted U.S. troops fed piece by piece into their forces because it would bring Americans into the war faster. Desperate for relief after four years of bloody fighting, Britain and France did not want to wait for the United States to establish and train its own independent fighting force. Throughout early 1918 they pressed American representatives and the Wilson administration to accept amalgamation.

Some Americans, notably Admiral William Sims and Bliss, favored amalgamation because of their concern over the depleted strength of the Allies. But Pershing, whose original orders from Baker expressly commanded him to retain independence, opposed the concept. His opposition was based on national pride, the desire for military glory, and a disapproval of Allied inefficiency. In addition, he believed the United States would have more influence at the peace conference if it fought the war in cooperation with, but independent of, the Entente powers. Wilson found Pershing's reasoning more persuasive than that of Bliss and Sims. Consequently, the American Expeditionary Force retained its own identity, fighting alongside British and French armies in its own sector of the western front.[37]

The controversy over amalgamation diverted the Supreme War Council's attention from the issue of unity of command. Little was done about that until Germany launched its last, great offensive at the end of March 1918. This threat helped stifle nationalistic objections to a single command structure. Consequently, on April 14 General Ferdinand Foch was appointed commander of the Allied armies. By putting the tactical direction of the war under unified control, the Allies were better able to thwart Germany's offensive. At about this time, the United States began flooding France with ever-increasing numbers of troops. This levy of fresh forces quickly turned the tide of war against Germany.

The U.S. Navy, even more than the army, looked forward to a unified effort with the British. When Daniels dispatched Admiral Sims to England in February 1917, he instructed the admiral that American policy depended on "hearty cooperation" with England and France. "I have assumed that our mission was to promote the maximum cooperation with the allies in defeating a common enemy," Sims informed the secretary in July. To this end, he viewed the U.S. fleet as but part of an Allied-British fleet, which, he urged, required the creation of a single command. Indeed, Sims showed so much enthusiasm for cooperation with the British admiralty that Wilson and Daniels chided him for viewing British opinion on strategy as "sacrosanct." But this showed only that the administration was determined to be an equal partner, not a junior to the Royal Navy.[38]

The establishment of convoys to guard ships against submarine attacks as they brought supplies and men from the United States to battlefields in Europe exemplified British-American cooperation. The Northern Barrage, too, proved how comfortably the two navies worked together. Although incomplete at the time of the armistice in November 1918, the Northern Barrage resulted in the laying of 70,263 mines in the North Sea. Of these, 56,611 were American mines laid by the United States Mining Squadron.[39] Working together, the British and American navies established effective control over the sea-lanes between the western front and the United States. During the war, not a single troop ship was lost to submarines.

Following the lead of the Allied and Associated armies, the navies established an Allied Naval Council, which the United States joined on January 8, 1918. As David Trask, who has written the best history of the council, has pointed out, "Although the Allied Naval Council by no means accomplished all that was expected of it, it was a useful institution through which the Allied and Associated Powers arranged those overall naval plans on which they were able to agree. It also helped to clarify the circumstances that precluded effective cooperation on other matters."[40] The council helped establish overall strategy for the naval war against Germany and its allies. In addition, it set priorities on the use of equipment and supplies and provided a vehicle through which the cooperating nations could be kept informed of each other's activities.

In only the activities in the Mediterranean Sea were the members unable to achieve any cooperation, but even in this failure the American desire to create unity of effort with Britain, France, and Italy is shown clearly. Prior to American entrance in the war, the Allies were unable to agree on either policy or strategy in the Mediterranean. Franco-Italian rivalry in the area was the major obstacle, but Anglo-Italian and Anglo-French suspicions also played an important role in precluding effective action. As Trask has shown, the British were interested in protecting their imperial obligations, particularly their communications with Asia. Italy and France were desirous of advancing their interests and power in the Mediterranean at the expense of Germany and of each other. Thus, Trask concluded, "a common interest and a common danger were not sufficient to overwhelm significant conflicts of interest." Unfortunately, the Mediterranean was a vital area of operations during the war. It served as the communication link for Great Britain, France, and Italy with their colonies and territories. In addition, the Mediterranean provided the supply line to Allied armies in Palestine, Mesopotamia, and Macedonia.[41]

Throughout the war, effective action against Germany and Austria was blocked in the Mediterranean by Allied suspicions of each other. Only the United States had no real interests to protect in the area. During the first half of 1918, Sims looked about for some way that the American Navy could take offensive action against the enemy. The Mediterranean struck him as an ideal location. Nothing was being done there because of Allied rivalries, yet he did not think that the Allies would suspect American motives. In effect, he tried to play the role of "honest broker" in formulating some action against the enemy in the Mediterranean. In January 1918 Sims's command developed a plan to attack Austria through the Adriatic Sea. The plan detailed a raid on the Austrian base at Cattaro in present-day Yugoslavia. The Americans wanted to mine the line of communications with Pola in combination with air raids and a land attack. The plan divided the responsibilities for this mission between Italy and the United States. After obtaining approval from Washington, Sims submitted the plan to the Allied Naval Council, and he immediately felt the heat of Allied suspicions and distrust of each other. Britain supported the American plan, but the representatives of France and Italy began picking it apart. They criticized the tactics outlined, the estimated number of men requested, and other details. By focusing on the minutae of the plan, both nations avoided an outright rejection of Sims's idea. Instead, they stalled approval of the plan through several meetings of the council. Finally, in June 1918 Sims dropped his efforts to gain their approval.[42]

Despite the final outcome of the proposal, Sims's effort to get it approved underlined the general American approach to establishing cooperation with its associates. Seeking some offensive operation in which the American Navy could participate, Sims was attracted to the Mediterranean precisely because the United States had no substantial interests to protect or advance there. At the same time, its importance to the war effort made it a vital area of operation. Sims hoped that the Allies would go along with the plan because they could trust the United States. Cooperation with Italy would be in line with the overall approach to the war. At the same time, the United States, as honest broker, would protect British and French interests from Italian ambitions. Unfortunately, the purity of his motives could not overcome the deep-bred suspicions that the Mediterranean generated in the French and Italians.

The failure to take the offensive in the Mediterranean ultimately proved to have little bearing on the outcome of the war. The German spring offensive in 1918 was a last gasp, a desperate gamble to overwhelm the Entente powers before the full strength of the United States could be brought into play. But the gamble was taken too late. By the spring of 1918 American mobilization was gathering momentum. Men and material streamed across the Atlantic in ever-increasing quantities. In July the one-millionth American soldier stepped onto French soil. The fortunes of war shifted against Germany and its allies while the fresh transfusions of power from the United States reinvigorated the Allies. Acting independently, but in close cooperation with French and British armies, the American Expeditionary Force helped halt the

German advance at Belleau Wood and the Second Battle of the Marne in June.

That summer the Allied and Associated nations launched their own offensive. Under French command, the Somme offensive began on August 8. This attack was followed by the Oise-Aisne offensive, also spearheaded by the French, on August 18, and the Ypres-Lys offensive, under the British, the next day. In each of these operations, American soldiers fought beside French and British troops. By mid-September Pershing was ready to lead American forces in their own offensive. He began by cutting off German troops at the St. Mihiel Salient, followed by the Meuse-Argonne offensive on September 26. By war's end, American battle casualties totaled 48,909 dead and 230,074 wounded.

And the Germans were defeated. In early October, General Eric von Ludendorff, second in command of the German army, pressed the new German government, headed by Prince Max of Baden, to sue Wilson for an armistice. Working through the Swiss, the new government asked Wilson for "the immediate conclusion of a general armistice." The president, in an unnecessary and potentially damaging aberration from his general policy of cooperation with the Entente powers, acted alone in negotiating the terms of the armistice. He wanted no interference in arranging the peace based on the Fourteen Points and the other principles he had defined. Claiming that the German request was yet too vague, Wilson refused to invite the Allies into the discussions. They would be invited, he determined, after he had obtained German agreement to his vision of the peace.

On October 8 Wilson posed three questions to the new German government. He asked, first, if Germany was willing to base the peace talks on the Fourteen Points and related principles. Second, he inquired if Germany would withdraw its armies from all invaded territories. Third, Wilson wanted assurances that the new government spoke for the German people, not for the militarists who had conducted the war. The Germans capitulated. Their answers to each question gave Wilson hope that the war could soon be concluded.

In a second note, Wilson demanded "absolutely satisfactory safeguards and guarantees of the maintenance of the present military supremacy of the Allies." The Germans agreed to withdraw their armies back into German borders. In a third note, Wilson reiterated that the Allied and Associated powers must have military supremacy. He added that he was ready to turn the correspondence over to the Allied governments for their approval and for the preparation of armistice agreements.[43]

Wilson expected the Allies to accept these terms. The military representatives to the Supreme War Council set to work drafting the military aspects of the ceasefire to assure Allied military supremacy. Meanwhile, Colonel House began convincing the governments to accept the political terms. The Allies balked. From October 29 to November 4 House threatened and cajoled the various prime ministers to gain their approval of Wilson's vision of the peace. To their threats that they would repudiate the Fourteen Points in favor of harsher terms against the enemy, House announced Wilson's readiness to sign a separate peace. This tactic undermined Allied objections and the Allies agreed to an armistice based on Wilsonian principles, but with two exceptions. The British absolutely refused to agree to freedom of the seas as defined by Wilson. The French demanded that Germany pay for the civilian damages resulting from the war. Unable to overcome these reservations, Wilson gave in. On November 11 the Armistice with Germany went into effect and the western front was quieted.[44]

The Armistice specified that Allied and Associated forces would occupy certain portions of Germany, primarily the Rhineland. In November Pershing established the Third Army, consisting of the First, Second, Third, Fourth, and Fifth Divisions, the Thirty-second and Forty-second National Guard Divisions, and the Eighty-ninth and Ninetieth National Army Divisions, as the American component of the occupation. Selection to the occupation army was touted as a reward to the hardest fighting units, but it also guaranteed that the occupiers would have little sympathy for the Germans.[45] At the time, Wilson probably did not intend the occupation to last beyond the signing of the peace treaty. However, French fears of a resurgent Germany forced him to change his plans.

At Paris in 1919 Wilson agreed to a lengthy occupation of Germany as part of a bilateral security pact with France. The area around Cologne was to be occupied for five years, Colbeny was to be occupied for ten years, and Manence was to be occupied for fifteen years, provided that Germany faithfully executed the terms of the peace treaty. Eventually, the size of the Third Army was reduced to seventy-five hundred men. As Wilson had done with the American Expeditionary Force during the war, he insisted that the Third Army be separate from the Interallied Rhineland High Commission. Although the two cooperated in setting occupation policies, American forces retained their unique identity.[46]

Once he agreed to the lengthy occupation, Wilson justified it in several ways. He saw it as a way to preserve German national unity against French efforts to divide it into several small countries. Participation of American forces would also moderate the harshness of the occupation. In addition, the occupation would help ease French fears of

Germany, and, finally, it would assure that Germany lived up to its obligations under the treaty. Thus, American forces remained in Germany throughout the remainder of Wilson's presidency. After the Senate rejected the peace treaty, the troops were kept there as a possible diplomatic lever in negotiating a separate peace. At no time did either Wilson or his successor, Warren Harding, request congressional approval of the occupation, despite grumblings from Congress. Not until 1923 did Harding withdraw the Third Army after passage of a Senate resolution criticizing the occupation.[47]

The withdrawal of the occupation forces brought to an end the American military involvement in Europe begun with the declaration of war against Germany in April 1917. Throughout the war, Wilson consistently sought to cooperate with the Allied nations in defeating Germany. He hoped that this cooperation would provide a solid foundation upon which to erect a new international system based on collective security. Only in areas where he feared the Allies would diverge too much from his own vision of the peace, as in political discussions in the Supreme War Council or the early negotiations over the Armistice, did Wilson shy from cooperation. Clearly, however, the theme of cooperation permeated his approach to the war, at home and abroad. Selective service, naval strategy, the establishment of the Supreme War Council, and the appointment of a supreme commander evidenced Wilson's overriding desire to effect a cooperative approach to the war that would lead to international cooperation during the subsequent peace. Wilson's last two interventions, the expeditions to Siberia and northern Russia, show how cooperation evolved into collective security.

6.
THE POWER of COLLECTIVE SECURITY:
Russia

In response to the social, political, and economic changes incurred by industrialization, the American people stepped beyond mere democratic cooperation to organize themselves into varied collectives devoted to particular causes. The Progressive Era was an age of organization, a joiner's paradise during which special interest groups sprouted in the fertile soil of reform. It was a time for combining, for choosing a cause, enlisting in a group, and working toward common goals. Reform groups ranged from the petty to the sublime, from advocates for simplified spelling to women demanding the franchise. The Woman's Christian Temperance Union persuaded the nation to try prohibition of alcohol, a goal sought by various groups since the founding of the Republic, but which was achieved only through the Progressives' spirit of reform and experimentation. Populists collected farmers and workers together to protect their common interests. Labor unions came into their own during the period; union membership tripled between 1896 and 1910. The American Federation of Labor, for example, was founded in 1886 with an initial roster of 150,000 members. By 1914 it claimed a membership of 2,020,671. The common thread linking all the reform movements during the Progressive Era, no matter what the cause, was the reliance on collective action, which gave expression to the belief in democratic cooperation.

Even Progressivism's enemies—big business and political bosses—found collective action a convenient method. Businessmen, whether the lucky or the ruthless, responded to industrialization with attempts to stamp out competition by forming trusts, monopolies, and holding companies. Andrew Carnegie in the steel industry and John D. Rockefeller in oil typified the move toward gaining control of the market and keeping control through tight organization and combination. Political machines ruled cities and states by collecting supporters, ensuring their loyalty through favors, and getting out the vote for the chosen candidates and issues. For reformers and businesses, radicals and bosses, collective action promised collective security.

Woodrow Wilson understood the power of collective action. "Men as communities are supreme over men as individuals," he proclaimed in 1887. Throughout his life, he praised the tendency of Americans to join together to achieve their goals. His analyses of this spirit of community concentrated on the role played by leaders, for in Wilson's view, groups could do little unless they had effective leadership. The leader emerged from the collective through his ability to express the community's goals and spirit. "The only way in which we can preserve our nationality in its integrity and its old-time originative force in the face of growth and imported change," he warned, "is by *concentrating* it, by putting leaders forward vested with abundant authority in the conception and execution of policy." The emphasis on concentration and leadership was fundamental to Wilson's political thought. After writing the speech "Leaders of Men," he noted in his journal that "institutions have their rootage in the common thought and only those who share the common thought can rightly interpret them."[1] Later in his career, when he was first a national and then a world leader, Wilson believed that he best understood the common aspirations of his followers, whether at home or abroad. By the end of World War I, he sensed a worldwide movement toward organized internationalism. He tried to give form to this movement in the League of Nations.

Wilson applied his view of community and collective action to international affairs. As early as June 1887, he was sensing a "tendency . . . as yet dim, but . . . clearly destined to prevail, towards, first, the confederation of parts of empires like the British, and finally of great states themselves. Instead of centralization of power, there is to be wide union with tolerated visions of prerogative. This is a tendency towards the American type—of governments joined with governments for the pursuit of common purposes, in honorary equality and honorable subordination." Leadership of this new collection of states, Wilson hoped, would be assumed by the United States. In a survey of the contemporary scene in September 1901, Wilson recognized the potential for greatness for the country. "A nation hitherto wholly devoted to domestic development now finds its first task roughly finished and turns about to look curiously into the tasks of the great world at large, seeking its special part and place of power," he wrote. He added that "a new age has come which no man may forecast. But the past is the key to it; and the past of America lies at the centre of modern history."² America's central position became most important during World War I. At that time, Wilson hastened to exploit America's leading position by guiding the modern world into an association of all democratic nations wherein each would find security in the protection of all. The problem confronting him was how to get from the ideal to the real, from the vision of countries united to an actual collective organization.

During the war, the United States cooperated with the Entente powers to defeat Germany and its allies. Looking beyond the conclusion of hostilities, Wilson envisioned a new international system based on unity and collective security. He realized that he could not depend on Allied cooperation to transform this vision into actuality. The publication by the Bolsheviks of the secret treaties undergirding the Entente alliance merely confirmed Wilson's suspicions that America's goals radically differed from those of its associates. For this reason, he chose to remain outside the alliance as an associate in the coalition, a distinction that allowed cooperation to defeat Germany but freedom in designing the postwar international system.

Wilson hoped that the spirit of cooperation fostered during the war would carry over into the peace, but, if necessary, he was prepared to apply America's diplomatic, moral, and financial power to compel acceptance of his ideas. As he wrote House during the war: "England and France have not the same views with regard to peace that we have by any means. When the war is over we can force them to our way of thinking, because by that time they will, among other things, be financially in our hands; but we cannot force them now, and any attempt to speak for them . . . would bring on disagreements, which would inevitably come to the surface in public."³ Wilson clearly distinguished in his own mind the goal of defeating Germany from the goal of defining the postwar world. To achieve the first, he eagerly cooperated with the Allies. To realize the second, however, he prepared the United States to stand alone. Although Wilson was ready to challenge the aims of the Entente powers after the war, he preferred—as his policies revealed—to transform the war-time spirit of cooperation into a peace-time enlistment in collective action.

COLLECTIVE ACTION BEFORE WORLD WAR I

The breakdown of the balance of power system in August 1914 created a political vacuum in international affairs that Wilson determined to fill. In late 1914, he advised his brother-in-law, Stockton Axson, that "there must be an association of nations, all bound together for the protecton of the integrity of each, so that any one nation breaking from this bond will bring upon herself war; that is to say, punishment, automatically."[4] While the war continued, Wilson defined his originally inchoate proposal for an association of nations. During the period of American neutrality, he balanced defense of international law and American rights against the desire to mediate an end to hostilities, which would give the United States an entry into any peace conference. As a consequence, it was sure to have a hand in the design of the new international structure.

Toward the end of 1914, Colonel House proposed a Pan American pact to unite the nations of the Western Hemisphere for their collective protection. Wilson saw it as a precursor of the postwar international system. As House explained, the advantage of a Pan American organization was that it would "serve as a model for the European nations when peace is at last brought about." The prospect excited Wilson and he quickly commissioned House to open discussions with the three leading South American nations, Argentina, Brazil, and Chile. Such a pact, Wilson also understood, would help in dealing with such problems as the Mexican Revolution because it would bind republican governments together in common defense against the anarchy and chaos of social upheavals.[5]

During the course of the lengthy discussions over the Pan American pact, Wilson drew up the criteria he wanted incorporated in the hemispheric arrangement. He sought to bind the signatories to a "common and mutual" guarantee of territorial integrity, an assurance of political independence for member states, a requirement that members have republican forms of government, an agreement to arbitrate disputes, an acceptance of arms control, and a promise by all members to refuse assistance to "enemies of any signatory government." Each of these criteria was resurrected in the Covenant of the League of Nations four years later. During 1915 the governments of Argentina, Brazil, and Chile accepted these terms in principle, but neither House nor Wilson was ever able to get them to move from principle to practice. In large measure, Wilson's interventionary policies in Mexico doused whatever enthusiasm the three powers had for the proposal. House's numerous discussions with the representatives of each government never got beyond the talking stage. No agreement for a pact was signed during Wilson's tenure.[6]

Nevertheless, as Sidney Bell has pointed out, Wilson's efforts to form a Pan American pact indicated a move to "establish a pattern of cooperation."[7] Similarly, the de facto recognition of Carranza in October 1915 was preceded by extensive consultations with a group of Pan American states in order to hammer out a common response to the

Mexican Revolution. As it became clearer that a pact involving the entire Western Hemisphere could not be effected, Wilson's interest dwindled. Neither Argentina, Brazil, nor Chile (nor any other hemispheric nation) was asked to mediate the dispute with Carranza over the punitive expedition as they had been two years earlier over the occupation of Veracruz. Nor were any other nations consulted to any great extent over the occupations of Haiti and Santo Domingo. Instead, Wilson transferred his interest in collective security from the boundaries of the Western Hemisphere to the world stage.

In May 1916 Wilson publicly announced his support of a postwar association of nations. At that time, he was thinking of a "universal alliance to maintain freedom of the seas and to prevent any war begun either a) contrary to treaty covenants or b) without warning and full inquiry—a virtual guarantee of territorial integrity and political independence."[8] From May 1916 through the signing of the peace treaty with Germany at the Paris Peace Conference in June 1919, Wilson added further refinements to his vision of the postwar world. But spelling out his criteria for peace proved a far easier task than obtaining the agreement of the other nations concerned. This chapter addresses how the effort to gain the consent of the Entente powers influenced the decision to intervene in Russia. In the conclusion to this volume, we will return to Wilson's international program as it was codified in the peace treaty.

COLLECTIVE SECURITY AND THE INTERVENTIONS IN RUSSIA

In the late winter and early spring of 1918, British and French officials felt a growing desperation born of their four-year loss of men and national treasure. The demise of Russia as an active participant in the war added to their fears. The March 1917 revolution led by Alexander Kerensky had seriously interrupted Russia's military effectiveness, and the November Bolshevik Revolution destroyed the country's fighting ability. The Treaty of Brest-Litovsk, signed on March 3, 1918, stilled the eastern front. Peace between Imperial Germany and Bolshevik Russia meant to the Allies that Germany would be free to transfer battle-hardened troops to the western front. They searched for some way to block the arrival of these massive reinforcements. From this fear-driven desire to somehow keep the eastern front alive came the idea for the twin interventions in Siberia and northern Russia.

The events leading up to these interventions present a confusing array of misunderstandings between the countries involved, misinformation about events in Russia, and misfortunes for the Allied cause on the western front. Members of the British and French governments, longing for some way to relieve the pressure on their armies, fixed on the idea of reestablishing the eastern front through an intervention in Russia. Yet, they lacked the military wherewithal to carry it out themselves. Thus, they turned to Japan, assisted by the United States, to spearhead a landing in Siberia. Although suspicious of Japanese ambitions in the area, they hoped somehow to control the situation by making Japan the mandatory of the Allies. In the view of these officials, the chance of keeping German divisions on the eastern front was well worth the risk that Japan might exploit the breakdown of Russia to expand its territorial and commercial empire.

For many months, Wilson stood as the only barrier to intervention in Russia. Convinced that it was unnecessary and just plain bad strategy, the president resisted tremendous pressure from Britain and France to allow the Japanese to land in force in Siberia. In Wilson's view, the Japanese were the worst choice, particularly since American relations with Tokyo had been strained throughout his administration. One of his first major foreign crises concerned a dispute with Japan over California's enactment of a land act that discriminated against Japanese immigrants. Competition between the two countries in China and the Far East exacerbated tensions, which were further compounded by Japan's Twenty-one Demands on China in 1915. The demands confirmed Wilson's suspicions that Japan sought preeminence in that area of the world. The Lansing-Ishii Agreement, negotiated in the fall of 1917, recognized Japan's special interests in China in return for a promise that Japan would respect the Open Door and the independence, both political and territorial, of China.

Although the agreement resolved the dispute temporarily, it did little to relieve American suspicions. Japanese diplomacy during the war, which took advantage of Britain and France's need of help, increased Wilson's distrust. By taking the path of expediency to guarantee itself the German possessions in Shantung and the northern Pacific Islands, Japan further alienated the president. Giving the Japanese a free hand in Siberia seemed to Wilson an invitation to additional trouble. He wanted no part of any plan that might encourage their ambitions or allow them to carry out their machinations.

Yet, despite these grave reservations, in July 1918 Wilson not only consented to interventions by Japan in Siberia and by Great Britain in northern Russia, he also contributed troops to both expeditions. As George Kennan has shown, the story of how this came about is confusing and unclear, primarily because the participants were unsure themselves.[9] Driven by an irrational desire to divert Germany's attack on the western front, Britain and France begged Wilson's approval of their bizarre scheme to recreate the eastern front through Siberia. In the end, they wore the president down. Against his better judgment and against the advice of his military experts, Wilson finally went along with his allies' plan.

For this reason, American participation in the Russian interventions differed in style and form from Wilson's previous resorts to force. Unlike the occupations of Veracruz, Haiti, and Santo Domingo, the punitive expedition after Pancho Villa, and the decision to go to war against Germany, Wilson was dragged into the Russian imbroglio at the insistence of his allies. His policies reflected his discomfort, and the interventions followed a peculiar pattern. Essentially, the Russian interventions were not his; they lacked the Wilsonian touch that characterized the earlier instances of force.

But one theme emerges eventually. Wilson finally approved the proposals to emphasize the importance of going beyond simple international cooperation to establish a collective response to international events. By proving the utility of such collaborative action in Russia, he hoped to show how it could succeed in the postwar era. Viewed in this light, the interventions appear as the precursors of collective security. Only when Wilson perceived them thus did he go along with the projects.

Although each intervention in Russia was seen by Wilson and his advisers as a separate military action from the other, they are discussed together here because the same events influenced the decisions to intervene and because the two interventions influenced each other. But it must be kept in mind that Wilson and his subordinates perceived each intervention as distinct, despite the fact that both were in Russia. The president was much more receptive to the northern interventions through Archangel and Murmansk than he was to the intervention in Siberia through Vladivostok.

COLLECTIVE PRESSURES FOR INTERVENTION

At first the British, then the French and Japanese, proposed armed intervention in Siberia to keep the Siberian railroad open for use by the Allies and to prohibit Germany from taking possession of large stocks of war supplies stored at Vladivostok. Implicit in the proposal was the hope that a landing of Allied troops would convince Germany to keep its forces in the east to protect against the reestablishment of a fighting front. Increasingly, British and French officials pressured the

United States government to commit to the scheme. Their pleas originally met a chilly reception in Washington.

Intervention in Russia held no appeal to Wilson, who wanted to leave the Russians to settle their problems without armed interference. America's first duty, he believed, was to defeat Germany. Wilson had embraced the March revolution because of its promise to establish democracy in one of the last bastions of European autocracy. "I hope with all my heart that the new forces in Russia may be guided by the principles and objects it sets forth!" he exclaimed to Lansing in June 1917.[10] At that time, American policy encouraged as much as possible the democratic tendencies evinced by the Kerensky government. Wilson sent a commission headed by Elihu Root on a tour of Russia to express America's sympathy with the revolution. Although others in the administration, most notably Lansing, believed the situation there would "go from bad to worse," the president earnestly prayed for the success of the democratic forces.[11]

His prayers went unanswered. Internal crises diverted the Kerensky government from making a full contribution to the war, and the Russian people showed a growing disenchantment with further fighting. The decline in Russia's military effectiveness caused concern on the western front. "The Russian situation today is probably the most serious obstacle to our success," Pershing told Scott on October 1. "Unless they can pull themselves together and make some sort of showing, there is nothing to prevent a large number of German divisions from coming to the western front." Three days later, he estimated that the failure of the Kerensky government to participate adequately in the war would prolong the fighting through 1919.[12]

The Bolshevik Revolution, which began on November 7, 1917, increased the fear that Russia would soon be taken out of the war. Led by Nikolai Lenin and Leon Trotsky, the Bolsheviks overthrew the Kerensky government with relative ease, but they also threw Russia into the agony of civil war. The Allies watched helplessly, fearful that the new government would soon make a separate peace with Germany. Many of these observers were convinced that the Bolsheviks were, in truth, German agents loyal to the kaiser. At this point, few understood what Bolshevism meant as a political philosophy; still fewer cared. The major concern in every Allied capital was to keep the Russian front alive.[13]

The question, of course, was how to keep Russia in the war. Lansing suggested to Wilson early in December that they aid internal military groups against the Bolsheviks, whom he feared would soon sue the kaiser for peace. But he felt no great confidence in that strategy. "The

Russian situation is to me an unanswered and unanswerable riddle," he noted in his diary. The secretary suspected that the Bolshevik leaders were German agents whose mission was to end the war on the eastern front. Should that occur, it would keep the fighting going on the western front for at least two more years. Yet, despite these fears, Lansing could think of no satisfactory policy to pursue.[14]

On December 23 the military representatives to the Supreme War Council, except Bliss, recommended in Joint Note Number 5 that the Allies support "by all means in our power" any group in eastern Europe that promised to continue the war. With more confidence in this solution than Lansing showed, they argued that, unless the Bolsheviks were stopped, Russia would begin shipping oil and wheat to Germany. This would endanger the effectiveness of the Allied blockade. To carry out their recommendation, the military representatives urged the establishment of direct communications with "our friends in Russia either by way of Vladivostok and the Siberian Railway or by operations in Turkey."[15] Joint Note Number 5 was the first of many such notes the military representatives issued calling for some degree of Allied intervention in Russia. The Allies continued to press the Wilson administration for its approval, for none of the powers anxious to intervene were willing to take that step without American consent, primarily because they needed American help.

The issue put Wilson in a difficult quandary. He considered force an inappropriate response to the collapse of Russia, yet his emphasis on international cooperation made him hesitate to turn the Allies down. In his view, the western front should receive first claim on men and materials. The lack of shipping in the United States added further justification to his decision to concentrate on sending troops and supplies to France. Wilson wanted nothing to detract from the effort there.

But the Russian problem refused to go away. The longer it continued, the more it drew the Wilson administration toward intervention. On January 1, 1918, the American consul at Vladivostok, John Caldwell, cabled the State Department to request an American warship. Caldwell reported increasing trouble between Bolshevik forces, the Red Army, and their various opponents in the civil war, the White Army. In addition, the Japanese consul was also requesting ships from his government. Upon receipt of this message, Lansing asked Daniels to send the USS *Brooklyn,* flagship for the commander-in-chief of the American Asiatic Fleet, Admiral A. N. Knight, to Vladivostok. Knight's orders of January 3 advised him that "if possible avoid landing armed forces at Vladivostok unless necessary to preserve American lives." His mission was mainly to observe events, especially any action by the Japanese.[16]

The dispatch of Knight and the *Brooklyn* to the Siberian port indicated no change in the Wilson administration's attitude toward intervention. However, as the Bolsheviks negotiated with Germany to end Russia's part in the war, the pressure on Wilson from the Allies increased apace. Aware that they could not spare the military resources themselves, Britain and France nominated Japan to carry out Allied policy in Siberia. Early in February, Lansing cabled Bliss to ask his opinion of Britain's proposal to ask the Japanese to occupy the Trans-Siberian Railway. "From the political point of view I think this would be dangerous and would be used by the Germans to consolidate Russian opinion against the allies," Lansing wrote Bliss. "British Government, however, have urged the plan very strongly and before definitely stating I am opposed to it I should like to have your opinion on military advantages, which they think could be secured, in order to help us decide whether these are great enough to outweigh the political objections."[17] Bliss decided to take the question up with his colleagues among the military representatives to the Supreme War Council.

In Joint Note Number 16, dated February 19, 1918, the military representatives endorsed intervention by Japan acting as the representative of the Allies. They recommended that "the occupation of the Siberian Railway from Vladivostok to Harbin together with both terminals presents military advantages that outweigh any probable political disadvantages." Without detailing the advantages, the military representatives added that, in their opinion, Japan should carry out the intervention after giving "suitable guarantees" not to exploit the situation to its own benefit.[18] This answer, however, was not the response sought by the Wilson administration.

The advice of soldiers on the political aspects of the question offended Wilson's deeply held belief in civilian control of the military. It mattered little that Lansing had asked for Bliss's views. The administration cabled the general that it "urgently hopes that your associates will regard the matter as involving political and diplomatic questions to be settled by the governments, and to that end will refrain from urging views set forth" in Joint Note Number 16. The reprimand could only have confused Bliss, since the note was in direct response to the questions raised by the secretary of state. He later declined to participate in recommendations by the military representatives concerning action by Japan because he did not want the receipt of this advice by members of the administration "complicated by their belief that I have failed to comply with previous instructions."[19] Although typical of Wilson's reaction to the military, the incident did not settle the issue.

Unfortunately for Wilson, the military representatives merely expressed the views of their governments. Lord Reading, the British ambassador to the United States, endorsed the use of Japan as a mandatory representing the Allies by explaining to the president:

> I can only add that it is with the United States that the final decision appears now to rest. France is eager for the decision. It is favorably regarded in Italy. Since the complete surrender of the Bolsheviki, the British Government believe that there is no other alternative open. Common action will of course become impossible if a different view is taken by the United States. In that event, however, it is much to be feared that action will be taken by Japan alone and that, in taking action, sufficient extension will not, on the one hand, be given to her plans, nor, on the other, will she carry them out under the safeguards that would be provided by an Allied mandatory.

Although awkwardly phrased, Reading's argument was that each of the Entente powers wanted an intervention in Siberia. Since the Japanese would probably send an expedition anyway, it was better to make it a joint intervention with the United States. Otherwise, no one would be able to moderate Japanese ambitions in the area. In sum, the ambassador argued, the British wanted the Japanese, acting at the behest of the Allies, to occupy the Siberian railway. Concurrent with the occupation, the Allies should issue a joint declaration proclaiming that it was but a temporary expedient "rendered necessary in the interests of Russian independence." In letters to House and Wilson, Arthur Balfour, Britain's foreign secretary, justified the intervention as a means to help Russia overcome the German menace. "Since Russia cannot help herself she must be helped by her friends," he told Wilson.[20]

The French, too, pressed Wilson to permit the Japanese to intervene. On February 26 Lansing informed the president that the French regarded "the question of intervention in Siberia as of grave urgency." Their concern grew out of reported disruptions of the Siberian railroad, which was the "only access for counteracting German efforts, whether political or military," in the region. Several weeks later, the French ambassador to the United States, Jules Jusserand, confirmed the attitude of his government toward intervention by Japan. "No undertaking of such importance in these troublous days, can of course go without some drawbacks," Jusserand observed. "But in the eyes of my Government, they are not to be compared with the advantages, the chief of which is the keeping open for us all and the shutting to the enemy, of the transiberian route, for us henceforth the only means of access to Eastern and Southern Russia." He added that the French expected no trouble from internal Russian groups since in that area the military forces were few and poorly trained. In the name of his government, he urged Wilson to give America's consent.[21]

From Tokyo, Wilson learned through the American ambassador, Roland Morris, that the Japanese intended "to arrest the sinister activities of Germany in Siberia." They promised not to intervene without the "whole-hearted support of all the great powers." This statement put the onus directly on Wilson for refusing to approve action that all the Allies considered essential to the war effort. Many junior members of the administration also promoted intervention. David Francis, the former American ambassador in Russia, General William Judson, the former American military attaché there, various officers in the Military Intelligence Division of the War Department, Lansing's assistants, Breckinridge Long and Basil Miles, and others argued in favor of some form of military intervention.[22] This tremendous pressure on the president was difficult to withstand; yet, withstand it he did, at least for a while.

To all these advices, the Wilson administration responded negatively. Acting Secretary of State Frank Polk informed the Japanese that "a military mission to Siberia would have disastrous results." The United States, Polk explained, "feels very strongly that the common interests of all the powers at war with Germany demand from them an attitude of sympathy with the Russian people in their present unhappy struggle." An attempt to occupy Russian territory risked uniting all the Russian factions against the Allies. Intervention in Siberia, Polk added, would aid only German propaganda. The Wilson administration wanted to help the Russian people, but it feared any step that might be construed as hostile. Similar arguments were used in notes to the British and French governments.[23]

American objections to Allied intervention in Siberia centered on two points. First, it smacked too much of political interference in Russia's internal affairs. Lansing, for example, believed that intervention might be warranted if the Germans gained control of Siberia. "The restoration of order in Siberia when the confusion is due to civil strife between Russian factions is a very different reason for military action from the wresting of control of the territory from an organized body of troops operating under German officers," the secretary observed. "The former would be interpreted as interference with the domestic affairs of Russia; the latter, as the legitimate expulsion of an enemy from conquered territory and the freeing of the Russian people from foreign and hostile domination." Since Germany had yet to gain control of Siberia, intervention would be opposed by the Russian people. Indeed, Lansing was sure that Germany would use an Allied landing "to consolidate

Russian opinion against the allies." Thus, Lansing noted in his diary, "it would seem unwise and inexpedient to support the request for Japanese intervention in Siberia. To unite the various Russian factions against this country and thereby to deliver Russia into the hands of the Germans, for which there would seem to be no compensatory military equivalent, would seem to be most unwise." With this view, Lansing wrote, Wilson agreed completely.[24]

Lansing's opposition to a Siberian intervention differed from his endorsement of interventions in Haiti and Santo Domingo because Russia was, or recently had been, a developed power and it was far from American shores. Opposite conditions obtained in both Haiti and Santo Domingo, which were not politically developed (in Lansing's view). Both occupied a strategic location near the United States and astride the sea route to the Panama Canal. The United States, he assumed, had a duty to bring stability to the two chaotic countries that it did not have to Russia. Thus, Lansing saw no contradiction in approving intervention in Haiti and Santo Domingo while shunning it in Russia.

The second American objection to intervention in Siberia concerned the use of Japanese forces. Russian distrust of Japan persuaded many of Wilson's advisers that using Japan as a mandatory of the Allies would be a mistake. "I have never changed my opinion that it would be a great political mistake to send Japanese troops into Siberia," Colonel House advised the president. "There is no military advantage that I can think of that would offset the harm." He worried that it would alienate the Bolsheviks from the Allies and "arouse the Slavs throughout Europe because of the race question." As House explained on March 3, "We are treading upon exceedingly delicate and dangerous ground, and are likely to lose that fine moral position you have given the Entente cause. The whole structure which you have built up so carefully may be destroyed over night, and our position will be no better than that of the Germans." House was dismayed at the "fatuous determination" of France and Britain to promote Japanese intervention. He speculated that the French now hated the Russians for leaving the war and the English hated the Germans so much that they had lost perspective on the issue. In House's view, intervention offered little hope for any material gain to the Allied side. The gamble was too great to risk America's superior moral position by turning the Russian people against the United States.[25]

To protect its moral position, the Wilson administration argued that the Bolshevik Revolution had not altered America's relations with Russia, despite the U.S. refusal to recognize the Bolshevik government. American policy, the State Department informed Ambassador Francis, was "to assist Russia to restore her integrity and freedom." Polk told the Japanese government that "recent events have in no way altered the relations and obligations of this government towards Russia." The United States regarded Russia as neither a neutral nor an enemy, but as an ally still. "The government of the United States feels that it is of the utmost importance, as affecting the whole public opinion of the world and giving proof of the utter good faith of all the governments associated against Germany, that we should continue to treat the Russians as in all respects our friends and allies against the common enemy," Polk added.[26] This attitude essentially begged the question of intervention, for none of the Allied governments expressed any intention to treat Russia as an ally of Germany. Indeed, the Allies touted intervention as a way to free Russia from German domination.

Wilson also tried to wash his hands of the matter. He told Polk that the United States would not oppose intervention by Japan, but it would not join in a request that the Japanese land troops. Lansing, convinced that a landing would cause bitter resentment in Siberia, wanted Japan alone to bear the blame. Nevertheless, the administration recognized the danger of this position. In response to a suggestion from Long that the Allies co-opt Japan by closely associating it with their purposes, the president pointed out that it was unwise to rely exclusively on the Japanese. The lack of men and materials meant that the United States could not act alone in Russia; but cooperation with Japan "cuts in many directions." Wilson understood that the Japanese could co-opt the Allies to their selfish purposes as easily as the Allies could use Japan for their own reasons. As Lansing told Long, it was the "most complicated problem he has ever had. Biggest problem and most complicated."[27] The issue was soon to grow more complicated still.

Thus far, the discussions about intervention had concentrated on using the Japanese in Siberia. During March, reports of increased German activities in northern Russia drew attention to the ports of Archangel and Murmansk, which, like Vladivostok in Siberia, contained large stocks of war supplies. On March 6 a relatively small force of British marines, numbering around two hundred, landed in Murmansk to protect Allied interests from disorder. Sometime later, Leon Trotsky, the Bolshevik commissar for war, implied a willingness to cooperate with Allied forces against the Germans in Murmansk. This encouraged some hope among the British and French that the Bolsheviks would consent to intervention by Japan in Siberia, but these hopes were dashed by the ratification of the Treaty of Brest-Litovsk. Peace on the eastern front, combined with the opening of the German spring offensive in the west, drove the British and French to redouble their efforts to keep as many of the kaiser's men in the east as possible. This, they believed, could be done only by intervention and intervention required the active assistance of the United States.[28]

Originally, the Allies understood the difficulty of intervention at Archangel and Murmansk because of the lack of men and materials to carry it out. The military representatives to the Supreme War Council and their navy counterparts on the Inter-Allied Naval Council affirmed that "no military resources whatever are found to be available for an expedition to Archangel." Nor could any be found for Murmansk.[29] Yet, having raised the issue of intervention in northern Russia, the Allies continued to discuss it. From the end of March on, they and the United States debated two interventions in Russia: one in Siberia by the Japanese, the other at Archangel and Murmansk by the British.

This dichotomy further muddied an already confused situation. Wilson strongly opposed the Siberian expedition because he distrusted the Japanese, but he raised no serious objections to the northern intervention, provided it did not interfere with the military effort on the western front. He accepted the northern interventions because he saw them as a way to cooperate with the Allies. Uncomfortable with being the single obstacle in the way of Allied desires for intervention in Siberia, yet unable to approve of their plans because of his suspicions of Japan, Wilson leapt at the chance to prove the United States was a good partner. During the first week of April, he asked Daniels to send a ship to Murmansk if one was available without disrupting convoys to France. He specified that the ship "be of sufficient force to command respect and afford real cooperation" with Allied vessels already there. The dispatch of this ship indicated Wilson's willingness to work with the British.[30]

The lack of military resources temporarily settled the issue of landing troops in the north. By early April, Wilson believed that American opposition to an intervention by Japan had effectively laid that issue to rest as well. When Herbert Bayard Swope submitted a draft magazine article on the subject for Wilson's review, the president approved his formula that "America's non-assent to the suggestion of Japanese intervention in Siberia seems to have checked the original plan and that it is not likely that anything will be done along that line until there is actual military necessity for the step." Later in the month, Viscount Ishii, the Japanese ambassador to the United States, confirmed this understanding when he told Lansing that Japan should act in conjunction with the United States. "My interview with the Ambassador was in every way satisfactory," the secretary told Wilson. "He is most frank and evidently desirous to do only what is entirely acceptable to this Government, and he assured me that is the wish and purpose of his Government."[31] But the president's conclusion that he had squelched the move toward intervention was premature.

On April 5, in response to the murder of three Japanese nationals in Vladivostok, Admiral Kato, the commander of the Japanese naval squadron at the port, landed five hundred men. The British debarked fifty men to protect their consulate. Although the Bolsheviks deeply resented the landing, they offered no armed opposition and, for the moment, the situation calmed down again. Three days later, the military representatives to the Supreme War Council, except Bliss, again urged using the Japanese as the mandatory of the Allies in a Siberian expedition. In Joint Note Number 20, they outlined three objectives for such action. First, it would keep supplies of food and raw materials out of Germany's grasp. Second, it would check German military and political expansion into the area. Third, it would compel the Imperial Army to keep its troops on the eastern front. The military representatives suggested that the best method for accomplishing these objectives was to support "every element of the Russian people that is willing to organize itself on lines which will enable it to resist German penetration, and to every nationality or element in the non-Russian regions of the Russian empire, or in Persia, which is prepared actively to oppose the advance of the enemy or to reject his intrigues." Furthermore, the military representatives added, in Siberia "support can only be given effectively by the Japanese."[32] The landing of Japanese forces in Vladivostok and Joint Note Number 20 put Wilson on notice that the question of intervention was not going to go away.

But in late April 1918 a new element introduced into the situation not only complicated Wilson's resistance, but eventually gave him a persuasive justification to join the Allies in endorsing an intervention at Vladivostok. The new element was an army of Czechoslovakian troops over fifty thousand strong, some of whom were former Russian prisoners of war and some of whom were deserters from the Austro-Hungarian army; all were veterans of the eastern front. They were driven by the twin desires to defeat the hated Austro-Hungarian Empire and its allies and to prove, through fighting the Central Powers, the value of Czechoslovakia as an independent nation. After the signing of the Treaty of Brest-Litovsk, the Czechs determined to leave Russia by making their way through Siberia to the Pacific Ocean, then to the western front via the United States. This convoluted route rivaled in absurdity the British and French hope that they could recreate the eastern front by landing troops in Siberia. Nevertheless, the Czechoslovak Legion, as this force came to be called, constituted a wild card in the dangerous game of collective action in Russia.

The Czechs began their long trek to the western front in the spring of 1918 with the approval of the Bolsheviks, who were anxious to rid themselves of this large, hostile force. Little love was lost between them, not only because of political and philosophical differences, but also because the Czechs were disgusted with the Bolsheviks for making peace with the Central Powers. As the Czechs traversed Russia on the Trans-Siberian Railway, the Bolsheviks grew increasingly concerned over having a well-trained, well-armed, antagonistic military force loose in the heart of Russia. Sporadic incidents of hostilities between the Czechs and the Bolsheviks culminated in the Bolshevik attempt to disarm the Czechs. When they refused, open fighting broke out. All along the route to Vladivostok, Czechs allied themselves with forces of the White Army while the Allies watched with interest.[33]

The Allies recognized the usefulness of the Czechs in combating German and Bolshevik influences in Russia. The military representatives to the Supreme War Council, including Bliss, recommended in Joint Note Number 25, dated April 27, that "all Czech troops, which have not yet passed East of Omsk on the Trans-Siberian Railway, should be dispatched" to Archangel and Murmansk. Although the military representatives approved the plan to transport the Czechs to the western front, until adequate transportation could be arranged they wanted them "employed in defending Archangel and Murmansk and in guarding and protecting the Murman railway." In addition, Czech forces east of Omsk could be used "to co-operate with the Allies in Siberia." The appearance of the Czechs on the scene encouraged the Allies to escalate their pressure on Wilson to approve Allied expeditions in Siberia and northern Russia.[34]

The Supreme War Council approved Joint Note Number 25 at its fifth session on May 2. It resolved that the British government would approach Trotsky in order to secure his agreement to a concentration of Czech troops at Archangel and Murmansk. The British government also took responsibility to arrange transportation to the western front for those Czechs who had made their way to Vladivostok. The French agreed to take responsibility for these forces until they embarked from the port.[35]

The different missions in northern Russia and Siberia specified in Joint Note Number 25 were in line with the views of Wilson and his advisers. The Wilson administration went to some pains to distinguish between an intervention in Siberia and one in northern Russia. In this way, it could explain its disapproval of the former and its approval of the latter. As Lansing pointed out to Lord Reading early in May, the administration considered "that the problem had really become two problems in that intervention in western Russia [Archangel and Murmansk] in no way involved the racial difficulty which had to be considered in regard to Siberia." The United States, he said, viewed with greater favor an expedition to Archangel and Murmansk because "we could understand the military advantage of the former but had been unable, thus far, to find any advantage in sending troops into Siberia." In addition, Trotsky's allegedly favorable attitude toward intervention probably applied only to the northern ports, not Vladivostok. Although Lansing questioned "how far the reported invitation for intervention would go" in Archangel and Murmansk, he had little doubt that it did not stretch as far as Siberia.[36]

Wilson also approved Joint Note Number 25, except he made no mention of the Siberian aspects of the recommendations. Bliss informed his colleagues on June 1 that the "President concurs in recommendations of the note, but points out that if Allied military operations are in contemplation in Russia from Murmansk and Archangel these Czech contingents might be especially valuable in association with any such expeditions because of their familiarity with Russian language and previous employment on Russian Front." Bliss also passed on the statement of policy that he had received from Baker that "the President is in sympathy with any practical military efforts which can be made at and from Murmansk or Archangel, but such efforts should proceed, if at all, upon the sure sympathy of the Russian people and should not have as their ultimate objects any restoration of the ancient regime or any other interference with the political liberty of the Russian people."[37] Although he endorsed intervention in northern Russia, Wilson still opposed a Siberian expedition led by the Japanese.

None of the arguments thus far put forth by the Allies changed Wilson's original opinion that a landing in Siberia was impractical and fraught with the danger of alienating the Russian people. As long as he opposed the plan, the Allies were stymied. Not only did they want American assistance, both military and financial, but no one wanted to risk angering the U.S. president by acting against his wishes in Siberia. As it was, the more they pushed for intervention, the more they raised doubts in the minds of various American officials concerning their true intentions.

During May and June, Bliss, for example, reported his suspicions that the proposed expedition was taking on an anti-Bolshevik character that had been absent previously. In addition, he worried that Britain and

France were prepared to induce the Japanese to cooperate by offering them land and other prizes in Russia. The record prepared by Bliss and his assistants of the second meeting of the fifth session of the Supreme War Council, held on May 2 at Abbeville, France, included a fascinating review of the efforts to involve the United States in a Russian expedition. Both in tone and content, the account exemplified the growing distrust of British and French motives among American officials. For instance, it pointed out that:

> The plan for intervening in Siberia was essentially an English plan; certainly it was pushed by the British Government. The participation of America was very much desired, because it was thought that no other country could furnish any troops to the expedition (always excepting Japan) and that only by the participation of American troops could the inter-Allied character of the expedition be assured; also, because it was thought that a purely Japanese expedition would lose the advantage of being popular with a large part of the local population and of appearing like an attempt at rescue to the anti-Bolsheviks of European Russia. Although not stated, undoubtedly there was in the minds of those who were so eager for American participation in this intervention the thought that once embarked on the enterprise, the American Government would go to whatever limit became necessary to make it a success, and that its participation would not be limited to the sending of a few troops but would ultimately and by gradual degrees come to include the financing of the expedition and of the pro-Ally Siberian Government.

According to the report, five arguments were usually advanced in favor of a Siberian expedition. First, it would counteract German penetration into Russia, thereby limiting its influence. Next, a successful intervention would lead to the reestablishment of the eastern front, thus keeping large numbers of German troops away from France. Participation by Japan was important because "it would get Japan into the war and inflict on her losses and give her a stake in the war and an anti-German feeling, which seemed very desirable" because it would prohibit the Japanese from making a separate peace. In addition, intervention in Siberia would protect Persia, India, and Afghanistan from both German and Bolshevik propaganda. Finally, it would open a "direct channel for the support of the anti-Bolshevist forces then fighting and a way out for the Czechs and other pro-Ally troops and prisoners captured by the Russians."

The report also listed four arguments against intervention. First, American soldiers sent to Siberia would, by necessity, be taken from the western front, as would the shipping needed to get them to Russia. In order to have any real influence on the outcome of the war, the expedition would have to be very large, much larger than the six or seven divisions proposed by the British. Third, it would take too long to build up an eastern front again, particularly since the outcome of the war was being decided at that moment in France. Finally, since the United States could not contribute large numbers of troops without interfering with its efforts in France, the brunt of the intervention would have to be carried by Japan. In order to induce Tokyo to accept this, the Allies would have to offer it additional territory in Asia and Siberia, which violated promises to the Russians not to interfere with their independence.[38]

Bliss personally opposed intervention unless the Allies could positively ascertain that the Russian people would give it a "cordial welcome." He warned Baker that the Germans would exploit a Japanese intervention by turning the Russian people against the Allies. The result would be "the East combining with Middle Europe against the West." In addition, Bliss was still concerned that the proposal for intervention was becoming explicitly anti-Bolshevik, rather than keeping its original purpose as a move against Germany. "I hear only denunciation of the Bolsheviks and everything they stand for," he wrote. "I think most would like to see something like the old regime restored. It is from the old Russian regime that come declarations in favor of intervention." He asked Baker to give him some idea of how to respond to these proposals.[39]

Baker took the issue up with the president. Wilson was also disturbed at the anti-Bolshevik character the proposals for intervention were assuming, and neither Baker nor Wilson wanted Japan rewarded for its efforts at the expense of Russia. On May 28, Baker cabled Bliss that:

> The President's attitude is that Russia's misfortune imposes upon us at this time the obligation of unswerving fidelity to the principle of Russian territorial integrity and political independence. Intervention via Vladivostok is deemed impractical because of the vast distances involved, the size of the force necessary to be effective, and financing such an expedition would mean a burden which the United States at this time ought not assume. In order to be effective, either to create a military situation on the eastern front which would relieve the pressure on the western front or to prevent the Central Powers from exploiting the agricultural and other resources of Russia, such an intervening expedition would have to penetrate into European Russia, and, however such an expedition were safeguarded by the approval and concurrence of the Allies, its appearance would be such that German

propagandists would be able to persuade the Russian people that compensation at their expense and out of their territory was ultimately to be exacted. In this way and others Germany would be able to arouse Russian patriotic feeling and thus secure military and other aid from the Russians far outweighing any foreseeable advantage from so difficult an intervention.

The idea of compensating Japan by territory in Asiatic Russia is inadmissable. The President is heartily in sympathy with any practical military effort which can be made at and from Murmansk and Archangel, but such efforts should proceed upon the sure sympathy of the Russian people and should not have as their ultimate object any restoration of the ancient regime or any other interference with the political liberty of the Russian people.[40]

Wilson was already concerned that Japan would take advantage of the intervention, and he absolutely opposed any encouragement of its ambitions by offering territory or other gains. Nor was he willing to turn the intervention into an effort to depose the Bolsheviks. Certainly, talk of restoring the ancient regime of the czars was contrary to his attempts elsewhere to save democracy from autocracy and militarism.

Thus, Wilson's opposition to a Siberian expedition seemed complete and firm. He offered to go along with a northern intervention as compensation for his disapproval of action by Japan. Yet, during this last phase of American opposition to an intervention in Siberia, various officials within the administration showed a wavering attitude. The pressure from the Allies was beginning to take its toll. "From all sides there are now coming pleas for intervention in Siberia," Breckinridge Long observed on May 31. "Paris cables a meeting will be held there tomorrow between Lloyd George, Clemenceau, and Italian Premier on subject; Reinsch [the American ambassador to China] advises it from Peking; various cables from other ports, Russian and Siberia urge it; and a general sentiment of personnel all over the Northern Hemisphere seem setting toward Allied intervention." When Bliss requested instructions earlier in the month on how to respond to Allied promptings for Japanese intervention, Wilson told Baker that "as a merely military proposition, we approve, but that, inasmuch as delicate aspects of international policy are involved, the matter will be further considered by me from the standpoint of proper presentation by the Supreme War Council."[41] The answer reflected a general weakening in Wilson's original opposition to a Siberian expedition on the grounds that it was militarily impractical.

The administration was beginning to understand that, as Lansing pointed out to the president, "inaction causes concern both in Great

Britain and France." Even so, Lansing could not think of any action the United States could take that would improve the situation. "I am not so sure of the wisdom of intervention in Siberia," the secretary informed one correspondent, "but I can assure you that the subject is receiving very careful consideration both as to policy and as to the physical difficulties of transportation, which on account of lack of ships in the Pacific are very great."[42] The administration's confidence was crumbling.

The turning point for American policy came in June 1918. During that month, the pressure on Wilson from Britain and France, aided occasionally by Italy, reached its peak, leaving the United States clearly isolated as the single obstacle to intervention in Siberia. It was not a position in which Wilson felt comfortable because it endangered his efforts to foster close cooperation among the Entente powers. He did not want the United States to establish the precedent against collective action. Yet the president remained unconvinced that intervention was necessary. To agree to it after he had rejected all the reasons put forth to justify it would make the United States appear pusillanimous and a pawn of the stronger-willed Allies. In other words, Wilson, who was learning that coalition warfare sometimes involved distasteful duties, needed a new reason to explain American approval of the expedition.

During June, reports reaching the Allies seemed to indicate that German penetration of Russia was more extensive than they had believed earlier. Also, the Czechs were getting into deeper trouble with the Bolsheviks. At the same time, the Czechs expressed their willingness to cooperate with the Entente powers against the Central Powers in Russia. Wilson leapt at the chance to help them because it offered him a way out of his quandary. It was a convenient way to do what Britain, France, and Italy were urging him to do without the embarrassment of openly changing his mind. By claiming that he wanted to assist the Czechs, Wilson was saying, in effect, that the old arguments in favor of intervention were still no good, but a new, more persuasive reason had arisen. The Allies got American cooperation, the Czechs were helped, and the president avoided the appearance of yielding to pressure. In this way, Wilson tried to prove the utility of international cooperation among equals. Unfortunately, the course of the intervention reflected the confused process Wilson took in reaching his decision.

Wilson's retreat began in response to the increasingly apparent isolation of the United States from its associates on the question of intervention. At the sixth session of the Supreme War Council, held at Versailles from June 1 through June 3, Britain, France, and Italy went out of their way to identify the United States as the only opponent of Japanese intervention in Siberia. More than that, they asserted that American opposition effectively vetoed the entire scheme. Stephen Pichon, the French foreign minister, reported to the war council that the foreign ministers of the three nations agreed that "all the Allies with the exception of the United States thought Japanese intervention in Siberia desirable." As Bliss informed the War Department, Pichon told the council that "the three Foreign Ministers agreed that of course no final steps should be taken without the approval of the President of the United States because the Allied Governments would not wish to take any action in opposition to him." In order to reassure Wilson, the foreign ministers proposed, and the council approved, asking Japan its intentions in regard to an expedition in Siberia. Specifically, the Allies wanted promises from Tokyo that it would respect the territory of Russia, that it would not interfere with Russia's internal affairs, and that it would go as far into Russia as necessary to fight the Germans. Once Japan gave assurances on these issues, Pichon felt sure that "it would be possible to explain to the President of the United States exactly what were Japan's intentions and it might then be easier to overcome his evident reluctance to acquiesce in Japanese intervention."[43] The question of the Siberian intervention was then temporarily tabled awaiting Tokyo's reply.

In the meantime, the Allies took up the subject of the northern intervention. In Joint Note Number 31, which was approved by the Supreme War Council, the military representatives observed that "the general situation in Russia and especially in the Northern Ports has completely altered." The German threat against Murmansk and Archangel was "more definite and more imminent." Finland had fallen under German domination and the Imperial army was preparing to advance on Petrograd. "We are urged to occupy [Archangel and Murmansk] not only by the Allied Representatives in Russia but also by the majority of the Russian parties," the military representatives claimed. "Such occupation is an indispensable corollary of Allied intervention in Siberia." In addition, the Czech forces awaiting transportation to the western front were in danger of capture by the German-Finnish Armies. Their agreement to defend Archangel and Murmansk "will be conditional on the moral and material support of a few Allied units on the spot to co-operate with them against the Germans." Based on these considerations, the military representatives recommended "that a military effort be made by the Allies to retain in their possession, first in importance, the port of Murmansk; afterwards or even simultaneously if possible the port of Archangel." They added that the best way to limit this effort to the minimum number of Allied troops, which they estimated at four to six battalions, was to use the Czech forces already there.[44]

Still the Wilson administration hesitated. Although sympathetic to the northern interventions, primarily as a means to divert discussion of a Japanese expedition in Siberia, lack of manpower and shipping persuaded many officials to oppose it now, especially since the German spring offensive in France was at its height. The same considerations applied to an intervention in Siberia, particularly since no one wanted Japan to go in alone. "The creation of an Eastern front is a more colossal undertaking than I think anyone can have an idea of who is not dealing directly with questions of creating and supplying an army overseas," Wilson informed one correspondent. Secretary of State Lansing agreed completely. As he noted in his diary, "There are no ships to carry troops across the Pacific. We have literally swept that ocean of suitable vessels and sent them into the Atlantic." The lack of adequate transportation for an expeditionary force convinced him that the United States needed to concentrate on getting men and materials to the western front and not divert its strength with expeditions to Siberia and northern Russia.[45]

The American military also opposed intervention. "If I had my own way about Russia and had the power to have my own way," Baker told the president, "I would like to take everybody out of Russia except the Russians, including diplomatic representatives, military representatives, political agents, propagandists and casual visitors, and let the Russians settle down and settle their own affairs." He realized the impossibility of this, of course, but he wanted Wilson to ensure that whoever the Allies sent into Russia, whether for propaganda or for military assistance, "represent our feeling and point of view." Given the administration's suspicions of Tokyo's motives, this criteria ruled out a Japanese expedition. Bliss worried that the Russian peasantry would unite under Germany against a Japanese intervention. He also believed that intervention in either Siberia or northern Russia would require too large an investment of men and material, which would seriously detract from the "decisive theater of war." Admiral William S. Benson, the chief of naval operations, agreed with this reasoning. He advised Daniels that "this war must be won by the successful operations on the Western front by the Allied armies and to undertake any operations that would interfere with this effort would seem to be ill-advised." Benson strongly urged that the administration stick to the "well recognized principle of concentration of effort" as the best way to defeat Germany.[46]

Perhaps hoping for support of these views, the Wilson administration asked General Foch, the recently appointed commander-in-chief of the Allied armies, his attitude toward intervention if it interfered with the American effort to send troops and supplies to France. In three separate replies, Foch made clear, first, that he approved of intervention in northern Russia and in Siberia as a means to keep Germany from reinforcing the western front and, second, that he did not think that either intervention would "retard the arrival of American troops in France." He explained that the northern intervention would probably require only one or two American battalions because the Allies could depend on the Czechs for additional manpower. In Siberia, the Japanese could supply most of the necessary men. "The value of the occupation of the port of Murmansk by the Allies is indisputable," Foch told Bliss. In a letter to Wilson, Foch wrote that "more than ever, in the interest of military success in Europe, I consider the expedition to Siberia as a very important factor for victory."[47]

Foch's reply left Wilson with no more excuses for not going along with the northern interventions. Although still unconvinced about the Siberian expedition, the president decided to go along with the Allies in Murmansk and Archangel. The British were urgently requesting the United States to send forces to those two ports, but Wilson stipulated that the request had to come from all the Allies. The War Department informed Bliss that "the President will not consider any project for the use of American troops emanating from a single nation, but that such recommendation must come from the Military Representatives at Versailles representing all the nations." Since all the Allies had been urging such action, this presented no problem. Indeed, Wilson insisted on it only to emphasize the importance of collective action by the Allies. The Supreme War Council issued the proper request during its seventh session on July 2.[48]

Toward the end of June, the Japanese government replied to the war council's request for assurances in regard to the proposed Siberian intervention. The reply increased the pressure on Wilson, for the Japanese refused to take part in the intervention unless they were "assured of the approval and active support of the United States Government." Tokyo promised to respect the territorial and political integrity of Russia, but it refused to say whether Japanese forces would go beyond Irkutsk to fight the Germans. This was not the answer sought by the Allies. Although Wilson said that he read the reply "with genuine delight," he originally misunderstood its implications. Japan's answer further isolated him from America's partners in the war. The Allies had no intention of giving up on their project for a Siberian expedition.

Japan's answer meant that their efforts to get approval for it were concentrated once again on the president. As before, Wilson was singled out as the sole obstacle blocking the plans of his allies.[49] Thus, Wilson's desire to establish close cooperation among Germany's enemies was thrown onto the scales against his distrust of Japan's ambitions in Siberia. In the balance hung his vision of collective security to guarantee the peace of the postwar world.

At the end of June, the Czechs tipped the scales in favor of the cooperation of the United States with the Allies. Their battle with the Bolsheviks during their long trek to Vladivostok intensified throughout the month. On June 29 the Czech forces that had reached the port overthrew the local Soviet authorities and took control of the city. Immediately, they announced their intention to cooperate with the Allies, even to the point of establishing a new eastern front against Germany. The Supreme War Council moved quickly to exploit the Czechs' action. At its seventh session on July 2, the council approved a long note to Wilson that reviewed all the arguments in favor of intervention, discussed the action of the Czechs, and concluded that Foch and the other military advisers deemed intervention essential to victory against Germany. The note ended with a plea to Wilson to approve the proposal "and thus enable it to be carried into effect before it is too late."[50] This time, the plea for intervention met a receptive audience in Washington.

The take-over of Vladivostok by the Czechs allowed Wilson to interpret the Siberian intervention as a cooperative effort both with the Allies and with the Czechs. As Lansing pointed out, the capture of the port "materially changed the situation by introducing a sentimental element into the question of our duty." He added that "it seems to me that we are burdened with the responsibility of rendering them aid, and that, if we fail to do so, and if they are destroyed or frustrated, we will be held culpable or at least generally blamed, especially by their compatriots in this country and in western Europe." He suggested sending to the Czechs arms and other materials, as well as "some troops" to help them police the railroad and advance against the Germans. The previous suspicions about the motives of the Allies and Japan no longer applied, Lansing wrote, because "furnishing protection and assistance to the Czecho-Slovaks, who are so loyal to our cause, is a very different thing from sending an army into Siberia to restore order and to save the Russians from themselves. There is a moral obligation to save these men from our common enemies, if we are able to do so."[51] Wilson perceived the situation in much the same light as his secretary of state.

At a White House conference on July 6 attended by Wilson, Lansing,

Baker, Daniels, Chief of Staff General Peyton C. March, and Admiral Benson, the president approved the use of American troops in Siberia. The participants ruled out any attempt to reestablish an eastern front because it was "physically impossible." Instead, American policy was to cooperate with Japan and the other Allies to aid the Czechs. The decision to intervene was thus made on the "sentimental grounds" of assisting the Czechoslovak Legion.[52]

Only the American military continued to object. Chief of Staff General March, for instance, objected strenuously to the plan formulated on July 6. He believed it essential to the war effort to concentrate America's participation on the western front. In a discussion with one of Lansing's assistants, March left the impression that he believed "military intervention hazardous, extremely difficult, and unsound policy." Lansing would later complain that March had blocked the plan in every possible way.[53]

General Bliss also disapproved. The constant badgering for intervention from the Allies caused him to lose patience with them. "This Siberian expedition on a large scale," he observed, "was an expedient of desperation, the hobby of those who could not see any hope for an early favorable decision on the Western Front." When Baker asked his personal views on the issue, Bliss told him that he felt it best to concentrate the American effort in France. "It would then be obvious that our sole object is to defeat Germany and that we are not tying ourselves up with Allies who have many and different objects in view after defeat of Germany."[54] As Wilson often had in the past, he overruled his military advisers because he believed the decision was more political than military. It was more important to him to cooperate with the Allies than simply to defeat Germany.

Foch's support of the Siberian interventions settled the issue of their military utility for the Allies. Wilson was hesitant to challenge the Entente commander-in-chief. Although Foch's reasoning was probably more political than military, it added considerably more pressure on the besieged president to go along with the other coalition members. Thus, Wilson determined to join the interventions because the demands of cooperation and collective action seemed to require it.

Wilson intended to use the Russian interventions to prove the utility of collective action. Many years later, Secretary of War Baker explained his understanding of the president's motives:

> The North Russian and Siberian Expeditions were practically the only decisions of a military character made by President Wilson personally during America's participation in the World War. When President

> Wilson told me that he desired American soldiers sent in these allied expeditions I told him that the war had to be won on the Western Front, in the opinion of Pershing, Bliss and March. That every soldier sent elsewhere delayed the final victory by delaying allied preponderance in France and that the British and French morale, which demanded successful side-shows, could be adequately sustained by increasing speed in landing American soldiers and equipment in France. His reply was: "Baker, I wholly agree with all you say from a military point of view, but we are fighting this war with allies and I have felt obliged to refuse to do so many things they have asked me to do that I really feel obliged to fall in with their wishes here. I have, however, stipulated that the American contingent in both cases is to be small."[55]

Cooperation with the Allies and the Czechs, then, was the main determinant for Wilson in approving American participation in the interventions.

Wilson himself explained his motives to the Allies in an aide-memoire on July 23. The explanation made clear his intention to work jointly with them, provided they did not go beyond the limited aims of American policy. They had his cooperation, he implied, now he expected them to cooperate with him. In the aide-memoire, Wilson declared that:

> The whole heart of the people of the United States is in the winning of this war. The controlling purpose of the Government of the United States is to do anything that is necessary and effective to win it. It wishes to cooperate in every practicable way with the Allied Governments, and to cooperate ungrudgingly; for it has no ends of its own to serve and believes that the war can be won only by common council and intimate concert of action. It has sought to study every proposed policy or action in which its cooperation has been asked in this spirit.

The president then went on to review the government's preferred approach for winning the war, which was to concentrate the American effort on the western front. He explained his opposition to political interference in Russia, which he called "military intervention," by saying that "it would add to the present confusion in Russia rather than cure it, injure her rather than help her, and that it would be of no advantage in the prosecution of our main design, to win the war against Germany." But Wilson recognized the need for "military action" as a way to "help the Czecho-Slovaks consolidate their forces and get into successful cooperation with their Slavic kinsmen and to steady any effort at self-government or self-defense in which the Russians themselves may be willing to accept assistance." The only proper role for

American and Allied forces was to guard the military stores at the ports and to help the Czechs. Thus, the president intended to limit American cooperation to "these modest and experimental plans." He was putting the Allies on notice that he would not go along with more ambitious efforts to overthrow the Bolsheviks or in any other way interfere in the internal affairs of Russia.[56]

This statement of policy reflected Wilson's attitude throughout the intervention. The aide-memoire was used to explain the mission of American troops in Siberia to General William S. Graves, commander of the American troops there. It was the only set of orders he received to describe his mission. In a press release issued in early August, Wilson publicly pledged not to interfere in Russia's internal affairs. The purpose of the intervention was to guard the war supplies at the ports, to help the Czechs, and to act collectively with the Entente powers.[57]

The Allies did not entirely agree with the president. Throughout the intervention, the United States ran into difficulty in trying to curb the ambitions of Japan. The British, too, went beyond the limited aims of the American government. Trouble plagued the expeditions in Siberia and northern Russia from their earliest moments because cooperation with the Allies proved easier to talk about than to practice. "There could be no such thing as unity of action because the representatives of England, France, and Japan were partisans in the Russian conflict and I was not," General Graves wrote afterwards. "This made cooperation impossible as long as my orders remained as originally issued."[58] Japan caused most of the problems, but the other Allies also diverged from Wilson's limited goals. At the heart of the difficulties lay a profound difference in objectives.

Even before the troops landed, Japan caused a stir by insisting on command of the Allied forces in Siberia. Eventually, Wilson agreed to the request and to British command in northern Russia, but this solved only part of the problem. In addition, the United States and the Allies disagreed over the number of troops to send and the objectives of their mission. On August 1, 1918, Wilson complained to Daniels that, "unhappily, the Japanese Government is trying to alter the whole plan in a way to which we cannot consent." Although Tokyo claimed it had no intention of sending any more troops than those necessary to assist the Czechs and guard the supplies, its perception of what this required was far more ambitious than Washington's. As Lansing's assistant, Breckinridge Long, pointed out on August 17: "The situation in Siberia is developing in a direction which differs somewhat from the policy outlined by the President. The movement is towards a greater military activity than appeared to be necessary at the time the President formulated the policy. There are unmistakable signs that there is in the Japanese mind an intention to send a larger military force." Long recommended a change in American policy to allow for "an increased military expedition" to keep up with the Japanese, but these views were unacceptable to Wilson.[59]

Throughout the late summer and into the fall of 1918, the Allies urged the Wilson administration to reinforce the Russian expeditions. General Thomas Bridges of the British Military Missions to the United States, for example, wrote the secretary of war on July 25 to argue in favor of recreating the eastern front. Based on an exaggerated estimate of Germany's strength, Bridges assumed that "if we face the war solely from the Western Front standpoint (and I include the Italian and Salonica fronts) without recreating some kind of Eastern Front, we have to reckon, sooner or later, with the whole German army, including most of the 38 or 40 divisions now on the Eastern Front backed by the larger reservoir of manpower, supplies, and raw materials of Russia." By expanding the interventions in Siberia and northern Russia, the Allies would be able to "help Russia onto her feet again, deny her resources to Germany, and draw off German troops from the decisive theatre." Bridges recognized that Washington viewed the situation differently than the British. "We have for a long time regarded the Bolsheviki as completely in German hands," he wrote, adding that "we probably trust the Japanese more than you and we believe that once some sort of Russian Army is in being we can use unlimited numbers of Japanese in the field without disturbing Russia." Bridges warned that, if the United States allowed the opportunity in Russia to slip away, it would be responsible for "prolonging the years of the war, millions of American casualties, the expenditure of billions of treasure, and in fact the heavy additions to the human sum of misery that we shall hereby incur, as well as a great risk of an inconclusive peace."[60] But Wilson refused to cave in to this pressure from the Allies, for he had no intention of expanding the operations in Russia. Instead, he directed the American effort against Germany to the western front, and the majority of his advisers endorsed that decision.

Wilson envisioned a very limited action in Russia. "The other governments are going much further than we and much faster,—are indeed, acting upon a plan which is altogether foreign from ours and inconsistent with it," he told Lansing in late August. He asked the secretary of state to explain to the Allies that "we do not think cooperation in *political* action necessary or desirable in eastern Siberia because we contemplate no political action of any kind there, but only the action of friends who stand at hand and wait to see how they can help. The more plain and emphatic this is made the less danger will there be of subsequent misunderstandings and irritations." Wilson's policy of helping the Russians, rather than imposing a solution to their troubles upon them, was reminiscent of his perception that he had aided the Mexicans, Haitians, and Santo Dominicans to find a way to end the revolutions in their countries. Lansing believed that American assistance to the Czechs was both sufficient and beneficial to U.S. purposes. "Our confidence in the Czech forces has been justified," he told the president, adding that "assistance to the Czechs amounts to assistance to the Russians." He urged Wilson to increase support of these forces through additional supplies.[61] This alternative was far more attractive than the plans proposed by the Allies.

In mid-September, the French joined the allied chorus urging additional reinforcements. Bliss opposed the request because it would distract from the effort on the western front where, he believed, the war would be won or lost. Baker quickly endorsed the general's arguments. "Bliss and I agree that yielding to this request would only open the door to further diversion of American forces as French and British will not send theirs and will join in requests upon us," the secretary advised Wilson. "Could you not decline on ground that our energy is to be devoted to early and decided success on the Western Front?" These views coincided with those of the president. At the end of the month, he instructed Lansing to announce the imposition of a severe limitation on the size of the American expeditionary forces. "The ideas and purposes of the Allies with respect to what should be done in Siberia and on 'the Volga Front' are ideas and purposes with which we have no sympathy," wrote Wilson. Lansing spelled out this decision in a note to the Allied governments. As a consequence, Japanese forces eventually outnumbered the Americans by about ten to one. Washington sent approximately seven thousand men; Tokyo sent around seventy thousand. In northern Russia, the ratio of British to American troops was more nearly equal, primarily because the British, their manpower reserves decimated by four years of war, did not have many men to spare for the intervention.[62]

Yet, despite Wilson's firm rejection of the efforts to increase American involvement in Russia, the Allies continued to press the administration for additional forces. On October 8, for example, the military representatives to the Supreme War Council, ignoring the protests of Bliss, issued Joint Note Number 38, which called for renewed efforts to open an eastern front. The military representatives, minus Bliss, who refused to sign the note, outlined a plan for the widely dispersed Allied and Czech forces in Russia to link up with each other along the Trans-Siberian Railway. The plan included a request for five additional battalions from the United States to supplement the single regiment already in northern Russia.

General Bliss, in an appendix to the joint note, pointed to the "extreme reluctance with which [the United States] considered the proposition to send an Expedition to Murmansk and Archangel; and when it agreed to take part in this Expedition, it contributed its quota of troops for a very limited and very clearly defined purpose." This purpose, Bliss reminded his colleagues, was to help the Czechs get out of Russia and "to steady any effort at self-government or self-defense in which the Russians themselves may be willing to accept assistance, but not to help any party of Russians against any other party or against any form of Russian government or to help that government against them." In addition, American forces in northern Russia were to guard any military stores that might be there and "to make it safe for Russians to organize there of their own free will, but not to help them fight against any form of Russian government or against any other body of Russian people." As Bliss pointed out: "Thus, it appears that the United States, having reserved to itself the right to limit, as may seem to it wise, the use of its military forces, and having plainly declared the limitations which it has imposed upon their use in Russia, nevertheless leaves the European powers with which it is associated in the war against Germany absolutely free to form and carry out their policy; and without further reference to the government of the United States."[63] Since the Allies depended on the United States to supply the expeditions with men and materials, the offer to let them decide their own policy without consulting Washington was gratuitous. Allied policy to reopen the eastern front, both Bliss and Wilson knew, depended on American assistance. By withholding its cooperation, the Wilson administration attempted to influence the course of the intervention.

The Armistice on November 11 negated any need to increase the size of the Russian interventions to recreate an eastern front. For many in the Wilson administration, peace with Germany took away the rationale for the expeditions altogether. General Pershing, for example, assumed that peace robbed the interventions of their original purposes. Baker wrote the president early in November that "I heartily wish it were possible for us to arrange affairs in such a way as to withdraw entirely from that expedition."[64] On November 27 the secretary of war put forth his opposition to continuing the interventions in stronger terms. In doing so, he touched upon what would become the central question in discussions with the Allies about withdrawal. Increasingly after the defeat of Germany, the Russian expeditions took on an anti-Bolshevik coloring. For Baker, this was simply not a legitimate purpose.

Baker began his argument against prolonging the interventions by reviewing their original goals. "We went into Murmansk and Archangel in order to prevent accumulated military stores from falling into the hands of the Germans," he reminded Wilson. The Allies landed troops in Vladivostok to help the Czechoslovaks. "Neither military expedition was in theory hostile either to Russia or to any faction or party in Russia," Baker pointed out, adding that these purposes were legitimate. But the signing of the Armistice changed the circumstances. The Germans were withdrawing, and Baker believed it was time to transport the Czechs back to their homeland. Consequently, "our forces in both places are now, I am afraid, being used for purposes for which we would not have sent them in the first instance." Since the onset of winter had "frozen in" the troops in northern Russia, Baker turned his attention to the forces in Siberia.

He saw no reason for keeping them in that region. Baker feared that they "were being used by the Japanese as a cloak for their own presence and operations now taking place." The secretary suspected the Japanese of using the intervention to take control of the Chinese Eastern Railroad and to encourage a pro-Japanese faction among the Russians. In addition, the Japanese were constantly sending reinforcements. Already, their force had grown from seven thousand men to seventy thousand. Thus, each additional day the United States remained merely gave the Japanese more time to expand their operations and increase the size of their expedition. By withdrawing, the administration would expose Tokyo's ambitions and save itself from further complicity in Japan's designs.

Baker also discounted the argument that the presence of American troops assisted relief efforts in the area, including the promotion of democratic ideals. "I frankly do not believe this," he wrote, "nor do I believe we have a right to use military force to compel the reception of our relief agencies." Similarly, the United States had no right to use force against Bolshevism. Baker told Wilson, "I do not know that I rightly understand Bolshevism. So much of it as I do understand I don't like, but I have a feeling that if the Russians do like it, they are entitled to have it and that it does not lie with us to say that only ten percent of the Russian people are Bolsheviks and that therefore we will assist the other ninety percent in resisting it." For Baker, only one solution made sense. "I have always believed that if we compelled the withdrawal of the Germans and Austrians we ought then to let the Russians work out their own problems," he advised the president. "Neither the method nor the result may be to our liking, but I am not very sure that the

Russians may not be able to work it out better if left to themselves, and more speedily, than if their primitive deliberations are confused by the imposition of ideas from outside." Thus, Baker concluded, "my own judgment is that we ought simply to order our forces home by the first boat and notify the Japanese that in our judgment our mission is fully accomplished and that nothing more can be done there which will be acceptable or beneficial to the Russian people by force of arms." Because force offered only limited benefits, and then only when applied to particular purposes, Baker recommended that the United States rely on economic and moral aid to Russia. The troops had achieved all that could be expected of them, he assured Wilson; it was time to bring them home.[65]

But even Baker realized that the question of withdrawal could not be settled in November 1918. As Bliss pointed out to Pershing, the issue would have to be decided through discussions with the Allies at the peace conference, which was scheduled to open in Paris in January 1919. Quite simply, this was the price of international cooperation. Many in the administration understood that the topic of Bolshevism would be one of the most important items on the agenda. For Secretary of State Lansing, Bolshevism represented the "most hideous and monstrous thing that the human mind has ever conceived." Lansing, however, refrained from advocating continued intervention. Instead, convinced that this dangerous ideology was spreading westward into Eastern and Central Europe, the secretary believed it essential that "we must not go too far in making Germany and Austria impotent as we may give life to a being more atrocious than the malignant thing created by the science of Frankenstein." Germany, though defeated militarily, must be left economically and morally strong enough to resist the insidious spread of Bolshevism.[66] The answer, then, lay with the settlement to be reached at the Paris Peace Conference.

The next chapter describes the course of both interventions from the opening of the Paris Peace Conference to the eventual withdrawal of American and Allied forces from northern Russia in the summer of 1919 and from Siberia in the summer of 1920. At Paris, the purpose of the expeditions took on a more explicitly anti-Bolshevik character. This confronted Wilson with a clear challenge to his conception of the role of force in foreign policy. Thus, the discussions about Russia during the peace conference offer a convenient example with which to analyze what Wilson learned about the limits of force from the interventions that he undertook, not only in Russia, but in Mexico, Haiti, Santo Domingo, and World War I.

7.
THE LIMITS of FORCE:

Russia, Bolshevism, and the Paris Peace Conference

World War I interrupted the domestic reforms of the Progressive movement by diverting attention to the defeat of German militarism. The American people accepted the new challenge eagerly, with high hopes for building a better world. United among themselves and with the other democracies, they expected to change the international system as they had reformed American government and society. Opposition to the war on the home front was not allowed, and objectors were silenced harshly. But the emphasis on unity and sacrifice spawned during the war did not survive long beyond the Armistice in November 1918. The brutal suppression of dissent unleashed all the doubts and uncertainties about the dramatic transformations wrought by Progressives. After two decades and more of agitation and reform, culminating in the brief experiment in restructuring the international system, the people of the United States retreated into more selfish pursuits. The great campaign to save the world for democracy ended in the belief that democracy could be preserved only at home, and interest in the salvation of Europe dwindled quickly. American troops returned from the front to devote themselves to personal business, not public crusades. They had found the limits of reform.

Bolshevism's infection of Russia, and the fear of its spread into Europe and across the Atlantic to the United States, encouraged this growing distrust of social and political change. The Red Scare of 1919–20, with its elements of xenophobia and resurgent conservatism, expressed the gnawing anxiety that the United States should avoid further contamination with European problems. As Arno Mayer has shown, this reactionary trend was not confined to America. Across Europe, the forces of movement confronted head-on the forces of order.[1] The ultimate defeat of the former induced a somnolence in liberal reform throughout much of the world.

In part, Woodrow Wilson, with his grand yet disturbingly vague promises of permanent peace and plenty, contributed to the somnipathy of liberalism. His inability to bring his program to fruition helped put to rest the faith in progressive change. The refusal of the American people to follow him into the League of Nations indicated that he had failed them as leader. But Wilson was victim, too, of the rejuvenated conservatism. The disavowal of membership in the league evidenced an overwhelming desire to renounce America's commanding position in world affairs. The denial of the president's dream signified a rejection of Wilsonian internationalism. Although the United States remained active in foreign affairs, Wilson's warning that it was better to try, at least, to control events, rather than merely to respond to the actions of other nations, went unheeded. Twenty years later, the next generation paid the price.

Thus, World War I represented, not the war to end all wars, but one episode in a continuing series of armed conflicts characterizing the relations between nations during the twentieth century. Force, not collective security and not the law, became the method of choice for regulating international affairs. For this, too, Wilson shared the blame. The interventions in Mexico, Haiti, Santo Domingo, World War I, and Russia illustrated the utility of armed power as a tool of foreign policy. Although presidents before him had turned to force to implement their policies, none had used it as freqently nor as consistently as Wilson. Tragically, because it was unintentional, Wilson confirmed for later generations of American leaders how convenient force could be in dealing with international problems.

Yet Wilson's successors often misunderstood the most important lesson he offered them. Wilson realized that force, as an aspect of power, must be limited in scope and invested with clear purpose and identifiable, realistic goals. One of the key elements in his employment of armed power was his ability to control the military. The president did not get carried away with armed power; he did not see it as the solution to international problems. In Wilsonian foreign policy, force provided just one way to achieve international goals and Wilson confined its uses to particular, well-defined aims. Once these were achieved, he turned to other forms of power, such as military (the threat of force), diplomatic, economic, and moral to implement his policies. In this way, force fit into a multifaceted approach to world affairs. Each tactic complemented the others to form an overall strategy of American internationalism.

THE LIMITS OF FORCE IN MEXICO, HAITI, SANTO DOMINGO, AND WORLD WAR I

Wilson knew the limits of force. Previous chapters of this study examine each intervention as it exemplifies a particular aspect of Wilson's understanding of the role of armed power in foreign policy. The occupation of Veracruz in 1914 and the punitive expedition two years later showed how Wilson bent the military to his purposes. Despite the protests of army and navy officers that fighting meant war, the president restrained their actions to the specific objectives he identified as important. He confined the occupation of Veracruz to the city limits, then used the presence of his soldiers on Mexican soil to inaugurate negotiations with the two leading factions in the country over the outcome of the revolution. Two years later, with Pershing deep in Mexico, yet under orders to do no more than chase bandits, Wilson again offered the presence of American troops as proof of his interest in the country's problems. As before, he arranged a conference with the leading power in Mexico in order to put forth American solutions to the crises racking the nation. Although both efforts to ingratiate American advice ultimately failed because of Mexican opposition, the attempts revealed Wilson's ability to limit the actions of the military and his desire to help in other lands.

The occupations of Haiti and Santo Domingo also expressed this longing to help. After months of trying to induce Haitian leaders to accept American assistance, the Wilson administration used the excuse of riots in Port-au-Prince to take over the entire country. Once the marines gained control, Admiral William S. Caperton sought a Haitian leader willing to follow orders. Finding such a man in Sudre Dartiguenave, Wilson used the presence of U.S. forces throughout the country to ensure his election as president. Afterwards, armed power played a minor role in the domination of Haiti. Instead, the United States relied on its diplomatic, economic, moral, and military power to effect social and governmental reforms. The organization of a marine-trained gendarmarie warded off further violent outbreaks, and ratification of a treaty between the two nations legitimized American actions at the same time that it guaranteed the U.S. a controlling say in Haitian affairs.

Less than a year later, the Wilson administration tried the same tactics in Santo Domingo. Although an occupation was carried out with relative ease after a revolt threatened the constituted government, the Dominican legislature refused to cooperate in the legitimization of

American control. Frustrated in the search for a docile Dominican, Wilson finally ordered a military government to rule the country. The military governor, an American naval officer, administered the affairs of the Republic until the Dominicans could learn the proper methods of self-rule. Part of his job was to teach them democracy.

The occupations of Haiti and Santo Domingo illustrate the depth of Wilson's democratic ideology and the lengths to which he went to help other peoples. In each instance, force gained him control of events, but once the navy and marines achieved this objective, Wilson switched to other forms of power to accomplish the larger goal of teaching democracy. He limited armed power to the crises of the moment: the quelling of revolution and the restoration of order. Even in Santo Domingo, where Dominican obstinacy compelled Wilson to establish an American military government, force was not needed to rule the country. With disorder subdued, military power sufficiently bolstered the occupation. Thus, as he had with the Mexican interventions, Wilson restrained the role of force in Haiti and the Dominican Republic.

The request to Congress for a declaration of war against Germany in April 1917 testified to Wilson's respect for international law. Throughout the period of neutrality, the president looked to the law as the standard with which to judge the actions of the belligerents. Although Great Britain was chided for its violations of the rules of blockade and contraband, Germany's reliance on submarine warfare seemed the greater offense against the laws of the sea. Wilson protested vigorously against the U-boat. Originally, the kaiser retreated by suspending submarine operations against unarmed and neutral vessels, but the hope of victory ultimately persuaded him to turn again to his fleet of U-boats. Germany's announcement of unrestricted submarine warfare in February 1917 left Wilson little choice but to break relations. Not long afterward, as submarines began the wholesale slaughter of all ships traveling in the war zone, Wilson determined on war as the only way to enforce the law.

Throughout the period of neutrality, Wilson also strove to substantiate his claim as impartial mediator of the dispute. Even as he protested German and British infringements on international law, he offered his services to negotiate an end to the war. These efforts led him to articulate a new system of international relations based on cooperation among the major industrial powers. The pain of declaring war on Germany was eased by the hope that, through the destruction of militarism, the relations between nations could be restructured to ensure the future peace. Wilson intended to avert future wars and strengthen international law by orchestrating a concert of nations.

During World War I, American domestic and foreign policies emphasized the necessity of cooperation. The selective service system engineered by General Enoch H. Crowder relied on the willingness of the citizenry to cooperate in the national effort. Crowder's "supervised decentralization" fostered this attitude by using local leaders to administer the draft in each community. Similarly, the organization of the country's industrial power depended on corporate and business leaders working together under the auspices of the War Industries Board. In the realm of military action, Wilson insisted that the army and navy, while retaining their national identities, join ranks with the Allied forces. The establishment of the Supreme War Council and its committee of military advisers and the selection of Ferdinand Foch as commander of the Allied armies signaled the success of cooperation.

The Allied proposal for an intervention in Russia offered Wilson an opportunity to test the utility of collective security. Although he originally opposed a military expedition to Siberia because he suspected the motivation behind it and doubted its military efficacy, he eventually went along with it to illustrate the ability of nations to work together. For this reason, too, Wilson agreed to a joint intervention with Great Britain in northern Russia. Siberia and Archangel became the laboratories wherein Wilson experimented with a multinational approach to the solution of international problems. Force helped him give expression to his faith in the proposed League of Nations. Wilson hoped to show that the democratic nations, by collective action, could deal with such renegade countries as Germany and Russia.

Thus, Wilson turned to armed power to promote American democratic ideology, enforce international law, establish international cooperation, and encourage collective security. Through his tight control of the military, the president limited his uses of force to clearly identified objectives. By achieving these, he opened new avenues along which other aspects of American power could be brought into action. That Wilson's policies ultimately failed showed that his reach far exceeded his grasp. Armed power contributed to this failure by arousing resentment in the hearts of the peoples against whom Wilson applied it. Carranza, for example, bitterly objected to the occupation of Veracruz despite the fact that it seriously interrupted Huerta's ability to wage war against the Constitutionalists. Two years later, Carranza again protested the help the United States extended to him with the punitive expedition against Pancho Villa. Wilson never understood that American assistance, particularly its military aid, was neither sought nor wanted in Mexico.

Similarly, Wilson's efforts to compel the peoples of Haiti and Santo

Domingo along the path to democracy failed because neither the Haitians nor the Dominicans went willingly. Force accomplished the physical subjugation of each country, but it extended no further. The refusal of the people to learn the lessons Wilson taught meant that armed power, regardless of its overwhelming advantages, offered little help when it came to the promotion of ideas. The ideal of democracy could not be crammed down their throats nor instilled with rifle butts. In spite of the limits Wilson put on force, his ambitions still exceeded even its abilities.

Wilson used force during World War I to defend an idea. By interpreting the war as an association of the democratic countries in battle against militarism and autocracy, the president transformed it into a fight to save democracy. He made the war a conflict between contrasting ideologies, a grand contest to protect the democratic way of life from its autocratic opposite. Unlike the interventions in Mexico, Haiti, and Santo Domingo, during which Wilson applied force offensively to promote the ideal of democracy, American intervention in the First World War was an essentially defensive attempt to preserve that ideal. Although force failed in the earlier interventions, it proved admirably suited to protect what already existed—the democracies of Britain, France, and the United States.

For as long as the interventions in Russia retained their original purposes—to guard large accumulations of war supplies, open a second front, and assist the Czechs—armed power lent itself to the efforts. Increasingly, however, as the war against Germany drew to a close, the Allies invested the Russian expeditions with an anti-Bolshevik character. Wilson, perhaps because of his previous experiences, realized the futility of combatting a political ideology with arms. He argued that Bolshevism, as an idea, could not be fought with force. Instead, he believed that other forms of power, primarily economic and moral, were more appropriate responses to the Russian revolution.

Wilson's opposition to the use of force against an ideology reflected his understanding of the limits of force. At the same time, the president's efforts to organize a League of Nations represented a refinement of his views on the role of force in international affairs. The president's belief in the ability of collective security to regulate the relations between nations merely carried into peacetime his emphasis on international cooperation during the war. These two themes, the restraint of force against Bolshevism and the promotion of collective security, are explored in this chapter. They illustrate the coming to maturity of Wilson's understanding of armed power.

COLLECTIVE FAILURE IN RUSSIA

As with most of the issues discussed at the Paris Peace Conference, confusion and ignorance of what was going on characterized the American delegation's approach to the Russian question. The fault for this lay with Wilson for failing to exercise adequate leadership over the other commissioners. The American commission consisted of Wilson at the head, House, Lansing, Bliss, and Henry White, the only Republican. Wilson listened to their advice on matters he considered within their respective areas of expertise, but he did not take them into his confidence in other areas nor share with them his general views on the course of the proceedings. Although, for example, Wilson and House established the Inquiry in 1917 to study possible terms of the peace, once the conference opened the president rarely sought its studied opinions, despite the fact that some of the brightest minds in the country participated in it. Lacking time and interest to consult his subordinates, Wilson tried to reshape the world single-handedly.

Each morning, Lansing, Bliss, and White met in their rooms at the Hotel Crillon to review the course of the conference, but the record of these meetings reveals that they seldom knew what was transpiring between the president and the heads of the other delegations. Rumor and gossip were often their only sources of information. House occasionally attended these meetings to pass on requests and instructions from Wilson, but he made little effort to keep his colleagues informed of the president's activities. Wilson and House mistakenly assumed that they could carry the burden of the negotiations alone, calling on the other commissioners only when they needed expert opinion. American policy and interests suffered from their arrogance.

As a consequence, members of the American Commission to Negotiate the Peace remained uncertain of Wilson's policies and often unaware until after the fact of agreements he reached with the other participants. Frustration and disenchantment were the result. When, for instance, the final draft of the treaty was presented to the Germans on May 7, few in the American delegation had read the document in its entirety. A rash of resignations among the junior members of the American commission protesting the terms of the settlement greeted the treaty's publication. William R. Bullitt, who served as an expert on Russia, resigned on May 17 because, he informed the president, the treaty would "deliver the suffering peoples of the world to new oppressions, subjections, and dismemberment—a new century of war." He included Russia, which had "not even been understood" at the conference, among his many examples of the treaty's failings. "It is my conviction," Bullitt charged Wilson, "that if you had made your fight in the open, instead of behind closed doors, you would have carried with you the public opinion of the world, which was yours." He indicted Wilson for losing faith, not only in the ideals he formerly espoused, but also in the millions of people who supported the president's program. Others shared Bullitt's disillusionment.[2]

Wilson took on too much of the work himself. Convinced that this was his only chance to mold the world according to his vision of the peace, he distrusted anyone else's competence to handle the negotiations. Wilson met daily with David Lloyd George of England, Georges Clemenceau of France, and, somewhat less frequently, with Vittorio Orlando of Italy. These leaders summoned witnesses, experts, and other representatives to Wilson's house, where they usually met during the last half of the conference, to confer on particular issues, but they negotiated among themselves on many of the final resolutions. The tremendous amount of work and enormous amount of detail involved in this schedule eventually overwhelmed the president. In the end, both his health and the treaty paid the price.

Even House ultimately failed to live up to the president's expectations. When Wilson returned briefly to the United States in mid-February, he left House in charge, believing the colonel alone understood his goals. Yet, arriving back at the conference a month later, Wilson found to his chagrin that House had given in too much. Thrown into despair by this seeming treason to his ideals, the president assumed even more of the work. Thus, House, too, was often left in the dark. At the end of June, with the treaty signed and ready for delivery to the Senate, Wilson took leave of the ubiquitous Colonel House, never to see his former confidant again. Their friendship, one of the most powerful partnerships in American political history, ran aground on the shoals of Wilson's conviction that he alone could redeem the peace.

By trying to pull all the strings, Wilson only succeeded in tying himself up in knots. He preserved his general vision of the postwar world, but lost his way amidst the details of the settlement. Faced with opposition from all sides, Wilson compromised again and again on specific issues, hoping all the while that his cherished League of Nations would solve the problems left over from the conference. Although he stood up to Italy's demand for Fiume, for example, he surrendered to Japan's insistence on possession of Shantung. The former decision left Italy disgruntled; the latter disillusioned many of Wilson's followers because it violated the principle of self-determination. Against the advice of the other commissioners, Wilson pledged to France protection against future German aggression. In the president's view, the league made this guarantee innocuous, but it handed his opponents sufficient ammunition for them to charge that he had disregarded America's traditional policy of no alliances. These compromises and special agreements gave the treaty an ungainly appearance. Wilson's lofty principles were brought down to earth by the greedy demands of other countries.

The question of Russia brought together all these problems. Two concerns, a pronounced desire to withdraw U.S. forces and an unwillingness to resort to force against Bolshevism, dominated the American delegation's considerations of the issue. The weather, combined with suspicion over Britain's plans, complicated the withdrawal from the northern region. The activities of Japan discouraged the United States from pulling out of Siberia. At the same time, the spread of Bolshevism across Russia and into Eastern and Central Europe panicked British and French officials, who proposed using force as the defense. The Americans, however, thought they knew better the limits of armed power. These three topics, though recognized as interrelated, were considered separately at the conference.

By the time the peace conference convened, arctic temperatures in northern Russia had frozen any substantial troop movements. Breckinridge Long, for instance, pointed out in a draft statement of policy on January 21 that the United States intended the northern expedition to protect Allied war supplies and "to safeguard the rear of the Czecho-Slovaks." Although peace brought an end to these missions, the administration allowed them to continue because of "physical necessity." Until the spring thaw, no ship could break through the ice blocking the port of Archangel. Even Tasker Bliss, one of the most ardent advocates of withdrawal, admitted that little could be done until the spring. The forces at Archangel, he advised Lansing and White at their daily meeting on January 30, could not be moved to Murmansk because of the "great difficulties which these troops would have in effecting a retreat during the winter." Nevertheless, Bliss, fearful that the Allies—particularly the British—might convince Wilson to expand American operations in the area, repeatedly pressed on the president the need to bring the troops home. On February 9, for example, he determined to tell Wilson that American soldiers should be "gotten out of Russia as soon as possible. They are not doing the slightest good there that I can see."[3] He hoped that by making American policy clear, the Allies would drop any plans for a more ambitious intervention.

Part of the urgency that Bliss and his colleagues felt resulted from a number of reports reaching Paris throughout the winter and spring of

1919 that indicated a serious deterioration in the morale of American troops stationed in Russia. For the first time in Wilson's experience as commander-in-chief, his officers talked of the possibility of mutiny among the troops. On at least one occasion, soldiers in Archangel temporarily refused to return to the front. The statements of the commanding officers involved showed a disenchantment with their mission. General Edward Ironside, the British commander of the Allied forces in northern Russia, described the expedition as "a side show of the Great War. It was a hasty improvisation conceived without much previous consideration by either political or military experts, almost in desperation, as it were, to prevent the Germans from winning the war in France." General Graves admitted that he had "never been able to come to any satisfactory conclusion as to why the United States ever engaged in such intervention."[4] One of the most bitter judgments came from N. A. McCully, the commanding officer of the U.S. naval forces in northern Russia. Writing to his superiors in the Office of Naval Intelligence in early June 1919, McCully observed:

> From indications at the present time, Allied Operations in Northern Russia, however righteous their intention, have accomplished little either in a Military way, in the way of gaining the good will of any considerable number of Russians, or even in the way of securing the safety of a population compromised by its friendship with the Allies, and now apparently on the verge of being abandoned by them.
>
> To be sure, the Allies, during the period of their Occupation, have fed the population, not thoroughly or generously, but sufficient to prevent starvation. . . .
>
> What has been needed before everything has been an Influence which has the Good of Russia at heart and only the Good of Russia, and of such an Influence the Russian has yet had no assurance. However, he is accustomed to suffer, and if this comes to pass the limits of his endurance, he meets at least this eventuality gracefully.[5]

These reports and complaints reinforced the Wilson administration in its determination to withdraw American forces from the northern expedition as soon as the weather permitted it.

The American delegation suspected that Great Britain wanted the American troops to stay. Its views, however, were based on hearsay and rumor, for British policy was by no means clear in the winter of 1919. Bliss noted that "the present expedition in North Russia is, to all intents, a British expedition. It is under British command and it is presumably executing plans approved by the British War Cabinet." He urged his colleagues to clarify American policy so that no one could misunderstand American intentions. "Has the United States any plan of its own, or will they continiue to send troops to Russia at the demand of the British commander?" he asked in one memorandum. The United States must encourage, he believed, "a distinct understanding between the Allies as to their military plans in Russia." Otherwise, American troops would be used for purposes not intended by the Wilson administration.[6]

Great Britain exacerbated these suspicions in February by asking for almost fifteen hundred troops to help repair the railroads in Murmansk. Wilson turned the request over to Bliss for his military advice. Seizing the opportunity, Bliss again urged withdrawal. "I doubt the political or military wisdom of sending any more troops to North Russia except for the purpose of enabling the force that we now have there to concentrate at Murmansk and Archangel at the earliest moment that it can do so with safety," he told the president on February 8. The only purpose for the additional troops should be to help evacuate the ones already there. Wilson approved the suggestion. Consequently, on February 13, Bliss informed the Allies that the United States would send technical troops "for the purposes of assisting in placing the Murmansk Railway in condition to render it efficient for the supply and maintenance of the American and Allied force in Northern Russia during the winter and facilitate the prompt withdrawal of the entire expedition as soon as weather conditions in the spring will permit."[7] The weather did not interfere with reinforcing the expeditions, as it did with withdrawing them, because it was a limited number of troops and they would be taken in at Murmansk. The British agreed to Bliss's conditions, which meant that he had, for the moment, won his point. In addition, he received some indication that American forces would be evacuated as soon as it was warm enough.

Despite other indications that the Allies now wished to withdraw from Archangel and Murmansk, the American commissioners did not rest easy. In their daily meeting on April 1, Bliss pointed out to Lansing and White that "although the American Delegation was absolutely in favor of having these troops withdrawn, it had not yet been possible to get the President to induce the other Associated Governments to commit themselves on this point." The next day, the American delegates received a report from their consul at Archangel that General Ironside intended to move troops into the interior in an effort to link up with the Allied forces in Siberia. Ironside reportedly felt that an Allied withdrawal from the region would lead to the collapse of the government there and its replacement by Bolsheviks. This and other reports of a similar nature convinced Bliss to take the subject up once again with Wilson. For some time, he had suspected the British of harboring anti-Bolshevik ambitions for the expedition. On April 21 he informed the president that the British had no intention of withdrawing. Nevertheless, he said, the United States should still pull out.[8]

This information bothered Wilson enough that, the next day during his meeting with Lloyd George and Clemenceau at his house, he brought up the subject. He asked the British prime minister if he were sending additional troops to Archangel. Mentioning the memorandum from Bliss, Wilson expressed his concern that "the local British Commander, instead of contemplating withdrawal, intended to take steps to link up the Russian forces in the north with those in Siberia." Was it also true, Wilson inquired, that twelve thousand reinforcements were being sent to Ironside?

Lloyd George pleaded that there must be some misunderstanding, yet he did little to clarify the situation. "Great importance was attached to secrecy in regard to the withdrawal from north Russia," he explained, "and possibly this was some local bluff to convey the impression that no withdrawal was intended." He also mentioned, in a reversal of his previous statement, that he "did not think that the reinforcements contemplated were nearly so large." At any rate, he promised Wilson that he would look into the matter. This answer seemed to satisfy the president, who informed Bliss that the Allies were "quite of our mind and purpose." He asked Bliss to cooperate with them in tracking down the source of these rumors since "they are anxious to cooperate with us in getting the troops out." A few days later, Lloyd George reported back to the president that only five thousand troops were being sent to Ironside. He offered no explanation of why reinforcements were going to northern Russia if withdrawal was the objective. Wilson failed to ask him to clarify the point.[9]

Soon enough, however, the British made their intentions clear. At one of their daily meetings at the end of April, Lloyd George expressed an interest in assisting militarily the organized group of Russians at Archangel friendly to the British. Wilson responded firmly that "the United States only had one regiment at Archangel, and United States public opinion would not tolerate sending any more troops." The prime minister replied haughtily that "the British Government had called for volunteers, and had received more offers than they could accept. The lists had had to be closed, because they were full." But his answer only heightened Wilson's suspicions. He later informed Admiral Benson that "so far as we are concerned, there are no plans whatever for active operations, and what is intended is merely to insure a safe withdrawal of our land forces." The president could no longer speak knowingly about the concerns of the Allies.[10]

With the coming of spring, the British increased their pressure on the United States not to end its participation in the intervention. Bliss, unsure of the effect this pressure would have on Wilson, wrote on May 29 to ask that the troops in Archangel be evacuated or, at the least, replaced with fresh forces. "I do not know what is to be the political policy of the United States in Russia," he advised the president, "but, even if such a policy should involve the use of American troops there, I believe that the present force should be withdrawn because we know from many reports that it has become largely disaffected." Bliss warned that if new troops were sent, they risked being trapped in Archangel or Murmansk during the next winter. He pleaded with Wilson to determine American policy so that appropriate dispositions of forces could be made.[11]

But Wilson had already made his decision, even though he failed to keep Bliss informed adequately. He successfully withstood Allied pressures to prolong the intervention because he was convinced that it would do little good. Having proven the utility of international cooperation by joining the intervention in the first place, Wilson felt no great compulsion to carry on with it. If the British intended to stay, they would have to go it alone. Benson reported on June 6 that the American troops had been withdrawn from Archangel. Four days later, Wilson assured the anxious Bliss that "I have not changed my mind in the least, and the withdrawal of our troops should be in no way interrupted or delayed." This settled American policy, but as late as July, the Allies again pressed for assistance in the northern expedition. Bliss, still in Paris, tried to discourage them. Meanwhile, the evacuation of the troops proceeded unabated.[12] Since the British, despite the overwhelming numbers of volunteers, preferred not to act alone, they, too, withdrew their forces during the summer of 1919. Collective action, Wilson taught them, worked two ways.

Wilson's method of handling the discussions on the northern intervention interfered with his policy. Bliss served as the president's expert on the subject because of his military background and his interest in the intervention, but he rarely knew what Wilson wanted since the president infrequently consulted with him. According to one historian, Wilson met only five times with Bliss during the entire six months of the peace conference.[13] Bliss had no idea until the very end just where Wilson stood, which caused him constant anxiety lest the Allies convince the president to continue the intervention. Ignorant of what both Wilson and Lloyd George planned, Bliss could offer little help to the president in responding in British pressures. His lack of information forced him to confine his advice to monotonously reiterating his views on withdrawal.

By cutting Bliss off, Wilson exposed himself to the brunt of the pressure from the British. Although within his prerogative as the man in charge of American policy, he left himself with no one to advise him on the facts or on what should be done. As Wilson admitted to his acquaintance, Norman Hapgood, his impressions of Russia were based on scanty and "indefinite information."[14] His egotistical refusal to delegate authority hurt himself and the national interest. It meant more work and more stress for him at a time when his attention was urgently needed on other issues pending before the conference. Since he had decided to withdraw American troops from Murmansk and Archangel, it seems odd indeed that he did not pass on to Bliss the distasteful task of dealing with British objections. Had he done so, Wilson might have spared himself a great deal of frustration and worry. This same arrogant attitude appeared in the way he handled other problems during the peace conference, including the intervention in Siberia.

Wilson never fully grasped the situation in Siberia. Pressed by other business, confused by faulty and conflicting reports from the men on the ground, and blinded by an abiding distrust of the Japanese, Wilson stumbled about in search of an escape from the imbroglio in which he and the country were enmeshed. The solution to the problem proved elusive, and Wilson clumsily jumped from one policy to another. In his previous interventions, Wilson had pursued reasonable policies—given his goals—with reasonable consistency, but the president never answered to his own satisfaction the most basic question about the Siberian intervention: Why are American troops there? As he admitted in a meeting of the Council of Four on May 20, he "did not feel the same chagrin that he had formerly felt at having no policy in regard to Russia. It had been impossible to have a policy hitherto." Even after May 20, however, he still could not offer a coherent approach to the intervention. He explained to his colleagues that the United States went into Siberia to help get the Czechs out of Russia, but that they "had refused to go."[15] The statement was misleading since little effort was ever made to evacuate the Czechs. Wilson's candid admission that he had no policy merely made explicit what his actions and decisions had implied throughout the intervention.

The president's subordinates reflected his confusion. Some believed the purpose of the intervention was to help the Czechs. Some said it was to curb the Japanese appetite for influence and control. Others wanted to use it as a base against the Bolsheviks. Still others hoped to keep the railroads running so the population could be fed and the White Army equipped. A few perceived it as a way to help Admiral Alexander Kolchak, head of the White Army, gain power over all of Russia. And some of Wilson's subordinates intended to use the intervention to teach Kolchak liberal, democratic methods.

In truth, Wilson chased all these policies, sometimes skipping from

The Limits of Force / 233

one to the other and sometimes following all at once. He wanted to help the Czechs, curb the Japanese, stop the Bolsheviks, keep the railroads running, and assist Kolchak to gain power as head of a democratic government. But most of all, Wilson wanted the whole mess to disappear. Unfortunately, it did not go away and he could never determine which of these policies was most important. In the end, poor health forced him to step back and let events play themselves out. The United States finally withdrew its forces from Siberia in the summer of 1920. Little success could be claimed for the intervention. "In a vastly confused situation your duties were frequently delicate and difficult," Baker told Graves in summing up the accomplishments of the general's mission, "because of the remoteness of your field of action from the United States, you were thrown completely upon your own resources and initiative."[16] Yet, this was small consolation for the troubles endured by Graves and his troops.

Baker correctly understood that Graves was much on his own in Siberia. The guiding hand that Wilson had exercised in Mexico, Haiti, Santo Domingo, World War I, and even in Murmansk and Archangel failed him in Siberia. Save for his original decision to cooperate with the Allies, Wilson never saw clearly just what he wanted from the Siberian intervention. When cooperation went as far as it could go, the president's policies ran out of steam. Though he stoked frantically, nothing could get things moving again. Thus, as he had shown the British the dual nature of international cooperation, so now he learned of its pitfalls from the Japanese.

The situation in Siberia differed significantly from American participation in the northern expedition. Most importantly, Japan was far more self-reliant than England, and, therefore, much less dependent on the cooperation of the United States. Wilson, realizing that American withdrawal would not coerce the Japanese to pull out as it had the British, felt compelled to continue the intervention. He did so in order to retain some measure of influence over Tokyo's policies. The next step, that of active political interference in the area, came naturally.

Occasionally, a report from Tokyo encouraged a belief that the civilians in the government wanted to bring Japan's policy into line with Washington's. This was, however, by no means evident in Japan's actions. If the United States pulled out and left it a free hand in Siberia, it would soon have complete control of the vital Siberian railways. In addition, the Americans had convincing evidence that Japan was interfering freely in the internal politics of the region. Graves, for example, considered that the Japanese and the "organized Russian Cossack troops east of Bakal constitute one force." According to Lansing, the strain in U.S.-Japanese relations resulted from Japan's goal of "eventual domination of Eastern Siberia."[17] This ambition directly contradicted America's traditional policy of the Open Door and Wilson's announced intention to avoid forcible intervention in Russia's internal affairs.

Thus, the desire to keep tabs on the Japanese became the prime motive for continuing the intervention after the signing of the Armistice. Peace with Germany also meant that the original aim of helping the Czechoslovak Legion reach the western front no longer obtained. At the end of March 1919, Graves recommended that the Czechs be withdrawn as soon as possible in order to avoid trouble between them and the Russians in the area. The American commissioners to the peace conference reached the same conclusion, though their reasoning was based on a fear that the Czechs would be contaminated by Bolshevism.[18] Although the Czechs were not withdrawn at this time, they no longer served as an adequate excuse for the presence of American soldiers. The administration needed a new reason to justify the continuance of the intervention. Consequently, in early 1919, it developed a plan for interallied control and operation of the Trans-Siberian Railway.

The proposal called for the establishment of a zone six miles wide along the length of the railroad. This zone would be policed jointly by Japanese and American forces. Despite the overwhelming distances involved and the refusal to send Graves the large number of reinforcements necessary to implement the plan, the administration pushed the proposal for two reasons. First, it offered a way to curb Japanese ambitions by enticing them to cooperate with the United States. Since the railroad would be operated by a commission of engineers headed by John F. Stevens, an American who had been advising the local Russian authorities on the maintenance and operation of the railroad since 1917, the Wilson administration entertained great hopes of dominating the control of the Trans-Siberian Railway. Secondly, the plan offered a legitimate purpose for continuing the intervention which would effectively deflect the growing number of domestic critics, particularly in the Senate, who were questioning Wilson's policies in Siberia.

The official excuse was that control of the rails best ensured keeping open the routes of commerce into Siberia and European Russia. "The [State] Department has believed the only solution of the Russian problem to be an attempt to restore normal conditions of economic life," William Phillips, an assistant secretary of state, cabled the American delegation to the peace conference on March 28. The railroad plan offered the best way to achieve this. If it failed, Phillips feared, the Japanese would intervene on a massive scale. Through the efforts of the American ambassador in Tokyo, Roland Morris, the Japanese government eventually approved the plan.[19]

On April 2 Wilson issued the following instructions for transmittal to Graves:

> General Graves should be instructed that the United States favors economic rehabilitation of the country and feels strongly that a policy of political moderation among the several Russian factions is a necessary condition. In particular General Graves should be told that his mission is to insure the cooperation with his Allies of uninterrupted operation of the Trans-Siberian and Chinese Eastern Railways and it is suggested that the movements of his forces be limited to a zone of say three miles on either side of the railway.

On Baker's recommendation, Graves's new orders were amended to limit the objectives of American policy to "the preservation of order about the railroad, its stations and trains, as those in charge of the railroad may request, and also stating definitely as one of late objects the common desire to bring about the cessation of local violence by conflicting Russian forces merely as such actions affect the dispatch of trains or operation of the railroad." Thus, the establishment of a zone was dropped in favor of simply keeping the rails operating. According to Baker, the advantage of this policy was that it limited Allied military activity to the railroad, it would not require expanding the intervention force, and it would "give no implied sanction to great increases by any nation or extension of its political or military activities."[20] He hoped that the Japanese would be as limited in their actions as the United States.

The railroad plan relieved much of the anxiety among administration officials concerning the decision to prolong the intervention. "While conditions in Eastern Siberia are reported to be still unsatisfactory," Polk reported to Lansing on April 24, "I believe that the situation will be relieved first, by the operation of the railways under Stevens, and second, by our present efforts to secure a unity of policy on the part of Japan and ourselves and also the other governments concerned in regard to the employment of military forces now in Siberia." Maintenance of the railroads became the official purpose—and excuse—for the intervention, replacing the earlier rationale of aiding the Czechs. "So far as I know," Bliss wrote on June 21, "the United States has committed itself to a military expedition in Siberia which, as I understand it, was originally intended to assist a force of Czecho-Slovaks in Siberia to escape from massacre by the Bolsheviks and which subsequently was instructed to guard a certain section of the Trans-Siberian Railroad." At the end of June, Wilson used American participation in the railroad plan to explain his policies to the Senate. "The purpose of the continuance of American troops in Siberia, is that we, with the concurrence of the great Allied powers, may keep open a necessary artery of trade and extend to the vast population of Siberia the economic aid essential to it in peacetime but indispensable under the conditions which have followed the prolonged and exhausting participation by Russia in the war against the Central Powers," Wilson informed the upper house. This statement temporarily satisfied the Senate, but Wilson's argument hid the basic confusion permeating his Siberian policies.[21]

Wilson's lack of a clear conception of what he wanted from the Siberian intervention robbed it of any chance for constructive work. Even the plan to keep the railroads open was racked by inconsistency and ambivalence. Keeping the lines clear and operating efficiently was a great help to the White forces in the area, particularly those of Admiral Kolchak, who was headquartered in Omsk. Yet, even as Wilson held out this bit of assistance to Kolchak, the president refused to go all the way. He insisted that Kolchak adopt a liberal platform of reforms before he receive further help, including diplomatic recognition, from the United States. At the same time, Wilson continued to press for a policy of noninvolvement among the Allies in the internal affairs of Siberia. These conflicting policies of helping Kolchak with the one hand while denying him enough assistance with the other merely reflected Wilson's lack of information and his indecision. It alienated America's allies and thoroughly confused Wilson's subordinates. For example, the American commissioners suggested issuing a declaration disclaiming any intention of interfering in Russia's internal affairs but adding that the United States desired to help the government in Siberia "until such time as all Russia may become united under a central government in which the whole country is represented." They offered no explanation of how this could be done without interfering in the internal affairs of the area because they themselves did not know.[22]

More than most other American officials, General Graves suffered from the confusion inherent in Wilson's contradictory policies. State Department representatives, both on the ground and in Washington, urged increased support of Kolchak, including diplomatic recognition. Graves, however, diligently pursued his original orders to avoid taking sides in the Russian civil war. This attitude exposed him to severe criticisms from the State Department. Polk complained to Lansing on March 13 that "General Graves is holding absolutely aloof from internal conflicts between Russian factions." Not only did this bring him into opposition with Japan, but it also weakened America's policy of supporting Stevens in the operation of the railroad. Quoting from various State Department representatives, Polk indicated that Graves, "without employing his forces to assist one Russian faction as against another, should be authorized definitely to throw the weight of such influence as he may have through the presence of American forces to insist upon a policy of moderation" among the Russians. Polk and others in the State Department believed the situation was beyond Graves's abilities, and they recommended his relief.[23]

These complaints eventually reached the president, who was concerned enough by them to ask Baker if Graves should be replaced in order to "relieve unnecessary friction" with the Japanese and the Russians. The secretary of war defended his subordinate by pointing out that Graves was following his orders. "Up to the present," Baker wrote Wilson, "he has no orders except to guard the railroads and preserve local order without taking sides" between the various factions. This answer appealed to the president's desire not to intervene in Russia's internal affairs, just as the State Department's complaints appealed to his desire to find a liberal substitute for Bolshevism. Graves stayed in command of American forces in Siberia, much to the chagrin of State Department officials, who continued their efforts to increase support for Kolchak. The episode revealed the split nature of Wilson's policies and his inability to reconcile his divergent motives.[24]

Kolchak represented the only hope, however slim, of replacing Bolshevism with a liberal Russian government. Part of the reason for Wilson's ambivalence toward the admiral resulted from the president's doubts about Kolchak's liberalism. State Department reports painted a rosy picture of Kolchak's political leanings and of his military strength, a view endorsed by British officials. But still Wilson remained skeptical. In a meeting with Lloyd George and Clemenceau on May 7, Wilson insisted that Kolchak should promise that he would institute reforms if he won the civil war. The president believed that Bolshevism would soon fail of its own weaknesses. What he feared most was that "Imperial Russia might remain." In order to determine Kolchak's true political colors and his chances for success, Wilson arranged for Ambassador Morris to travel to Omsk on a fact-finding mission.[25]

In the meantime, Graves reported that Kolchak, angered at America's policy of noninterference, might start fighting against U.S. troops. "We are now squarely up against the proposition of using force or getting out as the Russian military are coming to our sector and evidently are not only going to ignore us but practically attempt to take over our duties in guarding railroad," Graves warned in early May. In transmitting this message to Wilson, Baker added his opinion that "either General Graves should be directed to cooperate with the Kolchak government or he ought to be withdrawn." But Wilson was not yet ready to make that decision. The day after receiving this information, he told Lloyd

George and Clemenceau that he "had always been of opinion that the proper policy of the Allied and Associated Powers was to clear out of Russia and leave it to the Russians to fight it out among themselves." Still, he issued no orders to this effect, nor did he offer any direction to Graves on meeting Kolchak's forces. Instead, he waited to hear from Morris.[26] The immense distances involved and the confused nature of the situation delayed Morris's report. He visited Kolchak's headquarters in July and August, which meant that Wilson lacked accurate information in the interim. The president and the Allied powers continued to discuss the intervention. At Wilson's insistence, Kolchak was promised additional aid if he could give assurances concerning the establishment of a liberal, democratic government. Lansing, Bliss, and White, who heard only rumors of these discussions, feared that some sort of quid pro quo arrangement existed between the Allies and Kolchak over recognition. The president assured them that he knew nothing about any secret deal. Their concern showed once again the isolation in which Wilson worked during the peace conference.[27]

In early June, Kolchak issued a proclamation promising elections to a constituent assembly and land for the peasants, among other reforms, once the Bolsheviks were defeated. Wilson pronounced it "a very good proclamation," but it was, in fact, little more than a pipe dream. Internal dissension among the White forces and the growing strength of the Red Army doomed Kolchak to defeat. The Allies proposed a blockade of Russia in a last, desperate attempt to help the White Army, but Wilson declined to participate. Since the United States was not at war with Russia, he had no legal authority to impose a blockade. As he told his friend Vance McCormick on June 22, "the Russian people must solve their own problems without outside interference." In reverting to this stand, Wilson recognized that Kolchak, whose liberalism he continued to suspect, was teetering at the edge of defeat.[28]

Morris confirmed that Kolchak was on the verge of military defeat. In addition, the ambassador considered the admiral a reactionary who headed a corrupt military government. Nevertheless, he preferred even Kolchak to Bolshevism. But Wilson disagreed. The president informed the Council of Four that, since the United States had not recognized the Omsk government, it could provide only limited support. This stance infuriated State Department officials. Basil Miles, for instance, threatened to resign if the United States withdrew from Siberia before Kolchak was strong enough to stand alone. Unfortunately, neither Miles nor his colleagues understood that Wilson had gone as far as he intended to go in supporting the admiral.[29]

Wilson's policies toward Kolchak illustrate the confusion and indecision underlying the intervention. Unable to withdraw because of his fear of Japan's ambitions in the area, Wilson toyed with various schemes to help Kolchak, even though he was never comfortable with political interference in the area. Wilson insisted that Kolchak establish a liberal political platform, but he refused to offer full American support. Indeed, even after Kolchak gave the required assurances, Wilson continued to distrust him. Consequently, American policy was never more than half-measures that changed direction almost daily. At the end of July, for example, the administration again objected to Japanese policies in a note that some officials, particularly Baker, considered too harsh. The United States threatened to withdraw from the intervention unless Japan changed its ways. The threat, however, was clearly empty. Even Wilson finally admitted that he was perplexed as to what should be the future policy toward Russia.[30]

Still, American forces remained in Russia. The only aspect of the situation that crystallized in the late summer and fall of 1919 was the final decision not to recognize Kolchak. Even after that, Wilson considered sending the admiral a shipment of arms. Lansing recommended at the end of November that the United States should withdraw, but Wilson, who had suffered a debilitating stroke on October 2, was in no condition to reach a decision. American policy merely treaded water; the intervention continued on its own momentum. Only Graves seemed convinced that "the policy of the United States of non-interference in the internal affairs has been the only policy we could have safely followed."[31] Many in the administration would have been surprised that Graves could discern any policy at all amidst the confused twists and turns of Wilson's decisions. The withdrawal of American forces in 1920 came about almost as an afterthought. It signified an admission that they had no real purpose in Siberia.

The Siberian fiasco showed Wilson at his worst as military commander-in-chief. It evidenced little of the consistency of policy that characterized earlier interventions. The president himself gave no sign of the single-minded determination with which he had controlled previous instances of force. Yet, some aspects of the Siberian intervention were reminiscent of other interventions. The attempt, for example, to direct Kolchak along liberal democratic paths resembled the efforts to encourage Carranza to adopt various constitutional, agricultural, and political reforms in Mexico. In neither instance was Wilson successful in this type of interference. Carranza's obstinate nationalism doomed the earlier attempt; Wilson's indecision and inconsistency effectively destroyed the later one.

Wilson's poor showing in Siberia resulted from his general opposition to the intervention in the first place and his doubts that any success could come of it. Distracted by the more important task of establishing peace in Europe, the president had little time to formulate policies for the Siberian intervention. Caught in the tangled web of international cooperation, Wilson struggled futilely to retain America's freedom of action while controlling Japan. The essential conflict in these goals led to the contradictions and confusions of his policies. The power of collective action exerted an influence in both directions, for it controlled American policy as much as it controlled the Japanese. The restraints that international cooperation put on American actions frustrated Wilson and his subordinates, but it also offered a lesson—for those willing to learn—in the limits of force.

REACHING THE LIMITS OF FORCE

Wilson and the other American commissioners evinced a far better understanding of the limits of force in their approach to Bolshevism. Since the complex attitude of the Allies to the threat of Lenin and his policies did not result in an American use of force, its history lies beyond the reach of the present study. Nonetheless, the president's realization that armed power was inappropriate for combatting an ideology throws light on his understanding of force. Throughout the peace negotiations, the American delegation argued strenuously against employing arms to stop the spread of Bolshevism into Eastern and Central Europe. Their arguments rested on the proposition that force offered no help against a political doctrine. Wilson, for example, warned the Council of Four in March 1919 that:

> In my view, any attempt to check a revolutionary movement by means of deployed armies is merely trying to use a broom to sweep back a high tide. Besides, armies may become impregnated with the very Bolshevism they are sent to combat. . . . The only way to act against Bolshevism is to eliminate its causes. This is a formidable task: What its exact causes are, we do not know.
>
> In any case, one cause is that the peoples are uncertain as to their future frontiers, the governments they must obey, and at the same time, are in desperate need of food, transport, and opportunities for work. There is but one way to wipe out Bolshevism: determine the frontiers and open every door to commercial intercourse.

Other members of the American delegation also urged strengthening the exposed areas of Europe with food and other economic assistance. "Food is the real problem," Lansing noted in his diary in late October

1918. "Empty stomachs mean Bolsheviks. Full stomachs mean no Bolsheviks."[32] This simple truism became the constant refrain of the U.S. delegates in their opposition to intervention in European Russia. In adopting this attitude, Wilson underscored his recognition of the limits of force.

Bolshevism hung over the Paris Peace Conference like a shroud. Second only to the discussion of the peace treaty in monopolizing the attention of the conferees, the fear of this ideology seeped into all aspects of the negotiations. To meet the threat, various officials in the British and French governments proposed sending Allied armies across Europe. The suggestions came so frequently, the proposals seemed so outlandish, that Bliss could not contain his disgust. Suspicious of the actual motives underlying these plans, he complained bitterly to his fellow commissioners on February 26, 1919, that the Allies were "looking for opportunities to steal each others' land, to cut each others' throats, with assistance that they deliberately expect to receive from the United States. All of these plans will fall like a house of cards, if they are plainly told that no such assistance will be given."[33] Plain speaking, however, proved of little value. Despite consistent rejections by the United States of all the plans to use troops against Bolsheviks, the Allies persisted in dreaming up new ways to employ force. The details of the plans, for our purposes, are of less consequence than the rationale behind Wilson's unvarying opposition. Although he was no friend to Bolshevism or its goals, he understood that bullets were ineffective against ideas and that armies could not reverse the disenchantment with political and social conditions wherein those ideas bred. In his view, economic power, not armed power, was the more potent weapon.

The threat seemed real enough. "The American Commissioners are deeply concerned over the chaotic political conditions in the Central Empires and the progress toward anarchism or at least communism," the commissioners cabled the State Department on January 3. "The peril to Western Europe if Bolshevism prevails in Central Europe is very real." Polk, the acting secretary of state while Lansing was in Paris, agreed with this view. Reports reaching the department, he informed the U.S. delegates, "show the growing menace of Bolshevism outside of Russia."[34] The destruction of the war and the collapse of orderly government in Germany and the former Austro-Hungarian Empire ploughed fertile ground for the growth of Bolshevism. The debate at the peace conference centered on the best way to keep those seeds of anarchy from sprouting.

The solution, in the American view, lay in reconstruction, not further destruction with armed power. In their cable of January 3, the commissioners urged Polk to discuss with the secretary of the treasury, Carter Glass, a way to extend economic assistance to Central Europe. The danger from Bolshevism, they argued, "can only be met by aid from outside in relieving the food and economic situation. It is now exclusively a practical question of reestablishing sane governments capable of resisting the advance of Bolshevism from Russia and thus forming a bulwark to protect the west from coming into open conflict with the elements which frankly declare themselves enemies of all existing governments." Henry White, Wilson's token Republican, explained to Senator Henry Cabot Lodge, "Bolshevism thrives only on starvation and disorder." He urged the senator to support a one hundred million dollar appropriation for food relief.[35]

Some among the Allies, however, believed just as firmly that armed power offered the best defense. Marshal Foch, for example, urged the Allied and associated governments to sponsor a military intervention across Central Europe and into Russia. Bliss, Wilson's military expert on the commission, spoke adamantly against this proposal. He advised the president on January 7 that "we must regard Bolshevism in two lights; first, as an idea, however vague and inchoate and wild, and, secondly, as a propaganda by military force; that if we sent troops in sufficient numbers to occupy a given line, we could prevent *Bolsheviks* from crossing the line, but that we could not prevent *Bolshevism* from crossing it." Bliss recommended instead a policy of supplying the central sections of Europe with food and other economic assistance to help build up strong, democratic governments capable of resisting the temptations of communism on their own.[36]

Wilson accepted this reasoning. "The real thing with which to stop Bolshevism is food," he told Lansing three days later. On the same day, he wrote Tumulty that Bolshevism "cannot be stopped by force but it can be stopped by food." Peace, Wilson concluded, could not be achieved unless "this means of stemming the tide of anarchism is employed." At a meeting with Lloyd George and Clemenceau on January 12, the president expressed doubt "as to whether Bolshevism could be checked by arms." This was further confirmed by reports that fear of foreign intervention was uniting the people of Central Europe under the Bolshevik banner. Without this fear, Bolshevism could not succeed.[37]

In the face of such strong American opposition, the Allies began seeking other means to combat the spread of Russia's new philosophy. Lloyd George, for example, developed a plan to invite representatives of the various Russian factions to meet with the conferees. French objections compelled a change of venue to the Prinkipo Islands in the Sea of Mamara. The purpose of the meeting was to arrange a truce in the Russian civil war and to determine which was the strongest faction. The plan fell through, however, when the Allies and the Bolsheviks could not come to terms on diplomatic recognition and other conditions set by Lenin. Similarly, the Bullitt mission to Moscow, which was also an attempt to find a diplomatic solution to the problem, came to naught because the Allies could not bring themselves to accept Lenin's government as legitimate. These half-hearted exertions of diplomatic power merely affirmed the Allied view that armed power offered the only realistic solution.[38]

When the Prinkipo Conference and the Bullitt mission proved stillborn, various individuals again turned to force as the answer. Among American officials, several lower-level State Department and military advisers strongly urged their superiors to unleash the army against the Bolsheviks. Ernest L. Harris, the consul general at Irkutsk, for example, advised the State Department that "Bolshevism is no longer a Russian problem but one which endangers all humanity." The former consul at Moscow, DeWitt C. Poole, endorsed this view by advising the "forcible overthrow of the Moscow Government." H. E. Yarull of the Office of Naval Intelligence took an even more extreme position. He wanted not only a declaration of war against the Bolshevik government, but also the arrest and trial for treason of all those in the United States who spread communist propaganda. He suggested that foreign agitators be deported and that discontent among the enlisted men should be prevented, lest they, too, fall prey to the temptations of Bolshevism.[39]

These views, however, found an unsympathetic reception among U.S. officials in Paris. "Armies may stop Bolshevism," Bliss advised one of the advocates of force, "but they cannot stop Bolshevism provided there is any fertile ground of ignorance and hunger on which Bolshevism feeds." The best prophylactic, he believed, was to define the peace on Wilsonian concepts and to reinforce Europe with economic relief. The defeat of Bolshevism depended, not on armies, but on "the rehabilitation of the world, and the relief of misery and starvation everywhere."[40] No other plan promised any success.

Many of the Allies continued to disagree. Winston Churchill, England's secretary of war and air, proposed in mid-February a plan for the military overthrow of the Lenin government. The response of the American delegation was delayed until Wilson, who was making a brief trip to the United States, could be informed of the details. Lansing advised him that the American representatives unanimously rejected Churchill's plan. Bliss wrote Colonel House that "I think that it would be very unwise if anything should be done with the consent of the United States which could be construed by anyone as indicating an intent on the part of the United States to take part in an intervention in Russia." He sent a similar letter to Arthur Balfour, the British minister for foreign affairs, in order to drive the point home. In both letters, Bliss argued that the administration should decline to take part in such an intervention until the present war with Germany was ended by the signing of the peace treaty. Only then, he advised, could the American people be convinced that Russia was now their enemy. He also hoped that peace would so strengthen the nations of Europe that a battle against Bolshevism would be unnecessary.[41]

On February 17 the American commissioners discussed the latest British proposal. They agreed that the United States had no wish to intervene, preferring instead to "be of service to Russia in relieving her distress." Bliss repeated the views he had expressed to House and Balfour, which the other commissioners heartily endorsed. In addition, Bliss made the same arguments in meetings with the Allied military representatives, who also agreed with him that a full-scale intervention was impractical. Peace, they agreed, should be established first.[42]

In the meantime, Wilson found Churchill's proposal confusing, for he had understood Lloyd George "to say that there could be no thought of military action there." The president advised Lansing that "it would be fatal to be led further into the Russian chaos." House clarified the situation on February 19 by informing Wilson that Churchill's views were not representative of other officials in the Allied governments. Wilson refused to be soothed. "Hope you will be very plain and decided to the effect that we are not at war with Russia and will in no circumstances that we can now foresee take part in military operations there against the Russians," he instructed House. "I do not at all understand why Churchill was allowed to come to Paris on such an errand after what Lloyd George had said with regard to the British sending troops to Russia." This helped settle the issue, and on February 23 the American commissioners were able to inform the president that "Churchill's project is dead."[43] Its death was in the particulars of the plan only; the idea of intervening in Russia remained very much alive.

The several proposals for an Allied war on Russia confirmed the commissioners' suspicions that Britain and France intended to involve the United States in an armed intervention against Bolshevism to ensure America's continued presence in Europe. General Bliss told Lansing and White that the Allies planned "for continued military operations after the war, and that these plans include help from the United States." Specifically, Bliss outlined a proposal put forth by Marshal Foch to bring the nations bordering Russia together under

French direction for a war on the Bolsheviks. The plan depended on financial assistance from the United States. "With the best intentions in the world," Bliss told his colleagues, "The American philanthropic schemes for the new countries are enabling these countries to spend so much more on military preparation, and by so much more are contributing to the preparation for a new continental explosion." The solution, he suggested, was for the administration to announce plainly its intention to withdraw its armies once peace was signed.

Lansing and White agreed with this analysis, and the commissioners determined to send a telegram to Wilson, who was still in Washington, outlining their views. Lansing suggested that they encourage the president to declare that the United States intended "to cooperate through the League of Nations and not otherwise." Bliss accepted the task of drafting the telegram, which he promptly did, but Colonel House delayed giving his approval for so long the message was never sent. By the time it was ready for transmission, Wilson was well on his way back to Paris and the commissioners decided to explain themselves to him in person.[44]

The outbreak of a communist revolution in Hungary in March 1919 seemed to substantiate the Allied fears of the spread of Bolshevik influence into Eastern and Central Europe. Led by Béla Kun, a militant radical who made no effort to hide his encouragement of other revolutions, the Hungarian revolt complicated the American effort to discourage armed intervention against Bolshevism. Captain Nicholas Roosevelt reported to Wilson from Budapest on March 26 that "unless immediate and vigorous action is taken the Allies will be met with a disastrous state of affairs in Central Europe which it may take years to straighten out." As Roosevelt saw it, "Hungary has defied the Peace Conference and allied herself with the Bolsheviki. It is Germany's turn next." Others among Wilson's advisers also recommended a military expedition to topple the new regime, and on March 27 Marshal Foch proposed yet another plan to stop the spread of Bolshevism by military means.[45]

Wilson, however, kept a cooler head. He preferred to isolate Hungary with a blockade, for he feared that Bliss might be right that an intervention in Hungary would lead to a resumption of general war and the dissolution of the peace conference. United action with the Allies in boycotting the Béla Kun government, furthermore, would strengthen the principle of international cooperation and collective action on which he based the League of Nations.[46] Although Wilson recognized the Hungarian revolution as a challenge to his efforts to rebuild Europe along liberal, internationalist lines, he was unwilling to meet the threat with armed power. Economic and moral power appealed to him as the best means to prove the strength of his ideals.

Wilson's foreign colleagues understood the situation differently. Under French encouragement, if not outright sponsorship, a Rumanian army launched an attack against Béla Kun that eventually brought his government down in August. Wilson, relieved that Béla Kun no longer posed a danger, nevertheless objected to Rumania's actions. At one point, the American commission contemplated cutting off supplies to Rumania to compel it to cease the attack on Hungary, but no decision was reached. In Wilson's view, force should have been used only as a last resort. It was a poor first choice to use against revolutionary disruptions to the peace of Europe. Once again, however, the Allies worked against him, proving the complicated nature of international cooperation in a world in which the gun was more attractive than economic or moral power.[47]

The immediate effect of the Hungarian revolution was to encourage such Allied officials as Marshal Foch to press for acceptance of the plans for the armed overthrow of Bolshevism in Russia. They claimed this brutal method in the name of the salvation of Europe, but their arguments failed to convince the U.S. delegation. The Americans and their allies were separated by a large difference in perception of Bolshevism and what it meant to the peace of Europe. For the first time, Wilson recognized that an idea caused the turmoil. Previously, the president had failed to see the power of ideas different from his own. During the Mexican Revolution, for example, Wilson never understood that Carranza's ideals, which relied on Mexican nationalism and a program of agrarian and constitutional reforms to reduce the hold of the wealthy over the poor, were the motivating influence behind the call to arms. His failure to see the turmoil in Mexico in those terms not only convinced him that force could effect a solution, but it also resulted in the failure of his policy.

With Russia, Wilson came to see the power of ideas, even though he completely rejected the validity of communism as a political system. Consequently, he deduced that ideas could not be fought with armies. Instead, he adopted the views of many of his subordinates, among whom Bliss was the most vocal advocate, that Bolshevism could be destroyed only by changing the conditions of poverty, social disruption, and political degeneration in which it thrived. Reestablishing peace along the lines of liberal capitalism promised the best way to eradicate the desperate plight of Europe. By removing the causes of Bolshevism, the Wilson administration expected to remove its danger as well.

General Bliss, called upon by Wilson to address the military arguments put forth by Foch, expressed this view succinctly. On March 27 he addressed the Council of Four in response to a plan for military intervention outlined by Foch moments before. The fact that Wilson had asked him to be present indicated that the president approved of his opinion and depended on the general, as his military expert, to offset the authoritative views of the allied commander in chief. Bliss's remarks to the council not only represented the American position, but also expressed the Wilson administration's perception that force could not combat ideas. This understanding represented a major breakthrough in Wilson's insight into the role of armed power in foreign policy. The pity, of course, was that it came so late in his tenure.

"My conception of the origin and character of Bolshevism," Bliss began, "differs from that of the gentlemen here present." He urged the council to decide carefully what they intended to fight before they embarked on their crusade against Lenin. Otherwise, the general warned, "your military efforts are likely to result in failure." If they substituted the word "revolution" for Bolshevism, they would "get a more scientific viewpoint of the situation." Bolshevism was "the form which revolution takes among a people 95% of whom are in a state of civilization not much advanced from that of their predecessors in the time of Alaric and Attila." Because of the primitive state of the Russian people, their form of the revolution was "necessarily a bloody and brutal and unthinking form." If the movement spread westward across Europe, Bliss expected it to take a "gradually more etherealized form, due to the temperament and civilization and education of the peoples among which it may manifest itself." In the more civilized areas of Europe, Bolshevism would not express itself with violence and bloodshed.

Bliss argued that the present situation resembled that of Europe in the years after the Napoleonic Wars. Great armies, he told the council, exerted a democratizing influence on populations because they threw men from all levels of society together. The result a century before had been the establishment of "bourgeois governments for the preceding absolute and arbitrary governments." This occurred despite the efforts of the Holy Alliance. The war of 1914–18 achieved a similar result of bringing together "the entire able-bodied and able-minded population of each nation, with the usual democratizing influences in greater degrees than before." With the end of the war arose a universal disenchantment among the common people with their condition. "Governments of which they stood in awe," Bliss said, "have crumbled to pieces, and their respect for governmental authority has weakened." The result was a spirit of revolution, a desire for a change in existing conditions. "As is always the case," he continued, "the evils which people believe they are suffering from are attributed to the governments. These governments are bourgeois governments. The next and only change that the peoples can conceive of is a change from the bourgeois government to one of the proletariat." This explained the attraction of Bolshevism.

If the Council of Four would understand Bolshevism as the natural rejection of the old order, Bliss believed that they would realize that when they sent their armies to Russia, they would find Bolshevism appearing at home. The Foch plan could not meet that danger. Nor, Bliss advised, could any other plan. The plan proposed by Foch

> looks upon Bolshevism as a home-made product in Russia, as a thing which can be bottled up there by a great army extending from the Black Sea to the Baltic. The Marshal calls his army a "sanitary cordon." He says that if you wished to protect yourself from an epidemic of cholera starting in Russia you would place your sanitary agencies on the border of that country and prevent the disease from coming out. It is true that you can prevent an army of Bolsheviks from coming out of Russia by posting on its borders a sufficiently large military force. But you cannot in this way prevent Bolshevism from coming out. You cannot stop the progress of an idea, whether good or bad, by a line of bayonets. Nor could a line of sanitary police prevent the disease of cholera from coming out of Russia so long as there be a stream of water running from that country into Western Europe and bearing with it the germs of cholera.

The spread of Bolshevism could not be stopped by Foch's sanitary cordon because it was an idea, and ideas knew no borders.

Bliss refused to address the military qualities of the Foch plan, arguing that "it may be as good as any other." Instead, he urged the council to try other means. "If revolution is the expression of discontent on the part of the common people with their governments," he advised, "why not assure ourselves that there is no way in which we can relieve this discontent and have no other way than to kill the discontented people?" The immediate declaration of peace, the lifting of the blockade against Germany and its former allies, feeding the people, and assisting them to obtain the means to support themselves seemed the more sensible alternative. The limits of force made it an inappropriate response to the threat of Bolshevism.[48]

For Wilson and the other American commissioners, Bliss's views were eminently reasonable.[49] In resisting the efforts of the Allies to war on Bolshevism, Wilson tacitly recognized the power of ideas. He had, of course, relied on ideas himself during each of his previous interventions, but never before had he accepted the fact that other ideas, even those that directly contradicted his, could be persuasive to other peoples. Although he never understood the attraction of Bolshevism, he at least realized that it was attractive to some. He never sympathized with those who embraced it, but at least he recognized that their embrace could not be pried loose with force. Instead, he promoted liberalism as the democratic alternative to socialist ideas. Food, democratic governments, and international trade and intercourse, the president believed, offered a bloodless way to convert the frustrated and disgruntled populations of Europe from communists to democrats. Wilson believed that any reasonable man, once shown the proper way, could not long resist the inherent charms of his liberal internationalist world order.

Epilogue
THE WILSONIAN WAY of WAR:
Veracruz to Vladivostok

After the war, progressivism as a reform movement went underground. Elements of it surfaced a dozen years later during the presidency of Franklin Delano Roosevelt, who had been a junior member of the Wilson administration. But the end of World War I brought with it a desire to return to the "normalcy" that Warren G. Harding promised in his inaugural address in 1921. His policies indicated that he meant simply that the powers of the federal government would be curbed. Instead of trying to regulate business and the economy, as Wilson had done, Harding and his immediate successors, Calvin Coolidge and Herbert Hoover, cooperated with big businesses, helping them grow bigger and more powerful. The Great Depression at the end of the decade proved the failure of this approach in the modern world. Thus, the decade of the 1920s witnessed a return to the weak president. The Republican administrations much preferred a hands-off policy toward the nation's affairs. Wilson, sick in body and spirit, retired to a house on S Street in Washington. He died in 1924.

In foreign policy, the United States also tried to return to a more innocent era. Charles Evans Hughes, Wilson's opponent in 1916, took over the State Department under Harding and Coolidge. He was succeeded by Frank B. Kellogg, who, in turn, was followed by Henry L. Stimson. Although elements of Wilsonian internationalism appeared in their diplomacy, none of these secretaries of state followed it consistently. Under their leadership, American foreign policy followed a zigzag course with regard to events in other parts of the globe. Unwilling to join the League of Nations, for example, the Republican administrations of the 1920s sent observers instead. They did pursue a policy of international disarmament, which harked back to the Wilson period, but overall they seemed to want influence without responsibility, a say in world events without the burden of world leadership.

This attitude, of course, rejected most of what Wilson tried to do in office. Later presidents would return to the Wilsonian example when they accepted American leadership in the world, but Wilson was as often misunderstood as correctly interpreted. In the realm of armed power, for instance, force became a method of convenience, with little attention paid to its repercussions. With the wars in Korea and Vietnam, various presidents tried, rather unsuccessfully, to limit force without clearly defining their objectives. Harry Truman during the Korean War and Lyndon Johnson and Richard Nixon during the Vietnam War allowed the American military a far greater say in the political and diplomatic aspects of these wars than Wilson would ever have permitted. Indeed, the very fact that these two armed entanglements were popularly called wars instead of interventions showed how unlimited they became. In a sense, the United States learned from Wilson that force offered advantages, but it did not learn how he used it advantageously.

Nuclear weapons further complicated the dangers of armed power. Advances in military technology were of little concern to Wilson, primarily because the improvements in the tools of war during his time did not change the basic aspects of force. Nuclear weapons, however, increased the stakes of war. Their disuse since 1945 indicates quite clearly that no nation has been able to limit their impact. They have become weapons of diplomatic and military power, not armed. But their greatest influence is to underline the absolute necessity of limiting force. For this reason, the strategies that Wilson developed to restrict the interventions he undertook assume an importance beyond their historical interest. In the Wilsonian way of war, the limits of force were equal in importance to the power of force.

Collective security represented Wilson's mature understanding of the role of armed power in international relations. As such, it offers a convenient subject with which to conclude the present study, despite the inherent irony of ending an analysis of force with an examination of proposals for peace. Through collective security, Wilson offered the world a vision of the peace based on his own experiences with force. The insights he had gained from his military interventions helped him design the League of Nations based on a recognition of the strengths and limits of armed power. Incorporated into the covenant of the league and Wilson's promotion of it were many of the themes that ran through the interventions in Mexico, Haiti, Santo Domingo, World War I, and Russia.

Civilian control of the military, for instance, was transformed immediately after the war into an attack on militarism and a campaign for disarmament. Wilson's American democratic ideology appeared in his expressed belief that the war left the people of each nation in command of their own destinies; their leaders were their servants, not their masters. International law played a fundamental part since the covenant codified a new international order. Cooperation among nations was the foundation of the entire structure. The limits of force were recognized in the specifications of when and how force could be used appropriately. Thus, the covenant was Wilson's final attempt to define the uses of force as power in the relations between nations.

In the Wilsonian way of war, civilian control of the military provided the method by which Wilson employed the armed services to accomplish his purposes. In his own relations with the American military, Wilson insisted on the president's right to establish policy. He limited the advice of his uniformed subordinates to issues of tactics and fighting, only rarely allowing individual officers, such as Hugh Scott or Tasker Bliss, to discuss political questions. Wilson established the goals of force which the military was then expected to obtain without question or dispute.

At Paris in 1919, the president offered the League of Nations as the best way to eradicate the scourge of militarism. During the opening discussions of the covenant on January 25, 1919, Wilson explained the crusading impulse against military control that had brought the American people into the war. The peace would fail if it allowed the causes of World War I to survive, he said, adding that:

> We are here to see, in short, that the very foundations of this war are swept away. Those foundations were the private choice of small coteries of civil rulers and military staffs. Those foundations were the aggression of great powers upon the small. Those foundations were the holding together of empires of unwilling subjects by the duress of arms. Those foundations were the power of small bodies of men to work their will upon mankind and use them as pawns in a game. And nothing less than the emancipation of the world from these things will accomplish peace.[1]

Collective security promised the destruction of militarism. The need for large standing armies and the dependence of governments on the military would be relieved by the mutual protection afforded by the unity of nations.

Furthermore, Wilson urged a general reduction in armaments to reduce the influence of the military by limiting the ability of nations to wage aggressive war. Point four of the Fourteen Points, for example, called for "adequate guarantees given and taken that national armaments will be reduced to the lowest point consistent with domestic safety." Immediately after the signing of the Armistice in November 1918, the Wilson administration began a rapid demobilization of its armed forces. By January 1, 1919, seven hundred thousand men had been shipped home. The remainder followed quickly.[2] The speed of the demobilization confirmed Wilson's belief in disarmament.

Article X of the covenant encouraged an international reduction in arms because it guaranteed the territorial integrity of each nation. Henceforth, any aggression against one nation would be met by the united resistance of all nations. Immense, expensive armaments were unnecessary because the arms of all nations were linked together in self-defense. "Article X is the article which goes to the heart of this whole bad business," Wilson fervently believed, "for that article says that the members of the League (that is intended to be all the great nations of the world) engage to respect and to preserve against all external aggression the territorial integrity and political independence of the nations concerned." The article was essential to avoid the recurrence of another war caused by militarism run rampant.[3]

Wilson defended the large postwar naval building program of the United States in terms of disarmament. Admiral Benson, concerned by the size of the British fleets, advised him in February 1919 that peace depended on at least two powers with equal naval strength. Daniels endorsed this view, explaining to the president that "I feel, with Admiral Benson, that no nation ought to have a force, either on land or sea, to dominate, and in military and naval strength our country ought to be ready and willing to furnish, in proportion to its wealth and commercial importance, the necessary force to maintain the world's peace." Wilson acted on their advice, but the buildup of the navy did not, in his view, deviate from the disarmament program. Quite the contrary, in defending the policy begun in 1915 to create a navy equal to Britain's, Wilson explained to an audience at Coeur d'Alene, Idaho, on September 12, 1919, that Congress, "authorizing a great building program of ships and expenditure of vast sums of money to make our Navy one of the strongest in the world, paused a moment and declared in the midst of the appropriation bill that it was the policy of the United States to bring about disarmament."[4] Because the general goal of the building program was to stabilize the league, and because Wilson assumed that the United States would never use its navy aggressively, he saw no contradiction in working for a general reduction in arms at the same time that he strove to increase the size of the American navy.

The threat of militarism resuscitated in the United States became one of Wilson's favorite themes in his efforts to gain American acceptance of the Treaty of Versailles and the League of Nations. "You have the alternative," he told one audience on his lengthy western speaking tour in the fall of 1919, "armed isolation or peaceful partnership." He meant by this that the United States, should it refuse to enter the league, risked the dangers of militarism itself. He explained again and again on the tour that if America withdrew into itself, cutting off the rest of the world and reveling in its splendid geographic isolation, then "we must be physically ready for anything that comes." This would require the maintenance of a great standing army, with every man in America trained in the use of arms. This army would need large supplies of munitions and guns, which in turn would depend on high taxes. But the most serious threat, in Wilson's view, was that:

> You can not handle an armed nation by vote. You can not handle an armed nation if it is democratic, because democracies do not go to war that way. You have got to have a concentrated, militaristic organization of government to run a nation of that sort. You have got to think of the President of the United States, not as the chief counselor of the nation, elected for a little while, but as the man meant constantly and every day to be the Commander-in-Chief of the Army and Navy of the United States, ready to order them to any part of the world where the threat of war is a menace to his own people. And you can not do that under free debate. You can not do that under public counsel.

It would be impossible, Wilson threatened, to maintain a free government, responsible in its social reforms and progressive in its outlook, if it was at the same time required to keep up its military defenses without the protection of collective security. "You know how impossible it is, in short," he said, "to have a free nation, if it is a military nation and under military order."[5] The only alternative was to join the league.

Thus, the eradication of militarism and the preservation of democracy depended on the vitality of the League of Nations. Collective security promised not only the united protection of the world from further acts of aggression, but also protection from the threat of militaristic growths in democratic countries. Not even the United States enjoyed immunity against this disease. Unless it participated in the league, the U.S. would soon have "a military government in spirit if not in form."[6] For Wilson, civilian control of the armed forces, both in America and throughout the world, depended on the cooperation of all nations.

In the Wilsonian way of war, American democratic ideology defined the goals of force. Throughout each intervention, Wilson perceived his actions as assisting the downtrodden to achieve a democratic way of life. Since he defined America as the epitome of freedom-loving democracy, he used it as the model for other nations. The humanitarian impulse to help other peoples was distorted by a pervasive ethnocentrism. Wilson wanted not merely to free the poor and helpless from their misery, but to reshape their nations in the image of the United States. This resulted in a variety of peculiar actions designed to apply the American experience to a diverse range of peoples and cultures.

At Paris in 1919, Wilson's democratic ideology assumed several guises. First, he convinced himself that the national leaders gathered to negotiate the peace represented, not national interests or special classes, and certainly not the old European order, but the great mass of humanity which he called "the people." Evidence all around him, which he refused to see, indicated that this was not the case. Indeed, his own leadership was thrown into doubt by the congressional elections of November 1918. Despite his campaign appeal to the electorate to return Democratic majorities to the House and Senate, the Republican party gained a majority of fifty seats in the House and two seats in the Senate.

This apparent repudiation hardly gave Wilson pause. Arriving in Europe before the opening of the peace conference, he embarked on a grand tour of France, Britain, and Italy. At each stop he spoke eloquently to the people, urging them to require of their leaders the same selfless devotion to duty that he believed motivated the United States. By the end of the tour, his egotism fed by the applause and adulation of a grateful Europe, Wilson had convinced himself that he alone represented the true feelings of the world's peoples. By attributing to the Italians, French, and English his own ideals and purposes, Wilson grew confident that he could speak to them over the heads of their leaders. He alone was the interpreter of a new worldwide spirit of reform based on American principles of international justice and peace.

Throughout the negotiations and in his campaign to sell the treaty to the American people, Wilson reiterated the theme that finally, and at last, the peoples of the world controlled their own governments. The victory over Germany was a triumph for democracy. "We are assembled under very peculiar conditions of world opinion," Wilson announced at the opening deliberations over the league. "I may say without straining the point that we are not the representatives of Governments, but representatives of peoples." Returning to the United States part way through the conference, Wilson assured an audience in Boston that "the men who are in conference in Paris realize as keenly as any American can realize that they are not masters of their people, that they are servants of their people, and that the spirit of their people has awakened to a new purpose and a new conception of their power to realize that purpose, and that no man dare go home from that conference and report anything less noble than was expected of it." During his tour of the western United States, the president reiterated this theme. Speaking in Cheyenne, Wyoming, on September 24, Wilson claimed that World War I "was a people's war," the peace a "people's peace."[7] He could not bring himself to let down the millions of people who depended on him, nor would he allow their own governments to disappoint them.

Yet, if the peoples of the world had spoken, they spoke in favor of harsh terms against Germany and favorable terms for their respective countries. As Arno Mayer has shown, in every major nation that participated in the conference, including the United States, the parties of the Right—the conservatives and the defenders of the old order—were on the offensive while the parties of the Left—the reformers and the Wilsonians—were in retreat. Even Wilson admitted that the treaty as finally agreed upon was "undoubtedly very severe indeed," but he argued that it was not unjust considering the crimes committed by Germany. His commitment to the treaty and to the league blinded him to the selfishness of the other nations. As Lansing later observed, "Our idealism has shown that it is unable to overcome the passions of men."[8] Wilson could not see this; for him the treaty represented the culmination of democracy and American principles.

Indeed, Wilson assumed that American principles and ideals now guided the rest of the world. He considered the league an American conception based on the American example. The United States had no selfish interests to pursue, only ideals, justice, and democracy. It alone spoke objectively. As he explained at the opening discussions of the league on January 25:

> In coming into the war the United States never for a moment thought that she was intervening in the politics of Europe or the politics of Asia or the politics of any part of the world. Her thought was that all the world had now become conscious that there was a single cause which turned upon the issues of this war. That was the cause of justice and of liberty for men of every kind and place. Therefore, the United States should feel that its part in this war had been played in vain if there ensued upon it merely a body of European settlements. It would feel that it could not take part in guaranteeing those European settlements unless that guaranty involved the continuous superintendence of the peace of the world by the associated nations of the world.

As Lansing explained to Bliss, "We are peculiarly strong because we have no territorial cravings, no selfish interests to serve."[9] America's unselfish devotion to principle allowed it, the Americans believed, to take the unique position of sitting in judgment on the governments of other nations. Thus, Wilson assumed that the world after the war was somehow equally democratic, but that the United States was first among equals.

Because he believed that the peoples of the world accepted his vision, even if their leaders did not, Wilson acted on a grander stage than the other participants in the conference. His triumphant tour of Europe symbolized his vision of himself as spokesman of all people everywhere. He appealed to the citizens of other nations over the heads of their own governments to endorse his platform just as, nine months later, he would appeal to the citizens of individual states over the heads of their senators. During the conference, when the Italian delegation refused to surrender its claim to Fiume, Wilson issued a plea to the Italian people to reject their delegation's position in favor of Wilsonian principles. The immediate consequence of the appeal was that the Italian representatives withdrew temporarily from the negotiations. The Italian people did not respond as Wilson had hoped. His ethnocentrism, fed by his own ego, convinced him that America, with himself as its interpreter, alone could identify the principles upon which to build the peace. The cheering throngs of Europe prior to the conference encouraged this egotism, but the applause soon stopped as citizens in every nation looked expectantly for their spoils of war.

At least two aspects of the Covenant of the League of Nations underscored the American democratic ideology that defined Wilson's policies. The first was the decision to admit only democracies into the league; the second was the system of mandates. "No nation is admitted to the League of Nations that can not show that it has the institutions which we call free," Wilson explained. "Nobody is admitted except the self-governing nations, because it was the instinctive judgment of every man who sat around that board that only a nation whose government was its servant and not its master could be trusted to preserve the peace of the world." The criteria of democracy meant that the league would "advance civilization by substituting something that will make the improvement of civilization possible." The exclusion of autocracies and other governments that did not rule by the advice of the people reflected the league's basis in American principles. Henceforth, Wilson promised, autocratic governments were excluded from the "respectable society" upon which they depended for their survival.[10] As he had seen his interventions in Mexico, Haiti, and Santo Domingo earlier, Wilson saw the league as promoting democracy and self-rule for all the peoples of the world.

In those nations like Haiti and Santo Domingo with institutions and traditions too primitive to support democratic governments, the league offered the protection of mandates. This system, wherein a developed power took responsibility for an undeveloped power, represented the most blatant form of Wilson's ethnocentric humanitarianism as he applied it on a worldwide scale. In presenting the revised covenant to the peace conference, Wilson said:

> Then there is a feature about this Covenant which to my mind is one of the greatest and most satisfactory advances that have been made. We are done with annexations of helpless people, meant in some instances by some Powers to be used merely for exploitation. We recognize in the most solemn manner that the helpless and undeveloped peoples of the world, being in that condition, put an obligation upon us to look after their interests primarily before we use them for our interest; and that in all cases of this sort hereafter it shall be the duty of the League to see that the nations who are assigned as the tutors and advisers and directors of those peoples shall look to their interest and to their development before they look to the interests and material desires of the mandatory nation itself. There has been no greater advance than this, gentlemen.

This feature of the covenant made it "at one and the same time a practical document and a humane document." It had "a pulse of sympathy" and a "compulsion of conscience throughout it." The system of mandates, Wilson assured the delegates, was practical enough to work, but it was also "intended to purify, to rectify, to elevate."[11] As he had with the Mexicans, Haitians, and Santo Dominicans, Wilson never considered the possibility that the peoples coming under the mandate system might not need purification, rectification, or elevation.

Thus, Wilson's American democratic ideology, his impulse to push the American form of democracy into all corners of the globe, contributed to his perception that democracy now ruled the world. His vision was more hope than reality, but the two were now confused in his mind. He expected the other leaders with whom he met to obey the will of their citizens as he interpreted that will. The league brought this will to fruition, in Wilson's opinion, because it enshrined in its membership criteria and in its system of mandates the democratic principles of self-government, justice, and humanity. The policies he had pursued during earlier interventions were transformed at Paris into a grandiose vision of the way the world worked, but this vision ignored the central reality that other nations and their peoples cared more for the spoils of war than for the institution of democracy.

In the Wilsonian way of war, international law offered the rationale and the guidelines for the employment of force. During each intervention, Wilson looked to the law to explain his motives and purposes. In addition, he kept to the restrictions imposed by the law on various types of force. In time of war, the Wilson administration demanded that the belligerents respect America's international rights. Only with the occupations of Haiti and Santo Domingo did Wilson step beyond the bounds of international legality, but he explicitly excused these actions by appealing to the higher standards of morality. Consequently, the rules and regulations established over the centuries to guide the behavior of nations helped mold Wilson's interventions along certain lines.

At Paris in 1919, Wilson tried to enhance the power of international law by offering a revised code of right and justice supported by the moral and physical force of collective security. The Covenant of the League of Nations was itself a legal document that codified the rights and responsibilities of the member states. It also specified in detail the appropriate and inappropriate measures for the settlement of disputes and for changes in the international system.

The president understood the importance of the law to the league and the league's contribution to the "intelligent development of international law." In an address before the International Law Society at Paris on May 9, Wilson pointed out that:

> In one sense, this great, unprecedented war was fought to give validity to international law, to prove that it has a reality which no nation could afford to disregard; that, while it did not have the ordinary sanctions, while there was no international authority as yet to enforce it, it nevertheless had something behind it which was greater than that, the moral rectitide of mankind.
>
> If we can now give to international law the kind of vitality which it can have only if it is a real expression of moral judgment, we shall have completed in some sense the work which this war was intended to emphasize.

What was needed, Wilson argued, was a compassionate justice that expressed the desires and feelings of the common man. "To live and let live, to work for people and with people," he explained, "is at the bottom of the kind of experience which must underlie justice." The future of mankind depended on the way in which nations dealt with each other. To foster good relations, the covenant sought to exploit the "common brotherhood of man." Without this sense of justice and community, the world could not continue in its progressive development.[12]

For the American delegation, the Paris Peace Conference presented a unique opportunity to reform the international system that had spawned the war. The changes they proposed centered on creating a new system of relations based on common conceptions of justice and fair play. As House advised Wilson on January 19, "the League of Nations should promote the firm establishment of the understandings of international law as the actual rule of conduct among governments and the maintenance of justice and the scrupulous respect for all international obligations in dealings of organized peoples with one another." Lansing, too, agreed that the guiding principle for the new international system should be justice and respect for the territorial integrity of all nations.[13]

Wilson needed little encouragement on that approach. Throughout the period of American neutrality, he had moved steadily toward collective security as the best guarantee of international law and justice. In May 1916 he publicly endorsed American participation in a concert of nations. Over the winter of 1917, he and Lansing discussed in some detail the terms of a peace treaty with Germany. Its provisions included guarantees for political independence and territorial integrity of all nations, protections against economic warfare, disarmament, and a primitive system of cooperation.[14] During the war, the president further refined these terms, particularly with his Fourteen Points. By the time he arrived in Paris, he had a clear idea of the type of treaty he sought in the negotiations. International law and justice helped bring its details into focus.

The product of the conference, Wilson proudly announced on April 28, 1919, promised "to maintain justice in international relations and peace between the nations of the world." In particular, collective security as expressed in the league provided novel protections for the rights of all nations and all peoples. The beneficial results were so obvious to the delegates, Wilson stated, that it was unnecessary to draw their attention to "the capital significance of this covenant, the hopes which are entertained as to the effect it will have upon steadying the affairs of the world, and the obvious necessity that there should be a concert of the free nations of the world to maintain justice in international relations and peace between the nations of the world."[15] His task completed, Wilson returned to the United States intending to gain the Senate's ratification of the treaty. In order to speed this legal process along, the president spoke directly to the American people about the changes which the league wrought in international law. All of the reforms, he assured his constituents, were for the good of mankind.

He concentrated on the protections provided for the weak against the mighty, the meek against the aggressor states. Prior to the covenant, international law required that "no matter how deeply the United States is interested in something in some other part of the world that she believes is going to set the world on fire or disturb the friendly relations between two great nations, she can not speak of it unless she can show that her own interests are directly involved." Under the terms of Article XI, the situation was changed. With the league, any member could call the attention of the concert of nations to anything that might possibly disturb the peace. "Every aspiring people, every oppressed people, every people whose hearts can no longer stand the strain of tyranny that has been put upon them," Wilson claimed, "can find a champion to speak for it in the forum of the world." Thus, for example, any nation that considered an encroachment on China's rights could be "summoned to the bar of the world." The consequence of this reform in international law was to give legal recognition to the concern and interest of all nations in whatever affected the peace.[16]

This conception of the league as the natural defender of the weak grew out of Wilson's disgust with the previous system of relations which allowed strong nations to commit acts of aggression against less powerful states. The actions of Germany, of course, were the prime example of the abuses of the old order. "There never before has been provided a world forum in which the legitimate grievances of peoples entitled to consideration can be brought to the common judgment of mankind," Wilson advised an audience in Kansas City, Missouri, on September 6. The League of Nations overturned that state of affairs. The treaty, Wilson proudly told them, "is the first great international agreement in the history of mankind where the principle adopted has been, not the power of the strong but the right of the weak." It was a "charter of mankind."[17]

The treaty liberated the peoples of the world. Collective security guaranteed that the peace rested "on the rights of the weak, and only the power of the strong can maintain the rights of the weak." The foundation of justice, Wilson told his listeners in San Diego on September 19, demanded that the weak enjoy the same rights as the powerful. The league granted this privilege. "The principle of justice, the principle of right, the principle of international amity is this," Wilson said, "that there is not only an imaginary but a real equality of standing and right among all the sovereign peoples of the world." This ideal, though not always met, was the glory of the law; and the president promised to uphold it in the league.[18]

Thus, international law and its elements of right and justice permeated Wilson's conception of the League of Nations. The power of the law, as amended at Paris, lent itself to the protection of the powerless.

Wars of aggression and selfishness would be banned as all free nations worked together against aggression, tyranny, and exploitation. But the design of the league gave a different image since the major powers—the United States, Great Britain, France, Italy, and Japan—were given louder voices in the councils of the organization. As Lansing pointed out in his diary on May 8, 1919, the league was "an instrument of the mighty to check the normal growth of national power and national aspirations among those who have been rendered impotent by defeat." In addition, the treaty, through its mandate system, transferred people "against their wills into the hands of those whom they hate." In consequence, Lansing came away from the negotiations and the final settlement convinced that throughout the Treaty of Versailles, "justice is secondary. Might is primary."[19] These views were a particularly damning indictment of what Wilson thought he had accomplished during the conference.

In the Wilsonian way of war, cooperation among nations erected the conceptual framework for international relations. Wilson consistently sought allies whom he could support and who would help him. He did not fear independent action; rather, he believed that only through cooperation could peace be obtained. Even when he intervened on a limited scale, he sought internal groups in each country with which to join forces. Wilson wanted not to dominate, but to lead. International cooperation provided him with individuals, groups, and nations whom he could persuade and cajole to take the course outlined by him.

At Paris in 1919, Wilson strove to incorporate into the treaty with Germany the elements of international cooperation and collective action that he considered essential to the future maintenance of peace. He envisioned himself as embarked on a great task to build from the rubble of war a new system of relations based on unity and a community of interest. "Your work is not finished. Its character has only changed," Breckinridge Long told him on the day the Armistice was signed. "Instead of using the great force of this country as an agency for destruction, you can now use it in the other way you know so well, for construction."[20] Wilson accepted the duty gladly, for he was equally convinced that only he could instill in the hearts of the European powers the necessary sense of brotherhood. In his formulation of the League of Nations, Wilson offered the world what he considered its only hope to rise above the burden of the past to achieve a new order. The peace depended on a concert of nations willing to defend it against all challenges.

It was a difficult, perhaps impossible, mission. Few among the other powers believed as strongly as Wilson in the sanctity of cooperation and collective action. Although Lloyd George had endorsed a concert of nations even before Wilson did, the British seemed merely to go along with the scheme to appease the president. Italy and Japan tried to turn Wilson's intense desire for a league into a bargaining chip to gain their more provincial objectives. France sought protection against a revitalized Germany, showing little interest in Wilson's visionary scheme. "What the French really want is not a League of Nations for the maintenance of general peace," Bliss observed on February 14, 1919, "but an armed alliance of infinite duration against Germany."[21] Given these nationalistic goals of the other nations involved, Wilson grappled to overcome their selfishness. The irony, of course, was that having succeeded in Paris, he failed at home.

Wilson compromised again and again on the specific issues of the peace settlement in order to obtain international approval of the League of Nations. As he explained early in the proceedings of the conference: "There are many complicated questions connected with the present settlements which perhaps can not be successfully worked out to an ultimate issue by the decisions we shall arrive at here. I can easily conceive that many of these settlements will need subsequent reconsideration, that many of the decisions we make shall need subsequent alteration to some degree; for, if I may judge by my own study of some of these questions, they are not susceptible of confident judgments at present." The league was all the more necessary because of this, for only it offered a way to readjust continually the decisions reached at Paris. For the United States, the league represented "the keystone of the whole program which expressed our purposes and ideals in this war and which the associated nations have accepted as the basis of the settlement." The other matters before the conference assumed less importance in Wilson's eyes so long as it gave birth to the league to handle the problems left over from and caused by the peace treaty.[22]

The French desire to protect their country from future German aggressions exemplified Wilson's willingness to give in to the national claims of the other powers in order to gain their consent to the league. According to Admiral Benson, the military terms of the peace treaty made "the United States a member of a continuing alliance to curtail the sovereignty of Germany." Clemenceau demanded a military alliance against Germany between France, Great Britain, and the United States before he would consent to the league. Wilson, overriding the objections of the other American commissioners, agreed to these terms, provided that Britain and the United States enter into separate arrangements with France. The proposed alliance caused an uproar in the United States because it violated America's traditional policy of no entangling alliances. Wilson failed to understand the objections because in his view it merely supported the work of the league. "Happily there is no mystery or privacy about what I have promised the government here," he wrote Tumulty in April. "I have promised to propose to the Senate a treaty in which we shall agree, subject to the approval of the Council of the League of Nations, to come immediately to the assistance of France in case of unprovoked attack by Germany, thus merely hastening the action to which in any case we should be bound by the covenant of the League of Nations."[23] On other issues, such as the Japanese demand for Shantung, Wilson also gave in because he trusted the league to solve any resultant problems.

The importance of the league grew from the international cooperation and collective security that undergirded it. The peoples of Europe, Wilson explained, were buoyed up with hope in the league because it promised a new era "when nations will understand one another; when nations will support one another in every just cause; when nations will unite every moral and every physical strength to see that right shall prevail." He did not intend for America to fail them in achieving this hope. In announcing the signing of the peace treaty to the American people, Wilson proclaimed that it "associates the free Governments of the world in a permanent League in which they are pledged to use their united power to maintain peace by maintaining right and justice." He simply could not conceive that the United States would refuse to join the league and thereby destroy the foundations of international cooperation and collective action. "The League of Nations is the child of this great war," Wilson told the Belgian Parliament, "for it is the expression of those permanent resolutions which grew out of the temporary necessities of this great struggle, and any nation which declines to adhere to this covenant deliberately turns away from the most telling appeal that has ever been made to its conscience and to its manhood."[24] American participation presented the United States with its greatest opportunity to supply to the world the leadership and moral suasion for which the nation was born.

In presenting the Treaty of Versailles to the Senate on July 10, 1919, Wilson defined the purposes of the league and the reasons why the United States had no choice but to join. "The League of Nations was not merely an instrument to adjust and remedy old wrongs under a new treaty of peace; it was the only hope of the world," he told the Senate. He added that the United States had formulated the principles that guided the league and was expected to represent them at the conference. Having recently achieved its age of majority as a world power, the United States had a duty to continue to uphold the principles and ideals for which it fought. This new role and new responsibility brought new burdens, but also great opportunities. In conclusion, he spoke of the greatest of his ideals, the future role of America:

> The stage is set, the destiny disclosed. It has come about by no plan of our conceiving, but by the hand of God who led us into this way. We cannot turn back. We can only go forward, with lifted eyes and freshened spirit, to follow the vision. It was of this that we dreamed at our birth. America shall in truth show the way. The light streams upon the path ahead, and nowhere else.[25]

He urged the Senate to seize the chance, but neither his eloquence nor his arguments persuaded the necessary two-thirds majority.

Convinced that he could appeal over the heads of the senators to the people whom they represented, Wilson toured the western United States in the fall of 1919. At every stop, he reviewed the terms of the treaty in simple language. He explained the vision that it contained and the requirements of international cooperation and collective security that it entailed. Furthermore, he argued that the league offered the United States its greatest chance to assume the moral leadership of the world.[26] Throughout the tour, he suffered from grueling headaches as his body finally caved in under the pressures he exerted on it. On his way from Pueblo, Colorado, to Wichita, Kansas, Wilson collapsed. Rushed back to Washington, he suffered a stroke on October 2, 1919.

The Senate offered to compromise by putting various restrictions and reservations on the entry of the United States into the league. But Wilson refused to negotiate over America's destiny. "My clear conviction is that the adoption of the Treaty by the Senate with reservations would put the United States as clearly out of the concert of nations as a rejection," he explained to Tumulty. "We ought either to go in or to stay out."[27] In the end, the United States chose the latter course.

Yet, Wilson's vision survived. Such disparate leaders as Franklin Roosevelt, John Foster Dulles, and Richard Nixon have looked to his ideals, if not his methods of obtaining them, for guidance in their own foreign policies.[28] Force, too, has played an overriding role in America's participation in world affairs since Wilson. The example he set in his reliance on force as an aspect of foreign policy continues to obtain. The pity, perhaps, is that the wrong lessons have been learned from Wilson's experiences.

He tasted the bitter fruit of failure when he applied force to promote ideals, when he used force to spread the American vision, and when he relied on force to prove America's commitment to collective action. Yet, he learned from his experiences that force is limited and that its limitations must be made an explicit part of foreign policy. The Covenant of the League of Nations attempted to express this lesson. As he told the conference on February 14, 1919:

> Throughout this instrument we are depending primarily and chiefly upon one great force, and that is the moral force of the public opinion of the world,—the cleansing and clarifying and compelling influences of publicity; so that intrigues can no longer have their covers. . . .
>
> Armed force is in the background in this programme, but it *is* in the background, and if the moral force of the world will not suffice, the physical force of the world shall. But that is the last resort, because this is intended as a constitution of peace, not as a League of War.

Accordingly, the covenant established severe restrictions on the employment of force to settle international disputes. As he explained to an audience in Helena, Montana, on September 11, "The heart of the covenant of the League of Nations is this: Every member of the League promises never to go to war without first having done one or other of two things, either having submitted the matter to arbitration, in which case it agrees absolutely to abide by the award, or having submitted it to discussion by the council of the League of Nations."[29] Aggressive war was outlawed, and all nations pledged their cooperation to come to the aid of any state threatened by aggressive acts. Force was limited essentially to defense, either of national territory or of the integrity of the new international system.

Thus, after four years of interventions and war, Wilson came to see that force offered few benefits. Between April 1914 and July 1918 he dispatched American troops around the globe. From Veracruz to Vladivostok, Wilson sought through armed power to impose his principles of democracy and freedom on Mexicans, Haitians, Santo Dominicans, Europeans, and Russians. If, as he told the Senate in July 1919, the United States had lately achieved its majority as a world power, it reached that adulthood in ceremonies of blood and violence. Through Wilson's actions, America became not the representative of high ideals and grandiose principles, but an overbearing power intent on forcing other states to accept its solutions to their problems.

But Wilson did not invent force, nor was he the first nor the last to use it to achieve national objectives. In a violent world, he at least strove for a better, less selfish cause than other leaders before or after him. His example teaches the appropriate—and inappropriate—applications of armed power, that force can defend an idea better than it can promote one. Wilson recognized the importance of international law in regulating the methods of force and the vitality of international cooperation as a means of curbing the power of renegade nations. Further, and perhaps most importantly, Wilson's example illustrates how to control the military and not allow it to get carried away with force merely because the distinction between war and limited intervention is not always clear. The principle of civilian control that he embraced so dearly offers some hope that force, if it must be used, can be used carefully and wisely. Wilson understood what later generations have tended to forget: it is only through the limitations on force that civilization survives.

NOTES

INTRODUCTION

1. Woodrow Wilson, "Speech," Jan. 27, 1916, in Donald Day, ed., *Woodrow Wilson's Own Story*, 202.
2. George Kennan, *American Diplomacy, 1900–1950;* Robert Osgood, *Ideals and Self-Interest in American Foreign Policy;* Arthur Link, "Wilson: Idealism and Realism," in Link, ed., *Woodrow Wilson: A Profile*, 163–77.
3. N. Gordon Levin, Jr., *Woodrow Wilson and World Politics: America's Response to War and Revolution,* 1; Arno J. Mayer, *Political Origins of the New Diplomacy, 1917–1918,* and *Politics and Diplomacy of Peacemaking: Containment and Counterrevolution at Versailles, 1918–1919.*
4. Arthur Link, *Wilson;* Robert E. Quirk, *An Affair of Honor: Woodrow Wilson and the Occupation of Veracruz;* Jack Sweetman, *The Landing at Veracruz, 1914;* Frank Tompkins, *Chasing Villa: The Story Behind the Story of Pershing's Expedition into Mexico;* Donald Smythe, *Guerrilla Warrior: The Early Life of John J. Pershing;* David Healy, *Gunboat Diplomacy in the Wilson Era: The U.S. Navy in Haiti, 1915–1916;* Hans Schmidt, *The United States Occupation of Haiti, 1915–1934;* Sumner Welles, *Naboth's Vineyard: The Dominican Republic 1844–1924;* Bruce J. Calder, *The Impact of Intervention: The Dominican Republic During the U.S. Occupation of 1916–1924;* among the best general sources on World War I, see the works of Arthur Link, E. H. Buehrig, *Woodrow Wilson and the Balance of Power,* and Patrick Devlin, *Too Proud To Fight: Woodrow Wilson's Neutrality;* George Kennan, *The Decision to Intervene;* Betty Miller Unterberger, *American Intervention in the Russian Civil War,* and *America's Siberian Expedition, 1918–1920.*

1. THE POWER OF IDEALS: The Wilsonian Framework

1. Wilson to M. A. Hulbert, Feb. 1, 1914, in Arthur Link, ed., *The Papers of Woodrow Wilson* 29:211–12; Arthur Link, *Woodrow Wilson: Revolution, War, and Peace,* 2.
2. Wilson to Hulbert, Sept. 21, 1913, in Day, *Wilson's Own Story,* 148; Woodrow Wilson, *Leaders of Men,* ed. T. H. Vail Motter, 42, 29, 53–54, 23–24, 25, 26, 45, 43–44.
3. Wilson to Ellen Axson, Dec. 18, 1884, in Link, *Papers of Woodrow Wilson* 3:552–53.
4. Wilson, "Speech," Sept. 28, 1915, in Day, *Wilson's Own Story,* 199.
5. John W. Blassingame, "The Press and American Intervention in Haiti and the Dominican Republic," 43, 29–30.
6. Woodrow Wilson, *Congressional Government: A Study in American Politics,* 266, 260.
7. Woodrow Wilson, "The Ideals of America," Dec. 1902, in Ray S. Baker and William E. Dodd, eds., *The Public Papers of Woodrow Wilson: College and State* 1:441;

Woodrow Wilson, *Constitutional Government in the United States*, 77–79, 59–60.

8. George Creel, *The War, the World, and Wilson*, 18; Wilson, "Statement," Jan. 3, 1915, in Day, *Wilson's Own Story*, 178; Wilson to A. Mitchell Palmer, Feb. 5, 1913, in Ray S. Baker and William E. Dodd, eds., *The Public Papers of Woodrow Wilson: The New Democracy* 1:23–24; Arthur Link, *Wilson: The New Freedom* (Princeton, N.J.: Princeton Univ. Press, 1956), 147–52; Arthur Link, *Woodrow Wilson and the Progressive Era: 1910–1917*, 25–81; Arthur Walworth, *Woodrow Wilson*, 287–342.

9. Wilson, "Notes on Administration," ca. Nov. 15, 1885, in Link, *Papers of Woodrow Wilson* 5:49; Wilson, "The Art of Governing," Nov. 15, 1885, in Link, *Papers of Woodrow Wilson* 5:50–54.

10. Wilson, "The Study of Administration," ca. Nov. 1, 1886, in Link, *Papers of Woodrow Wilson* 5:363, 376.

11. Editorial note, "Wilson's Lectures on Administration at The Johns Hopkins, 1890," in Link, *Papers of Woodrow Wilson* 6:482–84; Wilson, "Notes for Lectures on Administration," Feb. 3–Mar. 10, 1890, in Link, *Papers of Woodrow Wilson* 6:484–521; Wilson, "Notes for Lectures at The Johns Hopkins," ca. Jan. 26, 1891–Feb. 27, 1894, in Link, *Papers of Woodrow Wilson* 7:115–59; Wilson, "Notes for Lectures at The Johns Hopkins," ca. Feb. 1, 1892–Feb. 27, 1895, in Link, *Papers of Woodrow Wilson* 7:381–436.

12. John M. Mulder, *Woodrow Wilson: The Years of Preparation*, 168–69.

13. Link, *Revolution, War, and Peace*, 14.

14. Samuel Wells, "New Perspectives on Wilsonian Diplomacy: The Secular Evangelism of American Political Economy," 400–401; Mulder, *Years of Preparation;* Arthur Link, "Woodrow Wilson and His Presbyterian Inheritance," in Link, ed., *The Higher Realism of Woodrow Wilson and Other Essays*, 3–21.

15. Wilson, "Democracy and Efficiency," Mar. 1901, in Baker and Dodd, *College and State* 1:414, and "A New Latin American Policy," Oct. 27, 1913, in Baker and Dodd, *The New Democracy* 1:67–69.

16. Wilson, "A Speech Accepting a Statue of Philip Kearney," Nov. 11, 1914, in Link, *Papers of Woodrow Wilson* 31:562.

17. William Allen White, *Woodrow Wilson: The Man, His Times, and His Task*, 38; John W. Davidson, ed., *A Crossroads of Freedom: The 1912 Campaign Speeches of Woodrow Wilson*, 135–36; "Report of a Speech," Dec. 14, 1899, in Link, *Papers of Woodrow Wilson* 11:298–99.

18. Wilson, "Ideals of America," in Baker and Dodd, *College and State* 1:422; Harley Notter, *The Origins of the Foreign Policy of Woodrow Wilson*, 117–18, 186; Woodrow Wilson, *History of the American People* 3:217, and *Division and Reunion, 1829–1909*, 149–50; Notter, *Origins of the Foreign Policy*, 56; Wilson, *Division and Reunion*, 242, and *History of the American People* 5:300.

19. Wilson, "What Ought We To Do?" ca. Aug. 1, 1898, in Link, *Papers of Woodrow Wilson* 10:574–76; Wilson, "Ideals of America," in Baker and Dodd, *College and State* 1:427–28; Notter, *Origins of the Foreign Policy*, 103; "Report of a Speech," Dec. 14, 1899, in Link, *Papers of Woodrow Wilson* 11:298–99; "A Newspaper Report of a Speech in Brooklyn," Jan. 14, 1900, in Link, *Papers of Woodrow Wilson* 11:374–75; "A Newspaper Report of a Public Lecture and an Alumni Meeting in Harrisburg, Pa.," Feb. 24, 1900, in Link, *Papers of Woodrow Wilson* 11:440; Wilson, "Ideals of America," 435; P. Edward Haley, *Revolution and Intervention: The Diplomacy of Taft and Wilson with Mexico, 1910–1917*, 5–7; Notter, *Origins of the Foreign Policy*, 118–19, 69–70.

20. William Diamond, *The Economic Thought of Woodrow Wilson*, 132; Wilson, "Ideals of America," in Baker and Dodd, *College and State* 1:441–42.

21. Wilson, "The Interpreter of English Liberty," in Woodrow Wilson, *Mere Literature and Other Essays*, 145–46; Notter, *Origins of the Foreign Policy*, 82–83, 80–81.

22. Wilson, "Address before Press Club in New York," June 30, 1916, in Baker and Dodd, *New Democracy* 2:219–20.
23. Wilson, "Address to Joint Session of Congress," Nov. 11, 1918, in Ray S. Baker and William E. Dodd, eds., *The Public Papers of Woodrow Wilson: War and Peace* 1:361, and "Address at Rome," Jan. 3, 1919, in Baker and Dodd, *War and Peace* 1:361.
24. Wilson, "Address to National Press Club," May 15, 1916, in Baker and Dodd, *New Democracy* 2:171.
25. Wilson, "Bible and Progress," May 7, 1911, in Baker and Dodd, *College and State* 2:294; Notter, *Origins of the Foreign Policy*, 186.
26. Wilson, "Address before Manhattan Club," Nov. 4, 1915, in Baker and Dodd, *New Democracy* 1:385–86; Day, *Wilson's Own Story*, 200; Wilson, "A Commencement Address," June 5, 1914, in Link, *Papers of Woodrow Wilson* 30:146, and "Address at Overflow Meeting at Soldiers Memorial Hall, Pittsburgh," Jan. 29, 1916, in Baker and Dodd, *New Democracy* 2:29; Notter, *Origins of the Foreign Policy*, 303–4; Wilson, "Address at Biltmore Hotel," May 17, 1915, in Baker and Dodd, *New Democracy* 1:332.
27. Wilson, "Address at Seventh Annual Dinner of the Railway Business Association," Jan. 27, 1916, in Baker and Dodd, *New Democracy* 2:8–9; Wilson, "Address at Soldiers Hall, Pittsburgh," in Baker and Dodd, *New Democracy* 2:26; see also Wilson, "Speech at Omaha," Oct. 5, 1916, in Baker and Dodd, *New Democracy* 2:346–47, and "Speech at Cincinnati," Oct. 26, 1916, in Baker and Dodd, *New Democracy* 2:382.
28. Wilson, "Third Annual Address to Congress," Dec. 7, 1915, in Baker and Dodd, *New Democracy* 1:411, and "Speech at Cincinnati," in Baker and Dodd, *New Democracy* 2:380; see also Wilson, "Memorial Day Address, Arlington," May 30, 1916, in Baker and Dodd, *New Democracy* 2:194.
29. Wilson, "Address before Salesmanship Congress, Detroit," July 10, 1916, in Baker and Dodd, *New Democracy* 2:229, and "Speech at Omaha," in Baker and Dodd, *New Democracy* 2:348.
30. Wilson, "Address at Peace Conference," Feb. 14, 1919, in Day, *Wilson's Own Story*, 322; *Hearings Before the Committee on Foreign Relations, United States Senate: Treaty of Peace with Germany: Testimony of President Woodrow Wilson*, 66th Cong., 1st sess., 1919, pp. 524–25.
31. Clarence H. Cramer, *Newton D. Baker*, 82; Newton Baker to George F. Peabody, Nov. 28, 1917, Newton D. Baker Papers.
32. John A. S. Grenville and George Young, *Politics, Strategy, and American Diplomacy*, 323.
33. Josephus Daniels, *The Cabinet Diaries of Josephus Daniels, 1913–1921*, 26; Josephus Daniels to Ray S. Baker, Nov. 29, 1933, Josephus Daniels Papers.
34. Robert Lansing, "Force and Material and Moral Impulses," May 23, 1922, Robert Lansing Papers; see also Daniel M. Smith, *Robert Lansing and American Neutrality, 1914–1917*, 8.

2. THE POWER OF CIVILIAN CONTROL: Mexico

1. Richard Challener, *Admirals, Generals, and American Foreign Policy, 1898–1914*, 364–400.
2. Wilson, quoted in Ernest May, *The Ultimate Decision*, 3–4; Wilson, "Address at Biltmore Hotel," in Baker and Dodd, *New Democracy* 1:331. See also Wilson, "A Commencement Address," June 5, 1914, in Link, *Papers of Woodrow Wilson* 30:147, 146.
3. Minutes, Joint Army and Navy Board, May 5, 1913, Records of the Joint Army and Navy Board, Old Army and Navy Branch, RG 225, National Archives, Washington,

D.C.; Daniels Diary entry, May 17, 1913, Daniels Papers; Joint Board Minutes, May 15 and Oct. 9, 1913, RG 225, Records of Joint Board; Fiske Diary entry, Nov. 5, 1914, Bradley Fiske Papers; Joint Board Minutes, Jan. 15, 1915, RG 225, Records of Joint Board; Joint Board Minutes, Apr. 26, 1919, RG 225, Records of Joint Board; Challener, *Admirals, Generals,* 364, 55: Grenville and Young, *Politics, Strategy, and American Diplomacy,* 321–23; Ernest May, "The Development of Political-Military Consultation in the U.S."; Wilson to Daniels, Dec. 22, 1913, Daniels Papers; Report of Frank McIntyre, J. R. Aleshire, and P. B. Howard to Lindley Garrison, Dec. 16, 1913, Daniels Papers; Maj. W. E. Horton to Wilson, Nov. 19, 1913, and Wilson to Horton, Nov. 22, 1913, Wilson Papers, Ser. 2; Challener, *Admirals, Generals,* 365; Frederick Palmer, *Bliss, Peacemaker: The Life and Letters of General Tasker Howard Bliss,* 106–7; Challener, *Admirals, Generals,* 364–65.

4. Documentary evidence on the Scott truce at Naco can be found in the Wilson Papers; the Hugh Scott Papers; the Tasker Bliss Papers; the Adjutant General's Office file, Old Army and Navy Branch, RG 94, National Archives, Washington, D.C.; and the Records of the Department of State Relating to Internal Affairs of Mexico, 1910–29, RG 59, for the period from Nov. 1914 to Jan. 1915. The Scott-Obregón conference of Apr. to May 1916 is discussed in chapter 2.

5. Wilson to Daniels, Aug. 11, 1913, Wilson Papers, Ser. 3; Daniels to Wilson, Sept. 7, 1913, enclosing Adm. Frank Fletcher to Secy. of the Navy, Aug. 26, 1913, Wilson Papers, Ser. 2; see also Challener, *Admirals, Generals,* 366.

6. Leonard Wood to Frank McCoy, Feb. 1, 1913, quoted in Jack C. Lane, *Armed Progressive,* 178; John J. Pershing to Frederick Palmer, Oct. 23, 1916, John J. Pershing Papers.

7. The bibliography on the Mexican Revolution and Wilson's policies toward it is extensive. Of particular help in preparing this brief summary of Wilson's initial reaction to the revolution were: Peter Calvert, *The Mexican Revolution, 1910–1914: The Diplomacy of Anglo-American Conflict;* Challener, *Admirals, Generals;* Kendrick A. Clements, "Woodrow Wilson's Mexican Policy, 1913–1915"; Howard F. Cline, *The United States and Mexico;* Mark T. Gilderhus, *Diplomacy and Revolution: U.S.-Mexican Relations Under Wilson and Carranza;* Kenneth J. Grieb, "The Lind Mission to Mexico," and *The United States and Huerta;* Friedrich Katz, *The Secret War in Mexico: Europe, the United States, and the Mexican Revolution;* Link, *The New Freedom;* Michael C. Meyer; *Huerta: A Political Portrait;* Robert Freeman Smith, *The United States and Revolutionary Nationalism in Mexico, 1916–1932.*

8. Wilson to Ellen Wilson, Aug. 19, 1913, in Link, *Papers of Woodrow Wilson* 28:190; Daniels, *Cabinet Diaries,* Apr. 11 and 18, 1913, pp. 29–30, 43–44; House Diary entry, Aug. 10, 1913, in Link, *Papers of Woodrow Wilson* 28:139; Challener, *Admirals, Generals,* 382–83; William Jennings Bryan to Wilson, July 19, 1913, Wilson Papers, Ser. 2.

9. Wilson, press release, Mar. 12, 1913, Wilson Papers, Ser. 2; Daniels Diary entry, Mar. 11, 1913, Daniels Papers.

10. Wilson to John Lind, July 30, 1913 (draft), Wilson Papers, Ser. 2; Wilson to Lind, Aug. 4, 1913, The Mexican Mission Papers of John Lind (hereafter cited as Lind Papers); Bryan to Lind, Aug. 13, 1913, Lind Papers.

11. Wilson, "Draft of a Joint Resolution," ca. Oct. 31, 1913, in Link, *Papers of Woodrow Wilson* 28:478–79; Wilson, "Draft of an Address to Congress," ca. Oct. 31, 1913, in Link, *Papers of Woodrow Wilson* 28:479–81; House Diary entry, Oct. 31, 1913, in Link, *Papers of Woodrow Wilson* 28:476–78; Augustus Brown to Wilson, Nov. 4, 1913, in Link, *Papers of Woodrow Wilson* 28:488–90; Link, *The New Freedom,* 379–84; Berta Ulloa, *La Revolución Intervenida,* 92–94; Haley, *Revolution and Intervention,* 114–15; Clements, "Wilson's Mexican Policy," 118; Bryan to Wilson, Oct. 28, 1913, quoted in William Jennings Bryan

and Mary Bryan, *Memoirs of William Jennings Bryan,* 360–61, and Bryan to Nelson O'Shaughnessy, Nov. 1, 1913, in Link, *Papers of Woodrow Wilson* 28:482–83.

12. Wilson to Bryan, Nov. 23, 1913, Correspondence of Secretary of State Bryan with President Wilson (hereafter cited as Wilson-Bryan Correspondence), RG 59; International Note, "Our Purposes in Mexico," Nov. 24, 1913, Wilson-Bryan Correspondence; see also Link, *The New Freedom,* 379–88; Clements, "Wilson's Mexican Policy," 122.

13. The reason for the army's predominant interest in and responsibility for war with Mexico is clear: Mexico had no navy. At a meeting of the Joint Board on Apr. 15, 1912, an agreement was reached between the two services that remained in force, with minor modifications, throughout the Wilson period. Under the terms of the settlement, the navy's responsibilities were: (1) the seizure and temporary occupation of Veracruz until the army relieved the naval forces in three days; (2) seizure and blockade of the Mexican ports on the Pacific and Gulf coasts. Joint Board Minutes, Apr. 15, 1912, RG 225, Records of Joint Board. This agreement was included in the War College's War Plan portfolios, Military Intelligence Division files, Old Army and Navy Branch, RG 165, National Archives, Washington, D.C.

The closest that the War College came to a plan for a limited intervention in Mexico was a plan drawn up in Jan. 1916 for the immediate occupation of the state of Chihuahua in the event of war; Memo to Chief of Staff from Gen. M. M. Macomb, Jan. 31, 1916, RG 165, WCD 6474-371. In Mar. 1916 a plan was formulated for the occupation and pacification of Northern Mexico; Memo to Chief of Staff from Macomb, Mar. 25, 1916, RG 165, WCD 6474-376. An accepted modification to the general war plan was approved in Feb. 1912 that proposed the take-over of northern Mexico, but this strategy depended on a large American army moving on Mexico City via Veracruz; Memo to Chief of Staff from Gen. A. L. Mills, Feb. 23, 1912, RG 165, WCD 6474-30 (this memo was repeated as Part 6, War Plan of Apr. 15, 1912, RG 165, WCD 6474–93). These plans were of very little use for the type of limited interventions in which Wilson engaged the military.

14. The quote is from "Strategic Study and War Plans," presented by Mills, Mar. 25, 1912, RG 165, WCD 6474-66. It is repeated in War Plan No. I, Strategic Study 1910, received by Chief of Staff, Apr. 4, 1911; RG 165, WCD 6474-5; Memorandum: Mexico, Military Situation on Southern Border, Apr. 1911; Proposed Lines of Action, May 8, 1911, RG 165, WCD 6474-17; Memo to Chief of Staff from Mills, Feb. 15, 1912, RG 165, WCD 6474-27; Memo to Chief of Staff from Mills, Apr. 15, 1912, RG 165, WCD 6474-93, Part I (note that this plan pointed out that the Mexican Army was "much demoralized," but it still argued that Mexico could muster 140,000 men in the federal army alone); Mexican War Plan, July 29, 1913, RG 165, WCD 6474-275; Gen. W. W. Wotherspoon to Adm. R. P. Rodgers, Apr. 22, 1911, RG 165, WCD 6474-9.

15. Memo to the War Plans Committee, "Armed Intervention in Mexico," from General William Crozier, June 24, 1913, RG 165, WCD 6474-270.

16. Memo to Chief of Staff from Gen. Hunter H. Liggett, July 14, 1913, WCD 6474-274; Adm. Frank Fletcher, Mexican War Plan, July 29, 1913, RG 165, WCD 6474-275.

17. Adm. Frank Fletcher, Private Notes, Oct. 1913, WQE-5, Misc. File, Old Army and Navy Branch, RG 45, National Archives, Washington, D.C.; Fletcher to Adm. Charles Badger, Feb. 24, 1913, Area File C: Caribbean, Old Army and Navy Branch, RG 45, National Archives, Washington, D.C.; Fletcher to U.S. Consul, Tampico, Dec. 12, 1913, RG 45, Area Files; "Estimate of the Situation," Feb. 28, 1913, RG 45, Misc. File; Lt. G. M. Courts, "Discussion of Intervention—Armed and Financial," Apr. 13, 1913, Subject File, Old Army and Navy Branch, RG 45, National Archives, Washington, D.C.; Clayton B. Vogel, "Outline of Plan for Taking Veracruz" (Vogel was a marine serving with Fletcher), Feb. 28, 1913, C. B. Vogel Papers, P.C. 2; Tasker Bliss to Adj. Gen., Apr. 25, 1913, RG 94, AGO 2151731B, filed with 2149991; Bliss to Liggett, Aug. 15, 1913, RG 165, WCD 6474-347, Inc. 4.

18. Sweetman, *Landing at Veracruz*, 151.
19. Fletcher to Secy. of the Navy, Apr. 16, 1914, WE-5, Dispatches File, Old Army and Navy Branch, RG 45, National Archives, Washington, D.C.; Daniels to R. S. Baker, Apr. 13, 1929, R. S. Baker Papers. For the facts leading up to the occupation, see Fletcher to Secy. of the Navy, Apr. 9, 1914, RG 45, WE-5, Dispatches File; William Canada to Secy. of State, Apr. 12, 1914, RG 59, 812.00/11478; Fletcher to Secy. of the Navy, Apr. 13, 1914, RG 45, WE-5, Dispatches File; Adm. Henry T. Mayo to Fletcher, Apr. 14, 1914, RG 45, WE-5, Dispatches File; Leonard Wood, Diary entry, Apr. 20, 1914, Wood Papers. The best secondary accounts are Quirk, *An Affair of Honor;* Sweetman, *Landing at Veracruz;* Challener, *Admirals, Generals,* 379–97; and Link, *The New Freedom,* 394–416.
20. Wood Diary entry, Apr. 26 and 29, 1914, Wood Papers, record his conversations with the French ambassador during which the latter discussed his participation in arranging for the offer of mediation. The British believed that Wilson had suggested mediation by the ABC powers. Grieb, *The United States and Huerta,* 159. The British ambassador told Henry Cabot Lodge on Apr. 25 "that Jusserand [the French ambassador] had hinted to Brazil, Argentina, and Chile to move." Henry Cabot Lodge, *The Senate and the League of Nations,* 20. Finally, an American aide to the Mexican delegation to the ABC conference wrote Emilio Rabasa, a member of that delegation, on Apr. 24, 1914 that the ABC powers "offered their services on account of an insinuation from Bryan." Ulloa, *La Revolución Intervenida,* 188; Rose to Bryan, May 29, 1914, Bryan Papers; Chargé d'Affaires to Argentina Lorillard to Secy. of State, Apr. 27, 1914, RG 59, 812.00/11737, and Apr. 29, 1914, RG 59, 812.00/12096; Mediators to Secy. of State, Apr. 25, 1914, RG 59, 812.00/11744c.
21. Daniels to Fletcher, Apr. 21, 1914, Daniels Papers. See also Bryan to O'Shaughnessy, Apr. 21, 1914, 6 A.M., RG 59, 812.00/11564 (in which Bryan explained that war had not been declared); Bryan to George Carothers for Carranza, Apr. 21, 1914, 9:50 P.M., RG 59, 812.00/11608a (in which Bryan defended the occupation as a reprisal, not an act of war); Josephus Daniels, *The Wilson Era: Years of Peace, 1910–1917,* 191. See also Frank Freidel, *Franklin D. Roosevelt: The Apprenticeship,* 229.
22. Badger to Daniels, Apr. 16, 1914, Wilson Papers, Ser. 2. See also Scott to Bliss, Apr. 20, 1914, Bliss Papers.
23. Badger to Secy. of the Navy, Apr. 23, 1914, RG 45, WE-5, Dispatches File; Mayo to Fletcher, Apr. 22, 1914, RG 45, WE-5, Dispatches File; Fletcher to Secy. of the Navy, Apr. 23, 1914, RG 45, WE-5, Dispatches File; Mayo to Badger, Apr. 30, 1914, RG 45, WE-5, Dispatches File. The confusion was not confined to the admirals. See, for example, Sweetman, *Landing at Veracruz,* 132; Frederic M. Wise, *A Marine Tells It to You,* 122; Freidel, *Franklin D. Roosevelt,* 232; Scott to Bliss, Apr. 24, 1914, Bliss Papers; W. A. Burnside to War College Staff, Apr. 25, 1914, RG 45, Subject File; James Parker, *The Old Army: Memories, 1872–1918,* 422; J. G. Harbord to Frederick Funston, Dec. 3, 1914, Funston Papers.
24. Garrison to Funston, original draft, Apr. 26, 1914, RG 94, AGO 2153594, and final draft, Apr. 26, 1914, RG 94, AGO 2153594, Inc. 2.
25. Garrison to Funston, May 14, 1914, RG 94, AGO 2160103. See also Garrison to Bliss, July 16, 1914, Bliss Papers.
26. Consul at Ciudad Juárez Edwards to Bryan, Apr. 21, 1914, RG 59, 812.00/11583; Carothers to Bryan, Apr. 21, 1914, RG 59, 812.00/11596, and Apr. 22, 1914, RG 59, 812.00/11618; Consul at Chihuahua, Letcher to Bryan, Apr. 22, 1914, RG 59, 812.00/11650; Bliss to Wotherspoon, Apr. 23, 1914, RG 94, AGO 2151395; Wotherspoon to Bliss, Apr. 23, 1914, RG 94, AGO 2151395B; Adj. Gen. Andrews to Bliss, Apr. 23, 1914, Bliss Papers; Bliss to Wotherspoon, Apr. 23, 1914, Bliss Papers; Wotherspoon to Bliss, May 19, 1914, Bliss Papers; Garrison to William G. McAdoo, Apr. 24, 1914, McAdoo Papers; McAdoo to Secy. of State, Apr. 24, 1914, Wilson Papers, Ser. 2; Wotherspoon to Bliss, Apr. 27, 1914,

274 / Notes

Bliss Papers; Bliss to Wotherspoon, May 14, 1914, RG 94, AGO 2165772; Bliss to Col. George Bell, Jr., July 22, 1914, Pershing Papers; Bliss to Gen. Robert K. Evans, Aug. 10, 1914, Bliss Papers; Andrews to Bliss, July 3, 1914, Bliss Papers; Bliss to Agwar, May 2, 1914, RG 94, AGO 2150626G; Dept. of State to Dept. of Justice, May 8, 1914, RG 59, 812.00/11940; Bliss to Adj. Gen., May 1, 1914, Bliss Papers; Two memos (unsigned) to Wilson, May 30, 1914, Wilson Papers, Ser. 2; Wilson to Bryan, July 7, 1914, Wilson Papers, Ser. 2; Memo to Wotherspoon from Gen. Enoch Crowder, Aug. 15, 1914, RG 94, AGO 2182228E; Bliss to Wotherspoon, Aug. 18, 1914, Bliss Papers; Garrison to Wilson, Aug. 20, 1914, RG 94, AGO 2182228; Bliss to Scott, Aug. 26, 1914, Bliss Papers; Wotherspoon to Bliss, Sept. 8, 1914, Bliss Papers; Adj. Gen. McCain to Bliss, Sept. 8, 1914, Bliss Papers.

27. Bliss to Wotherspoon, May 14, 1914, RG 94, AGO 2165772.

28. Wotherspoon to Bliss, June 15, Apr. 28, and May 12, 1914, Bliss Papers; Wotherspoon to Maj. Gen. Arthur Murray, May 19, 1914, RG 94, AGO 21633626; Wotherspoon to Bliss, May 26, June 4 and 17, 1914, Bliss Papers.

29. Bradley Fiske, *From Midshipman to Rear Admiral*, 550; Fiske Diary entries, Sept. 26 and Oct. 27, 1914, Fiske Papers.

30. Arthur Link, *Wilson: The Struggle for Neutrality* (Princeton, N.J.: Princeton Univ. Press, 1960), 239–41, 257–66, 457–94, 635–44; Katz, *The Secret War in Mexico*, 307–9.

31. Stone, "In re Villista Activities at Columbus, New Mexico," Mar. 18, 1916, RG 94, AGO 2378342; Friedrich Katz, "Pancho Villa and the Attack on Columbus, New Mexico," 334–36; Katz, *The Secret War in Mexico*, 307–8; Villa to Zapata, Jan. 8, 1915, RG 94, AGO 2384662AB.

32. Funston to Adj. Gen., #890, Mar. 10, 1916, RG 94, AGO 2377335J. See also Funston Report, Fiscal Year 1916, July 1916, RG 94, AGO 2480591; Bliss, "Facts about Villa's attack on Columbus," undated, RG 94, AGO 2387731.

33. No author, "The Military Strength for armed intervention in Mexico," Mar. 4, 1916, RG 165, WCD 6474-372. The War College did prepare a plan for the occupation of the state of Chihuahua at the request of Gen. Bliss in Jan. 1916, but this plan concluded that "the unwisdom of taking any step toward intervention without preparation for making it complete is therefore apparent. . . . In other words, partial intervention entails preparation for complete intervention, and should not be entered upon unless and until such preparation has been made." Memo to Chief of Staff from Macomb, Jan. 31, 1916, RG 165, WCD 6474-371. For the major war plans before the Columbus raid, see "Revision of plan of July 1913," June 1914, RG 165, WCD 6474-350, and "Mexican War Plan, revision of plan of July 1913," Oct. 1915, RG 165, WCD 6474-377.

34. Macomb, "Memo for file with 6474-374," Mar. 29, 1916, RG 165, WCD 6474-373.

35. Memo to Chief of Staff from Macomb and Bliss, Mar. 10, 1916, RG 165, WCD 6474-373; N. Baker to Wilson, Mar. 12, 1916, Wilson Papers, Ser. 2; Bliss to Parker, May 1, 1916, Bliss Papers. For Funston's plan, see Funston to Adj. Gen., Mar. 11, 1916, RG 94, AGO 2377632C.

36. Memo to Adj. Gen. from Bliss, Mar. 10, 1916, RG 94, AGO 2377632A; Scott to Col. W. E. Wilder, July 22, 1916, Scott Papers; Hugh L. Scott, *Some Memories of a Soldier*, 519–20; Memo to Adj. Gen. from Scott, Mar. 10, 1916, RG 94, AGO 2377632; Baker to Wilson, Mar. 10, 1916, Wilson Papers, Ser. 2.

37. Memo to Chief of Staff from Bliss, Mar. 13, 1916, Bliss Papers.

38. Bliss, "Report of patrol system along Mexican border," Apr. 17, 1913; Bliss, "Conditions along Mexican border and possible remedies for same," Apr. 19, 1913; Bliss to Crozier, May 12, 1913; Memo to Chief of Staff from Bliss, Mar. 13, 1916, all in Bliss Papers.

39. Memo to Chief of Staff from Macomb, Mar. 13, 1916, RG 165, WCD 6474-375; Scott to Secy. of War, Mar. 13, 1916, Scott Papers.

40. N. Baker to Wilson, enclosing Memo to Chief of Staff, Mar. 16, 1916, Wilson Papers, Ser. 2. See also Gen. Peyton C. March to Funston, undated, RG 94, AGO 2377632O; Memo to Chief of Staff from Bliss, Mar. 13, 1916, RG 94, AGO 2377632N.

41. Scott to Funston, Mar. 27, 1916, Funston Papers; Funston to Scott, Apr. 5, 1916, Scott Papers; Pershing to Funston, Apr. 16, 1916, RG 94, AGO 2379210A[113]; Scott to J. W. Pride, Mar. 17, 1916, Scott Papers; Pershing to Crowder, June 15, 1916, and Pershing to Wood, Aug. 20, 1916, Pershing Papers; Pershing to Scott, undated, Scott Papers; Funston to Scott, Apr. 5 and Mar. 24, 1916, Funston Papers.

42. Maj. Frank Tompkins to Pershing, Apr. 13, 1916, Bulky Files, AGO 370.22, Old Army and Navy Branch, RG 407, National Archives, Washington, D.C.; Tompkins, *Chasing Villa*, 137–44; Clarence Clendenen, *The U.S. and Pancho Villa: A Study in Unconventional Diplomacy*, 266–67.

43. Funston to Adj. Gen., quoting Pershing, #1327-A, Apr. 28, 1916, RG 94, AGO 2379201A[166]; Funston to Adj. Gen., quoting Pershing, Apr. 17, 1916, RG 94, AGO 2379210A[123]; Funston to Adj. Gen., quoting Pershing, #1611, June 13, 1916, RG 94, AGO 2379210A[225]; Funston to Adj. Gen., quoting two telegrams from Pershing, Apr. 15, 1916, RG 94, AGO 2379210A[111]; Funston to Adj. Gen., quoting Pershing, #1263, Apr. 16, 1916, RG 94, AGO 2379210A[113].

44. Pershing to Theodore Roosevelt, May 24, 1916; Pershing to Bird McGuire, June 15, 1916; Pershing to Frank P. Holm, June 19, 1916, all in Pershing Papers; Funston to Adj. Gen., quoting Pershing, #1238, Apr. 14, 1916, RG 94, AGO 2379210A[107]; Funston to Adj. Gen., quoting Funston to Pershing, May 19, 1916, RG 94, AGO 2379210A[194]; Funston to Scott, May 30, 1916, and Funston to James Parker, May 27, 1916, Funston Papers.

45. McCain to Funston, Apr. 14, 1916, RG 94, AGO 2379210A[108]; Memo to Scott from Baker, Apr. 19, 1916, Scott Papers; McCain to Funston, Apr. 16, 1916, RG 94, AGO 2379210A[112].

46. Scott and Funston to Adj. Gen., Apr. 22, 1916, RG 94, AGO 2379210A[139]; Scott and Funston to Adj. Gen., Apr. 22, 1916, RG 94, AGO 2379210A[144]; Scott to Baker, Apr. 24, 1916, RG 94, AGO 2394312A[14].

47. McCain to Scott, Apr. 23, 1916, Scott Papers; N. Baker to Scott, Apr. 22, 1916, RG 94, AGO 2394312; McCain to Scott, Apr. 22 and 24, 1914, Bliss to Scott, Apr. 27, 1916, and McCain to Scott, Apr. 27, 1916, RG 94, AGO 2394312A[14]; Scott to Mary Scott, Apr. 24 and 26, 1916, Scott Papers.

48. McCain to Scott, Apr. 26 and 30, 1916, RG 94, AGO 2394312A[14]; Baker to Scott, Apr. 30, 1916, RG 94, AGO 2394312; Baker to Scott, May 1, 1916, Scott Papers; McCain to Scott, May 1, 1916, RG 94, AGO 2394312A[14].

49. Scott and Funston to Secy. of War, Apr. 29, 1916, Scott Papers; May 2, 1916, RG 94, AGO 2394312A[14]; May 2, 1916, RG 94, AGO 2394312M; and May 3, 1916, Scott Papers.

50. N. Baker to Chief of Staff, May 4, 1916, RG 94, AGO 2394312Q; Scott to Secy. of War, May 8, 1916, RG 94, AGO 2394312A[14]; Scott and Funston to Secy. of War, May 8, 1916, RG 94, AGO 2394312X.

51. McCain to Funston, May 9, 1916, RG 94, AGO 2394312A[14]; Memo to Adj. Gen. from Bliss, May 9, 1916, RG 94, AGO 2394312Y; Baker to Gov. George W. P. Hunt, May 9, 1916, RG 165, WCD 6474-379; Scott and Funston to Secy. of War, May 9, 1916, RG 94, AGO 2394312A[14]; no author, "Description of Scott-Obregón conference of May 8 and 9, 1916," Scott Papers; Scott and Funston to Secy. of War, May 11, 1916, RG 94, AGO 2394312A[16]; Scott, "Border Conference with General Obregón," May 12, 1916, Bliss Papers; Scott and Funston to Secy. of War, May 11, 1916, RG 94, AGO 2394312A[8].

52. Secy. of Foreign Relations, Mexico, to Robert Lansing, May 22, 1916, U.S. Dept. of State, *Foreign Relations of the United States, 1916* (Washington, D.C.: Government Printing Office, 1928–).

53. Memo to Chief of Staff from Macomb, June 7, 1916, RG 165, WCD 6474-380; Memo to Chief, War College Division, from Scott, June 16, 1916, WCD 6474-383; no author, "Mexican Situation, 1916," June 10, 1916, RG 165, WCD 6474-381; Memo to Chief of Staff from Macomb, June 15, 1916, RG 165, WCD 6474-382; Macomb, "Notes by the Chief, WCD, of his Interview with the Chief of Staff, June 15, 1916," June 16, 1916, RG 165, WCD 6474-384. The plan finally drawn up in response to Scott's June 16 request was submitted in three installments, June 19, 20, and 23, 1916, RG 165, WCD 6474-385.

54. Funston to Adj. Gen., quoting Pershing, June 16, 1916, RG 94, AGO 2379210A[228]; Clendenen, *U.S. and Pancho Villa,* 277–78; Scott to Col. H. J. Slocum, June 20, 1916, Scott Papers.

55. Memo by Bliss, June 5, 1916, Bliss Papers; Bliss to Lansing, June 6, 1916, enclosing memo signed by Scott, but obviously written by Bliss, Scott Papers; Memo to Chief of Staff from Bliss, June 19, 1916, Bliss Papers; Memo to Adj. Gen. from Scott, June 19, 1916, RG 94, AGO 2414482AB.

56. Lansing to Secy. of Foreign Relations, Mexico, June 20, 1916, *Foreign Relations, 1916,* 581–92.

57. Funston to Adj. Gen., quoting Pershing, June 22, 1916, RG 94, AGO 2416172E; Funston to Adj. Gen., quoting Pershing, June 23, 1916, RG 94, AGO 2416172G; Funston to Adj. Gen., June 22, 1916, RG 94, AGO 2417328A; Memo to Chief of Staff from N. Baker, June 22, 1916, RG 94, AGO 2416172E.

58. N. Baker to Scott, June 22, 1916, RG 94, AGO 2416998; Memo to Adj. Gen. from Bliss, June 25, 1916, RG 94, AGO 2418482A.

59. Funston to Adj. Gen., quoting Pershing, June 25, 1916, RG 94, AGO 2416172O; William M. Ingraham to Wilson, Oct. 9, 1916, Wilson Papers, Ser. 2.

60. Donald Smythe, *Guerrilla Warrior: The Early Life of John J. Pershing,* 279.

61. Pershing to Col. Mark L. Hersey, June 15, 1916; Pershing to Charles R. Cameron, June 15, 1916; Pershing to Wood, Aug. 20, 1916; Pershing to Palmer, Oct. 23, 1916; Pershing to Wood, Sept. 10 and Oct. 21, 1916, all in Pershing Papers; Pershing to Funston, Nov. 2, 1916, RG 94, AGO 249052O; N. Baker to Wilson, enclosing Funston to Adj. Gen., quoting Pershing to Funston, Dec. 9, 1916, Wilson Papers, Ser. 2; Pershing to Col. Bertram T. Clayton, Oct. 15, 1916, and Pershing to Col. Melvin-Hill Barmon, Aug. 30, 1916, Pershing Papers; Pershing to Scott, Sept. 23, 1916, Scott Papers; Pershing to Bliss, Aug. 8, 1916, Bliss Papers.

62. Scott to Wood, Mar. 11, 1916, and Scott to Carothers, Mar. 17, 1916, Scott Papers; Scott to M. M. Parker, Mar. 18, 1916, RG 94, AGO 2381631; Scott to Col. J. T. Dickman, Apr. 8, 1916, and Scott to Col. E. J. Spencer, May 16, 1916, Scott Papers; Scott and Funston to Secy. of War, May 7, 1916, RG 94, AGO 2394312T; Scott to Capt. Oscar J. Charles, May 16, 1916, Scott to Garrison, May 19, 1916, Scott to Col. H. T. Allen, May 31, 1916, Scott to Capt. R. M. Thomas, Aug. 7, 1916, and Scott to Pershing, Oct. 9 and 30, 1916, all in Scott Papers.

63. Scott to Maj. J. A. Ryan, Sept. 5, 1916, Scott Papers.

3. THE POWER OF IDEOLOGY: Santo Domingo and Haiti

1. Link, *Revolution, War, and Peace,* 6.
2. Wilson, "Speech," Jan. 27, 1916, in Baker and Dodd, *New Democracy* 2:8; Wilson, "Speech," July 4, 1914, in Baker and Dodd, *New Democracy* 1:147; Link, *Revolution, War, and Peace,* 6.
3. Wilson, "Speech," Jan. 27, 1916, in Baker and Dodd, *New Democracy* 2:9–10; Link, *Struggle for Neutrality,* 548.

4. Mediators to Secy. of State, Apr. 25, 1914, and Bryan to Mediators, Apr. 25, 1914, RG 59, 812.00/11744c; "Confidential Memorandum," unsigned, undated, Wilson Papers, Ser. 2; Lansing to Bryan, May 1, 1914, RG 59, 812.00/11800 1/2; American Commissioners to Bryan, May 31, 1914, RG 59, 812.00/11631 1/2; Lodge, *Senate and League*, 19.

5. Bryan to American Commissioners, May 21 and June 1, 1914, RG 59, 812.00/12631 1/2; American Commissioners to Secy. of State, May 29, 1914, RG 59, 812.00/12631 1/2; Grieb, *The United States and Huerta*, 165–77; Link, *The New Freedom*, 409–13; Larry D. Hill, *Emissaries to a Revolution: Woodrow Wilson's Executive Agents in Mexico*, 182–85.

6. American Commissioners to Secy. of State, June 16 (not sent), and 18, 1914, RG 59, 812.00/12631 1/2.

7. Bryan to Lind, July 4, 1914, Lind Papers; Cleveland Dodge to Bryan, July 6, 1914, RG 59, 812.00/12432; John R. Silliman to Secy. of State, July 10, 1914, RG 59, 812.00/12469; Leon J. Canova to Secy. of State, July 6, 1914, RG 59, 812.00/12429.

8. Frank Polk to Rodgers, July 20, 1916, RG 59, 812.00/18749; Lansing to Wilson, July 3, 1916, RG 59, 812.00/17714 1/2.

9. Polk to Dr. John R. Mott, quoting Wilson, Aug. 18, 1916, RG 59, 812.00/24300a; Lansing to Richard Olney, Aug. 15, 1916, RG 59, 812.00/24300.

10. The records of the Joint Mexican-American Commission can be found in the State Dept. files, including United States Participation in International Conferences, Commissions, and Expositions: U.S. Commissioners of the American and Mexican Joint Commission, 1916, Memoranda Furnished by the State Dept., RG 43; Dispatches of John R. Silliman, Mexico City, 1914–15, RG 43. Other materials on the commission are located in the Wilson, Lansing, Baker, and Bliss papers. See also Frederick R. Rowe to Lansing, "Report on the Proceedings of the Commission with Accompanying Papers by the Secretary of the American Commissioners," Apr. 26, 1917, RG 59, 812.00/20849.

11. Bryan to American Legation, Santo Domingo, Sept. 4, 1913, RG 59, 839.00/860, National Archives, Washington, D.C.; John E. Osborne to American Legation, Santo Domingo, Sept. 6, 1913, RG 59, 839.51/1091; Charles B. Curtis to Secy. of State, July 2, 1913, RG 59, 839.00/853, and Sept. 3, 1913, RG 59, 839.00/880; Boaz Long to Bryan, Sept. 4, 1915, RG 59, 839.00/872.

12. Bryan to James M. Sullivan, Sept. 9, 1913, RG 59, 839.00/912a; Charles M. Hathaway to Secy. of State, Oct. 6, 1913, RG 59, 839.00/943.

13. Boaz Long to Bryan, Sept. 11, 1913, and Bryan to American Legation, Santo Domingo, Sept. 11, 1913, RG 59, 839.00/872; Osborne to John Bassett Moore, Sept. 20, 1913, RG 59, 839.00/885.

14. Walker Vick to Gen. Frank McIntyre, Sept. 25, 1913, DCR 277, Dept. of the Army, Records of the Dominican Customs Receivership, RG 139; Sullivan to Secy. of State, Sept. 18, 1913, RG 59, 839.00/882, Sept. 22, 1913, RG 59, 839.00/889, Sept. 24, 1913, RG 59, 839.00/911, Oct. 6, 1913, RG 59, 839.00/913, Oct. 7, 1913, RG 59, 839.00/930, Oct. 10, 1913, RG, 839.00/919, Oct. 12, 1913, RG 59, 839.00/920, and Oct. 16, 1913, RG 59, 839.00/946; Bryan to American Legation, Santo Domingo, Oct. 13, 1913, RG 59, 839.00/921; Vick to M. E. Beall, Sept. 26, 1913, RG 139, SD 229-13; Vick to McIntyre, Oct. 6, 1913, RG 139, DCR Outgoing Correspondence file.

15. Sullivan to Secy. of State, Oct. 31, 1913, RG 59, 839.00/961; Sullivan to Vick, Nov. 8, 1913, RG 139, DCR 39/16; Sullivan to Secy. of State, Nov. 21, 1913, RG 59, 839.00/976, and Nov. 22, 1913, RG 59, 839.00/973; Bryan to Daniels, Sept. 23, 1913, RG 59, 839.00/885.

16. Bryan to American Legation, Santo Domingo, Nov. 24, 1913, RG 59, 839.00/972a; Bryan to Wilson, Nov. 20, 1913, RG 59, Wilson-Bryan Correspondence.

17. Curtis to Boaz Long, Nov. 25, 1913, RG 59, 839.00/1465; Sullivan to Secy. of State, Nov. 30, 1913, RG 59, 839.00/975; Vick to Bryan, Dec. 1, 1913, RG 139, DCR 483/734; Long to Bryan, Dec. 1, 1913, RG 59, 839.00/975.

18. Bryan to Wilson, Dec. 1, 1913, RG 59, Wilson-Bryan Correspondence; Bryan to American Legation, Santo Domingo, Dec. 2, 1913, RG 59, 839.00/975; Boaz Long to Bryan, Dec. 4, 1913, RG 59, 839.00/1005; Sullivan to Secy. of State, Dec. 2, 1913, RG 59, 839.00/978; Bryan to Wilson, Dec. 4, 1913, Wilson Papers, Ser. 2.

19. Sullivan to Secy. of State, Dec. 5, 1913, RG 59, 839.00/989; Bryan to Wilson, Dec. 6, 1913, and Wilson to Bryan, ca. Dec. 7, 1913, Wilson Papers, Ser. 2; Bryan to Sullivan, Dec. 7, 1913, RG 59, 839.00/992b; Bryan to Daniels, Dec. 8, 1913, RG 59, 839.00/1001f; Sullivan to Secy. of State, Dec. 10, 1913, RG 59, 839.00/1002.

20. Sullivan to Secy. of State, Dec. 23, 1913, RG 59, 839.00/1041; Jordan Stabler, Frederick Sterling, and Hugh Gibson to Secy. of State, Dec. 20, 1913, RG 59, 839.00/1026.

21. Sullivan to Secy. of State, Jan. 10, 1914, RG 59, 839.51/1204; Sullivan to John (no last name given), Jan. 31, 1914, RG 59, Wilson-Bryan Correspondence; Sullivan to Secy. of State, Jan. 9, 1914, RG 59, 839.00/1040. For the negotiations over the appointment of an American comptroller to oversee American finances, see the State Dept. records, RG 59, 839.51 series, particularly document numbers 839.51/1178 through 839.51/1350. In addition, see Vick to McIntyre, Jan. 17, 1914, RG 139, DCR 88; Bryan to Wilson, Jan. 27, Feb. 3, 5, 9, and Apr. 11, 1914, all in RG 59, Wilson-Bryan Correspondence. For the suggestions on constitutional reforms, see Bryan to Sullivan, Jan. 18 and 27, 1914, RG 59, 839.011/3; Bryan to American Legation, Santo Domingo, Feb. 19, 1914, RG 59, 839.00/1069.

22. Vick to McIntyre, Jan. 23, 1914, RG 139, SD 69-11.

23. Sullivan to Secy. of State, Feb. 12, 1914, RG 59, 839.00/1065, and Feb. 12, 1914, RG 59, 839.51/1202; Link, *Struggle for Neutrality*, 511–12, 541–42.

24. Bryan to Wilson, Feb. 26, 1914, RG 59, Wilson-Bryan Correspondence; Bryan to Sullivan, Feb. 27, 1914, RG 59, 839.00/1071.

25. Vick to McIntyre, Mar. 24, 1914, RG 139, DCR 88, and Apr. 9, 1914, RG 139, V-Personnel; Beall to Vick, Mar. 6, 1914, RG 139, DCR 85/4, and Apr. 23, 1914, RG 139, DCR 85/20; Frank Anderson Henry to Secy. of State, Mar. 11, 1914, RG 59, 839.00/1100, and Feb. 24, 1914, RG 59, 839.00/1079.

26. Sullivan to Secy. of State, Mar. 20, 1914, RG 59, 839.00/1102; Sullivan, Blount, and Dickey to Secy. of State, Mar. 29, 1914, RG 59, 839.00/1119; Sullivan to Secy. of State, Mar. 19, 1914, RG 59, 839.00/1101; Bryan to American Legation, Santo Domingo, Apr. 2, 1914, RG 59, 839.00/1124, Apr. 4, 1914, RG 59, 839.00/1136, and Apr. 16, 1914, RG 59, 839.00/1153; Sullivan to Secy. of State, Apr. 5, 1914, RG 59, 839.00/1402; J. A. Cernuda to Boaz Long, Apr. 4, 1914, RG 59, 839.00/1141; Bryan to Wilson, Apr. 4, 1914, RG 59, 839.00/1141. For the negotiations over increasing the funds to the Dominican government, see State Dept. files, RG 59, 839.00 files, particularly documents 839.00/1071 through 839.00/1170. See also, Sullivan to Secy. of State, Mar. 5, 1914, and Bryan to Sullivan, Mar. 5, 1914, RG 59, 839.51/1258.

27. Sullivan to Secy. of State, Apr. 17, 1914, RG 59, 839.00/1192, and Apr. 21, 1914, RG 59, 839.00/1172; Lansing to Daniels, May 5, 1914, RG 59, 839.00/1201. For the navy's effort to effect a truce at Puerto Plata, see Capt. E. W. Eberle to Bordas, ca. May 1914, RG 45; Subject File, 1911–27, RG 45; Daniels to Eberle, May 5, 1914, Franklin D. Roosevelt to Eberle, May 7, 1914, and Eberle to Secy. of the Navy, May 12, 1914, RG 45, WA-7; Capt. Bierer to Secy. of the Navy, May 15, 1914, Wilson Papers, Ser. 2; Report of Eberle, May 25, 1914, and Eberle to Secy. of the Navy, July 31 and Aug. 17, 1914, RG 45, WA-7. For the State Dept.'s promise of support for Bordas in a blockade of Puerto Plata, see Sullivan to Secy. of State, Apr. 30, 1914, RG 59, 839.00/1194; Bryan to Sullivan, May 5, 1914, RG 59, 839.00/1194, and May 9, 1914, RG 59, 839.00/1211; Eberle to Secy. of the Navy, May 10, 1914, RG 45, WA-7; Lansing to Cernuda, May 16, 1914, RG 59, 839.00/1225; Bryan to American Legation, Santo Domingo, May 16, 1914, RG 59, 839.00/1229, and May 16, 1914, RG 59, 839.00/1222.

28. Wilson to Bryan, May 13 and 24, 1914, Wilson Papers, Ser. 3.
29. Sullivan to Secy. of State, May 20, 1914, RG 59, 839.00/1230; Bryan to Sullivan, May 23, 1914, RG 59, 839.00/1244a; Sullivan to Secy. of State, May 28, 1914, RG 59, 839.00/1253; Bryan to Sullivan, May 28, 1914, RG 59, 839.00/1245.
30. Lansing to Bryan, May 30, 1914, RG 59, 839.00/1520. For Jordon Stabler's continued urgings to intervene, see Stabler to Secy. of State, July 9 and 10, 1914, RG 59, 839.00/1424, July 17, 1914, RG 59, 839.00/1425, and July 20, 1914, RG 59, 839.00/1416. Members of the customs receivership also urged the Wilson administration to intervene. See, for example, John R. Vance to McIntyre, May 18, 1914, RG 139, DCR 88; Vick to Bryan, May 30, 1914, and Vick to Sullivan, May 19, 1914, RG 139, DCR 85; Vick to McIntyre, May 21, 1914, RG 139, DCR 88.
31. Bryan to Wilson, July 2 and 8, 1914, Wilson Papers, Ser. 2.
32. Wilson to Bryan, July 23, 1914, Wilson Papers, Ser. 3; Proposed Memo on Wilson Plan, July 27, 1914, Wilson Papers, Ser. 2.
33. Bryan to Wilson, July 31, 1914, RG 59, Wilson-Bryan Correspondence; Bryan to American Legation, Santo Domingo, July 29, 1914, RG 59, 839.00/1451a; Bryan to American Legation, Santo Domingo, Aug. 10, 1914, conveying final draft of the Wilson Plan, RG 59, 839.00/1582; Bryan to Fort Commission, Aug. 10, 1914, Wilson Papers, Ser. 2, and Aug. 13, 1914, RG 59, 839.00/1476a; Stabler to Bryan, Aug. 14, 1914, RG 59, 839.00/1552; Sullivan to Secy. of State, Aug. 4, 1914, RG 59, 839.00/1472.
34. American Commissioners to Secy. of State, Aug. 16, 1914, RG 59, 839.00/1480, Aug. 18, 1914, RG 59, 839.00/1481, Aug. 18, 1914, RG 59, 839.00/1485, Aug. 21, 1914, RG 59, 839.00/1488, and Aug. 23, 1914, RG 59, 839.00/1489; Bryan to American Commissioners, conveying instructions from Wilson, Aug. 23, 1914, RG 59, 839.00/no number; Bryan to American Commissioners, conveying Wilson directive on negotiations, Aug. 27, 1914, RG 59, 839.00/no number; American Commissioners to Secy. of State, Aug. 24, 1914, RG 59, 839.00/1489, Aug. 25, 1914, RG 59, 839.00/1490, Aug. 27, 1914, RG 59, 839.00/1490 1/2, and Aug. 27, 1914, RG 59, 839.00/1518; Bryan to American Commissioners, Aug. 27, 1914, RG 59, 839.00/1490; American Commissioners to Secy. of State, Aug. 28, 1914, RG 59, 839.00/1518; Bryan to American Legation, Santo Domingo, Aug. 28, 1914, RG 59, 839.00/1498a; Eberle to Secy. of the Navy, Sept. 2, 1914, RG 45, WA-7.
35. American Commissioners to Secy. of State, Sept. 8, 1914, RG 59, 839.00/1548, and Sept. 9, 1914, RG 59, 839.00/1507; Lansing to Bryan, Sept. 24, 1914, RG 59, 839.00/1528a. For information on the Dominican elections, see State Dept. files, RG 59, 839.00 file, particularly documents 839.00/1541 through 839.00/1791; Navy Dept. records, RG 45, WA-7, for the dates Oct. through early Nov. 1914. For American policy after the elections, see Daniels to Commanding Officer, *Hancock*, Dec. 5, 1914, RG 59, 839.00/1644; John F. Fort to Joe Tumulty, Nov. 16, 1914, Wilson Papers, Ser. 4, CF398; Bryan to American Legation, Nov. 14, 1914, RG 59, 839.00/1608; Bryan to Wilson, Dec. 12, 1914, RG 59, Wilson-Bryan Correspondence.
36. Bryan to American Legation, Santo Domingo, Dec. 14, 1941, RG 59, 839.00/1652a; Fifth Regiment, U.S. Marine Corps, "Haiti and Santo Domingo—Plan of Occupation," Dec. 1914, RG 45, WA-7; Vance to Vick, Aug. 27, 1914, RG 139, 27112; N. L. Orme to Vick, Sept. 2, 1914, RG 139, DCR 85/130; White to Roosevelt, Sept. 9, 1914, quoted in Freidel, *Franklin D. Roosevelt*, p 272; Vick to Maj. Hunt, Sept. 10, 1914, RG 139, DCR 289; Orme to Vance, Sept. 10, 1914, RG 139, DCR 85/135.
37. Lansing to Daniels, Dec. 12, 1914, RG 59, 839.00/1648; Schmidt, *U.S. Occupation of Haiti*, 60–61.
38. Bryan to Wilson, Jan. 21, 1914, RG 59, Wilson-Bryan Correspondence.
39. Bryan to Wilson, June 14, 1913, Wilson Papers, Ser. 4, CF612; Bryan to Wilson, June 20, 1914, RG 59, Wilson-Bryan Correspondence; Wilson to Bryan, June 23, 1914,

Wilson Papers, Ser. 3; Challener, *Admirals, Generals,* 379–81; Link, *Struggle for Neutrality,* 517; John E. Osborne to Bryan, Feb. 3, 1914, Wilson Papers, Ser. 2; State Department Memo on Conditions in Haiti, May 14, 1914, RG 59, 838.00/1; Schmidt, *U.S. Occupation of Haiti,* 56; Challener, *Admirals, Generals,* 381, 45; Link, *Struggle for Neutrality,* 517; Adm. William Caperton to Secy. of the Navy, Nov. 23, 1915, Records of the General Board of the Navy.

40. William Phillips to Bryan, Mar. 23, 1914, RG 59, 838.51/361; Dana G. Munro, *Intervention and Dollar Diplomacy in the Caribbean 1900–1921,* 331; Melvin Small, "The United States and the German 'Threat' to the Hemisphere, 1905–1914," 257; Roger Farnham to Bryan, Mar. 6, 1914, RG 59, 838.51/328; Schmidt, *U.S. Occupation of Haiti,* 52–53; Bryan to Wilson, Mar. 24, 1914, and Wilson to Bryan, Mar. 26, 1914, Wilson Papers, Ser. 2; Lansing to Sen. Cyrus McCormick, May 4, 1922, U.S. Congress, Senate, *Inquiry into the Occupation and Administration of Haiti and Santo Domingo, Hearings before a select committee on Haiti and Santo Domingo, pursuant to SR 112,* 67th Cong., 1st and 2d sess., Appendix B, 32–34; Challener, *Admirals, Generals,* 399; Schmidt, *U.S. Occupation of Haiti,* 59.

41. Boaz Long to Phillips, May 16, 1914, RG 59, 838.00/1669. See also Bryan to German ambassador, Sept. 16, 1914, RG 59, 838.51/354.

42. For discussions of the Wilson administration's racist attitude toward Haiti, see John H. Allen, "An Inside View of Revolutions in Haiti," 325; Schmidt, *U.S. Occupation of Haiti,* 48.

43. Gen. George Barnett, "Report on the Affairs in the Republic of Haiti, June 1915–June 30, 1920," Subject File 1911–27, ZWA-7, Box 850, RG 45, p. 469; Memo to McCormick from Maj. Edwin N. McClellan, Senate Inquiry, 63; Caperton testimony, Senate Inquiry, 310; Stabler memo, Feb. 9, 1914, RG 59, 838.00/no number.

44. Boaz Long to Bryan, Jan. 23, 1914, and unsigned memo from Division of Latin American Affairs, ca. Jan. 23, 1914, Wilson Papers, Ser. 2.

45. Stabler to Bryan, Feb. 3, 1914, Wilson Papers, Ser. 2; Farnham to Bryan, Mar. 5, 1914, RG 59, 838.51/335; State Department Records Relating to Internal Affairs of Haiti, RG 59; Memo dictated by Farnham, Mar. 6, 1914, RG 59, 838.51/328; Charles C. Smith to Secy. of State, Mar. 6, 1914, RG 59, 838.51/327; Schmidt, *U.S. Occupation of Haiti,* 48–52, 54, 60, 61; Link, *Struggle for Neutrality,* 517–18.

46. Bryan to Wilson, Feb. 21, 1914, Wilson Papers, Ser. 2; Bryan to American Legation, Haiti, Mar. 7, 1914, RG 59, 838.51/327a; Farnham to Bryan, Mar. 13, 1914, RG 59, 838.51/329; Boaz Long to Osborne, Mar. 21, 1914, RG 59, 838.00/929; Memo, probably by Farnham, Mar. 25, 1914, RG 59, 838.00/no number.

47. Wilson to Bryan, June 25, 1914, Bryan Papers; Link, *Struggle for Neutrality,* 521–22.

48. Bryan to Wilson, July 1, 1914, Wilson Papers, Ser. 2; Farnham to Bryan, July 1, 1914, RG 59, Wilson-Bryan Correspondence; Bryan to Arthur Bailly-Blanchard, July 2, 1914, RG 59, 838.00/341a.

49. Link, *Struggle for Neutrality,* 523; Bryan to Daniels, July 10, 1914, RG 59, 838.00/954; Press Notice on Marines to Haiti, July 13, 1914, RG 59, 838.00/no number; Bryan to Wilson, ca. July 1914, Wilson Papers, Ser. 2; Memo by R.B., Oct. 23, 1914, RG 59, 838.00/1; Wilson, "Remarks at a Press Conference," July 23, 1914, in Link, *Papers of Woodrow Wilson* 30:296.

50. Bryan to American Legation, Haiti, July 10, 1914, RG 59, 838.00/947a, and July 9, 1914, RG 59, 838.00/949a.

51. J. T. Cleary to Bryan, July 10, 1914, RG 59, 838.00/1129; Lemuel W. Livingston to Secy. of State, July 12, 1914, RG 59, 838.00/948, July 18, 1914, RG 59, 838.00/958, and July

23, 1914, RG 59, 838.00/962; Blanchard to Secy. of State, July 24, 1914, RG 59, 838.00/964; Boaz Long to Bryan, July 21, 1914, RG 59, 838.00/971; Bryan to Daniels, for transmission to Blanchard, July 24, 1914, RG 59, 838.00/967a; Bryan to Blanchard, Aug. 28, 1914, RG 59, 838.00/980a.

52. Bryan to American Legation, Haiti, Dec. 12, 1914, RG 59, 838.51/379; Blanchard to Secy. of State, Oct. 21, 1914, RG 59, 838.00/995; Lansing to Wilson, Oct. 26, 1914, RG 59, 838.00/1002, and Oct. 28, 1914, Wilson Papers, Ser. 4, CF612; Lansing to Daniels, Oct. 28, 1914, RG 59, 838.00/1059b; Lansing to Wilson, Oct. 28, 1914, RG 59, 838.00/1078; Lansing to Fiske, Oct. 29, 1914, RG 59, 838.00/1078a; Lansing to American Legation, Haiti, Oct. 29, 1914, RG 59, 838.00/1005a; Blanchard to Secy. of State, Oct. 29, 1914, and Lansing to American Legation, Haiti, Oct. 30, 1914, RG 59, 838.00/1006; Blanchard to Secy. of State, Oct. 30, 1914, and Lansing to Blanchard, Oct. 31, 1914, RG 59, 838.00/1008; Blanchard to Secy. of State, Oct. 31, 1914, RG 59, 838.00/1009; Lansing to Blanchard, Nov. 4, 1914, RG 59, 838.00/1157b; Bryan to American Legation, Haiti, Nov. 12, 1914, RG 59, 838.00/1020; Blanchard to Secy. of State, Nov. 18, 1914, Lansing to American Legation, Haiti, Nov. 21, 1914, and Bryan to American Legation, Haiti, Nov. 24, 1914, RG 59, 838.00/1028; Blanchard to Secy. of State, Nov. 25, 1914, and Lansing to Blanchard, Nov. 28, 1914, RG 59, 838.00/1039; Blanchard to Secy. of State, Dec. 1, 1914, RG 59, 838.00/1040, and Dec. 2, 1914, RG 59, 838.00/1041.

53. Bryan to American Legation, Haiti, Dec. 12, 1914, RG 59, 838.51/379; Bryan to Wilson, Dec. 12, 1914, RG 59, Wilson-Bryan Correspondence.

54. Blanchard to Bryan, Dec. 17, 1914, RG 59, 838.00/1093; Bryan to Wilson, Dec. 18, 1914, Wilson Papers, Ser. 4, CF612; Bryan to Blanchard, Dec. 19, 1914, RG 59, 838.00/1065.

55. Fifth Regiment, USMC, "Plan of Occupation," Nov. 9, 1914, RG 45, WA-7.

56. Henry W. Wakrhave to Bryan, Jan. 4, 1915, RG 59, 838.00/1377; Bryan to Wilson, Jan. 7, 1915, Bryan Papers; Munro, *Intervention and Dollar Diplomacy,* 345–46.

57. Wilson to Bryan, Jan. 13, 1915, Wilson Papers, Ser. 3; Bryan to Wilson, Jan. 15, 1915, RG 59, Wilson-Bryan Correspondence; Wilson to Bryan, Jan. 16, 1915, RG 59, 838.00/1382.

58. Bryan to Livingston, Jan. 16, 1915, RG 59, 838.00/1080; Memo written by unknown author, USS *Washington,* ca. Jan. 1915, RG 45, WA-7; Rear Adm. William B. Caperton, "History of U.S. Naval Operations under the command of Rear Admiral William B. Caperton, U.S.N., commencing January 5, 1915, ending April 30, 1919," RG 45, Subject File 1911–27, ZN, Box 802, pp. 2, 3; Caperton testimony, Senate Inquiry, 294, 296–97, 292, 295; Campaign Order No. 1 by Commander R. C. Moody, Jan. 31, 1915, RG 45, Area File C; Caperton Report, 10, 14; Memo to McCormick from McClellan, Senate Inquiry, 64; Caperton to Secy. of the Navy, Jan. 23, 1915, Moody to Caperton, Jan. 25, 1914, Caperton to Moody, Jan. 26, 1915, Moody to Caperton, Jan. 28, 1914, Caperton to Moody, Feb. 2, 1914, J. H. Y. Blakely, USS *Des Moines,* to Caperton, Feb. 19, 1915, Caperton to Blakely, Feb. 19, 1915, and Blakely to Caperton, Mar. 20, 1915, all in RG 45, Area File C.

59. Fort to Tumulty, Feb. 19, 1915, Wilson Papers, Ser. 4, CF398; Bryan to American Legation, Haiti, Feb. 20, 1915, RG 59, 838.00/1080, and Jan. 16, 1915, RG 59, 838.00/116a; Blanchard to Bryan, Feb. 24, 1915, RG 59, 838.00/1119, and Feb. 27, 1915, RG 59, 838.00/1122.

60. Bryan to Wilson, Feb. 25, 1914, Bryan Papers; Bryan to Blanchard, Feb. 27, 1914, RG 59, 838.00/1382; Bryan to American Legation, Haiti, RG 59, 838.00/1119.

61. Bryan to Fort, Feb. 27, 1914, RG 59, 838.00/1382.

62. Daniels to Caperton, quoted in W. C. Twining, USS *Tacoma,* to Moody, Mar. 10, 1915, RG 45, Area Files C; Twining to Secy. of the Navy, Mar. 9, 1915, RG 45, Area File C;

Fort to Secy. of State, Mar. 12, 1915, RG 59, 838.00/1140; Fort to Bryan, Mar. 13, 1915, and Wilson to Bryan, Mar. 13, 1915, RG 59, Wilson-Bryan Correspondence; Bryan to Wilson, Mar. 23, 1915, and Fort to Bryan, ca. Mar. 23, 1915, Bryan Papers.

63. Bryan to Wilson, Apr. 2, 1915, and Wilson to Bryan, Mar. 24, 1915, Bryan Papers; Bryan to Blanchard, Mar. 26, 1915, RG 59, 838.00/1151a; Moody to Caperton, Apr. 4, 1915, RG 45, Area Files C; Wilson to Bryan, Mar. 31, 1915, RG 59, Wilson-Bryan Correspondence.

64. Wilson to Bryan, Apr. 5, 1915, Bryan Papers; Fort to Bryan, May 5, 1915, RG 59, 838.00/1192; Wilson to Bryan, Apr. 6, 1915, RG 59, Wilson-Bryan Correspondence.

65. Bryan to Paul Fuller, May 6, 1915, RG 59, 838.00/1393a; Bryan to Wilson, May 6, 1915, RG 59, Wilson-Bryan Correspondence.

66. Fuller to Bryan, May 14, 1915, RG 59, 838.00/1175, May 22, 1915, RG 59, 711.38/16, May 25, 1915, RG 59, 711.38/17, and May 27, 1915, RG 59, 711.38/18; Bryan to Fuller, May 28, 1915, RG 59, 711.38/16; Bryan to Wilson, May 28, 1915 (two letters), Bryan Papers; Wilson to Bryan, May 28, 1915, Bryan Papers; Bryan to Fuller, May 29, 1914, RG 59, 711.38/19; Fuller to Bryan, May 30, 1915, RG 59, 711.38/19, June 2, 1915, RG 59, 711.38/20, and June 3, 1915, RG 59, 711.38/21; Bryan to Wilson, June 3, 1915, Bryan Papers; Bryan to Fuller, June 4, 1915, RG 59, 711.38/21; Fuller to Bryan, June 4, 1915, RG 59, 711.38/22; Bryan to American Legation, Haiti, June 7, 1915, RG 59, 711.38/22a.

67. Fuller to Secy. of State, June 14, 1915, RG 59, 838.00/1197.

68. "Description of Fuller's Report" by K. E. P., June 22, 1915, RG 59, 838.00/1197; Canova to Lansing, June 22, 1915, Daniels Papers; Wilson to Lansing, July 2, 1915, RG 59, 838.00/1196; L. H. W., Office of Counsellor, to Lansing, July 8, 1915, RG 59, 838.00/1197.

69. R. B. Davis to Secy. of State, July 27, 1915, RG 59, 838.00/1214; Capt. Edward L. Beach, "Admiral Caperton in Haiti," RG 45, Subject File 1911–27, ZWA-7, Box 850, pp. 2, 4; Caperton testimony, Senate Inquiry, 308; Gen. Cole testimony, Senate Inquiry, 672; Caperton to Secy. of the Navy, July 29, 1915, RG 45, Area File C; Lansing to American Legation, Haiti, RG 59, 838.00/1220; Boaz Long to Lansing, July 28, 1915, RG 59, 838.00/1385; Davis to Secy. of State, July 28, 1915, RG 59, 838.00/1221; Livingston to Secy. of State, July 28, 1915, RG 59, 838.00/1222.

70. Lansing to Daniels, July 28, 1915, RG 59, 838.00/1220; Caperton Report, 48; Barnett Report, 3.

71. Caperton testimony, Senate Inquiry, 307; Beach Report, RG 45, pp. 1–2; Lansing to McCormick, May 4, 1922, Senate Inquiry, 31, 32, 37, Appendix B; Capt. Shoup, USS *Eagle,* to Caperton, July 28, 1915, RG 45, Area File C; John H. Russell, "A Marine Looks Back on Haiti," unpublished manuscript, Maj. Gen. John H. Russell Papers, 3; Barnett Report, 4–5; Caperton Report, 47; Fort to Wilson, July 30, 1915, RG 59, 838.00/1276 1/2.

72. Caperton Report, 49; Lansing to Daniels, July 29, 1915, Daniels Papers, and July 30, 1915, RG 59, 838.00/1213a; Daniels to Lansing, July 30, 1915, RG 59, 838.00/1346; Daniels to Caperton, July 30, 1915, Caperton to Daniels, July 30, 1915, Benson to Naval Station, Guantánomo, July 28, 1915, Caperton to Daniels, July 29, 1915, and Daniels to Naval Station, Guantánomo, July 30, 1915, all in RG 45, Area File C; Davis to Secy. of State, July 30, 1915, RG 59, 838.00/1226.

73. Wilson to Daniels, July 31, 1915, Daniels Papers.

74. Blanchard to Lansing, July 31, 1915, RG 59, 838.00/1390; Boaz Long to Lansing, ca. July-August, 1915, RG 59, 838.00/1391; Division of Latin America Affairs, "Notes and Recommendations on the Political Situation in Haiti," ca. July-August 1915, RG 59, 838.00/1391; Lansing to Wilson, Aug. 2, 1915, Wilson Papers, Ser. 2.

75. Wilson to Fort, Aug. 2, 1915, Wilson Papers, Ser. 4, CP612; Lansing to Wilson, Aug. 3, 1915, RG 59, 838.00/1275b.

76. Wilson to Lansing, Aug. 4, 1915, RG 59, 838.00/1418; Wilson to Daniels, Aug. 4, 1915, Wilson Papers, Ser. 3.

77. Lansing to Wilson, Aug. 7, 1915, Wilson Papers, Ser. 2; Boaz Long to Lansing, Aug. 5, 1915, and Cone Johnson to Lansing, Aug. 6, 1915, RG 59, 838.00/1426; Lansing to Wilson, Aug. 10, 1915, Wilson Papers, Ser. 2.

78. Caperton Report, 61–144; Beach Report, 77–167; Caperton to Daniels, Aug. 5, 1915, and Caperton to Commanding Officer, USS *Connecticut,* Aug. 12, 1915, RG 45, Area File C; Caperton testimony, Senate Inquiry, 362; Caperton to Daniels, Aug. 21 and 24, 1915, RG 45, Area File C; Benson to Caperton, Aug. 25, 1915, Caperton Papers; Caperton to Durrell, Sept. 8, 1915, RG 45, Area File C; Caperton to Benson, Sept. 29, Oct. 26, and Nov. 1, 1915, Caperton Papers; Caperton to Durrell, Nov. 8, 1915, and Caperton to Secy. of the Navy, Nov. 11, 1915, RG 45, Area File C; Beach Report, 78–79.

79. Caperton Report, 217–18.

80. Caperton to Commanding Officer, USS *Connecticut,* Aug. 9, 1915, RG 45, Area File C; Caperton Report, 62; Russell, "A Marine Looks Back," 1; John H. Russell, "A Laboratory of Government," unpublished manuscript, Russell Papers.

81. Beach Report, 166–67; Smedley D. Butler testimony, Senate Inquiry, 518.

82. Sullivan to Secy. of State, Jan. 9, 1915, RG 59, 839.00/1658; Bryan to Wilson, Jan. 15, 1915, RG 59, Wilson-Bryan Correspondence; Bryan to American Legation, Santo Domingo, Jan. 12, 1915, RG 59, 839.00/1660a, Jan. 28, 1915, RG 59, 839.00/1663, and Feb. 1, 1915, RG 59, 839.00/1664; Lansing to Daniels, Jan. 28, 1915, RG 59, 839.00/1663.

83. Sullivan to Secy. of State, Feb. 1, 1915, RG 59, 839.00/1668, and Feb. 1, 1915, RG 59, 839.00/1678; Bryan to American Legation, Santo Domingo, Feb. 13, 1915, RG 59, 839.00/1678, and Feb. 2, 1915, RG 59, 839.00/1668; Henry to Secy. of State, Feb. 9, 1915, RG 59, 839.00/1680.

84. Bryan to American Legation, Santo Domingo, Apr. 20, 1915, RG 59, 839.00/1678, and Apr. 9, 1915, RG 59, 839.00/1684; Bryan to Wilson, Apr. 19, 1915, RG 59, Wilson-Bryan Correspondence; Bryan to American Legation, Santo Domingo, May 10, 1915, RG 59, 839.00/1700; Johnson to Secy. of State, July 14, 1915, RG 59, 839.00/1715; Lansing to American Legation, Santo Domingo, July 16, 1915, RG 59, 839.00/1714; Lansing to Daniels, July 16, 1915, RG 59, 839.00/1723a; Johnson to Secy. of State, July 21, 1915, RG 59, 839.00/1731; McIntyre to Clarence Baxter, June 4, 1915, RG 139, DCR 58; Baxter to Sen. James Phelan, Feb. 26, 1915, RG 139, DCR 68.

85. Bryan to Wilson, Mar. 10, 1915, RG 59, Wilson-Bryan Correspondence. For information on the State Dept.'s attempts to secure financial reforms and the confirmation of the financial adviser, see State Dept. files, RG 59, 839.00 files, particularly 839.00/1575 through 839.00/1706. The Wilson-Bryan Correspondence for the spring and summer of 1915 also contains some information.

86. Bryan to Wilson, Apr. 2, 1915, and Wilson to Bryan, Apr. 3, 1915, RG 59, Wilson-Bryan Correspondence; Wilson to William W. Russell, July 31, 1915, R. S. Baker Papers; [Illegible] to Boaz Long, Aug. 6, 1915, RG 59, 839.00/1731; Lansing to Daniels, Aug. 21, 1915, RG 59, 839.00/1766a; Stewart Johnson to Secy. of State, July 30, 1915, RG 59, 839.00/1737, Aug. 12, 1915, RG 59, 839.00/1738, Sept. 5, 1915, RG 59, 839.00/1749, Sept. 9, 1915, RG 59, 839.00/1765 1/2, and Sept. 4, 1915, RG 59, 839.00/1747.

87. Lansing to W. W. Russell, Sept. 17, 1915, RG 59, 839.51/1633a; Cone Johnson to Lansing, Sept. 11, 1915, RG 59, 839.51/1805; Polk to Wilson, Sept. 21, 1915, RG 59, 839.51/1834; Boaz Long and Russell to Secy. of State, Sept. 25, 1915, RG 59, 839.51/1805; Wilson to Polk, ca. Sept. 22, 1915, RG 59, 839.51/1834.

88. L. H. to Secy. of State, June 3, 1916, RG 59, 839.00/1896; W. W. Russell to Secy. of State, Oct. 22, 1915, RG 59, 839.00/1773, and Oct. 29, 1915, RG 59, 839.00/1776; Boaz

Long to Harrison, Nov. 4, 1915, RG 59, 839.00/1716; Wilson to Lansing, Nov. 17, 1915, RG 59, 839.00/1780; Russell to Foreign Minister, Santo Domingo, Nov. 19, 1915, RG 59, 839.51/1664; Russell to Secy. of State, Nov. 27, 1915, RG 59, 839.00/1656, and Dec. 27, 1915, RG 59, 839.00/1779.

89. Lansing to Wilson, Nov. 24, 1915, RG 59, 839.00/1776; Lansing to American Legation, Santo Domingo, Dec. 9, 1915, RG 59, 839.00/1653; Boaz Long to J. W. Wright, Nov. 18, 1915, RG 59, 839.00/1715; Lansing to American Legation, Dec. 2, 1915, RG 59, 839.00/1651.

90. W. W. Russell to Secy. of State, Jan. 19, 1916, RG 59, 839.00/1781; Latin American Division to Lansing, Jan. 22, 1915, RG 59, 839.00/1955; J. B. to Lansing, Jan. 24, 1916, RG 59, 839.00/1781; Lansing to American Legation, Santo Domingo, Jan. 24, 1916, RG 59, 839.00/1675, and Jan. 24, 1916, RG 59, 839.00,/1781.

91. W. W. Russell to Secy. of State, Feb. 18, 1916, RG 59, 839.00/1787, Feb. 18, 1916, RG 59, 839.00/1786, and Feb. 24, 1916, RG 59, 839.00/1789; Lansing to American Legation, Santo Domingo, Feb. 28, 1916, RG 59, 839.00/1789; L. H. Memo, Mar. 1, 1916, RG 59, 839.00/1798; Russell to Secy. of State, Mar. 3, 1916, RG 59, 839.00/1792; and Mar. 14, 1916, RG 59, 839.00/1795; Baxter to McIntyre, Mar. 4, 1916, RG 139, DCR 57.

92. W. W. Russell to Secy. of State, Apr. 15, 1916, RG 59, 839.00/1801, Apr. 16, 1916, RG 59, 839.00/1804, Apr. 17, 1916, RG 59, 839.00/1803, Apr. 27, 1916, RG 59, 839.00/1806, and Apr. 27, 1916, RG 59, 839.00/1821; Lansing to American Legation, Santo Domingo, Apr. 29, 1916, and Lansing to Daniels, Apr. 29, 1916, RG 59, 839.00/1806; Russell to Secy. of State, Apr. 29, 1916, RG 59, 839.00/1808; Lansing to Daniels, Apr. 29, 1916, RG 45, WA-7; W. S. Crosley to Caperton, May 16, 1916, RG 45, Area File C; Russell to Secy. of State, Apr. 30, 1916, RG 59, 839.00/1809; Vance to S. S. Behn, May 1, 1916, RG 139, DCR 99.

93. W. W. Russell to Secy. of State, May 1, 1916, RG 59, 839.00/1810; Lansing to American Legation, Santo Domingo, May 2, 1916, RG 59, 839.00/1803; Russell to Secy. of State, May 2, 1916, RG 59, 839.00/1811; Crosley to Secy. of the Navy, May 16, 1916, RG 45, Area File C; Russell to Secy. of State, May 5, 1916, RG 59, 839.00/1814; Daniels to Lansing, May 3, 1916, RG 59, 839.00/1812; Russell to Secy. of State, May 3, 1916, RG 59, 839.00/1815, and May 5, 1916, RG 59, 839.00/1817; Carl M. J. von Zielincki, "Observation of first day's fighting in the area occupied by the revolutionary forces," May 5, 1916, RG 59, 839.00/1834.

94. Caperton to Adm. William S. Benson, May 5, 1916, Caperton Papers; Benson to Caperton, May 5, 1916, Marine Corps, 1975-70/5-2 52655, Records of the U.S. Marine Corps, Office of the Commandant; Caperton to Secy. of the Navy, May 6, 1916, M.C., 1975-70/5-2 52655.

95. Caperton to Secy. of the Navy, May 6, 1916, RG 127, M.C., 1975-70/5-2 52655; Crosley to Caperton, May 6, 1916, RG 127, M.C., 1975-70/5-2 52655; Oral history interviews with Lt. Gen. Pedro Del Valle, 24, 28, with Maj. Gen. Julian C. Smith, 41–43, and with Maj. Gen. Omar T. Pfeiffer, 45, Marine Corps Oral History Collection; Capt. C. S. Freeman to McCormick, Senate Inquiry, 92; W. W. Russell to Secy. of State, May 6, 1916, RG 59, 839.00/1818.

96. Caperton to Secy. of the Navy, May 6, 1916, RG 45, Area File C, May 7, 1916, M.C., 1975-70/5-2 52655, and May 7, 1916, RG 45, WA-7; W. W. Russell to Secy. of State, May 7, 1916, RG 59, 839.00/1819, and May 7, 1916, RG 59, 839.00/1822; Jose Manuel Jiminez testimony, Senate Inquiry, 1094–95.

97. Lansing to W. W. Russell, May 7, 1916, RG 59, 839.00/1818; Benson to Caperton, May 6, 1916, RG 45, WA-7.

98. W. W. Russell to Secy. of State, June 5, 1919, RG 59, 839.00/2123; C. S. Freeman to Secy. of the Navy, Nov. 10, 1920, RG 45, Sec Nav 16870-561; Caperton, Campaign Order

No. 2, May 21, 1916, RG 45, Area File C; Caperton to Secy. of the Navy, May 17, 1916, RG 45, WA-7.

99. The documentary evidence for the period May to July 1916 is extensive. See the State Department records, RG 59, 839.00 files, the Records of the Navy, RG 45, Area File C, the Records of the Marine Corps, RG 127, the Caperton Report, and the personal papers of Caperton, Wilson, Daniels, and Benson.

100. Memo to Judge Adv. Gen., June 30, 1920, RG 45, Office of Secy. of the Navy, 5526-280; Memorandum Re Military Commissions in Haiti, July 3, 1920, RG 45, Office of Secy. of the Navy, 5526-280; Daniels to Lansing, Mar. 1, 1917, RG 59, 839.00/2006; F. Mayer to Lansing, Feb. 25, 1918, RG 59, 839.00/2075; Solicitor, State Dept., to Secy. of State, Mar. 18, 1918, RG 59, 839.00/2099, July 10, 1918, RG 59, 839.00/2099, Feb. 24, 1919, RG 59, 839.00/2121, and Mar. 31, 1919, RG 59, 839.00/2112; Polk to Secy. of Treasury, Apr. 10, 1919, RG 59, 839.00/2112.

101. Wilson to Lansing, Nov. 26, 1916, RG 59, 839.00/1951; Lansing to Daniels, Nov. 27, 1916, RG 59, 839.00/1952; no author, "Memorandum of Principal Events and Causes Leading up to American Occupation of Dominican Territory, September 17, 1915–," Nov. 29, 1916, RG 45, WA-7; H. S. Knapp to Brigade Commander, Second Provisional Brigade, Nov. 29, 1916, RG 45, WA-7 7083-17(N); Knapp to Secy. of the Navy, Nov. 30, 1916, RG 45, Area File C, and no date, RG 127, M.C., 1975-70/5-2 502362; Memo to Secy. of the Navy, no author, Dec. 7, 1916, and Knapp to Benson, Dec. 8, 1916, Benson Papers; Stabler to Lansing, Nov. 21, 1916, RG 59, 839.00/1952; Lansing to American Legation, Santo Domingo, Nov. 27, 1916, RG 59, 839.00/1951a; Brewer to Lansing, Nov. 29, 1916, RG 59, 839.00/1951.

102. Daniels to Lansing, Dec. 12, 1916, RG 59, 839.00/1965.

4. THE POWER OF THE LAW: *The Period of Neutrality*

1. See, for example, Sondra Herman, *Eleven Against War,* and Warren Kuehl, *Seeking World Order: The United States and International Organization to 1920.*

2. Notter, *Origins of the Foreign Policy,* 54; Wilson, "Notes for a Classroom Lecture—International Law," Mar. 8, 1892, in Link, *Papers of Woodrow Wilson* 7:453–57.

3. Wilson, "Address before the American Bar Association in Philadelphia," Oct. 20, 1914, in Baker and Dodd, *New Democracy* 2:195.

4. William Bishop, *International Law: Cases and Materials,* 902–3; Memo, unsigned, probably by Lansing, Apr. 14, 1914, RG 59, 812.00/11510 1/2; Wilson, Press Conference, Apr. 20, 1914, in Link, *Papers of Woodrow Wilson* 29:468, 452; Wilson, "Address to Congress," Apr. 20, 1914, in James B. Scott, ed., *President Wilson's Foreign Policy: Messages, Addresses, Papers,* 37. See also Link, *Papers of Woodrow Wilson* 29:468–70, 488, 493, 453; Daniel M. Smith, *Robert Lansing and American Neutrality,* 13–14; Daniels to Fletcher, Apr. 21, 1914, Subject File #536, Daniels Papers; Bryan to Judge Charles A. Douglass, undated, RG 59, 812.00/12631 1/2; Bryan to Carothers, Apr. 21, 1914, RG 59, 812.00/11637a; Garrison to Funston, May 14, 1914, RG 94, AGO 2160103, filed with 2149991; Judge Adv. Gen. to Chief of Staff, Oct. 22, 1914, RG 94, AGO 2218767A.

5. Macomb to Secy. of War, Apr. 13, 1916, RG 165, 9506-1; Lansing to all Consular Officers in Mexico, Mar. 10, 1916, RG 59, 812.00/17426a; Lansing, Memo of a Conversation with Mr. Arredondo, Mar. 9, 1916, RG 59, 812.00/17510 1/2; Lansing to Sullivan, Mar. 13, 1916, RG 59, 812.00/17415; J. Belt to Secy. of State, Mar. 13, 1916, and Polk to All Consuls, Mar. 14, 1916, RG 59, 812.00/17455; Arredondo to Secy. of State, Mar. 18, 1916,

and Polk to Arredondo, Mar. 19, 1916, RG 59, 812.00/17920; Polk to J. L. Rogers, Mar. 20, 1916, RG 59 812.00/17529; Polk to Wilson, Mar. 20, 1916, RG 59, 812.00/17743. Drafts of the agreement can be found at: Mar. 19 and 21, 1916, RG 59, 812.00/24290, and Mar. 27 and Apr. 4, 1916, RG 59, 812.00/17650 1/2. A final draft of a "hot pursuit" treaty was not agreed upon, but the subject became part of the negotiations of the Joint Mexican-American Commission.

6. See discussion of the legal problems with the occupation of Haiti in chapter 3.

7. Wilson, "Flag Day Address," June 14, 1917, in Baker and Dodd, *War and Peace* 1:61. See also Buehrig, *Balance of Power,* 84; Thomas A. Bailey, *Woodrow Wilson and the Lost Peace,* 1.

8. Wilson, "Remarks to the Associated Press in New York," Apr. 20, 1915, in Link, *Papers of Woodrow Wilson* 33:39–40. See also Wilson, "Address before the Southern Methodist Conference," Mar. 25, 1915, in Baker and Dodd, *New Democracy* 1:287.

9. Wilson, "Address to Naturalized Citizens in Philadelphia," May 10, 1915, in Baker and Dodd, *New Democracy* 1:321.

10. Wilson, "Address to DAR," Oct. 11, 1915, in Baker and Dodd, *New Democracy* 1:378, 381. See also Ray S. Baker, *Woodrow Wilson Life and Letters,* vol. 5, *Neutrality, 1914–1915,* 376; Buehrig, *Balance of Power,* 106, 118; and Link, *Revolution, War, and Peace,* 13.

11. Wilson, "Address before Interdenominational Meeting at Aeolian Hall, N.Y.," Jan. 27, 1916, in Baker and Dodd, *New Democracy* 2:1.

12. Wilson, "Address at Chicago," Jan. 31, 1916, in Baker and Dodd, *New Democracy* 2:68–69.

13. Bryan to Wilson, transmitting copy of Wilson to belligerent powers, Aug. 4, 1914, Wilson Papers, Ser. 2; Wilson to Col. Edward M. House, Aug. 6, 1914, Wilson Papers, Ser. 3; Lansing Memo, Aug. 9, 1914, Wilson Papers, Ser. 2; Wilson to Garrison, Aug. 6, 1914, in Link *Papers of Woodrow Wilson* 30:352; Smith, *Lansing and American Neutrality,* 20–21; Baker, *Neutrality,* 290.

14. J. B. Scott to Lansing, Feb. 16, 1915, Lansing Papers; Wilson to Hester E. Hosford, Jan. 21, 1915, Wilson Papers, Ser. 2.

15. Bryan to Wilson, Aug. 10, 1914, Wilson Papers, Ser. 2; Wilson to Bryan, Aug. 10, 1914, Bryan Papers. The ban on loans to belligerents was lifted in the fall of 1915.

16. Bryan to Wilson, Nov. 12, 1914, and Wilson to Bryan, Nov. 30, 1914, Wilson Papers, Ser. 2. Wilson did decide that it would be unneutral not to allow the belligerents to purchase arms in the United States; see Wilson to Bryan, Jan. 7, 1915, Bryan Papers.

17. Wilson to Hugo Munsterberg, Nov. 10, 1914, in Link, *Papers of Woodrow Wilson* 31:293. See also Wilson to Charles Eliot, Feb. 18, 1915, in Link, *Papers of Woodrow Wilson* 32:244–45, in which Wilson says, "Just now the United States stands as the chief custodian of neutral rights." See also Baker, *Neutrality,* 223; Wilson to Jacob Schiff, Dec. 8, 1914, Wilson Papers, Ser. 2.

18. Link, *Struggle for Neutrality,* 105–36, 171–90; Devlin, *Too Proud To Fight,* 156–216; Bryan to Wilson, ca. Sept. 30, 1914, Cecil Spring-Rice to Wilson, Oct. 12, 1914; Lansing to Wilson, Oct. 20, 1914, Spring-Rice to Wilson, Oct. 20, 1914, Walter Hines Page to Wilson, Oct. 21, 1914 (two letters), Lansing to Wilson, Oct. 23, 1914, House to Wilson, Oct. 24, 1914, Wilson to Page, Oct. 28, 1914, and Wilson to House, Oct. 29, 1914, all in Wilson Papers, Ser. 2; Memo by Garrison, Feb. 5, 1915, in Link, *Papers of Woodrow Wilson* 32:192–93, and Feb. 9, 1915, in Link, *Papers of Woodrow Wilson* 32:207; Page to House, quoted in House to Wilson, Oct. 20, 1914, Wilson Papers, Ser. 2; Page to Wilson, Oct. 15, 1914, quoted in John Milton Cooper, Jr., *Walter Hines Page: The Southerner as American,* 291, xxvii, 307–10; Spring-Rice to Wilson, Oct. 5, 1914, Wilson Papers, Ser. 2.

19. House to Wilson, Oct. 24, 1914, in Link, *Papers of Woodrow Wilson* 31:228; Wilson to Lansing, Oct. 22, 1914, Wilson Papers, Ser. 2; Wilson to W. H. Page, Oct. 28, 1914, Wilson Papers, Ser. 3. See also Charles Seymour, *American Neutrality, 1914–1917,* 123.

20. Bryan to Wilson, Mar. 23, 1915, Bryan Papers.

21. Wilson to Henry Garfield, Apr. 27, 1916, Wilson Papers, Ser. 2; Wilson, "Address Accepting Democratic Nomination," Sept. 2, 1916, in Baker and Dodd, *New Democracy* 2:282; Wilson to Congressman J. Thomas Heflin, May 27, 1917, in Baker and Dodd, *War and Peace* 1:47. See also Newton Baker, *Why We Went to War,* 46; Smith, *Lansing and American Neutrality,* 142.

22. Wilson to Garfield, Mar. 7, 1916, Wilson Papers, Ser. 2. See also Edward Grey to House, June 6, 1915, quoted in Charles Seymour, *The Intimate Papers of Colonel House* 1:54; Count Johann Bernstorff, *My Three Years in America,* 227; Buehrig, *Balance of Power,* 99–100. The attitude of the military as expressed in the pages of the *Army and Navy Journal* is discussed in Arthur A. Ekirch, Jr., *The Civilian and the Military,* 157.

23. Wilson, "Remarks at a Press Conference," Mar. 2, 1915, in Link, *Papers of Woodrow Wilson* 32:307; Bernstorff, *My Three Years,* 135–36; Baker, *Neutrality,* 261; Grenville and Young, *Politics, Strategy, and American Diplomacy,* 333–34.

24. See Link, *Struggle for Neutrality,* 320–24; Ross Gregory, *The Origins of American Intervention in the First World War,* 52–54; Lansing to Wilson, Feb. 7, 1915, Wilson Papers, Ser. 2; Buehrig, *Balance of Power,* 20–22.

25. Bryan to Wilson, Apr. 2, 1915, Bryan Papers, Apr. 6, 1915, Wilson Papers, Ser. 2, and Apr. 7, 8, 19, and 23, 1915, Bryan Papers; Bryan to American Embassy, London, Feb. 16, 1915, Bryan Papers.

26. Lansing to Bryan, Apr. 5, 1915, and Apr. 10, 1915, forwarding report by the Joint Neutrality Board, Wilson Papers, Ser. 2.

27. Wilson to Bryan, Apr. 6, 1915, Bryan Papers. See also Garrison to Wilson, Mar. 20, 1915, Wilson Papers, Ser. 2; Wilson to Bryan, Apr. 22, 1915, in U.S. Dept. of State, *Papers Relating to the Foreign Relations of the United States: The Lansing Papers,* 2 vols. (hereafter *Lansing Papers*), 1:378; Wilson to Bryan, Apr. 3, 1915, *Lansing Papers* 1:368; Bryan to Wilson, Apr. 23, 1915, Wilson Papers, Ser. 2; Wilson to Bryan, Apr. 28, 1915, Bryan Papers; Wilson to Bryan, Apr. 28, 1915, *Lansing Papers* 1:380.

28. Bryan to Wilson, forwarding memo by Lansing, May 1, 1915, Wilson Papers, Ser. 2.

29. Unsigned memo reporting conversation with Lindley Garrison, May 5, 1915, Enoch Crowder Papers. See also Lansing Memo, May 3, 1915, Lansing Diary, Lansing Papers.

30. Garrison to Wilson, May 10, 1915, Wilson Papers, Ser. 2. See also Garrison to Wilson, May 13, 1915, and William Howard Taft to Wilson, May 10, 1915, Wilson Papers, Ser. 2; Chandler Anderson Diary entry, May 11, 1915, Chandler Anderson Papers; House to Wilson, May 11, 1915, Wilson Papers, Ser. 2; House to Wilson, May 9, 1915, quoted in Seymour, *Intimate Papers of Colonel House* 2:433–34; House to Wilson, May 13, 1915, and May 14 (two letters), Wilson Papers, Ser. 2; Wilson to Bryan, May 14, 1915, Bryan Papers; Lansing to Wilson, May 17, 1915, and Wilson to House, May 23, 1915, Wilson Papers, Ser. 2; Lansing Diary entry, May 25, 1915, Lansing Papers; first draft of 2nd Lusitania note by Wilson, ca. May 30, 1915, and Lansing to Wilson, June 2, 1915, Wilson Papers, Ser. 2; Lansing to Dr. E. M. Gallaudet, June 2, 1915, Lansing Papers; Lansing to Bryan, June 3 and 7, 1915, Wilson Papers, Ser. 2; Charles Warren to Lansing, June 7, 1915, and Lansing to Warren, June 7, 1915, Lansing Papers; James W. Gerard to Wilson, June 8, 1915, second draft of 2nd Lusitania note, ca. June 1915 by Wilson, Lansing to Wilson, July 7, 1915 (two letters), Wilson to Lansing, July 7, 1915, Lansing to Wilson, July 8, 1915, Gottlieb von Jagow to Gerard, July 8, 1915, and House to Wilson, July 10, 1915, all in Wilson Papers, Ser. 2; Anderson Memo, July 13, 1915, Anderson Papers; Lansing to

Wilson, July 14 and 15, 1915, Wilson Papers, Ser. 2; Wilson to House, July 12, 1915, Wilson Papers, Ser. 2, and July 12, 1915, R. S. Baker Papers; Wilson to Gerard, May 27, 1915, Wilson Papers, Ser. 2.

31. Bryan to Gerard, May 13, 1915, in U.S. Dept of State, *Foreign Relations of the United States, 1915, Supplement,* 393–96; Lansing to Bryan, June 1, 1915, Wilson Papers, Ser. 2.

32. Wilson to Gerard, May 23, 1915, Wilson Papers, Ser. 2; Wilson to Bryan, June 2 and May 20, 1915, Bryan Papers; Wilson to House, May 20, 1915, quoted in Charles Seymour, *American Diplomacy During the World War,* 15.

33. Lansing to Gerard, June 9, 1915, *Foreign Relations, 1915, Supplement,* 436–38. See also Bernstorff, *My Three Years,* 150–51; Lansing to Gerard, July 21, 1915, *Foreign Relations, 1915, Supplement,* 480–82.

34. Bryan to Wilson, May 9, 1915, Wilson Papers, Ser. 2; May 12, 1915, Bryan Papers; May 12, 16, and 24, 1915, Wilson Papers, Ser. 2; June 2, 1915, Bryan Papers; June 2, 3 (two letters), 5, and 7, 1915, Wilson Papers, Ser. 2; Wilson to Bryan, June 8, 1915, and Bryan to Wilson, June 9, 1915, Wilson Papers, Ser. 2. See also C. Johnson to Lansing, May 15, 1915, Lansing Papers.

35. Bryan to Wilson, May 5, 1915, Wilson Papers, Ser. 2; House Diary entry, Jan. 24, 1915, in Link, *Papers of Woodrow Wilson* 33:452.

36. House to Wilson, May 25, 1915, Wilson Papers, Ser. 2; see also Seymour, *Intimate Papers of Colonel House* 1:281–82, 457, and 2:15–16; Lansing Diary entry, "Consideration and Outline of Policies," July 11, 1915, Lansing Papers; Robert Lansing, *War Memoirs of Robert Lansing,* 18, 128, 112; Lansing to Wilson, Aug. 18, 1915, *Lansing Papers,* 14; Smith, *Lansing and American Neutrality,* 19, 42, 168. Gerard felt much the same way; see Gerard to House, July 20, 1915, quoted in Seymour, *Intimate Papers of Colonel House* 2:23, and James W. Gerard, *My Four Years in Germany.*

37. Link, *Struggle for Neutrality,* 405–7; Devlin, *Too Proud to Fight,* 307–10; Gregory, *Origins of American Intervention,* 68–69; Ernest R. May, *The World War and American Isolation, 1914–1917,* 197–210. At the end of June, a submarine sank the British passenger liner *Armenian,* which caused a stir until the U.S. government learned that the ship had attempted to flee after the submarine surfaced to give warning, which justified the attack. Over two weeks later, a U-boat fired a torpedo at the *Orduna,* another passenger ship of British registry, but the missile went wide of its target. The German government refused to take official note of the incident and, since no injuries or damage resulted, the Wilson administration refrained from pressing a complaint. Devlin, *Too Proud to Fight,* 309.

38. Wilson to Edith Boling Galt, Aug. 19, 1915, Wilson Papers, Ser. 20.

39. Lansing to Wilson, Aug. 20, 1915, Wilson Papers, Ser. 12; Smith, *Lansing and American Neutrality,* 99; Tumulty to Wilson, Aug. 21, 1915, Wilson Papers, Ser. 12.

40. Wilson to House, Aug. 21, 1915, R. S. Baker Papers; Devlin, *Too Proud to Fight,* 320; Seymour, *Intimate Papers of Colonel House* 2:31–32.

41. Link, *Struggle for Neutrality,* 567–68; House to Wilson, ca. Aug. 22, 1915, Wilson Papers, Ser. 12.

42. Wilson to Galt, ca. Aug. 22, 1915, Wilson Papers, Ser. 12, and Aug. 22, 1915, Wilson Papers, Ser. 20.

43. Wilson to Galt, Aug. 25, 1915, Wilson Papers, Ser. 20; Link, *Struggle for Neutrality,* 551–87, 645–81; Devlin, *Too Proud to Fight,* 319–34; Smith, *Lansing and American Neutrality,* 103–4; Bernstorff, *My Three Years,* 152; Grenville and Young, *Politics, Strategy, and American Diplomacy,* 305–7.

44. Lansing to Hoke Smith, Sept. 14, 1915, Lansing Papers.

45. House to Wilson, June 26 and July 1, 1914, Wilson Papers, Ser. 2.

46. Wilson, "Remarks at a Press Conference," Aug. 3, 1914, in Link, *Papers of Woodrow Wilson* 30:332.
47. Wilson to Thomas Nelson Page, Jan. 28, 1915, Wilson Papers, Ser. 3. See also Baker, *Neutrality*, 269.
48. Wilson to House, Jan. 17, 1915, Wilson Papers, Ser. 2; Wilson letter of introduction for House, Jan. 18, 1915, Wilson Papers, Ser. 3.
49. House to Wilson, Feb. 11 and 15, Mar. 20 and 26, Apr. 18, and May 5, 7, 18, 1915; Wilson to House, May 18, 1915; House to Wilson, May 19 and 20, 1915; Wilson to House, May 20, 1915; House to Wilson, May 27 and 28, 1915, all in Wilson Papers, Ser. 2; House to Wilson, May 22, 1915, quoted in Seymour, *Intimate Papers of Colonel House* 1:285; Smith, *Lansing and American Neutrality*, 79, 146; Buehrig, *Balance of Power*, 201–2.
50. Arthur Link, *Wilson the Diplomatist*, 92.
51. House to Wilson, June 16, 1915, Wilson Papers, Ser. 2, and May 29, 1914, quoted in Seymour, *Intimate Papers of Colonel House* 1:249. See also pp. 469–70.
52. Wilson to House, Dec. 24, 1915, Wilson Papers, Ser. 2. See also Baker, *Neutrality*, 74.
53. House to Wilson, Jan. 8, 1916, Wilson Papers, Ser. 2; Wilson to House, Jan. 9, 1916, R. S. Baker Papers; House to Wilson, Jan. 11, 15, 16, Feb. 3, 9 (two letters), 10 (two letters), 11, 1916; Wilson to House, Feb. 12, 1916; House to Wilson, Feb. 16, 1916, all in Wilson Papers, Ser. 2; Seymour, *Intimate Papers of Colonel House* 2:85–86, 90–91, 118, 120, 163–65, 171, 472; Gerard, *My Four Years in Germany*, ix–x.
54. House to Wilson, Apr. 3, 1916, Wilson Papers, Ser. 2; Link, *Wilson the Diplomatist*, 63; Smith, *Lansing and American Neutrality*, 132.
55. Wilson, "Second Annual Address to Congress," Dec. 8, 1914, in Baker and Dodd, *New Democracy* 2:224.
56. Wilson, "Third Annual Address to Congress," Dec. 7, 1915, in Baker and Dodd, *New Democracy*, 1:410–13. See also Walter Mills, *Arms and Men: A Study in American Military History*, 235; House to Wilson, July 14, 1915, quoted in Seymour, *Intimate Papers of Colonel House* 2:19; John A. S. Grenville, "Diplomacy and War Plans in the United States, 1890–1917," 18–19; Seymour, *Intimate Papers of Colonel House* 1:vii.
57. Wilson, "Address at Cleveland," Jan. 29, 1916, in Baker and Dodd, *New Democracy* 2:44.
58. Wilson, "Address at Topeka," Feb. 2, 1916, in Baker and Dodd, *New Democracy*, 2:89, and "Address at Chicago," Jan. 31, 1916, in Baker and Dodd, *New Democracy* 2:59, 61, and "Address at Des Moines," Feb. 1, 1916, in Baker and Dodd, *New Democracy* 2:75.
59. Wilson, "Address at St. Louis," Feb. 3, 1916, in Baker and Dodd, *New Democracy* 2:109–10.
60. Lansing Diary entry, "Note on the Probable Renewal of Submarine Warfare," Jan. 24, 1916, Lansing Papers.
61. Wilson to Sen. William J. Stone, Feb. 24, 1916, in Baker and Dodd, *New Democracy* 2:122–24.
62. May, *The World War and American Isolation*, 191.
63. Devlin, *Too Proud to Fight*, 474; Seymour, *Intimate Papers of Colonel House* 2:226–30.
64. Wilson to Lansing, Mar. 30, 1916, quoted in Devlin, *Too Proud to Fight*, 475; Wilson to T. N. Page, Mar. 31, 1916, Wilson Papers, Ser. 3.
65. Devlin, *Too Proud to Fight*, 476, 478–80; Buehrig, *Balance of Power*, 229.
66. U.S. Dept. of State, *Foreign Relations, 1916, Supplement*, 227–29; Devlin, *Too Proud to Fight*, 478–80.

67. Wilson, "Message to Congress," Apr. 19, 1916, in Baker and Dodd, *New Democracy* 2:153–59.
68. *Foreign Relations, 1916, Supplement*, 257, 265; Devlin, *Too Proud to Fight*, 482.
69. Lansing to Wilson, May 6, 1915, Wilson Papers, Ser. 2.
70. Devlin, *Too Proud to Fight*, 482–83.
71. House to Wilson, May 9 and 19, 1916, Wilson Papers, Ser. 2; Lansing to Wilson, May 25, 1916, Wilson Papers, Ser. 2; Wilson, "Address to League to Enforce Peace," in Baker and Dodd, *New Democracy* 2:184–88; House to Wilson, May 28, 1916, Wilson Papers, Ser. 2; Lansing to Wilson, May 25, 1916, *Lansing Papers* 1:16–18.
72. House to Wilson, May 7, 10, 11, 14 (two letters), 1916; Tumulty to Wilson, May 16, 1916; House to Wilson, May 21, 1916; Grey to House, May 22, 1916; House to Wilson, May 26, 1916; Grey to House, May 29, 1916; House to Wilson, June 1, 1916; Polk to Wilson, June 6, 1916; House to Wilson, June 8, July 12, 14, 15, 1916, all in Wilson Papers, Ser. 2.
73. House to Wilson, Oct. 20, Nov. 6, 20, 30, 1916; Wilson, "Reasons why he should speak out," ca. Dec. 1, 1916; Wilson draft of note, ca. Dec. 1, 1916; House to Wilson, Dec. 3 and 4, 1916; Wilson draft of note, Dec. 9, 1916; Lansing to Wilson, Dec. 10, 1916; Wilson draft of note, Dec. 14, 1916; Lansing to Wilson, Dec. 14 and 16, 1916; Wilson note to belligerents, Dec. 18, 1916; Wilson outline for note to belligerents, ca. late 1916, all in Wilson Papers, Ser. 2.
74. House to Wilson, Dec. 20 and 27, 1916; Wilson to House, Dec. 28, 1916; House to Wilson, Dec. 28, 1916; Wilson to House, Jan. 5, 1917, all in Wilson Papers, Ser. 2; Seymour, *Intimate Papers of Colonel House* 2:327, 390–91, 393; Gregory, *Origins of American Intervention*, 112–13.
75. Count Johann Bernstorff to House, Jan. 31, 1917; Lansing to Wilson, Feb. 23, 1917; Bernstorff to House, Jan. 9, 1917; House to Wilson, Jan. 15, 16, 17, 18, 19, 20, 25, 1917; Wilson to Carnegie Foundation, Jan. 24, 1917; Lansing to Wilson, Feb. 8, 1917, all in Wilson Papers, Ser. 2.
76. Wilson, "Address to Congress," Jan. 22, 1917, in Baker and Dodd, *New Democracy* 2:407–14; see also Seymour, *Intimate Papers of Colonel House* 2:412; Link, *Wilson the Diplomatist*, 73.
77. Gregory, *Origins of American Intervention*, 121–27; Seward W. Livermore, *Politics Is Adjourned: Woodrow Wilson and the War Congress, 1916–1918;* Thomas W. Ripley, *A Little Group of Willful Men;* Samuel R. Spencer, *Decision for War, 1917*.
78. Gregory, *Origins of American Intervention*, 127–29; Spencer, *Decision for War, 1917;* Seymour, *Intimate Papers of Colonel House* 2:452; Small, "The German 'Threat'," 252–70.
79. See Grenville, "Diplomacy and War Plans," 17–21; Elting E. Morison, *Admiral Sims and the Modern American Navy;* Palmer, *Bliss*, 128, 132–35; Grenville, *Politics, Strategy, and American Diplomacy*, 319, 321, 325–27, 334–35; Challener, *Admirals, Generals*, 15–17, 24, 28–29; Seymour, *Intimate Papers of Colonel House* 3:6–7; Freidel, *Franklin D. Roosevelt* 1:267.
80. Buehrig, *Balance of Power*, ix; Seymour, *American Neutrality*, 171; Seymour, *American Diplomacy*, 24; Link, *Wilson the Diplomatist*, 87; Baker, *Why We Went to War*, 161; R. S. Baker, *Woodrow Wilson Life and Letters*, vol. 6, *Facing War*, 515; Mayer, *Political Origins of the New Diplomacy*, 167.
81. Wilson, "Speech to Congress," Apr. 2, 1917, in Baker and Dodd, *War and Peace* 1:7; Lansing Memo, Mar. 20, 1917, Lansing Papers. See also Gerard, *My Four Years in Germany*, x; Spencer, *Decision for War*, Preface; Baker, *Why We Went to War*, 5; Franklin K. Lane to George W. Lane, Apr. 1, 1917, in Anne W. Lane and Louise H. Wall, *The*

Letters of Franklin K. Lane, Personal and Political (hereafter cited as *Letters of Lane*), 242–43; William G. McAdoo, *Crowded Years: The Reminiscences of William G. McAdoo,* 369; Lansing to Edward N. Smith, Apr. 7, 1917, quoted in Smith, *Lansing and American Neutrality,* 165.

82. Wilson, "Speech to Congress," Apr. 2, 1917, in Baker and Dodd, *War and Peace* 1:6–11. See also Wilson to Dodge, Apr. 4, 1917, Wilson Papers, Ser. 2; David Trask, "Woodrow Wilson and the Reconciliation of Force and Diplomacy," 25; Buehrig, *Balance of Power,* 15–17, 55, 149; Smith, *Lansing and American Neutrality,* 168; Link, *Revolution, War, and Peace,* 71; Bailey, *Wilson and the Lost Peace,* 14; Palmer, *Bliss,* 137; Josephus Daniels, *The Navy and the Nation,* 38; Baker, *Facing War,* 208.

83. Wilson, "Speech to Congress," Apr. 2, 1917, in Baker and Dodd, *War and Peace* 1:11–16.

5. THE POWER OF COOPERATION: World War I

1. Wilson, "Democracy and Efficiency," Mar. 1901, in Baker and Dodd, *College and State* 1:398.

2. Wilson, "Democracy," Dec. 5, 1891, quoted in Link, *Papers of Woodrow Wilson* 7:347, 357, 363, 368, and Link's note, 344. See also Wilson, "Democracy and Efficiency," Mar. 1901, in Baker and Dodd, *College and State* 1:399.

3. Wilson, "Speech to Newly Naturalized Citizens" May 10, 1915, in *Presidential Messages and State Papers* 10:116. This was the famous "Too proud to fight" speech.

4. Wilson, "Democracy and Efficiency," Mar. 1901, in Baker and Dodd, eds., *College and State* 1:402, 404.

5. Wilson, "Address to Congress," Apr. 2, 1917, 10:376, 379, 382–83; "Address," 10:392; and "Proclamation of State of War and of Alien Enemy Regulations," Apr. 6, 1917, 10:384, in which he urged the American people to "give undivided and willing support" to the prosecution of the war; all in *Presidential Messages and State Papers,* pages cited.

6. Benson to Daniels, ca. Feb. 1917, Daniels Papers.

7. House to Wilson, June 5, 1917, Wilson Papers, Ser. 2; Ralph Hayes to A. M. Piper, conveying Newton Baker's statement on the purpose of war, Jan. 10, 1918; Baker to G. F. Peabody, Nov. 28, 1917; and Baker to Teddy Roosevelt, May 5, 1917, all in N. Baker Papers.

8. Daniels, *Years of Peace,* 273, 274–78.

9. Grosvenor B. Clarkson, *Industrial America in the World War: The Strategy Behind the Line, 1917–1918,* 97, 153, 8.

10. Quoted in Frederick Palmer, *Newton D. Baker: America at War* 1:192.

11. David A. Lockmiller, *Enoch H. Crowder: Soldier, Lawyer, and Statesman,* 152–53; Enoch H. Crowder, *The Spirit of Selective Service,* 23; Palmer, *Baker* 1:192–94, 206–12.

12. Gen. G. T. Ansell to N. Baker, Apr. 24, 1917, Crowder Papers; Crowder, *Selective Service,* 60, and see also pp. 57–58.

13. Crowder, *Selective Service,* 119–21; Hugh Johnson to Crowder, Spring 1917, Crowder Papers, Collection 1046. This was the same Johnson who later became head of NRA under Franklin Roosevelt.

14. Crowder to Lawrence F. Abbott, June 28, 1919, Crowder Papers, 1046, folder 155; Crowder, *Selective Service,* 224, 226.

15. Crowder to Selon Wilder, Feb. 2, 1920, f. 206; Crowder to C. T. Stagy, Mar. 19, 1920, f. 217; Crowder to William Daniels, Dec. 8, 1919, f. 192; Crowder to A. K. Cohen, May 28, 1920, f. 237; Crowder to F. Palmer, Jan. 28, 1931, f. 886, all in Crowder Papers, 1046; Wilson, "Proclamation Calling for Draft Registration," June 5, 1917, copy in Crowder Papers.

16. Crowder, *Selective Service*, 237; Palmer, *Baker*, 212–19; J. Miller to Crowder, Dec. 1, 1919, f. 190, and Crowder to Miss Miriam Jones, July 15, 1920, f. 246, Crowder Papers, 1046.

17. Crowder, *Selective Service*, 125, vii.

18. Wilson, "An Address to the Officers of the Atlantic Fleet," quoted in Link, *Papers of Woodrow Wilson* 43:428; Urs Schwarz, *American Strategy, A New Perspective*, 8; Josephus Daniels, *The Wilson Era: Years of War, 1917–1919*, 89.

19. Clarkson, *Industrial America*, 31, 111; Louis Smith, *American Democracy and Military Power*, 68.

20. Memo to Chief of Staff from Brig. Gen. J. E. Kuhn, Feb. 20, 1917, f. 74, and Memo to Chief of Staff from John Millis, quoting Kuhn, July 27, 1917, f. 903, Crowder Papers, 1046.

21. Bliss to Scott, Mar. 31, 1917, Bliss Papers; House to Wilson, Mar. 19, 1917, Wilson Papers, Ser. 2; Lane to George W. Lane, Apr. 1, 1917, *Letters of Lane*, 244.

22. Russell Weigley, *History of the United States Army*, 355–56; Bliss to Scott, May 25, 1917, Bliss Papers; N. Baker to Wilson, May 2, 1917, Wilson Papers, Ser. 2; Wilson to Baker, May 3, 1917, and Baker to Wilson, May 8, 1917, N. Baker Papers; Palmer, *Bliss*, 151.

23. N. Baker to Pershing, May 26, 1917, Wilson Papers, Ser. 2; Weigley, *History of U.S. Army*, 377; Smith, *American Democracy and Military Power*, 49–50; Maurice Matloff, *American Military History*, 381.

24. Newton Baker, "America's Duty," 453; Newton Baker, "America's Purpose in the War," 54; N. Baker to Wilson, May 27, 1917, N. Baker Papers.

25. Lane to George W. Lane, May 3, 1917, *Letters of Lane*, 250–51. See also Pershing to Wilson, Oct. 8, 1917, Wilson Papers, Ser. 2.

26. Robert Lansing Statement, July 28, 1917, and Lansing to Wilson, June 9, 1917, Lansing Papers.

27. Wilson, "Speech to Gathering of College Presidents," May 5, 1917, quoted in Newton Baker, *Frontiers of Freedom*, 30.

28. House to Wilson, Apr. 22, 1917, quoted in Seymour, *Intimate Papers of Colonel House* 3:37–38; House Diary entry, Apr. 22, 1917, 3:39, and Apr. 30, 1917, 3:54, both quoted in Seymour, *Intimate Papers of Colonel House*, pages cited; Wilson to House, Dec. 1, 1917, Wilson Papers, Ser. 2; Wilson, "Speech to Southern Society Banquet," Dec. 12, 1917, quoted in Daniels, *Navy and Nation*, 86–87. In the speech, Wilson added, "Freedom for all is not enough." See also House to Wilson, Aug. 24, 1917, quoted in Seymour, *Intimate Papers of Colonel House* 3:39; House Diary entry, Apr. 30, 1917, quoted in Seymour, *Intimate Papers of Colonel House* 3:54; Wilson, "Message to Russia," May 26, 1917, in Baker and Dodd, *War and Peace* 1:50.

29. Wilson, "The Fourteen Points," Jan. 8, 1918, quoted in Bailey, *Wilson and the Lost Peace*, 333–36; Mayer, *Political Origins of the New Diplomacy*, 352, 329–52.

30. Link, *Revolution, War, and Peace*, 85–86.

31. Wilson, "Speech to Alliance for Labor and Democracy," Feb. 22, 1918, quoted in Daniels, *Navy and Nation*, 127–28; Wilson to Mrs. H. H. Dyer Dermott, Sept. 20, 1918, Wilson Papers, Ser. 2.

32. Mayer, *Political Origins of the New Diplomacy*, 334–35.
33. John J. Pershing, *My Experiences in the World War* 1:43, 45–46, 95; Weigley, *History of U.S. Army*, 359–60; C. Joseph Bernardo and Eugene H. Bacon, *American Military Policy: Its Development Since 1775*, 355; Oliver Spaulding, *The U.S. Army in Peace and War*, 416–17.
34. N. Baker to Wilson, Oct. 4, 1917, N. Baker Papers; Baker to Wilson, Nov. 11, 1917, Wilson Papers, Ser. 2.
35. Bernardo and Bacon, *American Military Policy*, 361; Wilson to House, Nov. 2, 1917, and Wilson, "Note," ca. Nov. 15, 1917, Wilson Papers, Ser. 2; House to Wilson, Nov. 25, 1917, quoted in Seymour, *Intimate Papers of Colonel House* 3:281; Lansing to Wilson, June 29, 1918, Lansing Papers.
36. Schwarz, *American Strategy*, 13; Bernardo and Bacon, *American Military Policy*, 361.
37. David Trask, *Captains and Cabinets: Anglo-American Naval Relations, 1917–1918*, 183–84, 206.
38. Daniels to Adm. William S. Sims, July 18, 1918, Sims Papers; Sims to Daniels, July 16, 1917, Sims Papers; Daniels, *Wilson Era: Years of War*, 84–86.
39. Thomas Frothingham, *The Naval History of the World War* 3:236.
40. Trask, *Captains and Cabinets*, 180.
41. Trask, *Captains and Cabinets*, 362.
42. Trask, *Captains and Cabinets*, 362, 225, 240–51.
43. Walworth, *America's Moment*, 18–19, 25–30.
44. Link, *Revolution, War, and Peace*, 87; see also Walworth, *America's Moment*.
45. Keith L. Nelson, *Victors Divided: America and the Allies in Germany, 1918–1923*, 30.
46. Henry T. Allen, *The Rhineland Occupation*, iv, vi, 11, 127.
47. Nelson, *Victors Divided*, 257–58; Jolyan P. Gerard, "Congress and Presidential Military Policy: The Occupation of Germany, 1919–1923."

6. THE POWER OF COLLECTIVE SECURITY: *Russia*

1. Wilson, "Socialism and Democracy," ca. Aug. 22, 1887, 5:561; Wilson, "Nature of Democracy in the United States," May 13, 1889, 6:239; and Editor's note, all in Link, *Papers of Woodrow Wilson*, pages cited.
2. Quoted in Notter, *Origins of the Foreign Policy*, 43; Wilson, "The Significance of American History," Sept. 9, 1901, quoted in Link, *Papers of Woodrow Wilson* 12:184.
3. Quoted in Herman, *Eleven Against War*, 201.
4. Quoted in Richard N. Current, "The United States and 'Collective Security': Notes on the History of an Idea," in Alexander DeConde, ed., *Isolation and Security*, 36.
5. Quoted in Seymour, *Intimate Papers of Colonel House* 1:207–9; Herman, *Eleven Against War*, 190–91.
6. Sidney Bell, *Righteous Conquest: Woodrow Wilson and the Evolution of the New Diplomacy*, 95–96, 116.
7. Bell, *Righteous Conquest*, 97.
8. Wilson, "Address to League to Enforce Peace," in Baker and Dodd, *New Democracy* 2:184–88.
9. George Kennan, *The Decision to Intervene*.
10. Wilson to Lansing, June 1, 1917, *Lansing Papers* 2:338. See also Daniels to Arthur

Glasgow, Mar. 20, 1917, Daniels Papers; House to Wilson, Mar. 17, 1917, Wilson Papers, Ser. 2.

11. Wilson to Cyrus McCormick, Apr. 27, 1917, Wilson Papers, Ser. 2; N. Baker to the Chairman, Committee on Public Information, ca. 1917, N. Baker Papers; Baker to Wilson, Apr. 14, 1917, Wilson Papers, Ser. 2; Lansing Diary entry, "Memo on the Russian Situation and the Root Mission," Aug. 9, 1917, Lansing Papers; Pershing to Bliss, July 27, 1917, Bliss Papers.

12. Pershing to Scott, Oct. 1, 1917, and Pershing to Baker, Oct. 4, 1917, Pershing Papers.

13. For an expression of this view, see Pershing to Scott, Nov. 30, 1917, Pershing Papers. The early ignorance of what Bolshevism meant did not last long; indeed, the Bolsheviks complicated American opposition to intervention by issuing propaganda and political statements. The Wilson administration refused to recognize the new government, claiming that "this Government must continue for the present a silent witness of the internal confusion which prevails in Russia awaiting the time when the Russian people will manifest in no uncertain way their sovereign will." See the following: Lansing to Wilson, Jan. 2, 1918, Wilson Papers, Ser. 5A; David R. Francis to Lansing, Nov. 20, 1917, Lansing Papers; Lansing, "Memo on Nonrecognition of a Russian Government," Jan. 6, 1918, Wilson Papers, Ser. 5A; Breckinridge Long to Lansing, Feb. 22, 1918, Breckinridge Long Papers; Lane to George W. Lane, *Letters of Lane,* 245.

14. Lansing to Wilson, Dec. 10, 1917, Wilson Papers, Ser. 2; Lansing Diary entry, "Memo on the Russian Situation," Dec. 7, 1917, Lansing Papers.

15. Permanent Military Representatives to the Supreme War Council, Joint Note Number 5, Dec. 23, 1917, Bliss Papers.

16. Lansing to Daniels, Jan. 3, 1918, and Daniels to Commander in Chief, Asiatic Fleet, Jan. 3, 1918, Wilson Papers, Ser. 5A.

17. Lansing to Bliss, Feb. 2, 1918, Bliss Papers.

18. Permanent Military Representatives to the SWC, Joint Note Number 16, Feb. 19, 1918, Bliss Papers.

19. Bliss to Permanent Military Representatives to the SWC, Feb. 26, 1918, Bliss Papers; Notes from Second Meeting of Fifth Session of SWC, May 2, 1918, Bliss Papers.

20. Lord Reading to Wilson, Feb. 27, 1918, Wilson Papers, Ser. 5A; Arthur Balfour to House, Mar. 7, 1918, Wilson Papers, Ser. 2; Balfour to U.S. Government, Mar. 16, 1918, Bliss Papers; Balfour to Wilson, Mar. 18, 1918, Wilson Papers, Ser. 2.

21. Lansing to Wilson, Feb. 26, 1918, Wilson Papers, Ser. 5A; Jules Jusserand to Wilson, Mar. 13, 1918, Wilson Papers, Ser. 2.

22. Roland Morris to Secy. of State, Mar. 19, 1918, and Francis to Secy. of State, Feb. 24, 1918, Lansing Papers; Weekly Intelligence Summary, Jan. 26, 1918, 3:7, Mar. 2, 1918, 3:16, and Mar. 30, 1918, 3:23, all quoted in Richard D. Challener, ed., *United States Military Intelligence, 1917–1927,* pages cited; Breckinridge Long to Wilson, Mar. 4, 1918, Wilson Papers, Ser. 2.

23. Polk to American Legation, Peking, Jan. 21, 1918; Polk to American Embassy, London, Jan. 24, 1918; and Polk to American Embassy, Paris, Mar. 19, 1918, all in Breckinridge Long Papers; Lansing to Wilson, Mar. 18, 1918, Wilson Papers, Ser. 2; Wilson to John Sharp Williams, Aug. 13, 1917, in R. S. Baker, *Wilson Life and Letters: War Leader* 7:214.

24. Lansing Diary entries, "Memo on German Domination in Siberia and Possible Means of Overcoming It," Mar. 22, 1918, and "Memo on Proposed Japanese Military Expedition into Siberia," Mar. 18, 1918, Lansing Papers; Lansing to Wilson, Feb. 27 and Mar. 19, 1918, Wilson Papers, Ser. 5A; Lansing to Wilson, Dec. 10, 1917, 2:343–44, Wilson

to Lansing, Mar. 22, 1918, 2:353–55, 357, Lansing to Wilson, 2:357–58, and Wilson to Lansing, Mar. 22, 1918, 2:360, all in *Lansing Papers,* pages cited.

25. House to Wilson, Feb. 2 and Mar. 3, 1918, and House to Balfour, Mar. 4, 1918, Wilson Papers, Ser. 2.

26. Secy. of State to Francis, Mar. 13, 1918, Breckinridge Long Papers; Polk to American Embassy, Tokyo, Mar. 12, 1918, Breckinridge Long Papers.

27. Wilson to Breckinridge Long, Mar. 2 and 14, 1918, Wilson Papers, Ser. 2; Breckinridge Long, Diary entry, Feb. 26, 1918, Breckinridge Long Papers.

28. For listings of the war supplies stocked at Vladivostok, see War Department to Wilson, Mar. 2, 1918, and Polk to Wilson, Mar. 6, 1918, Wilson Papers, Ser. 2; John Caldwell to Secy. of State, Mar. 18, 1918, Breckinridge Long Papers; Daniels to Wilson, Mar. 27, 1918, Daniels Papers; Kennan, *Decision to Intervene,* 50–52, 123–29.

29. Note by Permanent Military Representatives to the SWC and Inter-Allied Naval Council, Mar. 23, 1918, and "Note by Allied Naval Council," Mar. 20, 1918, Annex A to Joint Report of Allied Naval Council, Mar. 23, 1918, Bliss Papers.

30. Wilson to Daniels, Apr. 8, 1918, Daniels Papers.

31. Wilson to Herbert Bayard Swope, Apr. 2, 1918, Wilson Papers, Ser. 2; Lansing to Wilson, Apr. 29, 1918, Wilson Papers, Ser. 5A.

32. Kennan, *Decision to Intervene,* 99–100; Permanent Military Representatives to the SWC, Joint Note Number 20, Apr. 8, 1918, Bliss Papers.

33. Kennan, *Decision to Intervene,* 136–65.

34. Permanent Military Representatives to the SWC, Joint Note Number 25, Apr. 27, 1918, Bliss Papers.

35. Minutes of Second Meeting of Fifth Session of SWC, May 2, 1918, Bliss Papers.

36. Lansing to Wilson, May 11, 1918, Wilson Papers, Ser. 2.

37. Bliss to Permanent Military Representatives to the SWC, June 1, 1918, Bliss Papers.

38. Minutes of Fifth Session of SWC, May 2, 1918, Bliss Papers.

39. Bliss to Agwar, May 26, 1918; Notes for Bliss from his staff, May 27, 1918; and Bliss to Agwar, May 30, 1918, all in Bliss Papers.

40. N. Baker to Bliss, May 28, 1918, Wilson Papers, Ser. 2; Baker to Bliss, May 28, 1918, N. Baker Papers.

41. Breckinridge Long Diary entry, May 31, 1918, Breckinridge Long Papers; House to Wilson, May 3, 1918, Wilson Papers, Ser. 2; Wilson to N. Baker, May 20, 1918, N. Baker Papers.

42. Lansing to Wilson, May 21, 1918, Wilson Papers, Ser. 2; Lansing to George Kennan, May 28, 1918, Lansing Papers.

43. Minutes of Third Meeting of Sixth Session of SWC, June 3, 1918; Bliss to Agwar, June 3, 1918; Bliss to Baker, June 3, 1918, all in Bliss Papers.

44. Permanent Military Representatives to the SWC, Joint Note Number 31, June 3, 1918, Bliss Papers.

45. Wilson to Thomas Dixon, June 26, 1918, Wilson Papers, Ser. 4, CP; Lansing Diary entry, "Memo on Intervention in Russia," June 12, 1918, Lansing Papers.

46. N. Baker to Wilson, June 19, 1918, Wilson Papers, Ser. 4, CF 64; Bliss to Col. D. E. Nolan, June 20, 1918, Bliss Papers; Memo by Stanley D. Embick, June 21, 1918, Bliss Papers; Bliss to Agwar, June 22, 1918, Bliss Papers; Benson to Daniels, June 22, 1918, Daniels Papers; Knight to Daniels, Mar. 18, 1918, quoted in Unterberger, *America's Siberian Expedition,* 38.

47. N. Baker to Bliss, June 15, 1918, and Bliss to Agwar, June 18, 1918, Bliss Papers;

Baker to Wilson, June 20, 1918, N. Baker Papers; Jusserand to Wilson, June 24, 1918, and Wilson to Jusserand, June 25, 1918, Wilson Papers, Ser. 2; Gen. Ferdinand Foch to Wilson, June 27, 1918, N. Baker Papers.

48. Wilson to Lansing, June 26, 1918, N. Baker Papers; Lord Reading to Wilson, June 28, 1918, Wilson Papers, Ser. 2; March to Bliss, June 24, 1918; Minutes of Seventh Session of SWC, July 2, 1918; Bliss to Agwar, July 5, 1918; Lord Milner to Lord Reading, July 5, 1918; Baker to Bliss, July 9, 1918; and Bliss to Agwar, July 13, 1918, all in Bliss Papers.

49. Bliss to Agwar, July 2, 1918, Bliss Papers; Kennan, *Decision to Intervene*, 389–90.

50. Kennan, *Decision to Intervene*, 391–94; Unterberger, *America's Siberian Expedition*, 60, 66; Lansing to Wilson, June 28, 1918, Wilson Papers, Ser. 2; Bliss to Agwar, July 2, 1918, Bliss Papers.

51. Lansing Diary entry, "Memo on Siberian Situation," July 4, 1918, Lansing Papers.

52. Lansing Diary entry, "Memo of a Conference at the White House in Reference to the Siberian Situation," July 6, 1918, Lansing Papers; Wilson to House, July 8, 1918, R. S. Baker Papers; Lansing to Wilson, July 8 and 9, 1918, Wilson Papers, Ser. 2.

53. Peyton C. March, *The Nation at War*, 113, 123–24; March, Memorandum, June 24, 1918, Peyton C. March Papers, Library of Congress Manuscript Division, Washington, D.C.; Basil Miles to Lansing, July 1, 1918, Wilson Papers, Ser. 2; Lansing to Breckinridge Long, Sept. 8, 1918, Breckinridge Long Papers.

54. Bliss Memo, July 2, 1918, and Bliss to Agwar, July 13, 1918, Bliss Papers; Palmer, *Bliss*, 169, 295–96, 303, 333, 374–75.

55. N. Baker to Mrs. Casserly, Nov. 15, 1924, N. Baker Papers; see also Newton Baker, "Foreword," in William S. Graves, *America's Siberian Adventure, 1918–1920*, ix–xii. The exact wording Baker attributes to Wilson should not be accepted as completely accurate since Wilson was usually careful to avoid referring to the Entente powers as America's allies, preferring, instead, to insist on America's status as an associate power. However, this minor discrepancy does not throw into question Wilson's intention as described by Baker.

56. Wilson, "Notes for Aide-Memoire," ca. July 17, 1918, Wilson Papers, Ser. 2; March to Bliss, July 23, 1918, Bliss Papers.

57. No author, "Draft Statement to Press," Aug. 3, 1918, R. S. Baker Papers; Wilson to Thomas Masaryk, Aug. 7, 1918, Wilson Papers, Ser. 2; Breckinridge Long Diary entry, Sept. 5, 1918, Breckinridge Long Papers; Wilson notes on assurances to Russia, ca. Aug. 3, 1918, and Polk to Wilson, July 20, 1918, Wilson Papers, Ser. 2; Unterberger, *America's Siberian Expedition*, 88, 232.

58. Graves, *America's Siberian Adventure*, 68. See also Lansing to Polk, Aug. 3, 1918, Lansing Papers, in which Lansing asserts that the British and French were aiding various factions in the Russian Revolution.

59. Wilson to Daniels, Aug. 1, 1918, Wilson Papers, Ser. 2. See also Lansing to Wilson, July 10, 1918, and Polk to Wilson, July 15, 1918, Wilson Papers, Ser. 2; Baker to Wilson, July 20, 1918, Baker Papers; Polk to Wilson, July 26, 1918, Wilson Papers, Ser. 2; Breckinridge Long to Lansing, Aug. 17, 1918, Breckinridge Long Papers; Polk to Wilson, Aug. 3, 1918, Wilson Papers, Ser. 2.

60. Gen. Thomas Bridges to N. Baker, July 25, 1918, N. Baker Papers. See also H. W. Studd, Acting British Military Representative, to Bliss, Aug. 16, 1918, and Statement by Military Representatives, Sept. 10, 1918, Bliss Papers, on the Allied purposes of the intervention in Siberia.

61. Wilson to Lansing, Aug. 23, 1918, *Lansing Papers* 2:378–79; Lansing to Wilson, Sept. 9, 1918, Breckinridge Long Papers.

62. N. Baker to Wilson, Sept. 15, 1918, N. Baker Papers; Remarks of Bliss to Perma-

nent Military Representatives to the SWC, Sept. 14, 1918, Bliss to Secy. of War, Sept. 15, 1918, and Bliss to Francis, Oct. 3, 1918, Bliss Papers. For information on Wilson's intention to limit the number of American troops in each intervention, see Wilson to Lansing, Sept. 26, 1918, Breckinridge Long Papers; and March to Bliss, Sept. 27, 1918, Bliss Papers.

63. Bliss to Permanent Military Representatives to the SWC, Oct. 7 and 8, 1918, Bliss Papers.

64. Pershing to Bliss, Nov. 19 and Dec. 1, 1918, Bliss Papers; Baker to Wilson, Nov. 6, 1918, N. Baker Papers.

65. N. Baker to Wilson, Nov. 27, 1918, Wilson Papers, Ser. 5A

66. Bliss to Pershing, Nov. 23, 1918, Bliss Papers; Bliss to N. Baker, Jan. 11, 1919, N. Baker Papers; Lansing Diary entry, "Memo on Absolutism and Bolshevism," Oct. 26, 1919, Lansing Papers; Lansing to E. N. Smith, Oct. 12, 1918, Lansing Papers.

7. THE LIMITS OF FORCE: *Russia, Bolshevism, and the Paris Peace Conference*

1. Mayer, *Politics and Diplomacy of Peacemaking.*
2. William R. Bullitt to Wilson, May 17, 1918, Wilson Papers, Ser. 5B.
3. Breckinridge Long, "Draft of Proposed Statement," Jan. 21, 1919, Long Papers; Minutes of Meeting of American Commissioners, Jan. 30, 1919, and Bliss Diary entry, Feb. 9, 1919, Bliss Papers. See also Bliss Diary entry, Jan. 8, 1919, Bliss Papers.
4. DeWitte C. Poole to American Commissioners, Feb. 13 and Mar. 31, 1919, Bliss Papers; Bliss to Wilson, Apr. 18, 1919, Wilson Papers, Ser. 5B; Phillips to American Commissioners, Apr. 4, 1919, Bliss Papers; Edward Ironside, *Archangel, 1918–1920,* 192; Graves, *America's Siberian Adventure,* 343. See also R. S. Baker interview with N. Baker, Apr. 6, 1928, R. S. Baker Papers, in which N. Baker describes his and March's opposition to the interventions.
5. N. A. McCully to Force Commander, ONI, July 9, 1919, Daniels Papers.
6. Memo by Bliss, Feb. 10, 1919, Bliss Papers.
7. Bliss Diary entry, Feb. 5, 1919; Gen. Sir Henry Wilson to Bliss, Feb. 5, 1919; Bliss to Woodrow Wilson, Feb. 8 and 12, 1919; Bliss to Gen. Emile Eugen Belin, Feb. 13, 1919; Bliss to Agwar, Feb. 14, 1919, all in Bliss Papers; Bliss to N. Baker, Feb. 14, 1919, N. Baker Papers. In June 1919, as the Allied forces were being withdrawn, the British asked Bliss to gain Wilson's approval for the railroad troops to remain temporarily. Neither Bliss nor Wilson had any objections to this provided the troops volunteered. The British promised to evacuate them by Sept. 1919. See Bliss telephone memorandum to Wilson, June 6, 1919, Wilson Papers, Ser. 5B; Bliss to Gen. H. Wilson, June 10, 1919, Bliss Papers; Wilson to Bliss, June 10, 1919, Bliss to Wilson, June 26 and 28, 1919, and Wilson to Bliss, June 28, 1919, all in Wilson Papers, Ser. 5B.
8. Minutes of Daily Meeting of American Commissioners, Apr. 1, 1919, Bliss Papers; Poole to American Commissioners, Apr. 2 and 15, 1918, Bliss Papers; Bliss to Wilson, Apr. 21, 1919, Wilson Papers, Ser. 5B. The American Commissioners recommended withdrawal of American troops from the northern intervention as early as Feb. 1, 1919. Minutes of Daily Meeting, Feb. 1, 1919, Bliss Papers. William Bullitt also recommended withdrawal of these troops. House approved the suggestion and recommended that Wilson should take it up with Lloyd George. Bullitt to House, Jan. 30, 1919, Wilson Papers, Ser. 5B.
9. Notes of a Meeting held at President Wilson's house in the Place des États Unis,

Paris, Apr. 22, 1919, Wilson Papers, Ser. 6A; Wilson to Bliss, Apr. 22, 1919, Bliss Papers; Notes of a Meeting, Apr. 25, 1919, Wilson Papers, Ser. 6A.

10. Notes of a Meeting, Apr. 30, 1919, Wilson Papers, Ser. 6A; Wilson to Benson, May 2, 1919, and Benson to Wilson, May 1, 1919, Wilson Papers, Ser. 5B.

11. Bliss to Wilson, May 29, 1919, Wilson Papers, Ser. 5B.

12. Benson to Wilson, June 6, 1919, and Wilson to Bliss, June 10, 1919, Wilson Papers, Ser. 5B; Bliss Diary entry, July 11, 1919, Bliss Papers. Earlier, Bliss described the pressures on him from the other military representatives to increase the size of the American expedition. "The expressed purpose for the increase in force urged was offensive Allied action by the Northern Russian expedition," Bliss explained to Baker, "and I consistently held to the view that the Murmansk and Archangel Expeditions were intended for a specific defensive purpose, namely, the retention of the ports of Murmansk and Archangel and for that purpose should not be augmented. Further I made it clear that the Government of the United States had definitely declined to take part in organized intervention in adequate force from Murmansk or Archangel." Bliss to N. Baker, Jan. 2, 1919, Bliss Papers.

13. Charles L. Mee, Jr., *The End of Order: Versailles, 1919,* 155.

14. Wilson to Norman Hapgood, June 20, 1919, Wilson Papers, Ser. 5B.

15. Notes of a Meeting, May 20, 1919, Wilson Papers, Ser. 6A.

16. Baker to Gen. William S. Graves, Aug. 31, 1920, N. Baker Papers.

17. Polk to American Commissioners, Dec. 30, 1918, and Polk to Lansing, Mar. 18, 1919, Bliss Papers; Lansing to Wilson, Mar. 22, 1919, Wilson Papers, Ser. 5B.

18. Phillips to American Commissioners, Mar. 29, 1919, American Commissioners to State Dept., Apr. 2, 1919, and Phillips to American Commissioners, Mar. 27, 1919, all in Bliss Papers. See also P. G. Kerr to Wilson, June 27, 1919, Wilson Papers, Ser. 5B; Phillips to American Commissioners, June 16, 1919, Bliss Papers; Notes of Meeting of Heads of Delegation, July 9, 1919, Wilson Papers, Ser. 6A.

19. Phillips to American Commissioners, Mar. 28, 1919, Bliss Papers; R. H. Lord to Bullitt, Jan. 19, 1919, Henry White Papers; Polk to American Commissioners, Jan. 11, 1919, White Papers; Wilson to Lansing, Mar. 28, 1919, Wilson Papers, Ser. 5B; Levin, *Woodrow Wilson and World Politics,* 200–202; Mayer, *Politics and Diplomacy of Peacemaking,* 338–39.

20. American Commissioners to Secy. of State, Apr. 2, 1919, and Phillips to American Commissioners, Apr. 4, 1919 (two letters), Bliss Papers.

21. Polk to Lansing, Apr. 24, 1919; Bliss Memo, June 21, 1919; Bliss to Col. Archibald Hopkins, June 10, 1919, all in Bliss Papers; President's Response to Senate Resolution as to the Reason for Retaining American Troops in Siberia, July 25, 1919, Breckinridge Long Papers; N. Baker to Tumulty, July 22, 1919, Tumulty to Baker, June 30, 1919, Baker to Tumulty, July 1, 1919, all in N. Baker Papers.

22. American Commissioners to State Dept., Jan. 8, 1919, Bliss Papers.

23. Polk to Lansing, Mar. 13, 1919, Bliss Papers. See also Phillips to American Commissioners, Mar. 28, 1919, Bliss Papers.

24. Wilson to N. Baker, May 20, 1919, and Baker to Wilson, May 20, 1919, N. Baker Papers.

25. Polk to American Commissioners, Mar. 9, 1919, and Phillips to American Commissioners, Mar. 29, 1919, Bliss Papers; McCormick Diary entry, Apr. 21, 1919, Wilson Papers, Ser. 14; Polk to American Commissioners, Apr. 28 and May 6, 1919, and Poole to American Commissioners, May 7, 1919, Bliss Papers; Notes of a Meeting of Big Four, May 10 and 19, 1919, and Notes of a Meeting, May 7, 1919, Wilson Papers, Ser. 6A; Wilson

to Tumulty, May 14, 1919 (two letters), and McCormick to Wilson, June 24, 1919, Wilson Papers, Ser. 5B.

26. Bliss to Wilson, May 8, 1919, Bliss Papers, and May 9, 1919, Wilson Papers, Ser. 5B; Notes of a Meeting of Big Three, May 9, 1919, Wilson Papers, Ser. 6A.

27. Levin, *Woodrow Wilson and World Politics*, 225; Draft of Message, Allied Powers to Kolchak, May 23, 1919, Wilson Papers, Ser. 5B; Notes of a Meeting of Big Four and Japan, May 24, 1919, and Notes of a Meeting of Big Four, May 23, 1919, Wilson Papers, Ser. 6A; Polk to American Commissioners, May 27, 1919, Bliss Papers; American Commissioners to Wilson, May 26, 1919, Wilson to Lansing, May 27, 1919, and Lansing to Wilson, May 28, 1919, Wilson Papers, Ser. 5B.

28. Notes of a Meeting of Big Four, June 7, 1919, and Notes of a Meeting of Big Four and Japan, June 17, 1919, Wilson Papers, Ser. 6A; McCormick Diary entry, June 22, 1919, Wilson Papers, Ser. 14; Wilson to Lansing, June 24, 1919, and Hapgood to Wilson, May 26, 1919, Wilson Papers, Ser. 5B; Notes of a Meeting of Heads of Delegation of Big Five, July 25, 1919, Notes of a Meeting of Big Five, June 25, 1919, and Notes of a Meeting of Heads of Delegation of Big Five, Aug. 8, 1919, Wilson Papers, Ser. 6A.

29. Levin, *Woodrow Wilson and World Politics*, 224–25, 228–29; American Commissioners to State Dept., June 25, 1919, Bliss Papers; Miles to Breckinridge Long, Aug. 26, 1919, Long Papers.

30. Lansing Diary entry, July 31, 1919, Lansing Papers; Lansing to American Embassy, Tokyo, Aug. 28, 1919, Breckinridge Long Papers; N. Baker to Lansing, Aug. 29, 1919, N. Baker Papers; Memo by Long, Aug. 29, 1919, Long Papers; Lansing to Wilson, Aug. 30, 1919, Wilson Papers, Ser. 2; Lansing to Baker, Aug. 30, 1919, N. Baker Papers; Wilson to Baker, Aug. 21, 1919, N. Baker Papers.

31. Lansing to Wilson, June 20, 1919, Wilson Papers, Ser. 5B; N. Baker to Graves, Sept. 26, 1919, N. Baker Papers; Lansing Diary entry, Oct. 9, 1919, and Lansing Memo, Nov. 30, 1919, Lansing Diary, Lansing Papers; Graves to Baker, Jan. 26, 1919, N. Baker Papers.

32. Link, *Wilson the Diplomatist*, 117–18; Lansing Diary entry, "Memo on Post-Bellum Conditions and Bolshevism," Oct. 28, 1919, Lansing Papers.

33. Bliss Diary entry, Feb. 26, 1919, Bliss Papers.

34. American Commissioners to Secy. of State, Jan. 3, 1919, and Polk to Lansing, Jan. 6, 1919, White Papers.

35. American Commissioners to Secy. of State, Jan. 3, 1919, Bliss Papers; White to Henry Cabot Lodge, Jan. 8, 1919, Wilson Papers, Ser. 5B; Palmer, *Bliss*, 368.

36. Bliss Diary entry, Jan. 7, 1919, Bliss Papers.

37. Wilson to Lansing, Jan. 10, 1919, and Wilson to Tumulty, Jan. 10, 1919, Wilson Papers, Ser. 5B; Notes of a Meeting of the SWC, Jan. 12, 1919, Wilson Papers, Ser. 6A; Edward Mezes to Wilson, Jan. 16, 1919, Wilson Papers, Ser. 5B; American Commissioners to State Dept., Feb. 3, 1919, Bliss Papers.

38. Mayer, *Politics and Diplomacy of Peacemaking*, 431–65, 464–71; Levin, *Woodrow Wilson and World Politics*, 206–18, 212–20. See also Bliss Diary entry, Jan. 19, 1919; American Commissioners to State Dept., Feb. 14, 1919; and Polk to Lansing, Jan. 12, 1919, all in Bliss Papers.

39. Polk to American Commissioners, Jan. 21, 1919, and Poole to American Commissioners, Jan. 22, 1919, Bliss Papers; Memo for CNO from H. E. Yarull, Feb. 6, 1919, Daniels Papers. See also Embick, "Aims of Russian Governments," Feb. 18, 1919, Bliss Papers.

40. Bliss to Hopkins, Feb. 12, 1919, Bliss Papers.

300 / *Notes*

41. Peace Conference Minutes, Feb. 15, 1919, Wilson Papers, Ser. 6A; Lansing to Wilson, Feb. 17, 1919, Wilson Papers, Ser. 5B; Bliss to House, Feb. 17, 1919, and Bliss to Balfour, Feb. 17, 1919, Bliss Papers.

42. Minutes of Daily Meeting of American Commissioners, Feb. 17, 1919; Notes on Policy Toward Russia after Prinkipo, Feb. 1919, Miscellaneous Memo File; Minutes of Daily Meeting of American Commissioners, Feb. 18, 1919; and Minutes of Conference of Military Representatives, Feb. 18, 1919, all in Bliss Papers.

43. Wilson to American Commissioners, Feb. 19, 1919; House to Wilson, Feb. 19, 1919; Wilson to House, Feb. 20, 1919; and American Commissioners to Wilson, Feb. 23, 1919, all in Wilson Papers, Ser. 5B.

44. Bliss to American Commissioners, Feb. 26, 1919, and Minutes of Daily Meeting of American Commissioners, Feb. 28, 1919, Bliss Papers. See also U. S. Grant to Wilson, Mar. 17, 1919, Wilson papers, Ser. 5B.

45. Nicholas Roosevelt, "The Hungarian Revolution," Mar. 26, 1919 (two documents); Stovall to Wilson, Mar. 27, 1919; Arthur Frazier to House, May 17, 1919; and Foch to Wilson, Mar. 27, 1919, all in Wilson Papers, Ser. 5B.

46. Bliss to Wilson, Mar. 28, 1919; Lansing to Wilson, Mar. 24, 1919; Herbert Hoover to Wilson, Mar. 28, 1919, all in Wilson Papers, Ser. 5B; Levin, *Woodrow Wilson and World Politics,* 191.

47. Levin, *Woodrow Wilson and World Politics,* 191–95; Mayer, *Politics and Diplomacy of Peacemaking,* 827–84; Notes of a Meeting, Apr. 26, 1919, Wilson Papers, Ser. 6A; Bliss to Wilson, June 10, 1919, Wilson Papers, Ser. 5B.

48. Bliss, "Remarks at Council of Four," Mar. 27, 1919, Bliss Papers; Bliss to N. Baker, undated and Oct. 5, 1919, N. Baker Papers.

49. Lansing to Wilson, Mar. 31, 1919, and Wilson to American Commissioners, ca. Apr. 1, 1919, Wilson Papers, Ser. 5B; Hugh Gibson to Bliss, Mar. 29, 1919, Bliss Papers; Lansing to Wilson, Aug. 7, 1919, Wilson Papers, Ser. 2.

EPILOGUE

1. Wilson, "Speech, Preliminary Peace Conference, Protocol Number 2," Jan. 25, 1919, Wilson Papers, Ser. 6A.

2. Wilson, "Address to Congress," Jan. 20, 1918, in August Hecksher, ed., *The Politics of Woodrow Wilson,* 303; Baker to Wilson, Jan. 1, 1919, Wilson Papers, Ser. 5B. For views of other administration personnel, particularly the military, on disarmament, see Bliss to Baker, Oct. 23, 1918, Bliss Papers; White to Wilson, Apr. 12, 1919, Wilson Papers, Ser. 5B; Pershing to Bliss, May 2, 1919, Bliss Diary entry, Dec. 22, 1918, Bliss to Lansing, Jan. 13, 1919, Staff memo to Bliss, Feb. 3, 1919, Bliss to Seward Prosser, Mar. 6, 1919, and Bliss to Hamilton Holt, Oct. 11, 1918, all in Bliss Papers; N. Baker to Wilson, Nov. 23, 1918, Wilson Papers, Ser. 5A; Bliss to Lansing, Dec. 16, 1918, Bliss Papers; House to Wilson, Jan. 25, 1919, Wilson Papers, Ser. 5B; Bliss to Lansing, Apr. 19, 1919, Bliss Papers.

3. Wilson, "Address at Indianapolis, Indiana," Sept. 4, 1919, in *The Messages and Papers of Woodrow Wilson* 2:746. For other speeches in which Wilson made this point, see the following from *Messages and Papers:* "Address at St. Louis, Missouri," Sept. 15, 1919, 2:765; "Address at Des Moines, Iowa," Sept. 6, 1919, 2:799; "Address at Omaha, Nebraska," Sept. 8, 1919, 2:809; "Address at Bismark, North Dakota," Sept. 10, 1919, 2:862; "Address at Helena, Montana," Sept. 11, 1919, 2:891; "Address at Spokane, Washington," Sept. 13, 1919, 2:913; "Address at Seattle, Washington," Sept. 13, 1919,

2:941; "Address at San Francisco, California," Sept. 17, 1919, 2:988; "Address at San Diego, California," Sept. 19, 1919, 2:1032; "Address at Reno, Nevada," Sept. 22, 1919, 2:1056; "Address at Salt Lake City, Utah," Sept. 23, 1919, 2:1071, 1080; "Address at Cheyenne, Wyoming," Sept. 24, 1919, 2:1090, 1094, 1097; "Address at Pueblo, Colorado," Sept. 25, 1919, 2:1120; and "Address to Pro-League Republicans," Oct. 27, 1920, 2:1209. See also Wilson to Lansing, May 24, 1919, Wilson Papers, Ser. 5B, and Bliss to Walter Willman, Dec. 30, 1918.

4. Benson to Daniels, Feb. 22, 1919, and Wilson to Daniels, Mar. 1, 1919, Daniels Papers; Daniels to Wilson, Mar. 4, 1919, Wilson Papers, Ser. 5B, and Mar. 4, 1919, Daniels Papers; Benson to Wilson, Apr. 28 and May 5, 1919, and Wilson to Benson, May 6, 1919, Wilson Papers, Ser. 5B; Wilson, "Address at Cour D'Alene, Idaho," Sept. 12, 1919, 2:909; "Address at Billings, Montana," Sept. 11, 1919, 2:875; and "Address at Seattle, Washington," Sept. 13, 1919, 2:944, all in *Messages and Papers,* pages cited.

5. Wilson, "Address at St. Louis, Missouri," Sept. 5, 1919, in *Messages and Papers* 2:773. See also from *Messages and Papers:* "Address at Des Moines, Iowa," Sept. 6, 1919, 2:799; "Address at St. Paul, Minnesota," Sept. 9, 1919, 2:844; "Address at San Francisco, California," Sept. 17, 1919, 2:966; "Address at San Diego, California," Sept. 19, 1919, 2:1030; "Address at St. Louis, Missouri," Sept. 5, 1919, 2:771–72; "Address at Sioux Falls, South Dakota, "Sept. 8, 1919, 2:821; "Address at Billings, Montana," Sept. 11, 1919, 2:870; "Address at Denver, Colorado," Sept. 25, 1919, 2:1108; "Address at Pueblo, Colorado," Sept. 25, 1919, 2:1127.

6. Wilson, "Address at Sioux Falls, South Dakota," Sept. 8, 1919, in *Messages and Papers* 2:821.

7. Wilson, "Opening Discussion of League of Nations," Jan. 25, 1919, 2:618; "Address at Boston, Massachusetts," Feb. 24, 1919, 2:639; "Address at Cheyenne, Wyoming," Sept. 24, 1919, 2:1037; all in *Messages and Papers,* pages cited.

8. Mayer, *Politics and Diplomacy of Peacemaking;* Wilson to Gen. Jan Smuts, May 16, 1919, and Wilson to Dr. George Herron, Apr. 28, 1919, Wilson Papers, Ser. 5B; Lansing Diary entry, "Greatest Loss Caused by the War Is Idealism Destroyed," May 6, 1919, Lansing Papers.

9. Wilson, "Address at Tacoma, Washington," Sept. 13, 1919, 2:931; "Address at Seattle, Washington," Sept. 13, 1919, 2:939–40; "Opening Discussion of League of Nations," Jan. 25, 1919, 2:620, all in *Messages and Papers,* pages cited; Lansing to Bliss, Dec. 16, 1918, Bliss Papers. See also Tumulty to Wilson, Dec. 31, 1918, Wilson Papers, Ser. 5B.

10. Wilson, "Address at St. Paul, Minnesota," Sept. 9, 1919, in *Messages and Papers* 2:852. See also Lansing to House, Apr. 8, 1919, and Lansing Diary entry, "Memo on League of Nations," Sept. 30, 1918, Lansing Papers; Wilson, "Address at Tacoma, Washington," Sept. 13, 1919, 2:927; "Address at Los Angeles, California," Sept. 20, 1919, 2:1040; "Address at Oakland, California," Sept. 18, 1919, 2:1011, all in *Messages and Papers,* pages cited. See also Lansing Diary entry, "Memo on an International Guaranty of Territory and Independence," Nov. 22, 1918, Lansing Papers; Bliss to Lansing, Dec. 15, 1918, Bliss Papers.

11. Wilson, "Report of Commission of the League," Feb. 14, 1919, in *Messages and Papers* 2:636, 637. See also Bliss to Baker, Jan. 21, 1919, Baker Papers.

12. Wilson, "Address at International Law Society," May 9, 1919, in *Messages and Papers* 2:668–70.

13. House to Wilson, Jan. 19, 1919, Wilson Papers, Ser. 5B; Lansing Diary entry, "Memo on Principle Which Should Govern the Congress of Paris," Nov. 18, 1918,

Lansing Papers; Lansing to Wilson, Jan. 22 and 31, 1919, Wilson Papers, Ser. 5B.

14. Lansing Diary entries, "President's Ideas of Peace in the Winter of 1917," July 29, 1919, and "Memo on Certain Essentials of a Stable Peace," Oct. 24, 1917, Lansing Papers.

15. Fifth Plenary Session, Apr. 28, 1919, Wilson Papers, Ser. 5B.

16. Wilson, "Address at Helena, Montana," Sept. 11, 1919, in *Messages and Papers* 2:896. See also from *Messages and Papers:* "Address at Reno, Nevada," Sept. 22, 1919, 2:1064; "Address at Cheyenne, Wyoming," Sept. 24, 1919, 2:1090; "Address at Denver, Colorado," Sept. 25, 1919, 2:1108.

17. Wilson, "Address at Kansas City, Missouri," Sept. 6, 1919, in *Messages and Papers* 2:784.

18. Wilson, "Address at San Diego, California," Sept. 19, 1919, in *Messages and Papers* 2:1017, 1024.

19. Lansing Diary entries, "Terms of Peace to Germany," May 8, 1919, and "Future Basis of Foreign Policies of U.S.," June 9, 1919, Lansing Papers.

20. Breckinridge Long to Wilson, Nov. 11, 1918, Long Papers.

21. Bliss to N. Baker, Feb. 14, 1919, N. Baker Papers.

22. Wilson, "Presenting Report on League," Feb. 14, 1919, in *Messages and Papers* 2:618, 621.

23. Benson to Wilson, Mar. 18, 1919, and Bliss to Wilson, Mar. 14, 1919, Wilson Papers, Ser. 5B; Lansing Diary entry, "Impressions as to the Present Situation," Mar. 20, 1919, Lansing Papers; Minutes of Daily Meeting of American Commissioners, Mar. 20 and 21, 1919, Bliss Papers; Notes Taken by Wilson at Big Four Meeting in Paris, Mar. 27, 1919, Wilson Papers, Ser. 6A; White to Wilson, Apr. 16, 1919, and Wilson to White, Apr. 17, 1919, Wilson Papers, Ser. 5B; "Discussion in Minutes about Guarantee to France," Apr. 22, 1919, Wilson Papers, Ser. 6A; Bliss to Holt, May 1, 1919, Bliss Papers; Wilson to Tumulty, ca. Apr. 23, 1919, Wilson Papers, Ser. 5B; "Discussion in Minutes about Guarantee to France," May 6, 1919, and "Discussion and Copy of Guarantee to France," May 6, 1919, Wilson Papers, Ser. 6A.

24. Wilson, "Address at Boston, Massachusetts," Feb. 24, 1919, in *Messages and Papers* 2:643; Wilson, Notes for speech at Boston, Feb. 24, 1919, Wilson Papers, Ser. 5B; Wilson, "Announcement of League of Nations," June 28, 1919, in *Messages and Papers* 2:693. See also Wilson, "Address on Return from Second Trip to Europe," July 8, 1919, 2:696, and "Address before Belgian Parliament," June 19, 1919, 2:689, both in *Messages and Papers*, pages cited.

25. Wilson, "Address before Senate," July 10, 1919, in *Messages and Papers* 2:709, 710–11, 712.

26. The speeches of Wilson's western speaking tour are quoted in *Messages and Papers* 2:727–1113.

27. Wilson to Tumulty, June 23, 1919, Wilson Papers, Ser. 5B.

28. Robert Dallek, *Franklin Delano Roosevelt and American Foreign Policy, 1932–1945*, 11–20, 29–30, 421, 438–39, 536; Townsend Hoopes, *The Devil and John Foster Dulles*, 32, 48, 55–56, 60, 61, 189, 199, 379, 431, 438, 439; Henry Kissinger, *White House Years*, 79.

29. Wilson, "Speech at Preliminary Peace Conference, Protocol Number 3," Feb. 14, 1919, Wilson Papers, Ser. 6A; Wilson, "Address at New York City," Mar. 4, 1919, 2:651; "Address before Belgian Parliament," June 19, 1919, 2:689; "Address at Reno, Nevada," Sept. 22, 1919, 2:1065; "Address at Helena, Montana," Sept. 11, 1919, 2:897, all in *Messages and Papers*, pages cited.

BIBLIOGRAPHY

Unpublished Personal Papers

Anderson, Chandler P. Library of Congress Manuscript Division, Washington, D.C.
Baker, Newton D. Library of Congress Manuscript Division, Washington, D.C.
Baker, Ray S. Library of Congress Manuscript Division, Washington, D.C.
Barnett, Major General George. Marine Corps Historical Center, Collections Branch, Navy Yard, Washington, D.C.
Benson, Admiral William S. Library of Congress Manuscript Division, Washington, D.C.
Bliss, General Tasker H. Library of Congress Manuscript Division, Washington, D.C.
Breckinridge, Henry. Library of Congress Manuscript Division, Washington, D.C.
Bryan, William Jennings. Library of Congress Manuscript Division, Washington, D.C.
Butler, General Smedley D. Marine Corps Historical Center, Collections Branch, Navy Yard, Washington, D.C.
Caperton, Admiral William B. Library of Congress Manuscript Division, Washington, D.C.
Church, William C. Library of Congress Manuscript Division, Washington, D.C.
Crowder, General Enoch H. Western Historical Manuscripts Collection, State Historical Society of Missouri Manuscripts, Columbia, Missouri.
Daniels, Josephus. Library of Congress Manuscript Division, Washington, D.C.
Dewey, Admiral George. Library of Congress Manuscript Division, Washington, D.C.
Fiske, Bradley A. Library of Congress Manuscript Division, Washington, D.C.
Funston, General Frederick. Kansas State Historical Society, Topeka, Kansas.
Garfield, James R. Library of Congress Manuscript Division, Washington, D.C.
Hoover, Irwin H. Library of Congress Manuscript Division, Washington, D.C.
Lansing, Robert. Library of Congress Manuscript Division, Washington, D.C.
Leahy, Admiral William D. Library of Congress Manuscript Division, Washington, D.C.
LeJeune, General John. Library of Congress Manuscript Division, Washington, D.C.
Lind, John. The Mexican Mission Papers of John Lind. Microfilm copy in

304 / *Bibliography*

Library of Congress of original in the Minnesota Historical Society, Minneapolis, Minnesota.
Long, Breckinridge. Library of Congress Manuscript Division, Washington, D.C.
McAdoo, William G. Library of Congress Manuscript Division, Washington, D.C.
McCoy, Frank Ross. Library of Congress Manuscript Division, Washington, D.C.
March, Peyton C. Library of Congress Manuscript Division, Washington, D.C.
Moore, John B. Library of Congress Manuscript Division, Washington, D.C.
Pendleton, General Joseph H. Marine Corps Historical Center, Collections Branch, Navy Yard, Washington, D.C.
Pershing, General John J. Library of Congress Manuscript Division, Washington, D.C.
Reid, General George C., Jr. Marine Corps Historical Center, Collections Branch, Navy Yard, Washington, D.C.
Russell, Major General John H. Marine Corps Historical Center, Collections Branch, Navy Yard, Washington, D.C.
Scott, General Hugh L. Library of Congress Manuscript Division, Washington, D.C.
Sims, Admiral William S. Library of Congress Manuscript Division, Washington, D.C.
Tumulty, Joseph. Library of Congress Manuscript Division, Washington, D.C.
Vandegrift, General Alexander. Marine Corps Historical Center, Collections Branch, Navy Yard, Washington, D.C.
Vogel, General C. B. Marine Corps Historical Center, Collections Branch, Navy Yard, Washington, D.C.
Waller, General L. W. J. Marine Corps Historical Center, Collections Branch, Navy Yard, Washington, D.C.
White, Henry. Library of Congress Manuscript Division, Washington, D.C.
Wilson, Edith B. Library of Congress Manuscript Division, Washington, D.C.
Wilson, Woodrow. Library of Congress Manuscript Division, Washington, D.C.
Wood, Leonard. Library of Congress Manuscript Division, Washington, D.C.

Unpublished Government Documents and Records

U.S. Department of the Army. Records of the Adjutant General's Office. Old Army and Navy Branch. Record Group 94. National Archives.
———. Records of the Bureau of Insular Affairs Relating to the Dominican Customs Receivership. Old Army and Navy Branch. Record Group 350. National Archives.
———. Records of the Dominican Customs Receivership. Old Army and Navy Branch. Record Group 139. National Archives.
———. Records of the Military Intelligence Division. Old Army and Navy Branch. Record Group 165. National Archives.

U.S. Department of the Navy. Bureau of Navigation General Correspondence, 1913–1925. Old Army and Navy Branch. Record Group 19. National Archives.
———. Naval Histories in the "Z" File. Old Army and Navy Branch. Record Group 45. National Archives.
———. Naval Records Collection of the Office of Naval Records and Library. Area File C (Caribbean). Old Army and Navy Branch. Record Group 45. National Archives.
———. Subject File, 1911–1927. Old Army and Navy Branch. Record Group 45. National Archives.
———. Subject File ZN (Personnel), 1911–1927. Old Army and Navy Branch. Record Group 45. National Archives.
———. WA-7 (Attachés Reports), 1911–1927. Old Army and Navy Branch. Record Group 45. National Archives.
———. WA-7, Dominican Republic-Santo Domingo. Old Army and Navy Branch. Record Group 45. National Archives.
———. Office of the Chief of Naval Operations. "Intervention in Haiti." Secretary's Files. Old Army and Navy Branch. Record Group 38. National Archives.
———. Records of the Military Government of Santo Domingo. Old Army and Navy Branch. Record Group 38. National Archives.
———. Records of the General Board of the Navy. Operational Archives. Naval Historical Center, Navy Yard, Washington, D.C.
———. Records of the Joint Army and Navy Board. Old Army and Navy Branch. Record Group 225. National Archives.
———. Records of the Navy Secretariat, Joint Army-Navy Board. Operational Archives, Naval Historical Center, Navy Yard, Washington, D.C.
———. Secretary of the Navy General Correspondence, 1897–1915. Old Army and Navy Branch. Record Group 80. National Archives.
———. Secretary of the Navy General Correspondence, 1916–1926. Old Army and Navy Branch. Record Group 80. National Archives.
U.S. Department of the Navy, U.S. Marine Corps. Marine Corps Adjutant and Inspector's Office. General Correspondence, 1913–1932 (Haiti). Old Army and Navy Branch. Record Group 127. National Archives.
———. Records of the U.S. Marine Corps. Office of the Commandant. Documents Selected from the Records of Various Organizations in Haiti and Nicaragua. Old Army and Navy Branch. Record Group 127. National Archives.
———. General Correspondence. Old Army and Navy Branch. Record Group 127. National Archives.
———. Haiti: General Correspondence of Headquarters. Gendarmerie d'Haiti, 1916–1919. Old Army and Navy Branch. Record Group 127. National Archives.
———. Haiti: General Correspondence of Headquarters. Gendarmerie d'Haiti, 1915–1926. Old Army and Navy Branch. Record Group 127. National Archives.
———. Haiti: General Correspondence of the Expeditionary Commander and

1st Brigade, 1915–1920. Old Army and Navy Branch. Record Group 127. National Archives.

———. Haiti: Reports of Conditions, 1918–1920. Old Army and Navy Branch. Record Group 127. National Archives.

———. Haiti: Special Correspondence of the Chief of the Gendarmerie d'Haiti, 1919–1920. Old Army and Navy Branch. Record Group 127. National Archives.

———. Records of Overseas Brigades, Battalions, and Regiments, 1889–1914. Old Army and Navy Branch. Record Group 127. National Archives.

———. Security: Classified General Correspondence, 1915–1937. Old Army and Navy Branch. Record Group 127. National Archives.

U.S. Department of State. Correspondence of Secretary of State Bryan with President Wilson, 1913–1915. State Department Branch. Record Group 59. National Archives.

———. Personal and Confidential Letters from Secretary of State Lansing to President Wilson. State Department Branch. Record Group 59. National Archives.

———. Records . . . Relating to Internal Affairs of Haiti, 1910–1929. State Department Branch. Record Group 59. National Archives.

———. Records . . . Relating to Internal Affairs of Mexico, 1910–1929. State Department Branch. Record Group 59. National Archives.

———. Records . . . Relating to Internal Affairs of the Dominican Republic, 1910–1929. State Department Branch. Record Group 59. National Archives.

———. U.S. Commissioners of the American and Mexican Joint Commission, 1916. Memoranda Furnished by the State Department, 1916. Gray-Lane Files, E-319. State Department Branch. Record Group 43. National Archives.

———. United States Participation in International Conferences, Commissions, and Expositions. U.S. Commissioners of the American and Mexican Joint Commission, 1916. Dispatches of John R. Silliman, Mexico City, 1914–1915, E-320. State Department Branch. Record Group 43. National Archives.

———. Dispatches from James Lewis Rodgers, 1916, E-326. State Department Branch. Record Group 43. National Archives.

———. Telegrams of James Lewis Rodgers, 1916, E-326. State Department Branch. Record Group 43. National Archives.

Oral History Interviews

Oral history interviews with the following are to be found in the Oral History Collection, Marine Corps Historical Center, Navy Yard, Washington, D.C.: Lieutenant General Edward A. Craig, Major General Pedro Del Valle, Brigadier General Lester A. Dessez, General Graves Ershine, Colonel William Lee, Major General DeWitt Peck, Major General Omar T. Pfeiffer, General Edwin A. Pollock, Major General Ford O. Rogers, Lieutenant General Christian F. Schilt, Major General Julian C. Smith, and Lieutenant General William J. Wallas.

Secondary Sources

A Chronicler. *Archangel: The American War With Russia.* New York: A. G. McClurg and Co., 1924.
Allard, Dean C. "Admiral William S. Sims and United States Naval Policy in World War I." *American Neptune* 35 (Apr. 1975): 97–110.
Allen, Henry T., *The Rhineland Occupation.* Indianapolis, Ind.: Bobbs-Merrill Co., 1927.
Allen, John H. "An Inside View of Revolutions in Haiti." *Current History* 32 (May 1930): 325–29.
Ancher, W. M. "The Imperialistic Mercenaries." *Marine Corps Gazette* 60 (Mar. 1976): 60.
Anderson, David D. *Woodrow Wilson.* Boston: Twayne Publishers, 1978.
Bailey, Thomas A. *Woodrow Wilson and the Lost Peace.* Chicago: Quadrangle Paperbacks, 1963.
Baker, Newton D. "America's Duty." *National Geographic* 31 (May 1917): 453–57.
———. "America's Purpose in the War." *Current History* 7 (Jan. 1918): 54–57.
———. *Frontiers of Freedom.* New York: Doran, 1918.
———. *Why We Went to War.* Reprint. Freeport N.Y.: Books for Libraries Press, 1972.
Baker, Ray S. *What Wilson Did at Paris.* Garden City, N.Y.: Doubleday, Page and Co., 1920.
———. *Woodrow Wilson Life and Letters.* 9 vols. Reprint. Westport, Conn.: Greenwood Press, 1968.
Baker, Ray S., and William E. Dodd, eds. *The Public Papers of Woodrow Wilson: College and State.* 2 vols. New York: Harper and Brothers, 1925.
———. *The Public Papers of Woodrow Wilson: The New Democracy.* 2 vols. New York: Harper and Brothers, 1926.
———. *The Public Papers of Woodrow Wilson: War and Peace.* 2 vols. New York: Harper and Brothers, 1927.
Balch, Emily. *Occupied Haiti.* New York: The Writers Publishing Co., 1927.
Bane, Suda L., and Ralph H. Lutz, eds. *The Blockade of Germany After the Armistice, 1918–1919.* Stanford, Calif.: Stanford Univ. Press, 1922.
Baughman, C. C. "United States Occupation of the Dominican Republic." *U.S. Naval Institute Proceedings* 51 (Dec. 1925): 2306–7.
Baughman, F., et al. *The Seizure of Haiti by the United States.* New York: Foreign Policy Association, 1922.
Beacker, Thomas. "The Arms of the 'Ypiranga': The German Side." *The Americas* 30 (July 1973): 1–17.
Beaver, Daniel R. *Newton D. Baker and the American War Effort, 1917–1919.* Lincoln: Univ. of Nebraska Press, 1966.
Beers, Burton F. *Vain Endeavor: Robert Lansing's Attempts to End the American Japanese Rivalry.* Durham, N.C.: Duke Univ. Press, 1962.
Beers, Henry P. *U.S. Naval Forces in Northern Russia (Archangel and Mur-*

mansk), *1918–1919*. Washington, D.C.: Navy Department, Administrative Reference Service Report, No. 5, 1943.

Bell, Sidney. *Righteous Conquest: Woodrow Wilson and the Evolution of the New Diplomacy.* Port Washington, N.Y.: Kennikat Press, 1972.

Bernard, L. L. *War and Its Causes.* New York: Henry Holt and Co., 1944.

Bernardo, C. Joseph, and Eugene H. Bacon. *American Military Policy: Its Development Since 1775.* Harrisburg, Pa.: Military Publishing Service, 1955.

Bernstorff, Count Johann. *The Memoirs of Count Bernstorff.* London: William Heinemann, Ltd., 1936.

―――. *My Three Years in America.* New York: Charles Scribner's Sons, 1920.

Bishop, William. *International Law: Cases and Materials.* Boston: Little, Brown and Co., 1971.

Blessingame, John W. "The Press and American Intervention in Haiti and the Dominican Republic." *Caribbean Studies* 9 (July 1969): 27–43.

Blum, John Morton. *Woodrow Wilson and the Politics of Morality.* Boston: Little, Brown and Co., 1956.

Blumenson, Martin, ed. *The Patton Papers.* 2 vols. Boston: Houghton Mifflin Co., 1972–74.

Blythe, Samuel G. "The Record of a Conference with President Woodrow Wilson." *Saturday Evening Post* 186 (May 23, 1914): 383–91.

Braddy, Haldeen. *Pershing's Mission in Mexico.* El Paso: Texas Western Press, 1966.

Bradley, John F. N. *Allied Intervention in Russia.* New York: Basic Books, Inc., 1968.

Branson, Leon, and George W. Goethals, eds. *War: Studies from Psychology, Sociology, Anthropology.* New York: Basic Books, Inc., 1964.

Breen, William J. *Uncle Sam at Home: Civilian Mobilization, Wartime Federalism, and the Council of National Defense, 1917–1919.* Westport, Conn.: Greenwood Press, 1984.

Brinkley, George A. *The Volunteer Army and Allied Intervention in South Russia, 1917–1921.* Notre Dame, Ind.: Univ. of Notre Dame Press, 1966.

Bryan, William Jennings, and Mary Bryan. *Memoirs of William Jennings Bryan.* Philadelphia: John C. Winston Co., 1925.

Buehrig, E. H. *Woodrow Wilson and the Balance of Power.* Bloomington: Univ. of Indiana Press, 1955.

Buell, Raymond L. *The American Occupation of Haiti.* New York: Foreign Policy Association Information Service, 1929.

Bullitt, William C. *The Bullitt Mission to Russia: Testimony Before the Committee on Foreign Relations, U.S. Senate.* Westport, Conn.: Hyperion Press, Inc., 1919.

Bunyan, James. *Intervention, Civil War, and Communism in Russia, April–December 1918.* New York: Octagon Books, 1976.

Burks, Arthur J. *Land of Checkerboard Families.* New York: Coward-McCann, Inc., 1932.

Calder, Bruce J. *The Impact of Intervention: The Dominican Republic During the U.S. Occupation of 1916–1924.* Austin: Univ. of Texas Press, 1984.

Calero, Manual. *The Mexican Policy of President Wilson as it Appears to a Mexican*. New York: Press of Smith and Thomason, 1916.
Callahan, James M. *American Foreign Policy in Mexican Relations*. New York: Macmillan, 1932.
Callcott, Wilfred H. *The Caribbean Policy of the United States, 1890–1920*. Baltimore, Md.: The Johns Hopkins Press, 1942.
Calvert, Peter. *The Mexican Revolution, 1910–1914: The Diplomacy of Anglo-American Conflict*. Cambridge: Cambridge at the University Press, 1968.
Canfield, Leon H. *The Presidency of Woodrow Wilson: Prelude to a World in Crisis*. Rutherford, N.J.: Fairleigh Dickinson Univ. Press, 1966.
Challener, Richard D. *Admirals, Generals, and American Foreign Policy, 1898–1914*. Princeton, N.J.: Princeton Univ. Press, 1973.
―――, ed. *United States Military Intelligence, 1917–1927*. New York: Garland Publishing Co., 1978–.
Clarkson, Grosvenor B. *Industrial America in the World War: The Strategy Behind the Line, 1917–1918*. Boston: Houghton Mifflin Co., 1923.
Clausewitz, Carl von. *On War*. Edited by Michael Howard and Peter Paret. Princeton, N.J.: Princeton Univ. Press, 1976.
Clements, Kendrick A. "Woodrow Wilson's Mexican Policy, 1913–1915." *Diplomatic History* 4 (Spring 1980): 113–36.
Clendenen, Clarence C. *Blood on the Border: The U.S. Army and the Mexican Irregulars*. New York: Macmillan Co., 1969.
―――. *The U.S. and Pancho Villa: A Study in Unconventional Diplomacy*. Ithaca, N.Y.: Cornell Univ. Press, 1961.
Cline, Howard F. *The United States and Mexico*. Cambridge: Harvard Univ. Press, 1953.
Coffman, Edward M. *The War to End All Wars*. New York: Oxford Univ. Press, 1968.
Cooper, John Milton, Jr. *The Vanity of Power: American Isolationism and World War I*. Westport, Conn.: Greenwood Press, 1969.
―――. *Walter Hines Page: The Southerner as American*. Chapel Hill: Univ. of North Carolina Press, 1977.
―――. *The Warrior and the Priest: Woodrow Wilson and Teddy Roosevelt*. Cambridge, Mass.: Belknap Press, 1983.
Cotner, Thomas E., and Carlos E. Castaneda, eds. *Essays in Mexican History*. Austin: Univ. of Texas Press, 1958.
Craige, John Houston. *Cannibal Cousins*. New York: Menton, Balch and Co., 1934.
Cramer, Clarence H. *Newton D. Baker*. Cleveland, Ohio: World Publishers, 1961.
Creel, George. *The War, the World, and Wilson*. New York: Harper and Brothers, 1920.
―――. *Wilson and the Issues*. New York: The Century Co., 1916.
Crowder, Enoch H. *The Spirit of Selective Service*. New York: The Century Co., 1920.

Crozier, William. *Ordnance and the World War: A Contribution to the History of American Preparedness.* New York: Charles Scribner's Sons, 1920.

Cumberland, Charles. "Border Raids in the Lower Rio Grande Valley—1915." *Southwestern Historical Quarterly* 55 (July 1953): 285–311.

Current, Richard N. "The United States and 'Collective Security': Notes on the History of an Idea." In Alexander DeConde, ed., *Isolation and Security*, 33–56. Durham, N.C.: Duke Univ. Press, 1957.

Dallek, Robert. *The American Style of Foreign Policy.* New York: Alfred A. Knopf, 1983.

———. *Franklin Delano Roosevelt and American Foreign Policy, 1932–1945.* New York: Oxford Univ. Press, 1979.

Danache, B. *Le Presidente Dartiguenave et Les Americaines.* Port-au-Prince, Haiti: Imprimière de l'état, 1950.

Daniels, Josephus. *The Cabinet Diaries of Josephus Daniels, 1913–1921.* Edited by E. David Cronon. Lincoln: Univ. of Nebraska Press, 1963.

———. *The Life of Woodrow Wilson.* Westport, Conn.: Greenwood Press, 1971.

———. *The Navy and the Nation.* New York: George H. Doran Co., 1919.

———. *Our Navy at War.* Washington, D.C.: Pictorial Bureau, 1922.

———. "The Problem of Haiti." *Saturday Evening Post* 32 (July 12, 1930): 32.

———. *The Wilson Era: Years of Peace, 1910–1917.* Chapel Hill: Univ. of North Carolina Press, 1944.

———. *The Wilson Era: Years of War, 1917–1919.* Chapel Hill: Univ. of North Carolina Press, 1944.

Daniels, Winthrop. *Recollections of Woodrow Wilson.* New Haven, Conn.: Privately Printed, 1944.

Davidson, John W., ed. *A Crossroads of Freedom: The 1912 Campaign Speeches of Woodrow Wilson.* New Haven, Conn.: Yale Univ. Press, 1956.

Davis, Harold P. *Black Democracy: The Story of Haiti.* New York: Dodge Publishing Co., 1936.

Day, Donald, ed. *Woodrow Wilson's Own Story.* Boston: Little, Brown and Co., 1952.

Devlin, Patrick. *Too Proud to Fight: Woodrow Wilson's Neutrality.* New York: Oxford Univ. Press, 1975.

Diamond, William. *The Economic Thought of Woodrow Wilson.* Baltimore, Md.: The Johns Hopkins Press, 1943.

Douglas, Paul H. "The American Occupation of Haiti." *Political Science Quarterly* 42 (1927): 228–58, 368–96.

Dunn, Frederick S. *The Diplomatic Protection of Americans in Mexico.* New York: Columbia Univ. Press, 1933.

Ekrich, Arthur A., Jr. *The Civilian and the Military.* New York: Oxford Univ. Press, 1956.

Emmett, Cris. *In the Path of Events with Colonel Martin Labor Crimmins.* Waco, Tex.: Jones and Morrison, Publishers, 1959.

Fagy, John Edwin. *Cuba, Haiti, and the Dominican Republic.* Englewood Cliffs, N.J.: Prentice-Hall, Inc., 1967.

Fellowes, Edward A. "Training Native Troops in Santo Domingo." *Marine Corps Gazette* 8 (Dec. 1923): 215–33.
Fischer, Fritz. *Germany's Aims in the First World War.* New York: W. W. Norton and Co., 1967.
Fiske, Bradley A. *From Midshipman to Rear Admiral.* New York: The Century Co., 1919.
———. *The Navy as a Fighting Machine.* New York: Charles Scribner's Sons, 1917.
Forster, Merlin H. "U.S. Intervention in Mexico: The 1914 Occupation of Veracruz." *Military Review* 57 (Aug. 1977): 88–96.
Freidel, Frank B. *Franklin D. Roosevelt: The Apprenticeship.* Boston: Little, Brown and Co., 1952.
Frothingham, Thomas G. *The Naval History of the World War.* 3 vols. Cambridge: Harvard Univ. Press, 1924–26.
Fuller, Stephen M., and Graham A. Cosmas. *Marines in the Dominican Republic, 1916–1924.* Washington, D.C.: History and Museums Division, Headquarters, U.S. Marine Corps, 1974.
Gardner, Lloyd C. *Wilson and Revolutions, 1913–1921.* Edited by Harald M. Hyman. New York: J. B. Lippincott Co., 1976.
Gelfand, Lawrence E. *The Inquiry: American Preparations for Peace, 1917–1919.* Princeton, N.J.: Princeton Univ. Press, 1957.
George, Alexander, and Juliette L. George. *Woodrow Wilson and Colonel House: A Personality Study.* New York: Dover Publications, Inc., 1964.
Gerard, James W. *My Four Years in Germany.* New York: Grosset and Dunlap, 1917.
Gerard, Jolyan P. "Congress and Presidential Military Policy: The Occupation of Germany, 1919–1923." *Mid-America* 56 (Oct. 1974): 211–20.
Gerlack, Allen. "Conditions Along the Border—1915: The Plan of San Diego." *New Mexico Historical Review* 43 (July 1968): 195–212.
Gilderhus, Mark T. *Diplomacy and Revolution: U.S.—Mexican Relations Under Wilson and Carranza.* Tuscon: Univ. of Arizona Press, 1977.
———. "The United States and Carranza, 1917: The Question of De Jure Recognition." *The Americas* 24 (Oct. 1972): 214–31.
Glaser, David. "1919: William Jenkins, Robert Lansing, and the Mexican Interlude." *Southwestern Historical Quarterly* 74 (Jan. 1971): 337–56.
Goebel, Julius. "The Recognition Policy of the United States." *Columbia University Studies in History, Economics, and Public Law* 66 (1915).
Goldwert, Marvin. *The Constabulary in the Dominican Republic and Nicaragua.* Gainesville: Univ. of Florida Press, 1962.
Goodelk, Stephen. "Woodrow Wilson in Latin America: Interpretations." *The Historian* 28 (Nov. 1965): 96–127.
Graves, William S. *America's Siberian Adventure, 1918–1920.* New York: J. Cape and H. Smith, 1931.
Grayson, Cary T. *Woodrow Wilson: An Intimate Memoir.* New York: Holt, Rinehart and Winston, 1960.

Greene, Fred. "The Military View of American National Policy, 1904–1940." *American Historical Review* 66 (Jan. 1961): 354–77.

Gregory, Ross. *The Origins of American Intervention in the First World War.* New York: W. W. Norton and Co., 1971.

Grenville, John A. S. "Diplomacy and War Plans in the United States, 1890–1917." *Royal Historical Society Transactions, 5th Series* 2 (1961): 1–21.

Grenville, John A. S., and George Young. *Politics, Strategy, and American Diplomacy.* New Haven, Conn.: Yale Univ. Press, 1966.

Grieb, Kenneth J. "The Lind Mission to Mexico." *Caribbean Studies* 7 (Jan. 1968): 25–43.

———. *The United States and Huerta.* Lincoln: Univ. of Nebraska Press, 1969.

Hackett, Charles W. *The Mexican Revolution and the United States, 1910–1926.* Boston: World Peace Foundation, 1926.

Hager, William H. "The Plan of San Diego: Unrest on the Texas Border in 1915." *Arizona and the West* 5 (Winter 1963): 327–36.

Haley, P. Edward. *Revolution and Intervention: The Diplomacy of Taft and Wilson with Mexico, 1910–1917.* Cambridge: The MIT Press, 1970.

Hall, William Edward. *A Treatise on International Law.* London: Clarendon Press, 1904.

Halliday, E. M. *The Ignorant Armies.* New York: Harper and Brothers, 1960.

Hammond, Paul Y. *Organizing for Defense: The American Military Establishment in the Twentieth Century.* Princeton, N.J.: Princeton Univ. Press, 1961.

Harris, Charles H., and Louis Sadler. "The Witzke Affair: German Intrigue on the Mexican Border 1917–1918." *Military Review* 59 (Feb. 1979): 36–50.

Hauberg, Clifford. *Latin American Revolutions.* Minneapolis, Minn.: T. S. Denison and Co., 1968.

Healy, David. *Gunboat Diplomacy in the Wilson Era: The U.S. Navy in Haiti, 1915–1916.* Madison: Univ. of Wisconsin Press, 1976.

Hecksher, August. *The Politics of Woodrow Wilson.* New York: Harper and Brothers, 1956.

Heinl, Robert Debs, and Nancy Gardner Heinl. "The American Occupation of Haiti." *Marine Corps Gazette* 62 (Nov. 1978): 28–41.

———. *Written in Blood: The Story of the Haitian People, 1492–1971.* Boston: Houghton Mifflin Co., 1978.

Hendrick, Burton J. *The Life and Letters of Walter H. Page.* 3 vols. New York: Doubleday, Page and Co., 1922–26.

Herman, Sondra. *Eleven Against War.* Stanford, Calif.: Hoover Institution Press, 1969.

Hickey, Des, and Gus Smith. *Seven Days to Disaster: The Sinking of the LUSITANIA.* New York: G. P. Putnam's Sons, 1981.

Hill, Larry D. *Emissaries to a Revolution: Woodrow Wilson's Executive Agents in Mexico.* Baton Rouge: Louisiana State Univ. Press, 1973.

———. "The Progressive Politician as a Diplomat: The Case of John Lind in Mexico." *The Americas* 27 (Apr. 1971): 355–72.

Hines, Calvin Warren. "The Mexican Punitive Expedition of 1916." Master's thesis, Trinity University, 1961.
Hittle, James D. *The Military Staff, Its History and Development*. Harrisburg, Pa.: Military Service Publishing Co., 1949.
Hobbs, Richard. *The Myth of Victory: What is Victory in War?* Boulder, Colo.: Westview Press, 1979.
Holley, Irving B., Jr. *Ideas and Weapons*. New Haven, Conn.: Yale Univ. Press, 1953.
Hoopes, Townsend. *The Devil and John Foster Dulles*. London: Andre Deutsch, Ltd. 1973.
Hopkins, J. A. H., and Melinda Alexander. *Machine-Gun Diplomacy*. New York: Lewis Copeland Co., 1928.
Houston, David F. *Eight Years With Wilson's Cabinet*. 2 vols. Garden City, N.Y.: Doubleday, Doran and Co., 1926.
Huntington, Samuel P. *The Soldier and the State*. Cambridge: Belknap Press, 1957.
Inman, Samuel Guy. *Intervention in Mexico*. New York: George H. Doran Co., 1919.
Iriye, Akira. *Across the Pacific: An Inner History of American-East Asian Relations*. New York: Harcourt, Brace and World, Inc., 1967.
―――. *From Nationalism to Internationalism: U.S. Foreign Policy to 1914*. London: Routledge and Kegan Paul, 1977.
Ironside, Edward. *Archangel, 1918–1919*. London: T. A. Constable, Ltd., 1953.
Janowitz, Morris. *The Professional Soldier: A Social and Political Portrait*. New York: The Free Press of Glencoe, Crowell-Collier Publishing Co., 1960.
Jessup, Phillip C. *Elihu Root*. 2 vols. New York: Dodd, Mead, 1938.
Juarez, Joseph Robert. "United States Withdrawal from Santo Domingo." *Hispanic American Historical Review* 42 (May 1962): 152–90.
Katz, Friedrich. "Pancho Villa and the Attack on Columbus, New Mexico." *American Historical Review* 83 (Feb. 1978): 334–36.
―――. *The Secret War in Mexico: Europe, the United States, and the Mexican Revolution*. Chicago: Univ. of Chicago Press, 1981.
Kelsey, Carl. "The American Intervention in Haiti and the Dominican Republic." *Annals of the American Academy of Political and Social Science* 100 (Mar. 1922): 110–99.
Kendall, Sylvian G. *American Soldiers in Siberia*. New York: Richard R. Smith, Publisher, 1945.
Kennan, George. *American Diplomacy 1900–1950*. Chicago: Univ. of Chicago Press, Phoenix Books, 1970.
―――. *The Decision to Intervene*. Princeton, N.J.: Princeton Univ. Press, 1958.
―――. "Russia and the Versailles Conference." *The American Scholar* 30 (Winter 1960): 13–42.
―――. *Russia and the West under Lenin and Stalin*. Boston: Houghton Mifflin Co., 1960.

Kennedy, David M. *Over Here: The First World War and American Society.* New York: Oxford Univ. Press, 1980.
Keynes, John Maynard. *The Economic Consequences of the Peace.* New York: Harcourt, Brace and Co., 1920.
Kilpatrick, Carroll, ed. *Roosevelt and Daniels: A Friendship in Politics.* Chapel Hill: Univ. of North Carolina Press, 1952.
Kissinger, Henry. *The White House Years.* Boston: Little, Brown and Co., 1979.
Knight, Melvin M. *The Americans in Santo Domingo.* New York: Vanguard Press, 1928.
Kohle, Luis G. "Robert Lansing and the Recognition of Venustiano Carranza." *Hispanic American Historical Review* 38 (Aug. 1958): 353–73.
Kolko, Gabriel. *The Triumph of Conservatism.* Chicago: Univ. of Chicago Press, 1967.
Kuehl, Warren. *Seeking World Order: The United States and International Organization to 1920.* Nashville: Vanderbilt Univ. Press, 1969.
Kyre, Martin, and Joan Kyre. *Military Occupation and National Security.* Washington, D.C.: Public Affairs Press, 1968.
Lamar, Clarinda H. *The Life of Joseph Rucker Lamar, 1857–1916.* New York: G. P. Putnam's Sons, 1926.
Lane, Anne W., and Louise H. Wall. *The Letters of Franklin K. Lane, Personal and Political.* Boston: Houghton Mifflin Co., 1922.
Lane, Jack C. *Armed Progressive.* San Rafael, Calif.: Presidio Press, 1978.
Lane, Rufus. "Civil Government in Santo Domingo in the Early Days of the Military Occupation." *Marine Corps Gazette* 7 (June 1922): 127–46.
Lansing, Robert. *The Peace Negotiations: A Personal Narrative.* New York: Houghton Mifflin Co., 1921.
―――. *War Memoirs of Robert Lansing.* Westport, Conn.: Greenwood Press, 1970.
Latham, Earl, ed. *The Philosophy and Policies of Woodrow Wilson.* Chicago: Univ. of Chicago Press, 1958.
Lawrence, David. *The True Story of Woodrow Wilson.* New York: George H. Doran Co., 1924.
Lawrence, T. J. *The Principles of International Law.* 4th ed. London: Macmillan, 1910.
Leighton, John L. *Simsadus: London: The American Navy in Europe.* New York: Henry Holt and Co., 1920.
Levin, N. Gordon, Jr. *Woodrow Wilson and World Politics: America's Response to War and Revolution.* New York: Oxford Univ. Press, 1968.
Leyburn, James G. *The Haitian People.* New Haven, Conn.: Yale Univ. Press, 1941.
Lieurven, Edwin. *U.S. Policy in Latin America.* New York: Frederick A. Praeger, 1965.
Link, Arthur. *The Higher Realism of Woodrow Wilson and Other Essays.* Nashville, Tenn.: Vanderbilt Univ. Press, 1971.
―――. *Wilson.* 5 vols. Princeton, N.J.: Princeton Univ. Press, 1947–.

———. *Wilson the Diplomatist*. Chicago: Quadrangle Paperbacks, 1963.
———. *Woodrow Wilson: Revolution, War, and Peace*. Arlington Heights, Ill.: A. H. M. Publishing Corporation, 1979.
———. *Woodrow Wilson and the Progressive Era: 1910–1917*. New York: Harper and Row, 1954.
———, ed. *The Papers of Woodrow Wilson*. 35 vols. Princeton, N.J.: Princeton Univ. Press, 1966–.
———, ed. *Woodrow Wilson: A Profile*. New York: Hill and Wang, 1968.
———. ed. *Woodrow Wilson and a Revolutionary World, 1913–1921*. Chapel Hill: Univ. of North Carolina Press, 1982.
Lippman, Walter. *Drift and Mastery: An Attempt to Diagnose the Current Unrest*. Englewood Cliffs, N.J.: Prentice-Hall, Inc. 1961.
Livermore, Seward W. *Politics Is Adjourned: Woodrow Wilson and the War Congress, 1916–1918*. Middletown, Conn.: Wesleyan Univ. Press, 1966.
Lockmiller, David A. *Enoch H. Crowder: Soldier, Lawyer, and Statesman*. The University of Missouri Studies, vol. 27. Columbia, Mo., 1955.
Lodge, Henry Cabot. *The Senate and the League of Nations*. New York: Charles Scribner's Sons, 1925.
Logan, Rayford. *Haiti and the Dominican Republic*. New York: Oxford Univ. Press, 1968.
———. "The United States Mission in Haiti, 1915–1932." *Inter-American Economic Affairs* 6 (Spring 1953): 18–28.
McAdoo, Eleanor. *The Woodrow Wilsons*. New York: Macmillan, 1937.
McAdoo, William G. *Crowded Years: The Reminiscences of William G. McAdoo*. Port Washington, N.Y.: Kennikat Press, 1971.
McCellen, Edwin N. "Operations Ashore in the Dominican Republic." *U.S. Naval Institute Proceedings* 47 (Feb. 1921): 235–45.
MacCorkle, Stuart A. *American Policy of Recognition Towards Mexico*. Baltimore, Md.: The Johns Hopkins Press, 1933.
MacCorkle, William A. *The Monroe Doctrine in Its Relation to the Republic of Haiti*. New York: Neale Publishing Co., 1915.
McCracklin, James H. *Garde d'Haiti, 1915–1934: Twenty Years of Organization and Training by the United States Marine Corps*. Annapolis, Md.: United States Naval Institute, 1956.
Machado, Manuel A., Jr. and James T. Judge. "Tempest or Teapot? The Mexican-United States of Intervention Crisis of 1919." *Southwestern Historical Quarterly* 74 (July 1970): 1–23.
Maddox, Robert J. *The Unknown War with Russia*. San Rafael, Calif.: Presidio Press, 1977.
Mahan, Alfred T. *The Influence of Sea Power Upon History, 1660–1783*. New York: Hill and Wang, 1957.
March, Peyton C. *The Nation at War*. Garden City, N.Y.: Doubleday, Doran and Co., 1932.
Matloff, Maurice. "The American Approach to War, 1919–1945." In Michael Howard, ed., *The Theory and Practice of War: Essays Presented to Captain Sir Basil Liddell Hart*, 213–46. London: Cassell, 1965.

———. *American Military History.* Washington, D.C.: Office of the Chief of Military History, U.S. Army, 1969.
May, Ernest R. "The Development of Political-Military Consultation in the U.S." *Political Science Quarterly* 70 (June 1955): 161–80.
———. *The Ultimate Decision.* New York: G. Brazeller, 1960.
———. *The World War and American Isolation, 1914–1917.* Chicago: Quadrangle Paperbacks, 1966.
Mayer, Arno J. *Political Origins of the New Diplomacy, 1917–1918.* New York: Vintage Books, 1970.
———. *Politics and Diplomacy of Peacemaking: Containment and Counterrevolution at Versailles, 1918–1919.* New York: Vintage Books, 1967.
Mee, Charles L., Jr. *The End of Order: Versailles, 1919.* New York: E. P. Dutton, 1980.
Merk, Frederick. *Manifest Destiny and Mission in American History.* New York: Vintage Books, 1966.
———. *The Monroe Doctrine and American Expansionism.* New York: Vintage Books, 1966.
Meyer, Michael C. "The Arms of the *Ypiranga.*" *Hispanic American Historical Review* 50 (Aug. 1970): 543–56.
———. *Huerta: A Political Portrait.* Lincoln: Univ. of Nebraska Press, 1972.
———. "The Mexican-German Conspiracy of 1915." *The Americas* 23 (July 1966): 76–89.
Miller, Charles I. "Diplomatic Spurs: Our Experiences in Santo Domingo." *Marine Corps Gazette* 19 (Feb. 1935): 43–50.
Mills, C. Wright. *The Power Elite.* New York: Oxford Univ. Press, 1956.
Mills, Walter. *Arms and Men: A Study in American Military History.* New York: Putnam, 1956.
Millspaugh, Arthur C. *Haiti Under American Control, 1915–1930.* Boston: World Peace Foundation, 1931.
Montague, Ludwell Lee. *Haiti and the United States 1714–1938.* Durham, N.C.: Duke Univ. Press, 1940.
Moore, John Bassett. *A Digest of International Law.* Washington, D.C.: Government Printing Office, 1906.
Morison, Elting E. *Admiral Sims and the Modern American Navy.* Boston: Houghton Mifflin Co., 1942.
Moskin, J. Robert. *The Story of the U.S. Marine Corps.* New York: Paddington Press, Ltd., 1979.
Motter, T. H. Vail. *Leaders of Men by Woodrow Wilson.* Princeton, N.J.: Princeton Univ. Press, 1952.
Mulder, John M. *Woodrow Wilson: The Years of Preparation.* Princeton, N.J.: Princeton Univ. Press, 1978.
Munro, Dana G. *Intervention and Dollar Diplomacy in the Caribbean, 1900–1921.* Princeton, N.J.: Princeton Univ. Press, 1964.
Nelson, Keith L. *Victors Divided: America and the Allies in Germany, 1918–1923.* Berkeley: Univ. of California Press, 1975.

Nelson, Otto L. *National Security and the General Staff.* Washington, D.C.: Infantry Journal Press, 1946.
Neubeck, Deborah K. *Guide to a Microfilm Edition of the Mexican Mission Papers of John Lind.* St. Paul: Minnesota Historical Society, 1971.
Nicolson, Harold. *Peacemaking 1919.* New York: Grosset and Dunlap, 1965.
Notter, Harley. *The Origins of the Foreign Policy of Woodrow Wilson.* Baltimore, Md.: The Johns Hopkins Press, 1937.
Olson, Keith W. *Biography of a Progressive: Franklin K. Lane, 1864–1921.* Westport, Conn.: Greenwood Press, 1979.
Oppenheim, Lassa Francis Lawrence. *International Law.* 2d ed. New York: Longmans, Green and Co., 1912.
Osborn, George C. "Woodrow Wilson Visits Mobile." *Alabama Historical Quarterly* 19 (1957): 157–69.
Osgood, Robert. *Ideals and Self-Interest in American Foreign Policy.* Chicago: Univ. of Chicago Press, Phoenix Books, 1965.
O'Shaughnessy, Edith. *A Diplomat's Wife in Mexico.* New York: Harper and Brothers, 1916.
———. *Intimate Pages of Mexican History.* New York: George H. Doran Co., 1920.
Padgett, James A. "Diplomats to Haiti and Their Diplomacy." *Journal of Negro History* 25 (July 1940): 265–330.
Palmer, Frederick. *Bliss, Peacemaker: The Life and Letters of General Tasker Howard Bliss.* New York: Dodd, Mead and Co., 1934.
———. *Newton D. Baker: America at War.* 2 vols. New York: Dodd, Mead and Co., 1931.
Palmer, John McAuley. *America in Arms: The Experience of the United States with Military Organization.* New Haven, Conn.: Yale Univ. Press, 1941.
Pappas, George S. *Prudens Future: The U.S. Army War College, 1901–1967.* Carlisle Barracks, Pa.: Alumni Association of U.S. Army War College, 1967.
Parker, James. *The Old Army: Memories 1872–1918.* Philadelphia, Pa.: Dorrance and Co., 1929.
Pearlman, Michael D. *To Make Democracy Safe for America: Patricians and Preparedness in the Progressive Era.* Champaign: Univ. of Illinois Press, 1984.
Pershing, John J. *My Experiences in the World War.* 2 vols. New York: Frederick A. Stokes Co., 1931.
Peterson, H. C., and Gilbert C. Fite. *Opponents of War, 1917–1918.* Seattle: Univ. of Washington Press, 1957.
Phillips, William. *Ventures in Diplomacy.* Portland, Maine: The Anthoesen Press, 1952.
Poetker, Joel S. *The Fourteen Points.* Columbus, Ohio: Charles E. Merrill Publishing Co., 1969.
Polk, James K. *Polk: The Diary of a President, 1845–1849.* Edited by Allan Nevens. New York: Longmans, Green and Co., 1952.
Posner, Walter H. "American Marines in Haiti, 1915–1922." *The Americas* 20 (Jan. 1964): 231–66.

Presidential Messages and State Papers, Vol. X: Wilson. New York: The Review of Reviews Co., 1917.

Quirk, Robert E. *An Affair of Honor: Woodrow Wilson and the Occupation of Veracruz.* Lexington: Univ. of Kentucky Press, 1962.

———. *The Mexican Revolution, 1914–1915: The Convention of Aquascalientes.* Bloomington: Indiana Univ. Press, 1960.

Radosh, Ronald. "John Spargo and Wilson's Russian Policy, 1920." *Journal of American History* 52 (Dec. 1965): 548–65.

Rausch, George J., Jr. "The Exile and Death of Victoriano Huerta." *Hispanic American Historical Review* 42 (May 1962): 133–51.

Ripley, Thomas W. *A Little Group of Willful Men.* Port Washington, N.Y.: Kennikat Press, 1975.

Rippy, J. Fred. "The Initiation of the Customs Receivership in the Dominican Republic." *Hispanic American Historical Review* 17 (Nov. 1937): 419–57.

———. *The United States and Mexico.* New York: Alfred A. Knopf, 1926.

Rodman, Selden. *Haiti: The Black Republic.* New York: Devin-Adair Co., 1954.

———. *Quisqueya: A History of the Dominican Republic.* Seattle: Univ. of Washington Press, 1964.

Rosenberg, Emily S. "World War I and 'Continental Solidarity,'" *The Americas* 30 (Jan. 1975): 313–34.

Rothberg, Robert J. *Haiti: The Politics of Squalor.* Boston: Houghton Mifflin Co., 1971.

Sandos, James A. "German Involvement in Northern Mexico, 1915–1916: A New Look at the Columbus Raid." *Hispanic American Historical Review* 50 (Feb. 1970): 70–88.

Schmidt, Hans. *The United States Occupation of Haiti, 1915–1934.* New Brunswick, N.J.: Rutgers Univ. Press, 1971.

Schoenrich, Otto. "The Present American Intervention in Santo Domingo and Haiti." In George H. Blakeslee, ed., *Mexico and the Caribbean,* 206–23. New York: G. E. Stechert and Co., 1920.

———. *Santo Domingo, a Country with a Future.* New York: Macmillan, 1918.

Schuman, Frederick L. *American Policy Toward Russia Since 1917.* Westport, Conn.: Hyperion Press, 1977.

Schwarz, Urs. *American Strategy: A New Perspective.* Garden City, N.Y.: Doubleday, 1966.

Scott, Hugh L. *Some Memories of a Soldier.* New York: Appleton Century, 1928.

Scott, James Brown, ed. *President Wilson's Foreign Policy: Messages, Addresses, Papers.* New York: Oxford Univ. Press, 1918.

Seligman, Herbert J. "The Conquest of Haiti." *Nation* 3 (July 10, 1920): 35–36.

Seymour, Charles. *American Diplomacy During the World War.* Baltimore, Md.: The Johns Hopkins Press, 1934.

———. *American Neutrality, 1914–1917.* New Haven, Conn.: Yale Univ. Press, 1935.

———. *The Intimate Papers of Colonel House.* 4 vols. Boston: Houghton Mifflin Co., 1926–28.

Shotwell, James. *War as an Instrument of National Policy.* New York: Harcourt, Brace and Co., 1921.
Sims, William S. *The Victory at Sea.* New York: Doubleday, Page and Co., 1920.
Singletary, Otis A. *The Mexican War.* Chicago: Univ. of Chicago Press, 1960.
Sklar, Martin. "Woodrow Wilson and the Political Economy of Modern United States Liberalism." In Ronald Radosh and Murray Rothbards, eds., *A New History of Leviathan,* 7–65. New York: E. P. Dutton and Co., 1972.
Small, Melvin. "The United States and the German 'Threat' to the Hemisphere, 1905–1914." *The Americas* 28 (Jan. 1972): 252–70.
Smith, Arthur. *Mr. House of Texas.* New York: Funk and Wagnalls, 1940.
Smith, Daniel M. *The Great Departure: The United States and World War I, 1914–1920.* New York: John Wiley and Sons, 1965.
———. "National Interest and American Intervention, 1917: An Historiographical Appraisal." *Journal of American History* 52 (June 1965): 5–24.
———. *Robert Lansing and American Neutrality, 1914–1917.* New York: Da Capo Press, 1972.
Smith, Louis. *American Democracy and Military Power.* Chicago: Univ. of Chicago Press, 1951.
Smith, Robert Freeman. *The United States and Revolutionary Nationalism in Mexico, 1916–1932.* Chicago: Univ. of Chicago Press, 1972.
Smythe, Donald. *Guerrilla Warrior: The Early Life of John J. Pershing.* New York: Charles Scribner's Sons, 1973.
Soutar, Andrew. *With Ironside in North Russia.* New York: Arno Press and the New York Times, 1970.
Spaulding, Oliver. *The U.S. Army in Peace and War.* New York: G. P. Putnam's Sons, 1937.
Spencer, Samuel R. *Decision for War, 1917.* Rindge, N.H.: Richard R. Smith, Publisher, 1953.
Stephenson, George M. *John Lind of Minnesota.* Port Washington, N.Y.: Kennikat Press, 1971.
Stone, Ralph. *The Irreconcilables: The Fight Against the League of Nations.* New York: W. W. Norton and Co., 1970.
Strakhovsky, Leonid Ivan. *Intervention at Archangel.* New York: H. Fertig, 1971.
———. *The Origins of American Intervention in North Russia (1918).* Princeton, N.J.: Princeton Univ. Press, 1937.
Sweetenham, John A. *Allied Intervention in Russia, 1918–1919.* London: Allen and Unwin, 1967.
Sweetman, Jack. *The Landing at Veracruz: 1914.* Annapolis, Md.: United States Naval Institute Press, 1968.
Taft, William Howard. *The United States and Peace.* New York: Charles Scribner's Sons, 1914.
Tate, Michael. "Pershing's Punitive Expedition: Pursuer of Bandits or Presidential Panacea?" *The Americas* 32 (July 1975): 46–72.
Taylor, A. J. P. *How Wars Begin.* New York: Atheneum, 1979.
Thomas, Llowell. *Old Gimlet Eye: The Adventures of Smedley Darlington Butler.* New York: Farrar and Rinehart, 1933.

Thomas, John W. *Fix Bayonets and Other Stories.* New York: Charles Scribner's Sons, 1970.

Thomas, Robert S., and Inez V. Allen. *The Mexican Punitive Expedition Under Brigadier General John J. Pershing, 1916–1917.* Washington, D.C.: U.S. Department of the Army, Office of Military History, 1954.

Thompson, John C. "Pershing's Mission in Mexico." Master's thesis, U.S. Army Command and General Staff College, 1975.

Thompson, John M. *Russia, Bolshevism, and the Versailles Peace.* Princeton, N.J.: Princeton Univ. Press, 1966.

Thornton, Willis. *Newton D. Baker and His Books.* Cleveland, Ohio: Western Reserve Univ. Press, 1954.

Thorpe, George C. "American Achievements in Santo Domingo, Haiti, and the Virgin Islands." In George Blakeslee, ed., *Mexico and the Caribbean,* 224–47. New York: G. E. Steckert and Co., 1920.

Tompkins, Frank. *Chasing Villa: The Story Behind the Story of Pershing's Expedition Into Mexico.* Harrisburg, Pa.: Military Service Publishing Co., 1934.

Toulmin, H. A. *With Pershing in Mexico.* Harrisburg, Pa.: Military Service Publishing Co., 1935.

Trask, David F. *Captains and Cabinets: Anglo-American Naval Relations, 1917–1918.* Columbia: Univ. of Missouri Press, 1972.

———. *General Tasker Howard Bliss and the "Sessions of the World," 1919.* Philadelphia, Pa.: American Philosophical Society, 1966.

———. *The United States in the Supreme War Council: American War Aims and Inter-Allied Strategy, 1917–1918.* Middletown, Conn.: Washington Univ. Press, 1961.

———. *Victory Without Peace.* New York: John Wiley and Co., 1968.

———. "Woodrow Wilson and International Statecraft: A Modern Assessment." *Naval War College Review* 36 (Mar.–Apr. 1983): 57–68.

———. "Woodrow Wilson and the Reconciliation of Force and Diplomacy, 1917–1918." *Naval War College Review* 27 (Jan.–Feb. 1975): 23–31.

Tumulty, Joseph P. *Woodrow Wilson As I Know Him.* New York: AMS Press, 1970.

Ullman, Richard Henry. *Anglo-Soviet Relations, 1917–1921.* Princeton, N.J.: Princeton Univ. Press, 1973.

Ulloa, Berta. *La Revolución Intervenida.* Guanajuato, Mex.: El Colegio de Mexico, 1971.

U.S. Congress. Senate. *Hearings Before the Committee on Foreign Relations, United States Senate: Treaty of Peace with Germany: Testimony of President Woodrow Wilson.* 66th Cong., 1st sess., 1919.

———. *Inquiry into the Occupation and Administration of Haiti and Santo Domingo. Hearings before a select committee on Haiti and Santo Domingo, pursuant to S. R. 112.* 2 vols. 67th Cong., 1st and 2d sess., 1922.

———. *Inquiry into the Occupation and Administration of Haiti and the Dominican Republic: Report.* Report No. 794. 67th Cong., 2d sess., 1922.

———. *Investigation of Mexican Affairs.* 2 vols. Report of the Subcommittee on Foreign Relations of the United States Senate. 66th Cong., 2d sess., 1920. Serial S. Doc. 285. 7665, 7666.

———. Committee on Foreign Relations. *Revolutions in Mexico.* 2 vols. 62d Cong., 2d sess., 1920.

U.S. Department of State. *Papers Relating to the Foreign Relations of the United States,* 1926–.

U.S. Department of the Navy. *Annual Report of the Navy Department for the Fiscal Year 1914,* 1915.

———. *Annual Report of the Navy Department for the Fiscal Year 1915,* 1916.

———. *Annual Report of the Navy Department for the Fiscal Year 1916,* 1917.

———. *Papers Relating to the Foreign Relations of the United States: The Lansing Papers.* 2 vols. Washington, D.C.: Government Printing Office, 1939.

U.S. Office of Naval Records and Library. *The Northern Barrage and Other Mining Activities.* Washington, D.C.: Government Printing Office, 1920.

Unterberger, Betty Miller. *American Intervention in the Russian Civil War.* Lexington, Mass.: Heath, 1969.

———. *America's Siberian Expedition, 1918–1920.* Durham, N.C.: Duke Univ. Press, 1956.

Vagts, Alfred. *A History of Militarism.* New York: Meridian Books, 1959.

Vandegrift, A. A. *Once a Marine.* New York: W. W. Norton and Co., 1964.

Vandiver, Frank E. *Black Jack: The Life and Times of John J. Pershing.* 2 vols. College Station: Texas A & M Univ. Press, 1977.

———. *John J. Pershing and the Anatomy of Leadership.* United States Air Force Academy, Colo.: United States Air Force, 1963.

Vierick, George S. *The Strangest Friendship in History: Woodrow Wilson and Colonel House.* New York: Liveright, 1932.

Waller, Willard, ed. *War in the 20th Century.* New York: The Revisionist Press, 1974.

Waltz, Kenneth. *Man, the State and War.* New York: Columbia Univ. Press, 1959.

Walworth, Arthur. *America's Moment: 1918.* New York: W. W. Norton and Co., 1977.

———. *Woodrow Wilson.* 2 vols. New York: Longmans, Green and Co., 1958.

Weigley, Russell. *The American Way of War, A History of U.S. Military Strategy and Policy.* New York: Macmillan, 1973.

———. *History of the United States Army.* New York: Macmillan, 1967.

———. *Towards an American Army: Military Thought from Washington to Marshall.* New York: Columbia Univ. Press, 1962.

Welles, Sumner. *Naboth's Vineyard: The Dominican Republic 1844–1924.* 2 vols. Mamoreneck, N.Y.: Paul P. Appel, 1966.

———. *The Time for Decision.* New York: Harper and Brothers, 1944.

Wells, Samuel F. "New Perspectives on Wilsonian Diplomacy: The Secular Evangelism of American Political Economy." *Perspectives in American History* 6 (1972): 389–419.

Weston, Rubin Francis. *Racism in U.S. Imperialism: The Influence of Racial Assumptions on American Foreign Policy, 1893–1946.* Columbia: Univ. of

South Carolina Press, 1972.

Wheaton, Henry. *Elements of International Law.* Edited by Richard Henry Dana, Jr. 8th ed. Boston: Little, Brown and Co., 1866.

White, Howard. *Executive Influence in Determining Military Policy in the United States.* Urbana: Univ. of Illinois Press, 1924.

White, John Albert. *The Siberian Intervention.* Princeton, N.J.: Princeton Univ. Press, 1950.

White, William Allen. *Woodrow Wilson: The Man, His Times, and His Task.* Boston: Houghton Mifflin Co., 1924.

Wick, Ned E. *Service in Siberia.* Rapid City, S.D.: Fenwigan Press, 1975.

Williams, T. Harry. *Americans at War: The Development of the American Military System.* Baton Rouge: Louisiana State Univ. Press, 1960.

―――. *The History of American Wars from 1745 to 1918.* New York: Alfred A. Knopf, 1981.

Williams, William Appleman. *American-Russian Relations, 1781–1947.* New York: Octagon Books, 1971.

―――. *The Tragedy of American Diplomacy.* New York: Dell Publishing Co., 1962.

Wilson, Edith Boling. *My Memoir.* Indianapolis: Bobbs-Merrill Co., 1939.

Wilson, Henry Lane. *Diplomatic Episodes in Mexico, Belgium, and Chile.* Port Washington, N.Y.: Kennikat Press, 1971.

Wilson, Joan Hoff. *Ideology and Economics: U.S. Relations with the Soviet Union, 1918–1933.* Columbia: Univ. of Missouri Press, 1974.

Wilson, Woodrow. *Congressional Government: A Study in American Politics.* Boston: Houghton Mifflin and Co., 1885.

―――. *Constitutional Government in the United States.* New York: Columbia Univ. Press, 1908.

―――. *Division and Reunion, 1829–1909.* New York: Longmans, Green and Co., 1912.

―――. *George Washington.* New York: Schocken Books, 1969.

―――. *History of the American People.* 5 vols. New York: Harper and Brothers, 1903.

―――. *Mere Literature and Other Essays.* Boston: Houghton Mifflin and Co., 1896.

―――. *The Messages and Papers of Woodrow Wilson.* 2 vols. New York: The Review of Reviews Co., 1924.

Wirkus, Fausten and Taney Dudley. *The White King of La Gonave.* New York: Garden City Publishing Co., 1931.

Wise, Frederic. *A Marine Tells It to You.* New York: J. H. Sears, Co., 1929.

Wright, Quincy. *A Study of War.* 2 vols. Chicago: Univ. of Chicago Press, 1942.

INDEX

ABC (Argentina, Brazil, and Chile) mediation, 47, 72–74, 158
Allied Naval Council, 180–81
Allies: relations among, 168–84
American Commission to Negotiate the Peace, 225, 232–33, 240–42, 260; suspicions of Allies, 228–29, 244–45; and Japan, 233–34; and withdrawal of Czechs from Russia, 234; and control of Trans-Siberian Railway, 234–36; and demands on Kolchak, 237–38; and Churchill plan, 243–44; and Hungarian revolution, 245–46
American democratic ideology: influence on Wilson, 22–23, 70–72; and occupation of Veracruz, 24–25, 72–74; and the punitive expedition, 74–75; and the occupation of Haiti, 24–25, 86–103; and the occupation of Santo Domingo, 24–25, 75–86, 104–12; and World War I, 24–25, 112–13; and the Siberian intervention, 112–13; and the Paris Peace Conference, 112–13
American Expeditionary Force, 181–82
Arabic, sinking of, 131–35
Archangel, intervention in, 191, 199, 201, 202, 207–18, 228–30, 231–32
Argentina: and mediation of occupation of Veracruz, 47, 72–74, 158; and proposed Pan American pact, 188–89
Arias, Desiderio, Gen., 76, 80, 86, 104, 108–9
Armed power, definition of, 1
Armistice, 183, 216
Axson, Ellen (later Ellen Axson Wilson), 10, 40, 84

Badger, Charles, 48–49

Báez, Ramón, 86
Bailly-Blanchard, Arthur, minister to Haiti, 91, 95, 101
Baker, Newton: as Wilson's adviser, 27, 28–29; views on force, 28–29; and the punitive expedition, 55, 57–59, 64; and World War I, 162, 171, 177; and formulation of selective service, 163–66; and Siberian intervention, 204–5, 210–11, 233, 237; opposition to Russian interventions, 208, 216–18; on Russian interventions as cooperative effort, 211–12; and Trans-Siberian Railway plan, 235–36; and note to Japan, 239
Baker, Ray S., 29
Balfour, Arthur: mission to U.S., 170–71; justifies Japanese intervention in Siberia, 195
Baxter, Clarence, 105
Beach, Edward L., Capt.: and Haitian policies, 102, 103
Belgium, invasion of, 124
Bennett, K. M., 105
Benson, William S., Adm.: appointed chief of naval operations, 37; and intervention in Santo Domingo, 109, 110; and World War I, 161–62; and Siberian intervention, 208, 210–11, 231; and naval buildup, 253; and U.S. alliance with France, 263
Bernstorff, Johann von: and sinking of *Arabic*, 132–35; and *Sussex* crisis, 145–49; and submarine warfare, 151
Bethmann-Hollweg, Theobald von: and submarine warfare, 131, 151
Bliss, Tasker H., Gen.: mentioned, 39, 63; and occupation of Veracruz, 44–45, 49–50; on punitive expedition, 54–56; on protection of border, 56, 63; and civil-

military relations, 67–68
—and World War I: plan for World War I, 169–70; Allied mission to U.S., 170–71; Pershing's orders, 171; mission to Europe, 177; creation of joint Allied council, 177–78; service on Supreme War Council, 178; amalgamation, 178–79
—and Russian interventions: views on Japanese intervention in Siberia, 194; Supreme War Council recommendations, 200; Czechoslovak Legion, 201; Joint Note Number 25, 202; views of Allies, 207, 244–45; opposition to intervention, 211, 215–16, 246–48; on Bolshevism, 242–43; Churchill plan, 243–44; on withdrawal from northern Russia, 227, 229–31; northern Russia as British expedition, 228–29; rumors of continued intervention, 231; Trans-Siberian Railway plan, 235

Bliss embargo, 49–50
Bliss plan, 56, 62–63
Bobo, Rosalvo, revolution of, 98
Bolshevik Revolution, 173–74, 192
Bolshevism: effect on Wilson's goals, 173–75; and Russian interventions, 189–218; effect on American reform, 219–20; and Paris Peace Conference, 240–49
Boquillas, raided by Mexicans, 61
Bordas Valdés, Jose: as president of Santo Domingo, 76, 80–82; on issue of American supervision of elections, 78–79; opposes Wilson Plan, 85–86
Boxer Rebellion, 44
Boyd, Charles T., Capt.: and fight at Carrizal, 64
Brandeis, Louis D., 34
Brazil: and mediation of occupation of Veracruz, 47, 72–74; and proposed Pan American pact, 188–89
Bridges, Thomas, Gen.: on reinforcing Russian interventions, 214
Bryan, William Jennings: as pacifist, 27–28; as Wilson's adviser, 27–28; demands dissolution of Joint Army and Navy Board, 37; policies toward Mexico, 40; and *Ypiranga*, 46, 47; attitude toward ABC mediation, 73–74; resignation, 99
—and Santo Domingo: response to Horacista revolt in Santo Domingo, 76–86; and American supervision of elections, 78–80; and Bordas, 81–82, 83; policy toward Santo Domingo, 83–85, 86; on Wilson Plan, 85–86; recommends supporting Jiménez with force, 104; explains American policy, 104–5; urges financial adviser, 105–6
—and Haiti: recommends purchase of Mole St. Nicholas, 87–88; fear of foreign interference, 88; recommends recognition of Oreste Zamor, 90; on customs receivership, 90–91, 92–93; opposes intervention, 92; offers American friendship, 92; new policy, 94; instructions to Fort Commission, 96; tempted to use force, 97; instructions to Fuller, 97
—and American neutrality: ban on loans to belligerents, 121; opposes sale of submarine parts, 121–22; sinking of *Falaba*, 125–27; and sinking of *Cushing*, 127; and sinking of *Gulflight*, 127; and sinking of *Lusitania*, 127–31

Bullitt, William R.: as Wilson's expert on Russia, 34–35; resignation of, 225–26; mission to Russia, 243
Bureau of Insular Affairs: and control of Dominican customs, 76. *See also* Vick, Walter
Burke, Edmund: influence on Wilson, 22–23
Burleson, Albert S., 34
Butler, Smedley, Maj.: in Haiti, 103

Cáceres, Ramón: assassination of, 76
Cacos: in Haitian revolutions, 89; brought under control, 102–3
Caldwell, John: requests American warship, 193
Cape Haitien, Haiti: in pattern of revolutions, 89; violent outbreak at, 92; taken over by Caperton, 103
Caperton, William B.: in Haiti, 67, 94–95, 100, 102, 103; and occupation of Santo Domingo, 109, 110
Carranza, Venustiano: leader of Constitutionalists, 39; opposition to occupation of Veracruz, 49–50, 223; split with Villa, 51–52; de facto recognition of, 52, 188–89; refuses to cooperate with punitive expedition, 57; policies toward ABC me-

diation, 73–74; disputes "hot pursuit," 117; and Zimmermann telegram, 151; and Wilson's efforts at cooperation, 158–59; ideals of, 246
Carrizal, battle at, 63–65, 74
Castine: dispatched to Santo Domingo, 105, 108
Chamberlain, George, Sen., 177
Chile: and mediation of occupation of Veracruz, 47, 72–74; and proposed Pan American pact, 188–89
China: 1900 intervention in, as precedent, 44; and Japanese relations with, 190
Churchill, Winston: on force against Bolsheviks, 243–44
City of Memphis, sinking of, 151
Civil-military relations, 35–39; during occupation of Veracruz, 39–51; during punitive expedition, 51–67; during interventions in Haiti, Santo Domingo, World War I, and Russia, 67–68
Civil War: Wilson's views on, 20; effect of failure of draft on selective service, 163–64
Clarkson, Grosvenor: and unpreparedness of military, 168–69
Clemenceau, Georges: meetings with Wilson, 226, 230, 238, 242; and French alliance with U.S., 263–64
Cleveland, Grover: influence on Wilson, 8, 13
Collective security: as motive of Wilson's policies, 185–89; and interventions in Russia, 189–218
Columbus, New Mexico: attacked by Villa, 52
Congressional Government (Wilson), discussion of presidency, 12–13
Constitutional Government in the United States (Wilson), discussion of presidency, 13
Constitutionalists, 40–42
Coolidge, Calvin: policies after Wilson, 250
Cooperation: established in U.S., 160–66; established abroad, 167–84
Covenant of the League of Nations: and legitimacy of force, 26; as formalization of international cooperation, 115; influence of proposed Pan American pact on, 188; discussion of, 219–49

Crosley, W. S., 109, 110
Crowder, Enoch H., Gen.: designs selective service, 163–66; and example of cooperation, 223
Crozier, William, Gen.: influence on Mexican war planning, 43–44
Curtis, Charles B.: recommends American supervision of Dominican elections, 78–79
Cushing, sinking of, 127
Czechoslovak Legion: in Russia, 200–201; trouble with Bolsheviks, 206, 210; as excuse for American intervention, 210–14

Daniels, Josephus: as Wilson's adviser, 27, 29–30; views on force, 29–30; and selection of Benson as chief of naval operations, 37; demands dissolution of Joint Army and Navy Board, 37; agrees with Wilson's Mexican policy, 40; explains occupation of Veracruz, 46; policies toward Haiti, 67, 87, 96, 102–3; on preparedness for war, 151; during World War I and Russian interventions, 152, 162, 179, 193
Dartiguenave, Sudre: elected president of Haiti, 102
Davis, R. B.: negotiates treaty with Haiti, 102
Declaration of London, 122
"Democracy" (Wilson), 156
Díaz, Porfirio: overthrown by Madero, 39
Dominican Convention of 1907: establishes customs receivership, 76; as model for Haiti, 91; foundation of U.S. policy, 104; as legal justification for occupation, 118
Dominican Republic. *See* Santo Domingo
Draft. *See* Selective service
Dulles, John Foster: influence of Wilson on, 265

Eberle, E. W., Capt.: mediates in Santo Domingo revolt, 82

Falaba, sinking of, 125, 126–27
Farnham, Roger L., 90
Farnham plan, 91–92
Fiske, Bradley, Adm., 48, 50–51
Fletcher, Frank F., Adm.: relationship

with Wilson, 38; and plan to seize Veracruz customshouse, 44–46; and arrest of mail orderly, 45–46; and occupation of Veracruz, 46–48

Foch, Ferdinand, Gen.: appointed commander-in-chief of Allied armies, 179; on issue of Siberian intervention, 209; on military intervention and force against Bolsheviks, 242, 246; and Hungarian revolution, 245–46

Force, definition of, 1

Fort, John F.: as Wilson's expert on Santo Domingo and Haiti, 34; mission to Santo Domingo, 85–86; mission to Haiti, 94–97

Fort Commission: to Santo Domingo, 85–86; to Haiti, 94–97

Fourteen Points, 174–75

France: receives credits, 121; wartime condition of, 168–70; and relations with U.S. during war, 171–84; and interventions in Russia, 189–218; and alliance with U.S., 263–64

Francis, David, 196

Fuller, Paul, Jr., 97–99

Funston, Frederick, Gen.: in Veracruz, 47, 48; response to Columbus raid, 53; on punitive expedition, 55, 57, 58; reaction to Parral attack, 59–60; and Scott-Obregón conference, 60–61; reaction to fight at Carrizal, 64

Galt, Edith Boling, (later Edith Boling Wilson), 100

Garrison, Lindley: as Wilson's adviser, 27–28; instructions to Funston, 49; reaction to Bliss embargo, 49–50; reaction to sinking of *Gulflight,* 127; and sinking of *Lusitania,* 128

Gerard, James W.: and sinking of *Lusitania,* 128; and sinking of *Arabic,* 132–33, 134; and *Sussex* crisis, 146

Germany: causes of war with, 11; Wilson's views on war with, 23; influence of American democratic ideology on policies toward, 112–13; infringement on U.S. neutrality, 118–35, 142–54; war with, 155–83; occupation of, 183–84; and fear of, in Russia, 189

Glenn Springs: raided by Mexicans, 61

Gore-McLemore resolution, 143–44

Graves, William S., Gen.: and intervention in Siberia, 213; on Japan's policies, 233–34; recommends withdrawal of Czechs, 234; and Trans-Siberian Railway plan, 235–36; criticisms of, 236–67; on intervention, 239

Gray, George, 75

Great Britain: hurt by ban on loans, 121; runs afoul of American neutrality, 122–23; and difference from Germany, 123–24; U.S. policy toward, 134–35; wartime condition of, 168, 170; relations with U.S. during World War I, 170–84; and interventions in Russia, 189–218; and Paris Peace Conference, 219–49

Grey, Earl: and Declaration of London, 122; correspondence with House, 137, 139; and *Sussex* crisis, 145–46; and mediation proposal, 149

Greytown, Nicaragua: shelling of, 117

Gulflight, sinking of, 127

Haiti: public interest in, 11–12; intervention in, 12, 22; civil-military relations during occupation, 67–68; effect of American democratic ideology on policy toward, 72, 86–103, 222; revolutions in, 89; customs receivership in, 90–103; influence of international law on intervention in, 117–18; as cooperative effort, 159–60; and limits of force, 221. *See also under* Wilson, Woodrow

Hale, William Bayard: as Wilson's expert on Mexico, 34; and Mexican fact-finding mission, 40–41

Hancock: ordered to support Jiménez, 36

Harding, Warren: withdraws American forces from Germany, 184; policies of, 250

Harris, Ernest L.: on force against Bolsheviks, 243

Healdton, sinking of, 151

Henríquez y Carvajal, Federico: elected president of Santo Domingo, 111

Hoover, Herbert: policies after Wilson, 250

Horacistas: opposition to Bordas, 76; alliance with Arias, 82

House, Edward M.: as Wilson's adviser, 27, 30; views on force, 30; as Wilson's expert on World War I, 34

—and American neutrality: role in period of neutrality, 120; and British violations

of neutrality, 122–23; effect of sinking of *Falaba* on mediation efforts, 127; and sinking of *Lusitania,* 127–31; and sinking of *Arabic,* 131–35; mediation efforts in Europe, 135–36; and plans for Wilson, 137; and changing view of war, 137–39; and *Sussex* crisis, 144–48; approach to Grey, 149; opposition to Wilson's fall peace campaign, 149–50
—and World War I: sees Wilson as spokesman of democracy, 162; recommends avoiding territorial discussions, 173; establishment of Inquiry, 176; mission to Europe, 177; urges creation of Allied military council, 177; and armistice, 183
—and Paris Peace Conference: opposition to Japanese intervention, 197; and Churchill plan, 244; and purpose of League of Nations, 260
House-Grey Memorandum, 139–40, 141, 145
Houseton, David F., 34
Huerta, Victoriano, overthrow of Madero, 39; refused recognition, 40; and promise of elections, 41; refusal to apologize, 46; resignation of, 47
Hughes, Charles Evan: as Republican presidential candidate, 149; and diplomacy after Wilson, 250–51
Hungary, revolution in, 245–46

Illinois, sinking of, 151
Inquiry, 176, 225
Interallied Rhineland High Commission, 183
International cooperation: as conceived by Wilson, 135; during World War I, 166–83
International power, forms of, 1
Ironside, Edward, Gen., 228
Ishii, Viscount: and Japanese intervention, 199–200
Italy: promised Fiume, 173; and proposed Mediterranean operation, 180–81; and withdrawal from peace conference, 257; provincial objectives of, 263

Japan: promised Shantung peninsula, 173; and intervention in Russia, 190–218; at Paris Peace Conference, 227–40; provincial objectives of, 263

Jiménez, Don Juan: elected president of Santo Domingo, 86; ends revolts, 86, 105; opposes financial adviser, 105–6; refuses amendments to customs convention, 107; settles Ferrer uprising, 108; requests American assistance, 109, 110–13, 118
Jiménistas: alliance with Arias, 82
Joffre, Marshal: mission to U.S., 170–71
Johnson, Lyndon: compared to Wilson, 251
Johnson, Stewart: endorses intervention in Santo Domingo, 106–7
Joint Army and Navy Board, 37
Joint Mexican-American Commission, 64–65, 74–75
Judson, William, Gen., 196
Jusserand, Jules: role in ABC mediation, 47; urges Japanese intervention in Siberia, 195–96

Kaiser. *See* Wilhelm II
Kato, Adm.: lands Japanese troops at Vladivostok, 200
Kellogg, Frank B.: diplomacy after Wilson, 250–51
Kerensky, Alexander, 189, 192
Knapp, H. S., Capt.: and military government in Santo Domingo, 111, 118
Knight, A. N., Adm., 193
Kolchak, Alexander, Adm., leader of White Army, 112, 236, 237, 238, 239
Korean War: compared to Wilsonian interventions, 251
Kuhn, J. E., Gen.: and U.S. reliance on Britain and France, 169
Kun, Béla, 245–46

LaFollette, Robert: opposes arming U.S. merchantmen, 151
Lamar, Joseph: and ABC mediation, 74
Lane, Franklin K., 75, 172
Lansing, Robert: as Wilson's adviser, 27, 30–32; views on force, 30–32; as Wilson's expert on World War I, 34; proposed Mexican policy, 52; attitude toward ABC mediation, 73–74; attitude toward Joint Mexican-American Commission, 75; and occupation of Veracruz, 116–17; in mediating Santo Domingo revolt, 82; on policy toward Santo Domingo, 83, 85,

105, 108, 110, 111; on removal of gold from Haiti, 87, 93; and occupation of Haiti, 100, 101, 102, 117
—and World War I: and U.S. neutrality, 120, 121; on submarines, 122, 125, 151–54; and sinking of *Falaba,* 125–27; and sinking of *Cushing,* 127; and sinking of *Gulflight,* 127; and sinking of *Lusitania,* 127–31; and support of Entente powers, 131; and sinking of *Arabic,* 131–35; perception of people's desire for peace, 143; and *Sussex* crisis, 144–48; opposition to Wilson's fall peacemaking campaign, 149–50; on World War I as cooperative effort, 171
—and Russian interventions: on keeping Russia in the war, 192–93; on Bolshevism, 193, 218, 239–40; asks for warship to Siberia, 193; and Bliss's opinion of intervention, 194, 195; on Japanese intervention, 196–97, 198, 233–34, 239; meeting with Ishii, 199–200; on inaction, 205–6; on problems with intervening, 208; on Czech take-over of Vladivostok, 210, 215
—and Paris Peace Conference: and Churchill plan, 243–44; suspicions of Allies, 245; and failure of peace treaty, 256, 260, 262; and American unselfishness, 256–57; and guiding principle of League of Nations, 260
Lansing-Ishii Agreement, 190
Law: domestic, as viewed by Progressives, 114; international, as viewed by Progressives, 114–15; as understood by Wilson, 115, 122; as foundation of neutrality policy, 119–35; and submarines, 125–35, 142–54
"Leaders of Men" (Wilson), 9–10
League of Nations: as heart of Wilson's program, 26–27, 175; codification of American ethnocentrism, 113; and end of reform, 220; and civilian control of military, 251–54; and disarmament, 252–53; and naval buildup, 253; and threat of militarism in U.S., 253–54; and American democratic ideology, 254–58; and international law, 258–62; and cooperation, 262–64; and limits of force, 266
League to Enforce Peace, 149
Leggett, Hunter H.: influence on Mexican war planning, 43–44

Lehman, Frederick: and ABC mediation, 74
Lenin, Nikolai: and Bolshevik revolution, 192; and Prinkipo meeting, 243
Lind, John: as Wilson's expert on Mexico, 34, 35; and Mexican mission, 40–41; plan for seizing customshouse in Veracruz, 44, 46
Livingston, Lemuel W.: as American consul at Cape Haitien, 91–92
Lloyd George, David: meetings with Wilson, 226, 230, 238, 242; on reinforcements to northern Russia, 230; and Prinkipo Conference, 242–43; and proposals for concert of nations, 263
Long, Boaz: attitude toward Santo Domingo, 77–78; fear of foreign interference in Haiti, 88; policy recommendations, 89–90, 92, 101; author of Russell's instructions, 107
Long, Breckinridge: on intervention in Siberia, 196, 198, 213–14, 227, 262
Ludendorff, Eric von, Gen., 182
Lusitania, sinking of, 127–31; as cause of Bryan's resignation, 27, 129–30

McAdoo, William G., 34
McCully, N. A.: and intervention in northern Russia, 228
Macomb, M. M., Gen.: on punitive expedition, 54–55, 56–57, 117
McIntyre, Frank, Gen.: as chief of Bureau of Insular Affairs, 76; explains American policy, 105
Madero, Francisco: overthrows Díaz, 39; overthrown by Huerta, 39
Mahan, Alfred Thayer: influence on U.S. Navy, 39
March, Peyton C., Gen.: and intervention in Siberia, 211
Mayo, Henry T., Adm.: and occupation of Veracruz, 45–46, 48
Max, Prince of Baden, 182
Mediation: American promotion of, in World War I, 135–42
Mediterranean: proposed operations in, 180–81
Meuse-Argonne offensive, 182
Mexican War: Wilson's views on, 20
Mexico: policies of Wilson toward, 39–42; War College Division's plans toward, 42–

44; situation in, 51–52. *See also* Veracruz and Punitive expedition
Mezes, Sidney: and the Inquiry, 176
Miles, Basil, 196, 238
Military Order of the Caraboa, 37
Military preparedness, 140–42
Mole St. Nicholas: importance of, in U.S.-Haitian policies, 87–88
Morey, Lewis, Capt.: and Carrizal fight, 64
Morris, Roland: as Wilson's expert on Russia, 35; on Japanese intervention in Siberia, 196; and control of Trans-Siberian Railway, 234; mission to Kolchak, 237–39
Mott, John R., 74–75
Murmansk: interventions at, 191, 198, 199, 201, 202, 207–18, 228–30, 231–32

Naón, Romulo S.: and mediation over occupation of Veracruz, 47
National Bank of Haiti: gold taken from, 87
Neutrality, U.S. defense of, 118–35, 142–54
Nicaragua: intervention in, as precedent, 44; as example of American democratic ideology, 72
Nixon, Richard M.: influence of Wilson on, 265
"Northern Barrage," 168, 179–80
Nouell, Msgr. Adolpho A.: as president of Santo Domingo, 76

Obregón, Álvaro: conference with Scott, 60–61
Oise-Aisne offensive, 182
Oreste, Michel, 88, 89, 90
Orlando, Vittorio, 226
Osborne, John E.: attempt to buy Mole St. Nicholas, 87–88
O'Shaughnessy, Nelson, 45

Page, Walter Hines: complaints against lawyers, 122; sabotage of Wilson's peace note, 150
Page, Thomas Nelson, 136, 145
Palmer, Frederick, 38
Pan-American conference, 52
Pan-American pact, 188–89
Paris Peace Conference: and Russia, 218, 225–40; and issue of Bolshevism, 240–49. *See also under* House, Edward M.; Lansing, Robert; League of Nations; Wilson, Woodrow
Parral, Mexico: attack on punitive expedition at, 58–59
Pershing, John J.: and punitive expedition, 55, 57–59, 64–65; and understanding of Wilson's policies, 65–66; and civil-military relations during war, 67–68; and World War I, 171, 176, 179, 183–84; and Russian interventions, 192, 216
Phelan, James, Sen.: investigation of Sullivan, 106
Philippines: Wilson's views on occupation of, 20–21
Phillips, William: and control of Trans-Siberian Railway, 234
Pichon, Stephen, 207
Platt Amendment: as example of American democratic ideology, 72
Plattsburg training camps, 141
Polk, Frank: attitude toward Joint Mexican-American Commission, 74; on Japanese intervention in Siberia, 196, 198; and Trans-Siberian Railway plan, 235; complaints about Graves, 236–37; on Bolshevism, 241
Poole, DeWitt C.: on force against Bolsheviks, 243
Port-au-Prince, Haiti: violent outbreak at, 92, 99; taken over by Caperton, 100; food shortage at, 101
Prinkipo Conference, 242–43
Progressive movement: description of, 2; the presidency during, 8; as beginning of age of experts, 35; and democratic ideology, 69–70; and importance of law, 114; and importance of cooperation, 155; as triumph of faith in democracy, 155; as age of organization, 185–86; interrupted by World War I, 219; after World War I, 250
Puerto Plata, Santo Domingo: falls to rebels, 82; revolt at, 104
Punitive expedition: causes of, 11; as example of limited intervention, 51; discussion of, 58–67; and civil-military relations, 65–67; influence of American democratic ideology on, 74–75; influence of international law on, 117; as co-operative effort, 158–59; and limits of

330 / Index

force, 221. *See also under* Wilson, Woodrow

Reading, Lord: and Japanese intervention in Siberia, 195
Religion: influence on Wilson, 7–18
Revolutionary War: Wilson's views on, 20
Roosevelt, Franklin D.: influence of Wilson on, 265
Roosevelt, Nicholas D., Capt.: on Hungarian revolution, 245
Roosevelt, Theodore: influence on Wilson, 2, 13; as activist president, 8; policies toward Santo Domingo, 76; and preparedness movement, 141
Root, Elihu: mission to Russia, 192
Rumania: attack on Hungary, 246
Russell, John H., Maj. Gen.: on occupation of Haiti, 103
Russell, William W.: as minister to Santo Domingo, 106, 108, 109–10
Russia: public interest in, 11–12; interventions in, 12, 189–218; interventions as issue at Paris Peace Conference, 225–49. *See also under* Siberian intervention; Wilson, Woodrow

Sam, Vilbrun Guillaume: revolution of, 93, 94; refuses to negotiate with Fort Commission, 96–97; and Fuller mission, 98; downfall of, 99
Santo Domingo: public interest in, 11–12; intervention in, 12, 23; civil-military relations during intervention in, 67–68; influence of American democratic ideology on occupation of, 75–86, 104–12, 222; American policies toward, 75–86, 104–12; influence of international law on, 118; as cooperative effort, 160; and limits of force, 221–22. *See also under* Wilson, Woodrow
Scott, Hugh L., Gen.: on punitive expedition, 54–57, 59–60; meeting with Obregón, 60–61; changes objective of Mexican War plans, 62; on understanding of Wilson's policies, 66; role as Wilson's adviser, 252
Scott, James Brown: and importance of international law, 121
Scott-Obregón conference, 57, 60–61

Selective service, 163–68, 223
Siberian intervention: effect of American democratic ideology on, 112–13; causes of, 189–218, 223; discussion of, at Paris Peace Conference, 225–40. *See also under* Russia; Wilson, Woodrow
Sims, William S., Adm., 151, 178–79, 180–81
Smith, Charles C.: as expert in Santo Domingo, 34, 85–86; in Haiti, 34, 94–97
Smith, Madison, minister to Haiti, 90
Somme offensive, 182
Spanish-American War: Wilson's views on, 20
Spring-Rice, Cecil: on neutrals, 122; mediation efforts of, 135, 149
Stabler, Jordan: on policy toward Santo Domingo, 83, 90
Stevens, John F., 234
Stimson, Henry L.: diplomacy after Wilson, 250–51
"Study of Administration" (Wilson), 15–16
Submarines: and effect on American neutrality, 124–35, 142–54
Sullivan, James M., American minister to Santo Domingo, 77; negotiations to end Horacistas' revolt, 78–79; on elections in Santo Domingo, 78–79, 80; urges support of Bordas, 80–81; financial involvement with Bordas, 81; resignation of, 106
Supreme War Council: establishment of, 178; term of peace drafted by military representatives of, 183; call for continuation of war in eastern Europe, 193; opposition to Bolsheviks, 193; and interventions in Siberia, 194, 200, 210; and Czechoslovak Legion, 201; Joint Note Number 25 of, 201–2; Joint Note Number 31 of, 207–8; Joint Note Number 38 of, 215–16
Sussex, sinking of, 144–48
Swope, Herbert Bayard, 199

Taft, William Howard: intervention in Nicaragua, ix; influence on Wilson, 2; policies toward Santo Domingo, 76
Tampico, Mexico: arrest of U.S. sailors at, 45
Théodore, Davilmar: revolt of, 90; as presi-

dent, 92; proposes concessions to U.S., 93; overthrown, 94–95
Thrasher, Leon: drowned on *Falaba,* 125; Wilson's reaction to death of, 126–27
Tompkins, Frank, Maj.: attacked at Parral, Mexico, 58–59
Trans-Siberian Railway: issue at Paris Peace Conference, 234–36
Treaty of Brest-Litovsk, 189, 198, 200
Treviño, Jacinto B., Gen.: orders Pershing out of Mexico, 62
Trotsky, Leon: and Bolshevik Revolution, 192; supports intervention in Russia, 198
Truman, Harry: compared to Wilson, 251
Tubantia, sinking of, 144
Tumulty, Joseph: Wilson's secretary, 95; and sinking of *Arabic,* 132
Twenty-One Demands, on China, 190

U-boat. *See* Submarines
United States Army: Third Army and occupation of Germany, 183–84
—War College Division of: war plans for Mexico, 42–44, 53–56, 62; war plans against Germany, 38, 168, 169–71, 177
United States Department of State: endorses Fuller's recommendations, 99
United States Marine Corps, Fifth Regiment: plans occupation of Santo Domingo, 86; and occupation of Haiti, 93, 102
United States Navy: and cooperation with British, 179; role of General Board in occupation of Veracruz, 48

Vásquez, Horacio, 76
Velásquistas: alliance with Arias, 82
Veracruz (Mexico), occupation of, 11, 39–42, 45–51; ABC mediation over, 46–47, 72–74; as understood by Wilson, 50; as lesson in limited intervention, 51; as negative precedent for punitive expedition, 53; influence of American democratic ideology on, 72–74; effect on policy toward Santo Domingo, 84; influence of international law on, 116–17; as cooperative effort, 158; and limits of force, 221. *See also under* Wilson, Woodrow
Vick, Walter, 79, 80, 81
Vietnam War: compared to Wilsonian interventions, 251

Vigilancia, sinking of, 151
Villa, Francisco (Pancho): leader of Constitutionalists, 39; split with Carranza, 51–52; decline in fortunes of, 52; attack on Columbus, New Mexico, 52; pursuit of, 52–67
Vladivostok: intervention at, 191, 200, 210–18

Wakrhave, Henry W., 94
War College. *See under* United States Army
War Industries Board, 162–63, 223
War of 1812: Wilson's views on, 20
Washington: role in Haitian intervention, 94–95
White, Henry: on Bolshevism, 242; and suspicions of Allies, 245
Wilhelm II, kaiser: and *Arabic* crisis, 134; and *Sussex* crisis, 148; and submarine warfare, 151
Wilson, Woodrow: influence on twentieth century U.S. foreign policy, ix–x, 4; on uses of force, 2, 3–4, 19–27, 33; general policies of, 2–3; as commander-in-chief, 4; as idealist, 5; views on leadership, 9–12; views on presidency, 12–14; theory of administration, 14–17; as president of Princeton, 16; as governor of New Jersey, 16; views on Revolutionary War, War of 1812, Mexican War, Civil War, Spanish-American War, and occupation of Philippines, 20–21; influenced by Edmund Burke, 22–23; understanding of limits of force, 22–23, 33; and League of Nations, 26–27; relationships with civilian advisers, 27–33; reliance on experts, 34–35; relationship with U.S. military, 35–39, 67–68, 168; stroke, and effect on policy, 239, 265
—and Mexican interventions: early policies toward Mexico, 39–43; relations with Huerta, 40, 42, 46; policy of "watchful waiting," 41; and lifting of arms embargo, 42; response to Tampico incident, interception of State Dept. telegram, and arrest of mail orderly, 45–46; decision to occupy Veracruz, 46–47, 50; control of military during occupation, 47–48; and Bliss embargo, 49–50;

policies toward Mexico in 1915, 51–52; and War College Division during punitive expedition, 53–56; policies toward punitive expedition, 57, 60; reaction to Parral attack, 59; policies toward Scott-Obregón conference, 60–61; endorses Bliss plan and sends Organized Militia to border, 63; answers Carranza's note, 63; reaction to fight at Carrizal, 64–65; and Joint Mexican-American Commission, 64–65, 74–75; and civil-military relations during punitive expedition, 65–67; influence of American democratic ideology on policies toward Mexico, 70–72; policies during ABC mediation, 72–74

—and intervention in Santo Domingo: policies toward Santo Domingo, 75–86, 104–13; on supervision of Dominican elections, 79; develops Wilson Plan, 83–86; effect of ethnocentric humanitarianism on policies, 112–13; legal justification for intervention, 118

—and Haitian intervention: policies toward Haiti, 86–103; Mole St. Nicholas, 87–88; fear of foreign interference, 88; supports customs receivership, 90–91; nonrecognition of Théodore, 92; response to Fuller's recommendations, 99; lack of legal justification for intervention, 101–2

—and period of neutrality: attitude toward international law, 115, 120; neutrality policy, 115–16, 118–35, 142–54; cause of war, 118; calls for mediation, 120–21; on submarine warfare, 121–22, 125, 151–52; British violations of neutrality, 122–23; German violations of neutrality, 123–24; sinking of *Falaba,* 125–27; sinking of *Cushing,* 127; sinking of *Gulflight,* 127; sinking of *Lusitania,* 127–31; sinking of *Arabic,* 131–35; role of U.S. in war, 135–36; second House mission to Europe, 136–37; vision of postwar world, 138–39; House-Grey Memorandum, 139–40; military preparedness, 140–42; midwestern speaking tour, 142–43; Gore-McLemore resolution, 144; *Sussex* crisis, 144–48; endorsement of concert of nations, 149; election of 1916, 149; peacemaking, 149–50; note to belligerents, 150; "peace without victory," 150–51; decision to enter war, 152–54

—and World War I: faith in democracy and cooperation, 155–57, 160–61, 166–67, 172–73; formulation of selective service, 163–66; cooperation with Allies, 168, 170–71; postwar territorial discussions, 173; reaction to secret treaties, 173; and Bolshevism, 173–74; postwar proposals, 174–75; establishment of Inquiry, 176; western front strategy, 177; sends House to Europe, 177; and Supreme War Council, 177–78; disapproves of amalgamation, 179; peace with Germany, 182–83; occupation of Germany, 183–84

—and Russian interventions: understanding of collective action, 186–87; and prewar policies of collective security, 188–90; view of Japan, 190; opposition to Siberian intervention, 192; supports Kerensky, 192; and Root mission, 192; and Joint Note Number 5, 193; objections to Japanese intervention, 196–98; different policies for Siberian and northern interventions, 199, 201–2; approves Joint Note Number 25, 202; opposed to rewarding Japan, 204–5; helping the Czechs, 206; overrules military, 211; use of interventions for cooperation, 211–12; continued trouble with Allies, 213–14; and question of command, 213–14; wants limited action, 214–15; summary of Siberian policies, 239–40

—and Paris Peace Conference: contribution to somnipathy of liberalism, 220; and uses of force, 220, 221–24; failure of leadership at Paris, 225–26, 231–32; pledge to protect France, 226–27; concerns with Russia, 227; possibility of mutiny, 228; on withdrawal from northern Russia, 231; lack of understanding of Siberian intervention, 232–33, 236; and control of Trans-Siberian Railway, 234–36; and Kolchak, 236; complaints about Graves, 237; Morris mission to Kolchak, 237–39; and understanding of limits of force, 240; accepts Bliss's view on Bolshevism, 242; and Churchill plan, 243–44; and Hungarian revolution, 245–46; recognition of power of ideas, 246, 249; accepts Bliss's view on limits of force,

246–48; and collective security, 251; and civilian control of military, 251–54; and American democratic ideology, 254–58; and elections of 1918, 255; and tour of Europe, 258; and World War I as triumph of democracy, 255–56; as world spokesman, 257; and Italy's claim to Fiume, 257; and mandate system, 257–58; and international law, 258–62; and plans for peace treaty, 260; and protection of weak, 260–61; and reform of international law, 261–62; and cooperation among nations, 262–64; and western speaking tour, 265; refusal to compromise, 265; and influence on subsequent leaders, 265; and the Wilsonian example of force, 266–67
Wilson Plan, for Santo Domingo, 83–86
Wood, Leonard: bemoans Democratic victory, 38; and preparedness movement, 141

World War I: effect of American democratic ideology on, 112–13; effect on policy toward Santo Domingo, 84; and period of American neutrality, 118–54; as cooperative effort, 157, 160–84; as part of series of wars, 220. *See also under* Wilson, Woodrow
Wotherspoon, W. W., Gen., 50
Wright, J. W., 108

Ypiranga: at Veracruz, 46
Ypres-Lys offensive, 182
Yurull, H. E.: on force against Bolsheviks, 243

Zamor, Charles, 89
Zamor, Oreste, 89
Zimmermann, Arthur: avoiding attacks on neutrality, 131; correspondence with House, 137; telegram to Carranza, 151
Zimmermann telegram, 151